Reading Plato in Antiquity

Reading Plato in Antiquity

Edited by
Harold Tarrant
and
Dirk Baltzly

Duckworth

First published in 2006 by
Gerald Duckworth & Co. Ltd.
90-93 Cowcross Street, London EC1M 6BF
Tel: 020 7490 7300
Fax: 020 7490 0080
inquiries@duckworth-publishers.co.uk
www.ducknet.co.uk

A catalogue record for this book is available
from the British Library

ISBN 0 7156 3455 0
EAN 9780715634554

Typeset by Ray Davies
Printed and bound in Great Britain by
MPG Books Ltd, Bodmin, Cornwall

Contents

Contents

Contributors

Hayden W. Ausland is Professor of Classics at the University of Montana. His many publications on Plato include 'On Reading Plato's Dialogues Mimetically', in the *American Journal of Philology* (1997).

Dirk Baltzly is Senior Lecturer in Philosophy at Monash University in Australia. His publications cover a wide area of Ancient Philosophy from the Presocratics to Proclus, and include volume III of *Proclus: Commentary on Plato's Timaeus* (2006).

Luc Brisson is Director of Research at the National Center for Scientific Research (Paris), and has published widely on philosophy and religions in Antiquity, including bibliographies, translations, and commentaries. Much of his work is devoted to Plato and Plotinus.

Tim Buckley received his doctorate from the University of Sydney in 2003, and has worked there in a number of capacities since then. He has also been involved in the Australian project preparing a translation of Proclus' *Commentary on Plato's Timaeus*.

John J. Cleary is Professor of Philosophy at Boston College, and Associate Professor at NUI Maynooth. He has published extensively on ancient philosophy, including *Aristotle on the Many Senses of Priority* (1988) and *Aristotle and Mathematics* (1995).

John Dillon is Regius Professor of Greek, Trinity College Dublin. He is author of *The Middle Platonists* (1977, 2nd. ed. 1996), *Alcinous: The Handbook of Platonism* (1993), and *The Heirs of Plato* (2003).

John F. Finamore is Professor and Chair of Classics at the University of Iowa. Among his publications on the Platonic tradition are *Iamblichus' De Anima: Text, Translation, and Commentary* (2002, with John Dillon) and (ed. with Robert Berchman) *History of Platonism: Plato Redivivus* (2005).

Lloyd Gerson is Professor of Philosophy in the University of Toronto. He has published widely in ancient philosophy, and recent books include *Ancient Epistemology* (forthcoming), *Aristotle and Other Platonists* (2005), and *Knowing Persons. A Study in Plato* (2003).

Contributors

Marije Martijn is a PhD student in Ancient Philosophy at the University of Leiden, the Netherlands. At an early stage she was involved, through Professor David Runia, in the work of the Australian team translating Proclus' *Commentary on Plato's Timaeus*.

Ken Parry is Senior Research Officer in the Department of Ancient History at Macquarie University and project director of 'City of Constantine' online. His recent publications include *The Blackwell Dictionary of Eastern Christianity* (1999) and *The Blackwell Companion to Eastern Christianity* (2006).

John Phillips is Professor of Classics and Philosophy at UT-Chattanooga. He has interests in Neoplatonism and the history of Platonism, including Atticus, and is about to publish *Order From Disorder. Proclus' Doctrine of Evil and its Roots in Ancient Platonism*.

Julius Rocca, recently Fellow at the Center for Hellenic Studies in Washington, is Honorary Research Fellow, Centre for the History of Medicine, University of Birmingham, and Research Affiliate at the University of Uppsala. His publications include *Galen on the Brain* (2003).

Richard Sorabji is a fellow of Wolfson College, Oxford, and the general editor of *The Ancient Commentators on Aristotle*, a series of some 70 volumes so far. Recent books include a three-volume Sourcebook on the commentators, second editions of *Aristotle on Memory* (2004), and *Philoponus and the Rejection of Aristotelian Science* (2006); the co-edited books *The Ethics of War: Shared Problems in Different Traditions* (2005), and *Greek and Roman Philosophy 100 BC to 200 AD* (2006); and *Self: Ancient and Modern Insights* (2006).

Atsushi Sumi is Lecturer of General Education at Hanazono University in Kyoto, Japan. He is the author of articles on Plato, Whitehead, and Plotinus, this last being his main focus of attention.

Harold Tarrant is Professor of Classics at the University of Newcastle, Australia, and the author of a number of books relating to ancient Platonism, including *Recollecting Plato's Meno* (2005) and volume I of *Proclus: Commentary on Plato's Timaeus* (2006).

Acknowledgements

In July 2002 a small symposium on the interpretation of Plato was held at the University of Newcastle, Australia. All contributors either gave, or expressed interest in giving, papers at that symposium. The resultant papers are much changed as a result of refereeing, updating, and editing. The Editors would like to thank the Australian Research Council who funded the wider project and part of the symposium; the University of Newcastle; and Monash University. We are also grateful to Nick Eliopoulos for preparing the Index Locorum.

November 2005   H.T. & D.B.

Introduction

Harold Tarrant and Dirk Baltzly

The place of classic texts in the study of philosophy is now assured. In the early days of Greek philosophy one might have had difficulty in giving such a guarantee, but not today. Certainly one may argue about the way such texts should be used and the proportion of time to be devoted to them, since independent argument and a willingness to develop new approaches must also be valued. One may also argue about what should be regarded as a 'classic text', though accomplished philosophers will want to return with some frequency to texts that they admire, puzzle over, or have a special desire to refute. For undergraduate study, moreover, what would philosophy be like in the absence of any texts – ancient, modern, or contemporary – which could not be regarded as specially recommended?

It is not surprising then that ancient philosophy itself made extensive use of texts for the purpose of developing the abilities of pupils. Clearly this happened less in the early days, when there was little that could be profitably prescribed for the new philosophic reader. The Presocratics had written in an enigmatic manner that made them difficult to understand. Consequently, in Plato's time the principal classic text was the same as for the rest of the Greeks, Homer himself, and one searched for whatever help it might provide for advancing philosophic debate. Hesiod and a range of other literary authors were also mined for what value one might extract from them. To dignify such exercises with the name 'interpretation' would seem premature, but texts were certainly being used for the advancement of philosophic goals. It is against that background that we should read the closing pages of Plato's *Phaedrus*, which shows how great a problem the independent life of the written word had become. An author should not expect the written text to continue doing the same work that it would have done under his own supervision.

Few texts have been as controversial as the closing pages of the *Phaedrus*, for the status that we afford Plato's writings – and hence the Plato that we feel we know – depends upon it. It was inevitable that such a text would be subject to divergent interpretations over the centuries. These issues of interpreting the one text, a fraction of a single dialogue, cannot easily be settled without appeal to a range of other issues: the overall purpose of this work, its relation to a vexed passage in the *Seventh Epistle*, the authenticity of that *Epistle*, the range of written works that it actually

1

applies to, and whether the dialogues adopt an approach that make them immune to the *Phaedrus'* criticisms.

How soon the works of Plato became classic texts is unclear. Aristotle, himself belonging to the next generation and an alumnus of Plato's Academy, often seems to engage with a vague memory of certain works, rather than with the letter of the text. One cannot expect to find in Aristotle any discussion of what the *ipsissima verba* of Plato meant. While Plato's *Protagoras* suggests that Plato thought debates over the meaning of a classic text unprofitable, we cannot expect his immediate pupils to have conducted similar exercises upon his own words: unless perhaps there was some political gain to be had from it. It may have been half a century after Plato's death that the first 'commentary' was written upon a Platonic work, and even then it did not come from the scholarch Polemo, but from his close associate Crantor. After that we know of no commentary on Plato written within the original Academy before it collapsed in the political upheavals of the early first century BC.

Substantial interest in Plato had been on the rise among Stoics for some time, and Posidonius (*c*. 135 – *c*. 50 BC) clearly engaged in interpretative exercises of some kind. A highly stoicized reading of the dialogues is to be found in the Epitome of Plato's doctrines referred to by John Dillon below (p. 21). Debates about wider aspects of one's approach to Plato appear in Cicero, though the level of detail is generally minimal. That does not mean, however, that they had not been preceded by detailed readings, as Tarrant's paper argues. Cicero had studied and made friends with various accomplished philosophers, most of whom would have had some use for Platonic texts. He spares his Roman audience anything that they would view as an obsessive exercise in interpretation, but his discussion of natural law appeals to a philosophic tradition that had thoroughly absorbed its own reading of key Platonic dialogues. That reading cannot be dismissed as the simplistic propaganda of a Stoic school.

With the advent of the Roman Empire the interpretative commentary flourished again, alongside handbooks and a variety of more literary Platonizing writings tracing their origins back to the *Symposium* and *Phaedrus*. Here Dillon examines the commentary within the Middle Platonic period, before Plotinus exercised his influence on the Platonic tradition. He argues that the period produced commentaries that were neither especially exciting nor wholly routine. Commentary is generally recognized as a product of reading texts within philosophical schools. These, though once concentrated in Athens, had flourished and spread more widely since Cicero's youth. Thus, in commentary, one sees into the interaction between the professional philosopher and his pupils. Indeed, the author of commentaries could be expected to be both professional in his work and concerned with the uncomplicated presentation of the essentials of Platonism to a relatively inexperienced audience.

By contrast John Finamore examines Apuleius' Platonizing theology, as demonstrated mainly in his handbook *On Plato and his Doctrines*, though partly in more stylish works such as the treatise *On the God of Socrates*. This reminds us that it was not solely specialist philosophers who wrote on Plato, Apuleius being better known for his 'novel' the *Golden Ass* (or *Metamorphoses*). Commonly seen against the background of the so-called 'Second Sophistic', he wrote the kind of performance-prose that would naturally be associated with a 'sophist'. He was also a dedicated latinizer of Greek culture, aiming to produce Latin examples of various essentially Greek 'genres', from ass-novel to philosophic handbook. In most cases this involves the complete rebuilding and embellishment of Greek originals, though the *De Mundo* is in parts little more than a translation of the well-known Pseudo-Aristotelian treatise *On the Cosmos*. It is a challenge for us, given what we possess, to respond to Apuleius as a philosopher, yet he was certainly in some sense a Platonist, and responded personally to the Platonist message and to related philosophic and religious influences. After all Plato himself had been successful as philosopher and literary author in the very same works, and sometimes the philosophic message remains exceedingly obscure. This combination of Platonist philosopher and literary artist had been seen shortly before Apuleius (fl. *c.* AD 160) in Plutarch of Chaeronea (*c.* AD 45-120), who demonstrated how a man of letters could also be a man of religion and a dedicated Platonist. Plutarch and Apuleius were not known as professional teachers of Platonism, nor were they authors of the usual commentaries, but they were still serious readers of Plato.

Another combination, this time combining philosophy with science, was to be found among the medical fraternity, responsible for some of the best critical thought of the second century. Though widely trained in philosophy, Galen developed a particular taste for Plato, and appealed often to his authority. As Rocca will show, his approach to the text is a somewhat literal one that comes close to denying that we should be interpreting at all, and yet it is distinctive.

For others Platonism was an important adjunct to their religious life. Among these were the Christian Platonists, dedicated first to their religion, but committed to explaining this to others in terms of traditional Greek thought, and particularly that of Plato. Such Christian philosophers made a considerable impact on Alexandria and its intellectual environs. Understanding other people's religions had been a natural part of understanding other people's societies and cultures, a process that Alexandria had fostered since its foundation. While Christianity's founder lived, Philo of Alexandria was already revealing his Jewish religion to the hellenized world by presenting it in terms that minimized its differences, where possible, from such philosophies as Stoicism and Platonism. The philosophy of Plotinus was also born in Egypt, and it was ultimately a 'fringe' figure of the Alexandrian world that turned him positively upon his philosophic path. Ammonius Saccas had inclinations toward the religious philosophies of Persia and India, and a different, more intuitive approach to the exegesis of texts from that of others. That, at least, is one interpretation of material in Porphyry (*VPlot.* 14), which stands tantalizingly close to Plotinus' condemnation of Longinus as a philologist. A shrewd guess might make Ammonius the defender of an intuitive response to a text in preference to its elucidation by primarily linguistic means.

As for Plotinus, we have his writings by which to judge his approach to Plato. These seldom exhibit a direct approach to Platonic texts, but are meditations on philosophic problems, problems that involve him in the interpretation of Plato (for the authority of Plato *required* his answers to be Plato-compatible), but would not demand this of others. A detailed understanding of central Platonic texts lies at the core of Plotinus' own philosophy, so that he could claim to be no more than an interpreter even though he is usually taken for an independent thinker in the Platonic tradition (the *first* Neoplatonist). If Plotinus had written commentaries and handbooks rather than meditation-literature, it could be claimed, he might seem less original, less of a turning-point, and more of a direct link between the exegetic activities discussed by Dillon and his own pupil Porphyry. But equally it is clear that his failure to produce collections of doctrines and straightforward exegesis is the natural result of Plotinus' approach to philosophy. Mechanical investigations of whole dialogues did not lead to the uplifting spiritual experience that Platonism demanded, and statements of doctrine, unaccompanied by a deeper understanding, would fail to communicate Platonic philosophy as he understood it. Regular Middle Platonism's obsession with words was an obsession with something of lowly metaphysical status.

Hence, what Plotinus gets out of Platonic texts is not just a reading of them, but a personal inward response that both validates and builds upon the original. It makes discussion of his treatment of Plato a complicated exercise, and consequently more papers in this collection bring in Plotinus than address his reading directly. Atsushi Sumi, however, deals with detailed matters of interpretation arising in one particular treatise (VI.2), and this discussion reveals the depth of Plotinus' knowledge of Plato and the extent to which issues of interpretation can lie at the root of his discussions – to the extent that anomalous passages must be regarded as 'riddling'. John Phillips, on the other hand, takes a philosophic problem that had become central to philosophy, the problem of evil's origin. He discusses the response of Plotinus among others in the light of Platonic texts, highlighting the importance of particular passages from the *Timaeus*, *Phaedrus*, and *Statesman*. It is no accident that, once one acknowledges that the whole of Timaeus' creation story is a kind of myth, the key passages all turn out to have the status of myths. It is to these that Plato's readers are now turning in an effort to penetrate to Plato's deepest insights.

Plotinus is one figure in whom we can witness the development of a multi-level theory of the virtues that was to sweep its way through centuries of Platonist thinking, undergoing transformations, yet still based upon a conviction that Plato's various statements about the virtues could not be reconciled so long as they were taken to apply to exactly the same sort of qualities. Luc Brisson examines this multilevel theory in special relation to Plotinus' pupil Porphyry, but with consideration of both what preceded and what followed. This exercise is crucial in defining the place of Porphyry in Neoplatonist moral theory – still an important part of philosophy in spite of the small amount of space that extant texts devote to it in comparison with metaphysics and theology. Since this theory of the virtues is intimately linked with the explanation of Platonic texts, particularly the *Republic*, *Theaetetus*, and *Phaedo*, the paper is also important for showing Porphyry's place in the exegesis of Plato's moral theory.

Mathematics had always been central to Platonism, especially among those who came to see Plato in terms of Pythagoreanism. We often react with some horror today at the extent to which mathematical considerations intrude into seemingly alien areas of philosophy, in both Plato and his successors. Mathematics can provide not just the basis for metaphysics, but also, via the details of harmonic theory, the basis of ethics. The wide-ranging paper of Hayden Ausland, important both for Plato and for his successors, relates especially to Pythagorean traditions of Platonic exegesis which reached their peak in the philosophy of Iamblichus, Porphyry's younger contemporary. He shows with new clarity how mathematical detail can have a direct bearing on a Platonist theory of justice.

One thing that was never expected of the great interpreters of Plato is that they should be for ever in agreement. At times their views could seem diametrically opposed. Often this is because they tried to go deeper into Plato's message, demanding that the real meaning was considerably different from any that could be derived from cursory reading. By refusing to be tied to the text like the 'philologist' Longinus or the pedantic Atticus, they were opening the gates to subjectivism in interpretation, a subjectivism that could only really work when the mind of the reader was somehow at one with that of Plato, the work's creator. Tim Buckley examines how Proclus related to his predecessors in the *Platonic Theology*, and the relationship that he postulated between Plato, those interpreters, and himself. In particular he discusses the concept of a Bacchic relationship linking Plato with Plotinus, Amelius, Porphyry, Iamblichus, Theodorus, Syrianus, and himself, and discusses the influence of the *Phaedrus* upon it. All these thinkers were thought to share in powers that were naturally conducive to Platonist insights, but still the majority fell significantly short of the truth.

The primary vehicle of philosophy available to Proclus, though by no means the only one, was the commentary. Of his commentaries the most widely used has long been the five books *On the Timaeus*. This is extensively discussed by Dillon, and two full papers are devoted to it. John Cleary examines how, in Proclus' hands, the investigation of Plato's work on physics (or rather on the natural world) turns out to have such serious consequences for matters of theology. He looks in detail at Proclus' principles of interpretation, seen mainly in book 1; the interlude on prayer in book 3; and interpretation of the divine craftsman's role as efficient cause of the sensible cosmos, also in book 3. Marije Martijn looks at some of the technicalities of commentary construction, but in so doing raises key questions of how Proclus was reading Plato. In particular she investigates Proclus' response (or perhaps lack of response) to today's serious issue of why Timaeus' cosmology should have been given the status of an *eikôs mythos*, explaining why a Neoplatonist did not need to see it as difficult.

Dirk Baltzly again gives precedence to Proclus' *Commentary on the Timaeus*, but with important discussion also of the *Commentary on the Alcibiades*, not to mention the treatment of Proclus' own progression in virtue to be found in his biographer Marinus. His paper returns to the issue of the levels of virtue that had been the subject of Brisson's paper, to which he makes reference. This time, however, one level, the cathartic or purificatory virtues, is singled out for special attention. Baltzly seeks a coherence in Proclus' treatment of the cathartic virtues, a coherence that became a real challenge for a Platonist who also recognized many non-Platonic religious texts as part of the canon of inspired literature.

Baltzly's paper touches on another huge issue for these later interpreters, the question of how Aristotle is to be seen as being, in some sense, a Platonist still. It is a strange irony that, whereas in recent times we have tended to see the history of western philosophy in terms of distinct Platonist and Aristotelian strands, using this to forge a fundamental distinction, a considerable amount of Aristotelian commentary from late antiquity came from the pens of Neoplatonists after Proclus, whose primary allegiance had been (at least nominally) to Plato. Commentators have usually left us works on only one of the two masters, though occasionally we have examples of their work on both, as from Olympiodorus. Commentaries on Aristotle were in any case inclined to make detailed reference to texts of Plato.

Plato and Aristotle were regularly held to be at least compatible *given their different approaches and concerns*, and sometimes altogether compatible, indeed in *harmony*. For us there are various ways of seeing their attempts to reconcile the two. Richard Sorabji provides an account that sees Plato and Aristotle, naturally, as philosophers with distinct positions, one of whom must usually lose out to some degree in any attempt to bring them into close relation. But it is also possible to argue the merits of either an Aristotelian reading of Plato, or, more commonly, a seemingly Platonist reading of Aristotle. It is the Platonist reading of Aristotle that dominates Lloyd Gerson's paper, and the acceptability and even merits of these readings are the primary focus here. These two papers complement each other, and take forward the issue of syncretism that has emerged in other papers in this collection.

At this point the central concerns of this volume conclude. However, the reading of Plato continued to be important, and Plato's most famous readers also acquired paradigmatic status, among them Proclus. Hence we conclude with Ken Parry's contribution to the debate over Platonizing influences in Byzantine Christian thought. Parry believes that Proclus was more influential in Byzantine times than is usually admitted by the Byzantines. Since some of his views would remain anathema to them, Proclus was not an authority to be embraced openly, but some aspects of his thought were nevertheless influential. In this context the place of the Platonizing figure of Pseudo-Dionysius is naturally important. We trust that seeing how the Byzantines read Proclus will nicely complement a volume such as this, much of which is given over to Proclus' own reading of Plato.

As we interpret ancient texts one factor that we seldom have before us is how the authors themselves expected to be interpreted in their own day. The lack of direct evidence is in most cases tantalizing, but in recent times effort has been made to discover how Homer and other literary figures tried to mould their audience's approach to reading their works. Plato himself was a communicator, acutely conscious of the fact that people would try to interpret his works in a variety of incompatible ways – as the *Phaedrus* shows. It is entirely plausible that the ancients were more sensitive to hints about how he should be interpreted than we shall ever be. We hope that readers of this volume will find exploring late antique readings of Plato useful, and we urge that this should not be seen as a kind of doctrinal archaeology uncovering fossils of long dead creatures, but rather as a way of sustaining a once-vibrant philosophy that was still alive in late antiquity – and is indeed still alive today in certain modes of philosophic inquiry and in a healthy openness to all the facets of Platonic philosophy.

Platonic interpretation and eclectic theory

Harold Tarrant

i. The response to Plato in Polemo's Academy

Recently we have recognized the importance in Roman times of the search for ancient authority – for a revelation from a time of superior wisdom.[1] Plato had practised philosophy during Greece's golden age, and thus became a revered authority. By the second century AD his influence extended over non-philosophic genres too. The struggle for Plato's authority had coloured Cicero's formative studies in philosophy, for his authority was being sought by (at least) two factions in the Academy, those of Philo of Larissa and Antiochus of Ascalon. Their followers were mischievously designated 'Fourth' and 'Fifth' Academies by Sextus Empiricus (*PH* 1.235), following a Pyrrhonist tradition that postulated successive doctrinal revolts in the Academy over two centuries. By questioning Academic fidelity to Plato, that tradition paved the way for any version of Plato others chose to promulgate. This freedom helped not only the Sceptics, for Plato's support could now be claimed by other doctrinal systems, like the Pythagoro-Platonic philosophy of Numenius.[2] When Plato's authority was so important, other schools gained by postulating a hiatus in the Platonic tradition, while legitimate heirs to the Academy preferred to deny this break-down – until Philo of Larissa, the last who could claim such legitimacy. Philo formally championed the thesis of one continuous Academic tradition, with the implication that his Academy had remained true to Plato.[3]

I now question the sharp changes of direction within the Academy claimed by the Pyrrhonists and others. Though the school did change, and leadership styles varied, over the two and a half centuries after Plato's death, nevertheless the Socraticism and resistance to straightforward teaching, which we associate with Arcesilaus, were there under his predecessors Polemo and Crates. I have recently argued this in relation to the Platonic *Theages*, showing that the work best reflects the educational ideology of Polemo's Academy.[4] 'Socrates' had become an inspirational, daemonic and erotic figure, who may or may not have some positive impact on pupils, failing to control the process himself. His intentions are good, but reason cannot determine his results. He influences by proximity, the closer the better. It helps if pupils listen, but it may work if they are in the next room! He has no methods, no elenchus, no midwifery, no dialectical procedures for imparting the truth, and does not teach in the ordinary sense.

Socrates generally represents the closest thing to a writer's ideal philosopher, and Plato's Socrates changes as his notion of how a philosopher should behave changes.[5] So the Platonic *Theages* should represent the outward face of the Academy at its time of composition, and the relationship between teacher and mentor was notoriously close in the Academy of Polemo, Crates, Arcesilaus, and Crantor. Polemo was a moderately high-profile leader, but little significant information survived until Cicero's time concerning his doctrines. Thus he contrasts sharply with his predecessor Xenocrates, who passed a rich legacy down to Roman times. This difference would be explicable if Polemo were more reluctant to communicate doctrine didactically.

Until recently Polemo had not been known as an interpreter of Plato either. This situation has changed thanks to an insight of David Sedley. Sedley argues that doxographical material concerning Plato's physics from Cicero's *Academica* (1.19-29) is not based on whimsical history of philosophy originating with Antiochus in the first century, but goes back to Polemo, the Academic scholarch to whom Antiochus gives disproportionate attention.[6] If this theory, now supported by John Dillon (2003), is correct, then it greatly improves our understanding of how interpretation of the *Timaeus* developed between Xenocrates and (a) the Stoics, and (b) the first formal commentator, Crantor. Polemo was a contemporary of Epicurus and Theophrastus, both of whom had responded to the *Timaeus* in puzzling ways that arguably reflect exegetical tendencies in the Academy. It seems that Polemo continued the non-literal reading of the *Timaeus* promoted by Xenocrates and Speusippus, according to which the world had no beginning, making the creation-process and creator-god of the *Timaeus* little more than expository devices for revealing forces eternally at work within the universe. Once the demiurge is factored out, we are left with various pairs, such as reason and necessity for instance, pointing to a basic dichotomy of cosmic powers that is also attested in Xenocrates. These are not opposing *active* powers, as the myth of the *Statesman* confirms; rather, one is essentially passive and somewhat resistant to the other's plans. The striking thing about the allegedly Polemonian interpretation is that it offers us a Plato whose physics is without transcendent powers. There is little left to separate his world from that of his more famous pupil, Zeno the Stoic.

The same similarities are not encountered when this account of Plato turns to epistemology. Here the Platonic Idea is introduced, and it is affirmed that for Plato the truth resided there, reached by mental power rather than by our unsatisfactory senses. Still, with no place of its own in physics, the Idea, at least as known to us, seems to be something belonging in the mind itself: 'knowledge they placed nowhere except in the notions and reasonings (*notiones, rationes*) of the mind' (1.32). Zeno's controversial 'apprehensible presentation' (*katalêptikê phantasia*), that strikes us as being of such a kind that it cannot fail to be true and accurate, is readily admitted to be an innovation. If this is still Polemo, then he had tried to preserve the Academy's historical link with the critique of the senses and with introspection. Such tactics might easily have accompanied a Socratic approach to education, reliant on the ideas in the pupil's mind rather than on acceptance of the master's doctrines as in other schools.

Under Polemo's leadership Arcesilaus, officially first of the Academic Sceptics, had been the close friend of the Academic Crantor. The enigmatic statement that he acquired Plato's books in his younger days[7] testifies to his interest in the school's connections with its founder. This is confirmed by his relationship with Crantor, regarded as the first Platonic commentator.[8] Crantor's work may have been prompted by the desire to come to Plato's defence against critics from other schools such as Epicurus and Theophrastus.[9] We know that he speaks of Plato's response to contemporary charges of plagiarizing the political theory of the Egyptians,[10] and that involves him too in the defence. While we can say little about Crantor's type of commentary, a commentary typically assumes that the original author had some worthwhile lesson to communicate *when correctly understood*. This seems to be a premise of the fragments in Plutarch's *De Animae Procreatione* and Proclus. But a lesson to communicate does not necessarily mean doctrine to communicate, while cryptic messages resisted *dogmatic* communication. I suggest that what held the early Academy together was a commitment to preserving not *doctrines* but *practices*. If practices under Polemo and Crates still privileged the spirit of inquiry and of self-examination, and assuming that a spiritual dimension to moral education[11] persisted, Arcesilaus was not an apostate. It is a later obsession with beliefs rather than practices that made Arcesilaus controversial.

ii. Antiochus and Cicero

By the time of Cicero the importance of school practice as opposed to school doctrine was diminishing, as might be expected when the Academy was no longer a living entity. It was natural to see the difference between schools in terms of doctrines, particularly after Carneades' efforts to distinguish (and allocate) various doctrinal positions. So by the first century BC it was of considerable interest to Antiochus, Cicero, and others that Plato and Aristotle often seemed to be suggesting the same doctrinal position as Zeno, while doctrinal differences clearly existed *within* each of their three schools, supposedly promoted by Arcesilaus, Theophrastus, and Aristo respectively.[12] Could it be that the great philosophers were at one on the key issues?

Now that we have reason to associate what seemed to be the appalling account of ancient Platonism in the *Academica Posteriora* with Polemo rather than with Antiochus' misunderstandings, the worst cloud over the latter's credentials as a reader of Plato has been removed, and it is time to reassess them. To that end I examine a passage treated more fully in my book on the interpretation of the *Meno*, which displays Antiochus' strong influence and interesting use of Plato – seen through stoic-tinted spectacles. This is from the first book of Cicero's *De Legibus* (*On Laws*). Cicero himself is conscious of writing in the Platonic tradition, choosing dialogue form[13] and treating his theologically related[14] legal system after discussion of his ideal constitution.[15] He follows Academic *communicative practice* rather than doctrine, for the Roman experience had new things to teach us, and he speaks (like a follower of Antiochus) for all respected philosophers, not for one. The history of philosophy at 1.38-9 mirrors the views of Antiochus,[16] who was convinced of the agreement between Plato and the Stoics on issues of importance, and above all in ethics, *in spite of differences in terminology*.

Though this text is clearly influenced by a reading of Plato, few passages are Platonic *as distinct from* Stoic. While its theme that law derives from divine nature is usually seen as Stoic, Cicero sees no contradiction with his consciously Platonic project. His syncretist approach means writing as a unitarian with regard to the Platonic corpus as well as to other bodies of philosophical writing, with all genuine works of approved philosophers seen as reflecting somehow a single philosophic vision. Consequently the philosophical parts of the book avoid references to particular works or authors.[17] Unattributed doctrines make it harder to dissect influences on Cicero's political works with precision, whether general Platonic influence or that of particular dialogues. Suggestive words and phrases show that Plato stands in the background, but the broader aim is to reawaken some seemingly ancient vision that was thought of as common property.

In trying to conjure up such a vision Cicero reverts to traditional Academic practice under Plato.[18] It is natural, then, that the so-called theory of recollection is among doctrines alluded to. Further, *De Legibus* I constantly postulates some innate awareness within us, which may be developed into something like knowledge (1.26, 59), and ultimately accounts for the good man (1.59: *bonus vir*). Many would call this awareness more Stoic,[19] but in the allegedly Polemonian history (*Academica* 1.32) it is *Platonists* who, after their rejection of the senses was established, were said to place knowledge only in the notions and reasoning of the mind, while *Zeno* was said to trust the senses, using them to account for notions in our minds – afterwards (42)! Hence Cicero, when writing from Antiochus' standpoint, sees *innate* ideas (essentially mental, regardless of whether sensation acts as a catalyst) as a Platonist feature. He needs this innate knowledge in the *De Legibus* to account for our grasp of divine or natural law, prior to all human law.[20]

Cicero's exposition of the legal philosophy 'of the most learned men' begins at 1.18. This phrase (*doctissimi viri*)[21] reflects Antiochus' inclusive way of referring to the groups to whom he claimed allegiance.[22] After a Stoic definition of law, we quickly feel the influence of Plato's *Laws* (713c-714a), where Plato, using a concept largely compatible with this definition, clearly derives law's Greek name (*nomos*) from the verb for 'distribute' (*nemo*), as Cicero does next (1.19). However, my principal interest here is in 1.24-32. I argue elsewhere that several Platonic texts, seamlessly interwoven, are combined in developing the picture of human beings born into this world with divine advantages and all the faculties they need to develop step by step towards perfect virtue. Among the texts involved are Protagoras' long speech from the *Protagoras*, and influential parts of the *Meno*. These are chosen because both deal with what one might call 'political excellence', a concept that Cicero, if anybody, would take seriously in his political works. Divine gifts play a part in explaining such excellence in both (*Meno* 99e, *Prot.* 321e-322d2), just as at 1.24.[23] Here, just as at *Protagoras* 322a, this gift will be the source of our kinship with, and recognition of, the gods.

Crucially, 1.25 begins with the claim that, because of our kinship with god, the man who knows god is the man who recollects (*recordetur*) his true origins. The origin in question is the heaven, identified in 1.26 as our former home and the site of our true family (*cognationis domiciliique pristini*). That context had been suggestive of *Timaeus* 90a-d, where the elevated position of the human head is for contemplation of the heavens, and the assimilation of our souls to the motions of the soul that drives the heavenly bodies. But what of the suggestion of the theory of recollection? Must it be intentional, and if so does it have something to do with the *Meno* or the *Phaedo*? Platonic recollection is again suggested by the phrase 'with nobody as teacher' (*nullo docente*) at 1.27. There will be other hints that both dialogues are relevant, and 'recollection' is here linked with naturally implanted common notions, as was usual in Platonist texts from late antiquity. As in many of these,[24] 'recollection' seems a two-stage process, involving first a non-technical awareness that gives all of us concepts, and then, for a few individuals, a further process of analysing the structure of these concepts by a process known as *diarthrôsis* in Greek and *enodatio* in Latin, both meaning literally the separation of limbs. Sadly, editors some-times conceal this at 1.26, by eliminating *enodavit* in favour of alternatives without manuscript authority.[25] It is *enodatio* that here supplies the foundations of knowledge (*scientia*). The same knowledge-giving process is later described as an illumination of the rudimentary notions (note *quibus inlustratis*, 1.59).

Common notions and recollection are employed in Cicero's source to explain the awakening of law within us, but humans cannot be given an *undisguised* awareness of what must be done. Right reason becomes law on being *developed* and *strengthened* within the human mind (1.18). We cannot all become lawgivers, only those who have achieved the highest regard. So Cicero, who offers himself here as an expert law-giver, needs innate knowledge to contribute to two different cognitive states, involving different levels of awareness of natural law. In Stoic terms law involves both those making progress (*prokoptontes*) and the sage (*sophos*), who is the only true legislator in early Stoicism.[26] The natural reading of the *Phaedo* makes innate knowledge subconsciously responsible for everybody's awareness of absolutes (74c-76a), while only Socrates is able to give a good account of them (76b-c), and the *Meno* is just as insistent on two levels of influence, one dream-like, the other involving knowledge (85c-86a).

Another standard Platonist feature here is the importance of assimilation to god in ethics.[27] It is by remembering our origins that we 'come to know god', and then it is by assimilating ourselves to this god that we can share in divine excellence too: 'for [excellence] is a human's likeness to a god' (1.25).[28] Assimilation to the divine was most clearly idealized at *Theaetetus* 176b, and then again at *Timaeus* 90a-d, a text which we have already found to be relevant here.

So some kind of Platonism, involving close interpretation of particular passages, has been interwoven with Stoic elements. The *Meno* is a key text, though recollection belongs also to the *Phaedo* and *Phaedrus*. The *Timaeus* is used to enhance the interpretation of the *Meno*, and other texts also operate in the background. The key role played here by the *Meno* is in suggesting the parallel roles of the common notions in cognition and moral development – especially in the political arena. The *Phaedo* (73-6) also enters into the equation, for Cicero assumes that recollectable knowledge is *of the universal* (*genera*, 1.26) just as it is *universally* shared among humans; and that the primary things being recollected are the great truths of a world beyond our sensations: truths about the virtues and the divine.[29]

iii. Common notions and 'eclecticism'

I return now to the idea of innate, recollectable knowledge. How, given the presence of natural and common notions, or 'incomplete intellections' as they are called at 1.27 and 30, do they not have the same results in all human beings? Would not uniform human doctrine arise from a uniform, naturally implanted notion? Yes, if they were perfected, but, given that they are incomplete, we can account for their differing results. The single example of a natural notion discussed by Cicero demands a belief that *x* exists without any commitment to the details of what *x* is like. Such an answer reflects a common situation in Plato's Socratic dialogues where Socrates and his interlocutor admit the existence of the *definiendum*, but cannot agree what it is. As for god, Cicero assumes that even savages acknowledge a god, having the required notion without knowledge of what he is like (1.24). Shared insight does not guarantee correct belief, unless one can analyse one's notions correctly. Another problem for humans is that the corrupting effects of evil can suppress their undeveloped notions, just as sparks of fire are quenched (1.33).

More important from the theoretical point of view is an answer suggested by 1.30, where we read that humans, who by definition have reason, share the same powers of sense and the same intellections. These undeveloped natural intellections are *stamped upon all in the same way*, but our mind's interpreter, speech, 'varies in words, while agreeing in opinions'. The *basis* for knowledge, therefore, is our common property, but confusion arises owing to our latitude of expression, presumably both internally as discursive thought, and externally as speech. This piece of epistemology underlies the eclecticism of the school of Antiochus, and at first sight it is reminiscent of Epicurus' attribution of human error to the discursive realm of opinion rather than to the senses or to the preconceptions.[30] But Antiochus and Cicero are not explaining error! The corruption of our natural notions or our failure to attend to them does that. He is explaining rather what the Sceptics would call *diaphônia*, or 'differences of voice' which are for them, but not for him, indications of conflicting doctrine and hence of error. Difference of voice may involve neither the corruption of the notions, nor our failure to dissect them limb from limb, and amount to no more than linguistic preference.

Antiochus' common appeals to the Old Academy, Aristotle, and Zeno involved the claim that their differences were in terminology rather than substance (as here at 1.38, 1.54-5).[31] Common tradition did not explain this alleged agreement, for others who belong to the same traditions, such as Theophrastus (*Ac.* 1.33), Aristo (*De Leg.* 1.55), and the New Academy (*Ac.* 1.43, 2.16; *De Leg.* 1.39), failed to adhere *either* in word *or* in doctrine to their predecessors. So another source of orthodox Platonic, Aristotelian, and Stoic agreement is needed, and this is their shared attention to the common notions. *Diaphônia* (difference of voice) arises from alternative ways of expressing these notions, but as long as the mind dissects them correctly, one will be an inheritor of the same philosophy, differently expressed. What this means is that no text of Plato, Aristotle, or Zeno, will require faithful adherence to a *literal* meaning. Doctrine must first be in tune with the notions acknowledged and dissected by Cicero and Antiochus; and then it must be able to be traced in the writings of those who had allegedly understood this doctrine through the common notions. Certain dialogues of Plato, including the *Meno*, *Protagoras*, *Phaedo*, and *Timaeus* were among these, with *equal* authority insofar as the same analysis of the uncorrupted common notions had informed them all.

We are now closer to determining how the influence of Plato operates. First, Platonic influence includes Platonic practice, particularly in regards to the overall project, the dialogue form, the type of conversation being presented, and the communicative strategy. Second, his authority is not something that Cicero wants to impress the reader with directly. He cannot say 'Listen to the voice of Plato', but allows that voice (and others) to permeate his work because the correct account will agree with Plato as properly understood. That he stands in the Platonic tradition is for the educated to quietly appreciate. Third, Plato is assumed to be whole and consistent, not on the surface at the verbal level, but at the level of the common notions – of which he and all persons of understanding are aware. This approach to Plato and to other authorities is underpinned by a theory that explains why this 'syncretism' should be right: all who were in touch with the common notions found the same truth, but expressed it through fundamentally different language. Words merely interpret and translate what the mind apprehends. The harmony of Plato, Aristotle, and Zeno the Stoic must be sought beyond the level of their verbal message, and concerns the fundamental shared ideas that are the basis of a deeper message – a message for which the Antiochian philosopher is obliged to seek an even greater clarity of expression. Only thus will he circumvent the dissensions of bickering philosophers, which had done so much to fuel the arguments of the Sceptics. And the Sceptics in turn had only discouraged the search for deeper understanding, by giving the impression that such an understanding could never exist. For Antiochus and for Cicero, it had existed, and it could still exist so long as we searched for it within ourselves. Through Plato's help we could recollect all that we needed to know – about ourselves and our place in the world that embraced us.

Notes

1. See in particular Boys-Stones (2001).
2. See fragments 24-8 (des Places).
3. See Brittain (2001), ch. 4.
4. See Tarrant (2005b).
5. See Long (1998).
6. See Sedley (2002).
7. His age at the time is omitted by Diogenes Laertius (4.32), but supplied by the Philodemus *Acad.* XIX 14-16.
8. See here the next contribution to this volume by John Dillon.
9. On Theophrastus see now Balthussen (2003) and compare Sedley (1998), 76-8, (2002). The range of sources in which Theophrastus' views on the *Timaeus* may be found (Taurus frs 22B, 23B, 24, 26B Lakmann, Plut. *Quaest. Plat.* 1006c, Proc. *In Tim.* I 120.30-121.1, 456.16-18, 2.6.21-2, 120.7-22, 122.10-17, 3.136.1-2, 151.1-9) suggests strongly that the commentary tradition had taken early account of his views. Proclus knows earlier critics of Theophrastus' complaints about the *Timaeus* (*In Tim.* II 120.22-8), who may well be identical with Crantor.
10. Proc. *In Tim.* I 76.2-8. On this passage see Dillon (2003), 219-20.
11. I associate this dimension with Socratic Eros, and with the adoption of works like *Alcibiades* I and *Theages* as authorities. See Tarrant (2005b).
12. See Cic. *Ac.* 1.43, 1.33, and 2.130.
13. The opening image of the oak tree is surely inspired by the image of the plane tree early in Plato's *Phaedrus* (229a-b, 230b). This dialogue is relevant, more concerned than any other with the problems of writing that worry Cicero at the

outset of his own work. These problems are there introduced as vital for Cicero's focal subject of law (*Phdr.* 277d, 278c-e, cf. *De Leg.* 1.17, 19, 42).

14. For the theological content of Cicero's work see below; for Plato's *Laws* as a theological text see Nightingale (1993) and Schofield (2003).

15. *De Leg.* 1.15: within the drama of the dialogue it is Atticus who introduces the idea of following the discussion of the state with one of law, adding the comparison with Plato as an added incentive; but Marcus then promises a discussion mirroring the *Laws* of Plato in its journey-like progress and three-sided discussion.

16. See Vander Waerdt (1994a), 4871-2; the key elements are the broad agreement of the Old Academy, Aristotle, and Zeno's Stoa; the inclusion of Polemo with Speusippus and Xenocrates, and Theophrastus with Aristotle; the insistence that Stoic ethics differ only in terminology; the separate mention of Aristo, and the privileging of Zeno over Chrysippus; the general dislike of Epicureans, and the destructive image (here tempered by Cicero's own reverence for it) attached to the New Academy.

17. This reflects Academic rejection of direct appeals to authority figures, as seen at *Ac.* 2.60, where the Academic uses reason rather than authority; cf. 2.7, with a reference to *antiquissimi et doctissimi* again. Might Antiochus once have shared this Academic belief that appeals should be addressed to the common notions (and hence to consensus, as in the *De Legibus*) rather than to authorities?

18. Take for instance the very introduction to the recollection passage at *Meno* 81a-c, which recalls through the mists of time certain religious and literary traditions in which Plato wishes to situate his present discussion; or the Water-Carriers Myth (*Gorgias* 493a), which becomes a similar remote trigger for some very this-worldly discussion of the dissolute life.

19. It might be useful to consider three features of Hellenistic concept-theory that Scott (1987), 365, thinks of as in conflict with Platonic recollection as correctly understood. First, these concepts develop in humans automatically and without effort; second, conceptual thought cannot take place without them; third, they act as criteria of truth. As I hope to show here, (1) they are seen by Cicero as available to all (1.30), but recovered fully *only by the sage*; (2) the Antiochian system seems to have been happy to postulate empirically formed concepts to account for some conceptual thought even without certain non-empirical concepts (*Ac.* 2.21), though all humans still have *some* concept of god (*De Leg.* 1.24) and *some* sense of justice (1.33), while generally lacking understanding of either; and (3) when they mature the concepts do indeed lead us to the truth, though quite a bit of effort may be required to avoid the vices and corruption that will undermine their influence (1.33). Scott's radical dichotomy between Platonic recollection and Hellenistic common notions breaks down in Cicero where the natural notions are doing a different level of work in the sage and in the ordinary human being. Hence, I reply to Scott that these concepts develop *to a low level* in humans automatically and without effort; second, conceptual thought cannot take place without them *at some level*; third, they act as criteria of truth *though only readily available at a high level*.

20. Note how another passage from Antiochus, *Ac.* 2.21, asserts that without the notions a thing can neither be understood nor searched for: a fairly clear allusion to *Meno* 80d.

21. I owe this to Vander Waerdt (1989); see more conveniently Vander Waerdt (1994a), 4871 n. 79.

22. Note that at 1.52 the term *doctissimi* cannot refer to philosophers of a single school.

23. The *divinum ... animorum munus* is a gift of *rational* soul, rather than soul pure and simple, since this gift is what separates us from ordinary animals and ensures our potential likeness to the gods.

24. Anon. *Tht.* 46.43-9, 47.37-48.8; Plut. *Quaest. Plat.* 1000e; Albinus, *Prol.* 6; Damasc. *In Phd.* 2.14.1 (cf. 1.263), 2.25. See Tarrant (2005a), 148, 153.

25. Dyck (2004), 139, sees the aptness of the verb, but chooses to use it instead in supplying *nec satis enodatos intellegentias*. Dyck's reasoning is that nature is not sufficient to achieve *enodatio*, but the end of 1.27 suggests otherwise.

26. *SVF* 3.332, 611, 614, 622. See Vander Waerdt (1994b), 274 with n. 8, for the lack of clear early Stoic references to natural law as such, and its early applicability to the sage alone. Vander Waerdt (1994a) also has much to say about the adaptation of Stoic theory, originally applicable to the sage, for those making progress also.

27. This becomes the standard goal for human beings in Middle Platonism, seemingly from Eudorus (Stob. *Ecl.* II 49.1-50.10) to Anon. *Tht.* (7.14-20), Albinus (*Prol.* 5) and Alcinous (*Didasc.* 28), and then Plotinus (*Enn.* I.2). If the source of *De Legibus* 1.25 is not already employing it as a goal, then it is on the verge of doing so.

28. This is not uncontroversial, but after *Est autem virtus ...* we expect the subsequent *est igitur ...* also to have *virtus* as its subject. To interpret the words *est igitur homini cum deo similitudo* as 'hence there is a similarity between man and god' is ridiculously weak. See further Tarrant (2006).

29. Note 1.60, where, following reference to the clarification of our shadowy intelligences that leads one to goodness under wisdom's guide, we read *cognitis perceptisque virtutibus* ('when the virtues have been recognized and understood').

30. See here D.L. 10.34; S.E. *Adv. Math.* 7.210-11.

31. Compare also *Ac.* 1.17, *Fin.* 5.88-9.

Pedantry and pedestrianism?
Some reflections on the Middle Platonic commentary tradition

John Dillon

Proclus, at the beginning of his *Platonic Theology*,[1] looking back, from a lofty perspective, over the whole sweep of the Platonic tradition, sees the divinely-inspired wisdom of Plato, after its original shining forth and later coming to completion (ἐκφαίνουσαν καὶ πάλιν ὕστερον τελειωθῆναι),[2] then entering upon a period of eclipse (ὥσπερ εἰς ἑαυτὴν ἀναχωρήσασαν), at which point it became unavailable to the great majority of those who professed philosophy, before it emerged once again into the light (αὖθις εἰς φῶς προελθεῖν). He does not make clear what he has in mind as regards a chronological sequence for these various stages, but it seems reasonable to suppose that the 'emergence once again into the light' is a reference to the appearance on the scene of Plotinus, and the deepening of insight into metaphysical realities consequent on that. The previous eclipse, therefore, would be most plausibly viewed as covering not only the period of Academic scepticism, but also the following couple of hundred years conventionally termed by modern scholars 'Middle Platonism'.[3]

Proclus is not, of course, entirely oblivious of the Middle Platonists. Such figures as Plutarch, Atticus, Severus, and Numenius, at least, figure repeatedly in the voluminous pages of his *Commentary on the Timaeus* – though always, I think, through the intermediacy of the learned Porphyry – but they do consistently come across, unless deemed to be plain wrong (as Plutarch and Atticus are on the question of the creation of the world in time), as operating on a lower level of understanding of the text; largely philological and antiquarian in their approach, and quite oblivious to deeper levels of meaning, as attained by the systematic practice of allegory, particularly in the post-Iamblichean period.

I have in the past been guilty myself of not being overly polite about Middle Platonic commentators. I do not intend to publish a full retraction here by any means, but I do think that a more balanced picture might be presented. After all, for all their faults, the pre-Plotinian commentators are considerably more in accord with our own view of the texts (unless, perhaps, we be rabid Straussians or devoted Heideggerians) than are Neoplatonists like Iamblichus or Proclus, and they largely established, for all subsequent ages, what role a commentary should perform, and what form it should take.[4]

Let us review, first of all, what we know of Middle Platonic exegetical activity. This took the form of commentaries on individual dialogues, essays on particular passages of central importance, and general accounts of Platonic doctrine. In the first category, the earliest commentator is probably Eudorus of Alexandria (fl. *c.* 25 BC).[5] We know from Plutarch (*Mor.* 1013b, 1020c) that he composed a fairly comprehensive commentary on the *Timaeus,* but we know of no comments from him on any other dialogue. Probably next chronologically is the *Anonymous Theaetetus Commentator,*[6] who, apart from his work on the *Theaetetus,* lays claim to commentaries on the *Timaeus* (35.12), the *Symposium* (70.12), and the *Phaedo* (48.10 – forthcoming!). His commentary does show the genre to be by his time well developed, with introductory discussion of the subject-matter, characters, and general background of the dialogue, and the commentary itself divided up into more or less continuous *lemmata.* We do not know of any commentaries on the dialogues from the hand of Plutarch, though we do have a most interesting monograph on a particular topic, to be mentioned shortly. On the other hand, the later Athenian Platonists L. Calvenus Taurus (fl. *c.* AD 140) and Atticus (fl. *c.* AD) did compose commentaries at least on the *Timaeus,*[7] as did Severus and, probably, Numenius of Apamea. I also regard the *Commentary on the Timaeus* of Calcidius, though it may it have been composed in the mid-fourth century, or even later, as essentially Middle Platonic, its main sources apparently being Numenius and the second-century Peripatetic Adrastus. Evidence of commentaries on other dialogues is unfortunately minimal, though we know of views that were held on many details of many of them.[8]

As regards monographs, there is the treatise of Plutarch mentioned above, *On the Generation of the Soul in the Timaeus,* and there would seem to have been a number of works on the Myth of Er in the *Republic,* if we may deduce this from the mention made by Proclus in his *Essays on the Republic* of a series of distinguished Platonists (τῶν Πλατωνικῶν οἱ κορυφαῖοι) who have written on the Myth, including Numenius, Albinus, Gaius, Maximus of Nicaea, Harpocration, and Euclides – though it is not clear in how many cases these commented in monographs rather than as part of more general works (in the case of Albinus, probably reporting Gaius, and Harpocration, at least, probably the latter). There also survives a monograph from Theon of Smyrna, of the early second century AD, on *Mathematical Principles Useful for the Study of Plato.*

This brings us to the more general works on Plato of which we have any record. Probably earliest is a work of Dercyllides which we shall have occasion to mention just below, *On the Philosophy of Plato.* Then we have Albinus' labour of love, in seven books, *Notes on the Lectures of Gaius* – his revered teacher, who seems to be a man who wrote little, if anything, himself. And then we have a mighty work by Atticus' pupil, Harpocration of Argos, *A Commentary on Plato*, in twenty-four books.[9] We also have, of course, two basic introductions to Platonism, in the form of the *Didaskalikos* of the rather shadowy Alcinous and the *De Platone et eius Dogmate* of the Roman rhetorician Apuleius of Madaura, both of the mid to later second century, from both of which many details of exegesis can be recovered. Last, but not, I think, least, we have, in Latin translation, an interesting work which was discovered by Raymond Klibansky back in the 1950s, but which has remained unpublished until now,[10] which goes through the Platonic dialogues, beginning (in the extant portion) with the *Republic,* and listing the *dogmata* presented in the various dialogues, including many which one would not have thought of at all. It is a fairly dismal production, in all truth, but by no means without interest. It is undoubtedly of Middle Platonic provenance, as there is no trace of any 'higher', Neoplatonic exegesis, though there are many traces of Stoic doctrine. It is high time that it was given a proper edition.

This, then, I think, completes the tally of Middle Platonic works of exegesis of which we have any knowledge. What I would like to do on this occasion is, by means of a judicious selection of examples, to survey the full range of types of comment indulged in by the various Middle Platonic commentators, in order to try to estimate how adequate or otherwise, from our point of view, their exegesis of the texts may have been.

I will begin – since it provides a good case-study for the differences in perspective between Middle Platonic and Neoplatonic commentary – with the *Timaeus*, which, throughout antiquity, from the Old Academy on, constituted one of the corner-stones of dogmatic Platonism. Let us start with the first sentence (17a): 'One, two, three – but where, my dear Timaeus, is the fourth of our guests of yesterday, our hosts of today?'

This little piece of Platonic foolery has provided a fine conundrum for scholars both ancient and modern.[11] Comment on the passage, albeit of a hostile nature, actually goes back to the period of the Old Academy, with Theophrastus' pupil Praxiphanes (in what context we have no idea) mocking Plato for making Socrates conduct a quite superfluous inventory of those present before pointing out that the fourth man is not there.[12] However, only much later do Platonist exegetes seem to have exercised themselves over the identity of the Absent Guest.[13] The first figure mentioned by Proclus as indulging in speculation over his identity, however, seems not to be a Platonist philosopher, but rather a *grammatikos* of the first century BC, one Aristocles of Rhodes.[14] This person, rather witlessly (in view of the chronological impossibilities),[15] proposes the mathematician Theaetetus, on the grounds that he was acquainted with philosophers of the Eleatic School (an allusion to the Eleatic Stranger of the *Sophist*). This proposal is, if anything, outdone in fatuity by that of a certain Ptolemy the Platonist[16] (Proc. *In Tim.* I 20.7-9), who proposed Clitophon –

he who plays a minor part in the *Republic,* as a hanger-on of the sophist Thrasymachus, and who has a (rather interesting) pseudo-Platonic dialogue called after him. I call the suggestion fatuous, but yet it is rather intriguing. Why on earth Clitophon? Ptolemy must have been reading the little dialogue, and something caught his eye, or his imagination, which made Clitophon seem suitable. At least one can say that there is no chronological impossibility involved.[17]

And then there is Dercyllides – that rather shadowy figure, perhaps of the first century AD, who edited the works of Plato before Thrasyllus, and wrote a work *On the Philosophy of Plato,* out of which this detail may have come.[18] Dercyllides proposes that the missing guest is none other than Plato himself, which is surely the silliest suggestion of all (Plato would have been still in diapers at the dramatic date of the dialogue); but even for this dotty proposal there is some glimmer of justification: Plato notoriously never puts himself into his dialogues, even when chronologically he could have been present, and Dercyllides may have seen a sort of analogy with Plato's excluding himself from the *Phaedo* (59b).

The only sensible proposal, though of a characteristically pedantic nature, is made by the second-century Platonist Atticus (fr. 16 des Places = Proclus *In Tim.* I 20.21-6): the Absent Guest must be a travelling companion of Timaeus, since it is Timaeus of whom Socrates enquires where he is, and it is Timaeus who makes excuses for him. Atticus, however, does not seem to be concerned as to why Plato should have marked him absent. To Atticus we shall return presently.

All this, then, is arguably not Middle Platonist exegesis at its best – and indeed the figures involved include only one of those whom we would think of as major Middle Platonic commentators – but it does seem to illustrate the different ways of looking at a text characteristic of pre- and post-Plotinian Platonists respectively. Porphyry, Iamblichus, and Syrianus, after all, are not at all interested in the identity of the Absent Guest; they are concerned, rather, with the arithmological significance of there being *three* guests rather than *four* on this occasion, and draw significant, if varying, symbolic conclusions from that.

But let us move on from this detail to consider the more general problem of the historicity and true meaning of the war with Atlantis (24e-25d). Here we may observe, once again, the stark contrast between a literal and an allegorical exegesis, but within the general framework of literal exegesis, there are subtleties.

This topic was actually broached first way back in the Old Academy, by Crantor of Soli, in his *Commentary.* The story he has to relate is a remarkable one. First of all, as Proclus tells us (*In Tim.* I 75.30ff.), Crantor declares that the Atlantis story is straightforward history (*historia psilê*), but he then seems rather to undermine this claim by his explanation of why Plato came to tell the story:

2. Pedantry and pedestrianism?

[Crantor] says that Plato found himself mocked (*skôptesthai*) by contemporary critics, with the allegation that he was not the inventor of his constitution (*politeia*),[19] but had based it on that of the Egyptians. He was so stung by this mockery that [in the *Timaeus*] he attributed to the Egyptians this story about the Athenians and the Atlantians, which indicated that the Athenians once lived under such a constitution: the prophets of the Egyptians, after all, he declares, say that these events are inscribed on stelae that are still preserved.

There is much that is peculiar about this anecdote, interesting as it is. First of all, who were the mockers, and why should Plato be stung by their mockery? As to the first question, one would think most naturally of contemporary sophists, such as Isocrates, but we have no evidence to go on. As to the second question, it is surely odd that Plato should be offended by the suggestion that he had borrowed an idea from the Egyptians, in view of his well-attested admiration of all things Egyptian; but an allegation of plagiarism is always annoying, no doubt, and it is conceivable that Plato should have been concerned in the *Timaeus* to deliver a literary counterblow.

Be that as it may, we have here a piece of literal exegesis, albeit of an oddly anecdotal nature. It would seem, in fact, that little attention was paid, in the Middle Platonic period, to the exegesis of the Proemium of the *Timaeus,* up to 27c. This is the point, at any rate, at which the Platonist Severus is stated (again by Proclus, *In Tim.* I 204.16f.) to have begun his commentary, regarding all before that point as unworthy of comment. This view would seem to have been shared by the Middle Platonic source or sources behind Calcidius, who begins his commentary only with the lemma 31c – which actually seems a little late. He says:[20]

About the beginning of the book, which contains merely the narration of deeds of long ago and a recapitulation of ancient history, I have said nothing, though I have deemed it relevant to set out the rationale of the whole work, the plan of the writer, and the structure of the book.

This he accordingly does, in the next two sections, but without dwelling on the Atlantis story at all. It would seem, on the whole, that, in earlier times, all that it was thought necessary to say about the Proemium was a brief summary of Plato's rationale in setting it up as a sort of sequel to the *Republic*.

However, this is not quite the whole story for Middle Platonic times. There are some authorities, Proclus tells us (I 76.10-17), who declare the tale of Atlantis to be 'a myth and fabrication with no historical basis, but containing a representation (*endeixis*) of permanent or regularly recurring features of the cosmos'.[21] These are not identified by Proclus, but he speaks of them in the way he normally speaks of pre-Porphyrian, Middle Platonic authorities. A further group, however, who do not seek to deny the historicity of the events, but still maintain their wider, cosmic, signifi-cance, are identified (I 76.17-77.6) as Numenius and the Platonist Origenes (though Plotinus' follower Amelius is also included, presumably following Numenius, as he often did). Numenius, we are told, refers the Atlantid War to a conflict of 'nobler souls' who are nurselings of Athena, with certain 'producers of generation' (*genesiourgoi*), who are protegés rather of 'the god who is the overseer of generation' (*tês geneseôs ephoros*), i.e. Poseidon.[22] These souls may be regarded as embodied (even as Odysseus in the *Odyssey* may be viewed as the human soul positioned between the forces of Athena and Poseidon), but Origenes, a little later, sees the conflict as one between two classes of daemon in the cosmos, one better, one worse, the former superior in power (*dynamis*), the latter superior in number (*plêthos*).[23]

Both these interpretations must appear to us a good deal more akin to Neoplatonic 'higher' (allegorical) exegesis than to the pedantry and pede-strianism which I am suggesting as the salient characteristic of Middle Platonic commentary, but Numenius is undoubtedly a Middle Platonist (though of the Neopythagorean persuasion), and Origenes arguably so.[24] The fact is, then, that there is a lot more going on, in the way of creative exegesis, in the Middle Platonic period than is generally recognized. Numenius, of course, is well grounded in the allegorical exegesis of Homer, as we can see from Porphyry's references to him in his essay *On the Cave of the Nymphs,* and he is the author of a work with the intriguing title *On the Secret Doctrines of Plato* – although the only detail we have preserved from this work (fr. 23 des Places) is, admittedly, not a very exciting one, albeit it does credit Plato with employing symbols. Numenius gives it as his opinion that Plato, in the *Euthyphro,* uses the character of the prepos-terous Euthyphro to symbolize the Athenian people in their beliefs about the gods, thus averting their wrath against him in the event that he had satirized them directly. Presumably Numenius, in the rest of the book, presented other instances of Plato saying one thing and meaning another, or at any rate of his concealing his true doctrine, but we unfortunately have no further details.

We see, then, that, at least at the latter end of the Middle Platonic period, there were developments in exegesis which anticipated to some extent the allegorizing of the Neoplatonists. This does not, however, alter the fact that the predominant impression we derive from the surviving remains of Middle Platonic commentary is something much less adventur-ous, though at the same time more akin to our own concerns. I would like now to turn to a number of salient passages from the dialogues on which we have some record of Middle Platonic comment, with a view to deriving a clearer view of their methods.

Sticking initially with the *Timaeus,* let us consider the exegesis of that key passage 28b, and, in particular, the key word: *gegonen.* Around the interpretation of this little word, uttered so baldly by Timaeus, a vast deal of discussion raged. If one did not accept the literal acount of the creation of the world, then it could not be allowed to mean what it appeared to mean. Even by the time of Crantor in the Old Academy, as we know from Proclus (*In Tim.* I 277.8-10 Diehl), the doctrine had been propounded that the cosmos is 'generated' only in the sense of 'being produced by a cause external to itself (ὡς ἀπ' ἄλλης αἰτίας παραγόμενον), and not self-generating nor self-substantiating'. Plainly, over the centuries, the debate went on, until in the mid-second century it results in the impressive *tour de force* of Calvenus Taurus in his *Timaeus Commentary*,[25] who assembles a list of no fewer than *four* possible meanings of *genêtos* other than the literal one: (1) that which is not in fact created, but is of the same genus as things that are created; (2) that which is in theory composite, even if it has not in fact been combined; (3) that which is always in process of generation (though it never had a beginning of generation); and (4) – Crantor's proposal – that which is dependent for its existence on an external cause. One could take one's pick. This would seem to be the sort of scholastic foot-slogging at which Middle Platonist scholars excelled. Proclus does not comment on Taurus, but he describes his successor Atticus, in various places, as 'a terrible fellow for quibbling about words',[26] and as 'most industrious' (*philoponôtatos*), and 'accustomed to follow the text very closely'[27] – this latter à propos an extraordinary suggestion by Atticus, on *Tim.* 41d, that one should postulate two mixing-bowls for the creation of souls (because Timaeus speaks at 41d4 of a 'former mixing-bowl' – so there must also, presumably, be a latter one!).[28]

But let us turn next to another key passage, 35a, on the composition of the soul. On this passage, of course, we have a surviving monograph by Plutarch, which is most informative, but also some information on the views of Atticus. Now Plutarch and Atticus, as we know, are repeatedly linked as sharing a common 'heresy' as to the temporal creation of the world, and the existence of a pre-cosmic chaos, presided over by a disorderly soul; but they are also credited[29] with a psychological theory that is a spin-off of that position, to the effect that the irrational soul within us is a distinct entity, though subordinated and harmonized with it (as distinct from being in conflict with it, as expounded by the doctrine of Numenius). From the exegetical perspective, attention must focus on the identification of the two components of the soul mentioned in 35a, 'the indivisible and always self-identical substance' (ἡ ἀμέριστος καὶ ἀεὶ κατὰ ταὐτὰ ἔχουσα οὐσία) and 'that which comes to be divisible about bodies' (ἡ περὶ τὰ σώματα γιγνομένη μεριστή). In the *De Procreatione Animae*, Plutarch first (1012d ff.) presents a critique of the views of his predecessors, in particular Xenocrates and Crantor, from the Old Academy, before presenting his own interpretation. In fact, Xenocrates' identification of the two soul-components with the Monad and the Dyad respectively might have been expected to suit Plutarch, but he objects to Xenocrates' denial of a pre-cosmic state of disorder and a disorderly soul to go with it. He himself, adducing the evidence of the 'maleficent soul' of *Laws* X, 896a-e, wishes to identify the 'substance that is divided about bodies' with this disorderly soul (1014b):

> For creation does not take place out of what does not exist at all, but rather out of what is in an improper or unfulfilled state, as in the case of a house or a garment or a statue. For the state that things were in before the creation of the ordered world (*kosmos*) may be characterized as 'lack of order' (*akosmia*); and this 'lack of order' was not something incorporeal or immobile or soulless, but rather it possessed a corporeal nature which was formless and inconstant, and a power of motion which was frantic and irrational. This was the disorderly state of a soul which did not yet possess reason (*logos*).

It is in fact still a subject of some discomfort for modern commentators as to how exactly these two components of the soul are to be identified, but they are disinclined to identify them with any definite cosmic principle. Cornford, for instance,[30] takes the 'indivisible substance' to be, broadly, Form or the Forms, while the 'divisible substance' would be the copies or images of the Forms immanent in the physical world, their blending, together with Sameness and Otherness, giving the soul the power of cognizing both levels of reality. Such a view is actually closest to that of Crantor in the Old Academy, who saw the soul as being composed of 'the intelligible substance' and 'that which is opinable in the sensible realm' (1012d), but it does not really address the problem of the origin of this *meristê ousia*.

At any rate, Atticus also, as Proclus tells us (*In Tim.* II 153.25ff. = fr. 35 des Places), takes the 'indivisible substance' to be the divine soul, and that divided about bodies as the irrational soul, both pre-existing the rational soul. What, we may wonder, does Atticus mean by the 'divine soul'? It would actually seem from other evidence (namely Syrianus, in his *Commentary on Metaphysics M*, p. 105, 35ff. Kroll) that Atticus, since he characterized the Forms as 'general reason-principles (*katholou logoi*) subsisting eternally in the essence of the soul',[31] must have situated the Forms at an ontological level inferior to the Demiurge, who was for him equivalent to the Good and the supreme God.[32] These Forms would therefore constitute the Paradigm, or Essential Living Being, which could be reasonably described as a 'divine soul'. God would then have mingled its essence with the refractory disorderly soul, to produce human souls. This account, if we can rely upon it, provides evidence of a degree of creative reinterpretation of the dialogue by Atticus, compatible both with his stance as staunch defender of Platonist orthodoxy (against Peripatetic encroachments) and of the temporal creation of the world, to which he was also committed.

Atticus' position on the relation between the Demiurge, the Paradigm, and the rational, or 'divine', World-Soul is actually rather difficult to work out with precision, since the impression which we may derive from his own words (preserved by Eusebius, *PE* XV 13 = fr. 9 des Places) conflicts starkly with reports relayed by Proclus (via Porphyry) in his *Timaeus Commentary*. In fr. 9 of his polemical tract *On Those who Claim to Interpret Plato through Aristotle*, Atticus clearly states that the Demiurge, as supreme God, is the father and creator of all things, and primarily of the Forms, which are his thoughts (*noêmata*); but from Proclus we hear Porphyry's criticism (*In Tim.* I 394.6ff. = fr. 28 des Places) that 'others (sc. Atticus), with their doctrine of the Forms subsisting by themselves and lying outside the (divine) intellect, present them to us as inert objects, like the models of the statuette-makers.'[33] There is something distinctly rhetorical about this passage, however; it may just be that Atticus, whom Porphyry would not much approve of anyway, in view of his other heresies, is falling victim to the much greater degree of sophistication which the issue as to whether the Forms were within or outside the divine Intellect took on in the next century, in the school of Plotinus. (Porphyry himself, we must recall, when he arrived to study with Plotinus in Rome, as he tells us himself, still held, following his former master Longinus, to the doctrine that the Forms were outside the Intellect, and had to be weaned from this by protracted argument, *VPlot.* 18.)

We can, then, derive from our sources quite a number of insights into Atticus' wrestlings with the central issues of the *Timaeus*. But this is not the only record we have of Middle Platonic interpretations of *Timaeus* 35a. We have notice, from Proclus (*In Tim.* II 153.15-25), of two varieties of mathematical interpretation of the two *ousiai,* that of Numenius (with whom is linked an otherwise quite unknown Aristander), looking back to the position of Xenocrates, which takes the two components to be the Monad and the Indefinite Dyad; and that of Severus, who preferred a geometrical model, the point and the principle of extension (σημεῖον καὶ διάστασις), which, if anything, goes back to the position of Speusippus, who defined the soul as the 'Form of the omnidimensionally extended' (ἰδέα τοῦ πάντη διαστατοῦ).[34] Numenius, however, held to a much more dualistic model of the human soul than had Xenocrates – more dualistic, even, that that of Plutarch and Atticus, if we may believe Iamblichus (*De An.* p. 375.12-15 Wachsmuth), so that for him the Indefinite Dyad is very much a principle of evil, or at least disorder, and there is within us an irrational soul, or psychic element, which continually wars against the reason.[35]

But it is time, I think, to move on from the interpretation of the *Timaeus,* interesting and central though it is, to take in a number of other notable pieces of Middle Platonic exegesis. If we turn to the *Phaedo,* for instance, we can discern various characteristic details preserved in the tradition. First, we may consider a response to an *aporia,* from Atticus' follower Harpocration, on the question as to why, at *Phd.* 70b, Socrates says to Cebes, 'Now what shall we do? Do you wish to keep on discussing this question, as to whether it is *likely* (*eikos*) or not (sc. that the soul survives departure from the body)?'[36] The *aporia* raises the question why

Plato had used the term *eikos* here, instead, presumably, of some such term as *alêthes*, 'true'. Harpocration's reply, as reported by the much later commentator Damascius (*In Phd.* I 182), is that this is simply because 'the proof rests on an inference' (ὡς ἀπὸ τεκμηρίου), while Damascius' own is rather that it is *eikos* as compared with the truth of the higher realm (ἡ ἐκεῖ ἀλήθεια). The *aporia* may or may not have been a deliberately troublesome one, of the kind that we have seen raised concerning the first sentence of the *Timaeus,* but Harpocration moves to neutralize it by philological means, whereas the later commentator derives a more metaphysical meaning from it. In between the two solutions is another, which is anonymous, and may or may not be Middle Platonic, to the effect that it is only being proved possible, but not necessary, that our souls continue to exist in Hades. This little detail, then, serves to remind us of the nuts and bolts of commentary. One must strive to defend Plato against any charges of inconsistency or incoherence.[37]

Another troublesome topic which concerns Harpocration, as it did many others, is the identity of the 'true earth' described by Socrates in the 'myth' at the end of the dialogue (108c). The history of the controversy is outlined by Damascius at *In Phd.* II 503-6:

> The earth of which Plato speaks here is incorporeal (*asômatos*) according to some, corporeal according to others; of the latter, Harpocration thinks that what is meant is the whole cosmos, and Theodorus [sc. of Asine] the sublunary world; of those who think of it as incorporeal, Democritus [sc. the Platonist] believes it to be Form (*idea*), Plutarch [sc. of Athens] to be Nature.

We have here an interesting mix of Middle and Neo-Platonic theorizing on this troublesome question. The Middle Platonists, Harpocration and Democritus,[38] are divided, one favouring a corporeal solution, the other an incorporeal one, but both prepared to allegorize Plato in this instance. Harpocration presumably means that the 'true earth' is a description of either a lunar or some other celestial paradise, while Democritus would seem to have plumped – rather incoherently, perhaps – for the Form of Earth. The problem, for modern as well as for ancient commentators, lies, after all, in the fact that Plato seems to be presenting this 'true earth' as in some way continuous with our earth, but composed of more refined substance. At any rate, we have here an instance where Middle Platonic and Neoplatonic commentators are not starkly opposed, but rather in relative continuity – and this, I think, if we had all the data before us, would probably reflect a good deal of the truth. Much of the substance of later Neoplatonic commentaries was in fact lifted more or less wholesale from their Middle Platonic predecessors, with only the allegorizing of the prefatory portions, and of the characters, and the imposition of a more rigid conception of a unitary *skopos* as the distinctively new features.

This has been a necessarily rather spotty survey of a large field of study, to which Harold Tarrant himself has made many distinguished contributions – most recently, of course, in his most stimulating book *Platos' First Interpreters*. I hope, however, that it may provide some food for thought. The title contained, as will have been noted, a question-mark. I trust that I have provided enough evidence to indicate that there is really no call to condemn the Middle Platonist commentators as unduly pedestrian or pedantic. Certainly we moderns are in no position to do so. The question of what commentary on a text should really be about has been the subject of some debate in recent years, but for most of us, I think, the virtues of a good commentary remain the answering of any questions that one might want to ask about a given text from a philological or historical point of view, together with some sober analysis of its structure and literary affiliations, if appropriate. Alternatives to this, in the form of 'hermeneutic' or post-modernist flights of fancy on the basis of the text, appear to me much more like the imposition upon the text of the ingenuity or prejudices of the commentator than a true exegesis of the author's intention (which some of these ingenious persons would actually dismiss as an invalid concept!). So far as can be discerned from the limited evidence, I should say that the Middle Platonists tended towards the former type of commentary rather than the second, while the Neoplatonists might be regarded as remote ancestors of the latter,[39] and that I would regard as being in their favour.

Notes

1. In the Preface, p. 5.6-16 Saffrey-Westerink.

2. What could this refer to? Could Proclus be viewing the period of the Old Academy as the 'completion' of Plato's teaching? He does not in general exhibit much interest in the Old Academicians, but he knows that they are there; cf. Tarán (1987).

3. Though an unsatisfactory term, it serves a purpose. George Boy-Stones has attacked it recently, in the preface to his stimulating book on the period (2001). I have said what I have to say on the question, Dillon (1996), 422-3.

4. A topic well dealt with by Tarrant (2000a).

5. I consider it highly unlikely that Antiochus of Ascalon composed commentaries as such.

6. I am now inclined to agree with Tarrant (1985), ch. 4, that he is much earlier than the second century AD slot into which I had placed him in *The Middle Platonists*, but I am still not quite prepared to identify him with Eudorus, as Tarrant might like to do.

7. We also have a passing reference, from Proclus (*In Tim.* III 247.15), to a commentary by Atticus on the *Phaedrus*.

8. The late Platonist Democritus (see below, n. 38) is credited with commentaries on the *Alcibiades*, and (possibly) on the *Phaedo*, and Longinus (quoted by Porphyry in his *Life of Plotinus*, ch. 20) speaks of his predecessor, Eubulus, the *diadochos* at Athens, as composing commentaries on the *Philebus* and the *Gorgias*, as well as a treatise *On Aristotle's Objections to Plato's Republic*'. This gives us what I am confident is only a glimpse of continuous pedestrian exegetical activity under way during these centuries.

9. Of which I have edited the fragments, Dillon (1971), repr. in (1990).

10. I have obtained a samizdat copy, by courtesy of my late friend Matthias Baltes.

11. I don't wish to exclude the possibility that Plato may have had some serious purpose in creating the Absent Guest, but I would despair of working out what it may have been. A.E. Taylor has a useful discussion at the beginning of his commentary, and in his *Prolegomena*, p. 25, but his positive suggestion (following his mentor Burnet – 'perhaps Philolaus') is hardly profitable. There is no specific indication, as he suggests, that Timaeus is merely standing in for this man; and when the question of an expositor of the cosmogony and anthropology is taken up at 20cd, there is no suggestion that Timaeus is in any way a second-best choice. The Absent Guest is simply forgotten.

12. Porphyry, ap. Procl. *In Tim.* I 14.20ff. Diehl. This criticism, fatuous though it is, is of considerable significance, indicating the interest being taken in details of this key text already in the early third century BC – the period when the Academician Crantor was composing his 'commentary' on the dialogue. Praxiphanes' perspective seems to have been primarily literary, since he is also reported by Porphyry as taking exception to the switch from cardinal to ordinal numeration, as between the counting of the first three and the mentioning of the absence of the *fourth.*

13. Crantor cannot, I think, have solved the mystery in his 'commentary' (whatever form that took), or we would have heard about it – and the later debate would have had no grounds.

14. If we are right to identify him, as Festugière would suggest (ad loc.), with the Aristocles of Rhodes who is quoted later, at I 85.28, à propos the date of the Bendideia, and not with the second century AD Peripatetic Aristocles of Messene, the teacher of Alexander of Aphrodisias.

15. Ibid. I 19.30-20.7. Theaetetus is portrayed in the dialogue called after him as being only a lad of about fifteen in 399 BC, whereas the dramatic date of the *Timaeus* is around the period of the Peace of Nicias, in the late 420s.

16. Not the well-known geographer, but (probably) a late Middle Platonist, whom Dihle (1957) would place around AD 300. There is no other trace, however, of a commentary on the dialogue by this person, so this conjecture must have occurred in some other context.

17. Proclus condemns this suggestion pretty roundly (παντελῶς ἄτοπον, 20.18), but only because, as he argues, Clitophon, while present at the first exposition of the *Republic,* was not present at its reprise to the present company, when he is spoken of in the third person.

18. He is also recorded as having some views on passages of the *Republic* (ap. Procl. *In Remp.* II 24.6-15 and 25.14-26 Kroll, probably from the same work rather than from a commentary. Tarrant, it must be said, argues stoutly (1993), 11-13, against the necessity of dating Dercyllides before Thrasyllus; but he is certainly Middle Platonic.

19. I.e. the ideal state of the *Republic.*

20. *Comm.* s. IV, p. 58, 26-59, 2 Waszink. '*Denique de principio libri, quo simplex narratio continebatur rerum ante gestarum et historiae veteris recensitio nihil dixi, rationem tamen totius operis et scriptoris propositum et ordinationem libri declaranda esse duxi.*' The *scriptoris propositum,* we may note, would represent the *skopos* of later Platonist exegetical theory, and this turns out to be (following on the *Republic,* which concerned justice in the individual and the state) 'natural justice' on the scale of the cosmos as a whole (s. VI, p. 59, 14-60, 3).

2. Pedantry and pedestrianism?

21. Οἱ δέ φασιν αὐτὴν μῦθον εἶναι καὶ πλάσμα γενόμενον οὐδαμῶς, ἔνδειξιν δὲ φέρον τῶν ἀεὶ ὄντων κατὰ τὸν κόσμον ἢ γιγνομένων.

22. This identification is made clear, if clarity were needed, by a passage from Porphyry's *De Antro Nympharum* (34), where Numenius is mentioned as contrasting Athena and Poseidon in a similar way, in the context of the *Odyssey*.

23. This sounds like a particular application of the principle put forward by Plotinus, and adopted by all Platonists after him, that, as one descends through the universe, a decrease in power corresponds to an increase in multiplicity.

24. He was, of course, a contemporary of Plotinus, and a fellow-student of Ammonius Saccas, but on the matter of postulating a One above Being, the distinctive innovation of Plotinus, Origenes plainly remains a 'Middle Platonist'.

25. Fr. 22B (Lakmann) = John Philoponus, *Aet. Mundi* 145.13ff. Rabe.

26. *In Tim.* I 284.13: δεινὸς γὰρ ὁ ἀνὴρ ἀντιλαβέσθαι τῶν ῥημάτων.

27. *In Tim.* III 247.12: καὶ ταῦτα εἰωθότα σφόδρα παρέπεσθαι ταῖς ῥήσεσι.

28. I call this proposal 'extraordinary', but in fact it is adopted by Plotinus, at *Enn.* IV.8.4.36ff., as a means of explaining why some souls are condemned to enter mortal bodies.

29. By Iamblichus, in his *De Anima,* p. 375, 1ff. Wachsmuth.

30. (1937), 59-66.

31. Τοὺς καθόλου λόγους τοὺς ἐν οὐσίᾳ τῇ ψυχικῇ διαιωνίως ὑπαρχόντας ἥγουνται εἶναι τὰς ἰδέας.

32. Cf. Procl. *In Tim.* I 305.6-16 = fr. 12 des Places. We also learn from *In Tim.* I 431.14-20 (= fr. 34 des Places) that Atticus, in giving an exegesis of *Tim.* 30d, where the Paradigm is stated to 'contain within itself all living creatures which are by nature akin to itself', argued that this cannot include the Demiurge, since that would imply that he was not perfect (*teleios*), so he must therefore be superior to it.

33. Οἱ δ᾽ ἀδρανεῖς τὰς ἰδέας τύποις κοροπλαθικοῖς ἐοικυίας ἐφ᾽ ἑαυτῶν οὔσας καὶ ἔξω τοῦ νοῦ κειμένας εἰσάγουσιν.

34. Cf. also Iambl. *De Anima* p. 363.26ff. Wachsmuth, where the connection between Severus and Speusippus is made more explicit.

35. Cf. fr. 52.44-75 des Places (from Calcidius).

36. ἀλλὰ τί ποιῶμεν; ἢ περὶ αὐτῶν τούτων βούλει διαμυθολογῶμεν εἴτε εἰκὸς οὕτως ἔχειν εἴτε μή;

37. There is in fact another of these apparently eristic *aporiai* recorded on an earlier passage of the dialogue, *Phd.* 66c, where it has been stated by Socrates that all wars take place 'for the sake of acquiring money', and some troublesome person has complained that that is not true: some are fought, for example, for other reasons, such as love of honour (*philotimia*). Harpocration (ap. Dam. *In Phd.* I 110) brushes this aside by claiming that Plato is speaking ἐπὶ τὸ πλεῖστον – *most* wars are fought for gain!

38. Democritus (nicknamed *Chnous*), who flourished in the early third century BC (see Luc Brisson's notice of him in the *Dictionnaire des philosophes antiques,* ed. R. Goulet, Paris [1989-ongoing], II 716-7) is a rather shadowy figure, but must count as a (late) Middle Platonist. Olympiodorus credits him with a commentary on the *Alcibiades* (*In Alc.* p.70 Westerink), and this entry would seem to provide some indication of a *Phaedo* commentary.

39. Admittedly, 'allegorical' commentary would be regarded nowadays as a quite improper way of approaching a text, but the hermeneuts and the post-modernists can be regarded as allegorizing in their way.

3

Apuleius on the Platonic gods

John F. Finamore

Apuleius is known mainly for his novel *The Metamorphoses* (or *The Golden Ass*) and for his rhetorical works, *Apology*, *Florida*, and *De Deo Socratis*. Less familiar are his philosophical works, *De Platone et Eius Dogmate* and *De Mundo*.[1] These two latter works display a Middle Platonic philosophical system that is in harmony with the glimpses of philosophy we receive in his other writings. I here investigate Apuleius' thinking on two topics of concern to Platonists of his time. The first concerns the Demiurge: his relation to the universe he designed, and whether he is the highest god. The second involves the role of the invisible gods as intermediaries. I hope to show that Apuleius is an independent Platonic philosopher creating his own Middle Platonic reading of Plato. I begin, however, by briefly addressing some questions about these two dialogues and their place in Apuleius' writings.

i. The *De Platone et Eius Dogmate* and *De Mundo*

Like the *Metamorphoses*, both of these works are adaptations of Greek originals. The *De Platone* is a re-working of basic handbook material, whose history is impossible to re-trace.[2] Of its two books, the first covers the life of Plato and then turns to matters of physics, including the roles of the gods, time, providence, and the soul and its effect on the body; the second book concerns ethics, including the virtues and the good state. The *De Mundo* (*On the Universe*) is a translation of the Pseudo-Aristotelian *On the Universe* (Περὶ Κόσμου), although the author misleadingly claims to be composing a work drawn from Aristotle and Theophrastus (*DM* 1.289).[3] The author follows his original closely, sometimes substituting Latin for Greek authors (as Ennius for Homer at 365). Book I takes us from the heavens with their divine planets and stars, through the four elements, to the earth and its phenomena, such as winds, clouds, volcanoes. Book II centres on the supreme god and ruler of the universe and the related topic of providence and fate.[4]

Apuleius here is not a mere translator. Although he certainly works from a Greek handbook, he does not follow it slavishly. Rather, he selects materials in harmony with his own philosophical beliefs. The *De Mundo* confirms this practice. Comparison of Περὶ Κόσμου 397b9-398b23 and *DM*

342-52 reveals a conscious effort to change the Greek original's emphasis on the transcendent god and his own power (δύναμις) at work in the universe to Apuleius' doctrine of an hierarchical chain of highest god, visible gods (stars and planets), and daemons.[5] Thus, Apuleius does not follow others uncritically, and, being attuned to the issues involved, realigns the original with his own reading of Platonic doctrine.

ii. The highest god

Apuleius discusses the highest god in four treatises: *De Platone* 190-1, 193-4, 204-6, and 219-20; *De Mundo* 341-52, 365-6, and 370-1; *Apology* 64; and *De Deo Socratis* 124.[6] He begins his discussion of Platonic doctrines in the *De Platone* with a division of three principles of things (*initia rerum*):

> god; matter that is incomplete, without form, with no distinct appearance or sign of quality; and the forms of things, which Plato calls 'Ideas' (ἰδέαι).
>
> *DP* 190[7]

This is straightforward interpretation of Plato's *Timaeus* (29d-31a), although Plato of course does not use the term 'principle' (ἀρχή), and what Apuleius interprets as 'matter' is in Plato 'all that was visible ... not at rest but in an inharmonious and disordered motion' (30a3-5), and the Form in question is the Form of Living Creature, which 'embraces all intelligible living creatures in itself' (*Tim.* 30c7-8). The tripartite doctrine is common in Platonic handbooks.[8]

Apuleius then turns to the god in this triad and characterizes it with fourteen epithets (190):

> But he [i.e. Plato] thinks these things about god, that he is incorporeal. He is one, he says, *aperimetros* (ἀπερίμετρος), maker and fashioner of all things, happy and cause of happiness, best, lacking nothing, himself conferring all things. He calls him heavenly, unnamed, ineffable, and, as he himself says, *aoraton, adamaston* (ἀόρατον, ἀδάμαστον).

Some of these epithets appear in other Apuleian works; others only here.[9] It should be noted that these terms, while not reproducing Platonic vocabulary precisely, accord with Platonic doctrine about the Demiurge.[10] Indeed, Apuleius continues (191) by stating that it is difficult to discover this god, and then quotes in Greek in truncated form *Tim.* 28c2-4: 'it is a task to discover god and having found him impossible to reveal to (the) many'.[11] Thus, it is the Platonic Demiurge that Apuleius has in mind when he speaks of the highest god. The epithet 'heavenly' (*caelestis*), however, seems odd.[12] For surely Plato envisioned the Demiurge as being above the cosmos he fashioned. Indeed, later, Apuleius himself calls him 'hypercosmic' (204):

3. Apuleius on the Platonic gods

> He [i.e. Plato] names three classes of gods, of which the first is that one and only highest, hypercosmic (*ultramundanus*), incorporeal, whom we have shown above to be the father and maker of this divine world.

Note that Apuleius is referring to *the same god* in both passages, the Platonic Demiurge, since he clearly refers in the second passage to the first when he says 'whom we have shown above the father and maker of this divine world.'[13] We must ask how the same god can be both 'of the heavens' and 'hypercosmic', *caelestis* and *ultramundanus*? Is that possible? Or could, perhaps, Apuleius be thinking of two higher gods: one supracelestial and the other heavenly?

Another two passages from the *De Platone* might (wrongly) seem to suggest this possibility. In section 193, Apuleius divides everything that exists into two kinds of substance (οὐσίαι, *essentiae*). 'Of these,' he says, 'one is conceived by thought alone; the other can be subjected to the senses' (193). This is clearly a Platonic dichotomy, which can be found in the *Timaeus* and other dialogues.[14] After explaining that the mind discerns substances of the first type and the senses those of the second,[15] Apuleius continues (193-4):

> And of the first substance and essence is the first god, mind, the forms of things, and the soul; of the second substance, all things which are informed, which come into being, which lead their origin from the exemplum of the superior substance, and which are able to be changed and transformed, slipping and fleeting like a river.

Apuleius gives four examples of substances of the first kind: god, mind, Forms, soul (*primum deum esse et mentem formasque rerum et animam*). At first blush, it would seem that Apuleius is presenting four examples in descending order of worth. If that were the case, then he might be distinguishing the first god from a lower, cosmic mind. Further evidence for this view might be sought in the second passage *DP* 220, where instead of the first and second substances Apuleius speaks of first and second goods:

> First goods are the highest god and that mind which [Plato] calls *nous* (*prima bona esse deum summum mentemque illam, quam* voῦν *idem vocat*).

In fact Moreschini[16] takes the words just this way, citing a similar passage in Alcinous' *Didaskalikos* (27.1, 179.36ff.): *Mens*, he says, is 'an allusion, therefore, to the Cosmic Noῦς, concerning which he barely speaks in the first book'. Others too have worried over the use of *mens* here. Gersh argues that mind should be identified with the Forms,[17] and then he argues that Apuleius could have associated the now unified Mind/Forms both with the first god and with soul. Dillon considers Apuleius' words in the second passage (*DP* 220) and suggests[18]

... that we have to do here not with two metaphysical entities but rather with the supreme God, the Good of *Republic* VI (who may or may not be an intellect) and our own intellect, which cognizes him.

These are both ingenious solutions to the problem, but both ultimately fail, I think, because they deny the due order of the four entities in the first passage. Whatever Apuleius is trying to say, it seems fairly certain that he is presenting these entities in order: god, mind, Forms, soul. If so, the mind in question is above the Forms, not equivalent to them or below them.

Most recently, Göransson has suggested a different solution to this dilemma, based upon the passage in the *Didaskalikos* to which Moreschini referred. Alcinous, like Apuleius in our second passage (*DP* 220), is discussing 'the most honourable and greatest good'.[19] About this highest good, Alcinous writes (27.1, 179.39-42):

Our good, if someone reads his [i.e. Plato's] writings accurately, is placed in the knowledge and contemplation of the first good, which someone might name *god and first intellect*.

Göransson, noting the similarity between the two authors' words, concludes that Apuleius has mistranslated his source, in which (as in the Alcinous passage) 'God and *nous* were identified.'[20] Now, although I agree that Apuleius has most probably reworked the material that Alcinous has reproduced, I cannot agree that this is a mistranslation. First, Apuleius knows Greek well and it is unlikely that he would make such an error.[21] Second, and more importantly, Apuleius has developed a Platonic doctrine of his own, one based not merely on compilations such as Alcinous' but on his reading of the texts of Plato himself. We know from his *Florida* (15.26, 18.15, 20.4) that he studied Platonic philosophy in Athens. We have preserved for us two fragments of a translation he has made of the *Phaedo*.[22] Translations of and references to Plato pepper his extant works. The obvious conclusion is that Apuleius knew his Plato well, and thus would have worked toward a consistent system of Platonic doctrine. Thus, just as he changed the emphasis of the pseudo-Aristotelian *De Mundo*, so too he would have re-worked the Platonic handbooks to better express his own interpretations of Plato.[23]

That said, what is Apuleius' doctrine here? First, taking the sequence of the four terms, we see that three (the highest god, mind, and Forms) are all supracosmic, whereas the soul exists in the cosmos. Apuleius, who shows knowledge of the *Phaedrus* myth, would be aware that the Forms reside in the 'hypercosmic place' (ὑπερουράνιος τόπος, 247c3).[24] In the *Timaeus*, both the Demiurge and the Forms (*Tim.* 27c-31a) are of the higher sorts of things that are invisible and eternal. Thus, the divine mind that is to cognize them must be equally transcendent. And it is in this sense, then, that Apuleius refers separately to the first god and to his mind – not because they are separate in actuality (for they are not) but because they are separable in thought. God, who is fashioner and governor of this world, is a mind but, in Apuleius' religious thought, he is the highest being in a truly personal religion. He is transcendent, but involved somehow with the cosmos (as we shall shortly see). Thus, it is this highest feature of the highest god – his transcendence but combined with his care for this world – that I suspect Apuleius is emphasizing here. His *nous* is just one aspect of him, and a lower one at that. Thus, I see Apuleius as differentiating between a higher religious status of the Demiurge and a lower philosophical one, but both of these aspects (like the unitary god itself) are supracosmic.[25]

We now return to the question of how god can be both *caelestis* and *ultramundanus*. The explanation is already hinted at in *DP* 204-5 (the passage in which the highest god is called *ultramundanus*), for there Apuleius introduces a tripartition of divinity into the highest god, the *caelicolae* (i.e. the visible gods: planets and stars), and the *medioximi* (i.e. daemons).[26]

In order to understand how these different classes of divine beings explain how the highest god can be called both *caelestis* and *ultramundanus*, we must turn to the *De Mundo*. We have already noted that Apuleius in the *De Mundo* reworks the doctrine of the Περὶ Κόσμου of god's transcendent οὐσία above the world and his δύναμις at work in it.[27] Like the unknown author of the Greek treatise, Apuleius sees god at work in the cosmos, but not directly.[28] Speaking specifically of the Demiurge *qua* creator, he says (*DM* 343):

> This is the saviour and creator of all who are born and made for the completion of the cosmos, but not in such a way that he constructed the world with his hands by employment of corporeal labor, but by a certain tireless providence he reaches all things placed at a distance and embraces those separated by the greatest intervals of distance.

Thus, even in the act of creation, god remains above the world. He acts, but not as a human artificer would with his hands. He embraces the world, but from a distance. This notion of distance plays an important role in the sequel.[29] Apuleius immediately adds that god 'holds a high and lofty seat' (*praestantem ac sublimem sedem tenere*) and 'occupies a hallowed throne in lofty citadels' (*in arduis arcibus habere solium consecratum*), and thus is supracosmic. He next turns to the entities beneath god (343):

> Those closer take more fully of his power: the heavenly bodies, by the degree to which they are close to him, partake of god the more; by much less do those who are second after these; and even to these earthly regions the benefits of god's bounty reach us by way of intervals of distance.

37

Those nearest to god are the visible gods and those second after them are the daemons,[30] beings foreign to the Pseudo-Aristotelian original. Thus, the power and providence of the transcendent god works through these intermediaries penetrating all the way down to the earth. As Apuleius says a little further on (344):

> That highest power consecrated in the temples of heaven, both to those who are far separated from him and to those nearest, in one and the same way, both through himself and through others,[31] brings the aid of salvation, neither penetrating nor approaching individually in each case nor dragging all things disgracefully while close at hand.

Apuleius goes on to compare god to military commanders, senators, and city officials who also delegate others to work on their behalf (345-6). The transcendent god is immanent in the world through his intermediaries, the gods and daemons. In this way, Apuleius can claim, the highest god is both above and in the heavens.

But how does the highest god act? We have seen that, although god is like a human craftsman, he does not create with his hands. An answer comes at *DM* 350-2, where Apuleius again discusses the chain from the highest god down to earth. Apuleius explains that the highest god while remaining enthroned on high 'dispenses his powers (*potestates*) through all parts of the cosmos' (350). These powers are placed in the charge of the visible gods within the cosmos, and the gods in turn govern the welfare (*salus*) of all on earth (350-1). After comparing the highest god to a puppeteer, who controls the puppet's movements by pulling on several strings,[32] Apuleius again explains the workings of the hierarchy (351-2):

> By no means differently the celestial power (*caelestis potestas*), when it begins to set things in motion (*initium mouerit*) by a knowing and salubrious effort (*sciente et salutifera opera*), insinuates the power of its own majesty by uninterrupted contact from the lowest to the second and then to the closest and then even to the supreme. One is moved by another, and the movement of one transfers its motion to another by its motion (*aliud alio commouetur motusque unius alteri mouendi se originem tradit*).

There are two points to notice here. First, Apuleius calls god a *caelestis potestas*. Since, a few lines above (350), Apuleius described god as dispensing his own *potestates* to the visible gods, one might think that the *caelestis potestas* is one of the planets or stars who has received the *potestas* from the Demiurge. The use of *maiestas*, however, rules that possibility out. For this *caelestis potestas* 'insinuates the power of its own *maiestas*' into the world below, and the word *maiestas* was just used above (350) of the Demiurge:[33]

> Thus one must think that he [i.e. the highest god] retains his rank and

maiestas, if he himself sits on the highest throne,[34] but he dispenses those powers through all parts of the cosmos.

Thus, the highest god is again called 'heavenly', even as Apuleius is describing the method of the immanence of this transcendent god. More evidence for this interpretation comes from the original Greek text (398b20-3), where, after the image of the puppeteer, the author continues by saying that 'the divine nature' (ἡ θεία φύσις), i.e. the highest god in his system, acts similarly.

The second point to notice is Apuleius' use of the words 'by a knowing and salubrious effort' (*sciente et salutifera opera*). These words are not in the Greek original.[35] Just as Apuleius added to the text that the Demiurge is a 'heavenly power,' i.e. one that acts within the heavens, so too he adds how the Demiurge acts. He acts 'knowingly' (*sciente*), i.e. through his intellect. This is not a new idea, of course. It is as old as Xenophanes fr. 25:

But without toil he [i.e. god] makes all things stir by his mind.

Xenophanes was arguing against the Homeric conception of the gods such as Zeus, who acted as human beings did, brandishing lightning bolts in his hands. Apuleius is making a similar argument against a different kind of anthropomorphizing tendency. As we have seen, the Demiurge does not create with his hands. Apuleius' god, like Xenophanes', acts through his mind. Thus it is likely that Apuleius has Xenophanes in mind when he was writing *sciente*.[36]

And he is most probably thinking of Anaxagoras fr. 13 as well. Anaxagoras' Mind was the force behind creation also. Anaxagoras says (fr. 13):

when Mind began to initiate motion, it was separated from all that was moved, and as much as Mind set in motion, all this was separated. And with this moving and dividing, the revolution caused it to be divided much more.

Thus, Mind initiated motion but remained separated from what it moved.[37] Here Apuleius' use of the expression *initium mouerit* ('began to set things in motion') accurately translates Anaxagoras' Greek (ἤρξατο ὁ νοῦς κινεῖν), more so than it does the Greek of the original. Further, the Anaxagoran doctrine that the Mind is separate to itself but also involved in the ordering of the cosmos (albeit through a 'revolution') is one for which Apuleius has sympathy, although his own metaphysics would explain god's immanence in a more refined manner. Apuleius would have been aware too of the criticism of Plato (*Phd.* 97b-99d, *Laws* 967bc) and Aristotle (*Met.* 1.4, 985a18-22) that Anaxagoras does not make proper use of this god in his system, relying instead on mechanical causes. Apuleius' highest god is, however, more than mere initiator of the motions of the cosmos.

We have seen that Apuleius distinguished the Demiurge's mind from the god himself. I argued that this was done to differentiate two features of god: the philosophical concept of god as pure intellect and the religious concept of god as saviour. Thus it is not surprising to find coupled with *sciente* the adjective *salutifera*. I have translated it 'salubrious', but the word has a wider range. On the primary level, it involves bringing well-being, but the word also has cult overtones for gods of healing.[38] Further, *salus* is what the god, acting through the visible gods, provides to humanity (*DM* 350), and what Lucius asked from Isis (*Met.* 11.1). Thus, just as the participle *sciente* represents the philosophical aspect of god (his role as Prime Mover), the adjective *salutifera* represents his religious, healing, salvific aspect. For Apuleius, of course, the salvific aspect is higher.[39]

This concludes our discussion of the highest god in Apuleius' writings. We have found that there is a remarkable consistency of outlook across the writings of Apuleius on this topic. The Demiurge is enthroned on high, in the hypercosmic realm. He acts on this realm through intermediaries: gods and daemons. He thus is both transcendent and immanent. Since Apuleius is both philosopher and priest,[40] he sees god in two aspects. The first, represented by the divine mind discussed by Xenophanes and Anaxagoras, is philosophical. God is the highest mind directing the universe with his thought. The second aspect is religious, god as saviour. God, at work through his intermediaries, is able to aid and protect those who reach out to him.

iii. Invisible gods

Apuleius, as we have seen, believes in visible gods (the stars and planets) and the intermediary daemons.[41] In the *De Deo Socratis* 121-3, however, he adds another category, that of the invisible gods. Apuleius begins this oration with a discussion of the gods, the highest of the threefold division of gods, daemons, human beings (116). After a discussion of the visible gods (116-21) and just before a short discussion of the highest god (124), Apuleius places a single, unique, brief study of the invisible gods. What are these gods and why has Apuleius included them in his system?

Beaujeu in his discussion of this passage (1973, 209-11) connects the invisible gods to Critias' discussion of the gods as basically unknowable (*Crit.* 107ab) and to the reference to 'Zeus, Hera, and all the others' in *Epinomis* 984de, although the *Epinomis* passage would seem to be about visible rather than invisible gods. Beaujeu concludes that for Apuleius the invisible gods 'are difficult to distinguish from daemons' (209). He also has concerns that the role of the invisible gods may conflict with Apuleius' insistence that the gods do not intervene directly in earthly matters (210).

3. Apuleius on the Platonic gods

Hijmans too (1987, 440-2) is hard pressed to explain the role of these gods in Apuleius' system:[42]

> Their several functions and competences are not discussed, however, and thus we cannot say exactly how their relationship with the visible gods should be described.

Gersh (1986, 1.302-8) has a good discussion of the invisible and visible gods, but like Hijmans worries about the relation of the invisible and visible gods, even suggesting 'the possibility of identifying the two groups' (306).

The problems raised by these three scholars can be addressed if we look at what Apuleius says in *DDS* 121-3 and compare it to Plato's *Phaedrus* myth, which was extremely important in Middle Platonic times, as it was later.[43] Although Gersh rightly sees (1986, 1.303-4 n. 318) that Apuleius begins his discussion of the invisible gods with a reference to the *Phaedrus*, he does not pursue the matter far enough. Apuleius writes (121):

> There is another class of gods, which nature has denied to our sight, yet we nevertheless contemplate, examining them closely with our intellect, contemplating more keenly with the acuity of the mind (... *nec non tamen intellectu eos rimabundi contemplamur acie mentis acrius contemplantes*).

Gersh notes the parallel with *Phdr.* 247c, where Plato is discussing the contents of the 'supracelestial place' (ὁ ὑπερουράνιος τόπος, c3), which 'can be observed by the intellect alone' (μόνῳ θεατῇ νῷ, c7-8). Thus the invisible gods, like the Forms, exist beyond the realm of the cosmos. Note, therefore, that the gods are clearly differentiated both from the visible gods (which exist in the cosmos) and the daemons (which live in the air).

It is worth comparing this passage with another about the stars in *DM* 292.[44] In the *De Mundo*, Apuleius is differentiating the fixed stars from the planets. Turning to the stars, he says that they do not roam as the planets do, but instead 'crown the single back of the ether with the nourishing and sacred pleasantness of light' (*simplex aetheris dorsum alma et sacrata amoenitate lucis coronant*). Now, the words *aetheris dorsum* derive not from the Greek of the original but from *Phdr.* 247b6-c2, where the souls of the gods in their winged chariots reach the top of the heavens (πρὸς ἄκρῳ), travel outside (ἔξω), take a stand 'on the back of heaven' (ἐπὶ τῷ τοῦ οὐρανοῦ νώτῳ), are carried with the circulation of the sphere of the fixed stars, and see what is outside of heaven (τὰ ἔξω τοῦ οὐρανοῦ). In Plato, the 'back of heaven' represents the boundary between the cosmos with the stars and planets and the supracelestial place, where the Forms are located. Apuleius is choosing to translate Platonic vocabulary here in the *De Mundo* so as to indicate clearly the place where the stars are located, i.e. at the very boundary between cosmos and supracosmos. Thus, this passage too provides evidence for the location of the invisible gods. Unlike the planets,

41

which revolve within the cosmos, and the stars, which revolve at the
boundary, the invisible gods exist in the supracosmic place, the better to
view the Forms.[45]

Returning to the *De Deo Socratis*, Apuleius next names twelve invisible
gods,[46] quoting two lines from Ennius' *Annales* (121):

*Iuno, Vesta, Minerva, Ceres, Diana, Venus, Mars,
Mercurius, Iovis, Neptunus, Vulcanus, Apollo*

This is a reference to the gods in the *Phaedrus* who (led by Zeus) travel
through the heavens in twelve groups, each god leading a train of
daemons and human souls (*Phdr.* 246e4-247a4).[47] Thus, Apuleius is
translating and adapting the *Phaedrus* myth to suit his purposes in the
De Deo Socratis.

It is simple enough to see why Apuleius thought that there was need for
a class of invisible gods. In the myth, Zeus and his fellow-gods begin the
journey 'within heaven' (ἐντὸς οὐρανοῦ, 247a5). They lead souls up to the
'high vault of heaven' (ἄκραν ἐπὶ τὴν ὑπουράνιον ἁψῖδα, *Phdr.* 247a8-b1)
and only then outside of it, as we have seen. This is a journey that celestial
gods cannot make, since they are obviously confined to the heavens. They
do not pass out of it. In fact, Apuleius most probably has the Platonic
phrase 'high vault of heaven' in mind, when he says just a little below (123)
that the invisible gods 'are located in the lofty zenith of the ether' (*hos
namque cunctos deos in sublimi aetheris vertice locatos*). Thus, the invisible gods are, as it were, amphibious, at home in the two realms. What we
have is a Middle Platonic attempt to solve a perceived dilemma in the text
of Plato. The gods in question cannot be visible gods and they are not the
Demiurge (who sits in ineffable splendour above all of this travelling), and
therefore another intermediary group was needed.[48]

Such then is Apuleius' conception of the highest and invisible gods.
We see in them the beginning of the system that allows the transcendent first principle to be present in his creation. Below the invisible
gods are a host of visible gods and daemons, all performing the will of
the Demiurge within the cosmos. The transcendent nature of the gods
necessitated the intermediary classes. The *Phaedrus* myth created the
need to find a place in his system for the invisible gods. The *Timaeus*
described the highest god. Both dialogues are treated relatively literally, more in the tradition of Plutarch than in that of Numenius for
instance. Thus, we see that Apuleius was a reader of Plato, carefully
building his system from hints in Platonic texts. Apuleius was indeed a
philosophus Platonicus, reading and interpreting Plato in a particular
Middle Platonic fashion.

Notes

1. The authorship of these two works is sometimes contested. Both *De Mundo* and *De Platone* come down in a group of manuscripts that also contain the *De Deo Socratis* and the *Asclepius* (see Beaujeu [1973], xxxvi-xli, and Moreschini [1991], iii-ix, and for an overview of Apuleian MSS Reynolds [1983], 15-18). The treatise Περὶ Ἑρμηνείας has a manuscript tradition separate from both the rhetorical and the philosophical works; see Moreschini (1991), xi-xiii. These manuscripts form a separate tradition from the *Metamorphoses* and the rhetorical works. (The *Apologia*, *Metamorphoses*, and *Florida*, together with the *Asclepius*, derive from a single eleventh-century MS F, on which see Vallette [1960], xxxii, and Reynolds [1983], 16.) That *Asclepius*, which it is not attributed to Apuleius in the manuscripts, is not Apuleian (*pace* Hijmans [1987], 411-12, and Hunink [1996], 288-308) is argued strongly by Harrison (2000), 12-13 with n. 49. Of the other rhetorical works *De Deo Socratis* is universally accepted as of Apuleian origin; the other two are doubted. The *DP* and *DM* are attributed to Apuleius in the manuscripts. Beaujeu (1973), who lists manuscripts with dates at li-lii (cf. also Moreschini [1991], iii-iv, Bajoni [1994], 1789-90 with n. 15), reports that 'the best manuscripts (BMV) attribute the two treatises to Apuleius by a *subscriptio* placed between' the two works (x). On the subscriptions and the naming of Apuleius in the MSS, see Redfors (1960), 9-10. Augustine also attributes the *DM* to Apuleius at *Civ.* 4.2, and there is a reference in Servius' commentary on Vergil's *Aeneid* to Apuleius' use of the word *medioximus*, which is found applied to daemons at *DP* 204-5. Dillon (1977), 309-10, and Hijmans (1987), 407-8, see here good evidence that Apuleius wrote both works.

Arguments against authenticity have focused on differences in style between the rhetorical works (including both the *Metamorphoses* and the *De Deo Socratis*) and the *De Mundo* and *De Platone*. These are explicable in terms of difference of content, but the matter is complex because of different distributions of final clausulae (see Axelson [1952], Redfors [1960], 75-113; Beaujeu [1973], xvi-xxiii; Harrison [2000], 178-80; and Bajoni [1994], 1790). Harrison (2000), 178, explains the issues succinctly. They are ultimately concerned with the date when new rhythms (the *cursus mixtus*) were introduced, but Apuleius could easily have been experimenting early with accentual rhythms in non-rhetorical works, particularly in view of his rhetorical skill. Axelson (1952), 18ff., cautiously suggests that the history of the clausulae should be revised rather than that authorship be denied, and Bajoni (1994), 1790, agrees. On the date of *DP* and *DM* see Harrison (2000), 179-80, who opts for a late date 'after 170, and perhaps rather later' based on the address to a son Faustinus (presumably mothered by Pudentilla) in the two works, and Dillon (1977), 310, who also prefers a date 'not much earlier than AD 170'. Evidence based on a supposed son, however, is tenuous at best, and it is better to agree with Hijmans (413 n. 62) that it 'cannot be pressed into service to establish the chronology' of the two philosophical works.

2. Here I owe a great debt to the work of Göransson (1995), who has (I believe) freed Apuleius' philosophy from the burden of the so-called teachings of Gaius. Göransson first shows (105-36) that the *Didaskalikos* itself is a compilation of several older texts and that parts of it are at odds with others. He then compares *De Platone* I (137-56) and II (157-81) with the *Didaskalikos*, showing that in book I Apuleius is not dependent on the *Didaskalikos* 'either as his only source, or as a source for any single section of the book' (156), but that in book II, chapters 1-2, 5-6, and 13-14, Apuleius and Alcinous share a common source. Finally, Göransson (182-26) makes a plausible case against the thesis that a work of Arius Didymus is the source of Apuleius (or indeed of Alcinous). On the relation between *DP* and the *Didaskalikos*, see also Harrison (2000), 195-203.

3. See Harrison (2000), 181, and Beaujeu (1973), 310.

4. For a convenient outline of the topics in *DP* and *DM*, see Harrison (2000), 198, 181-2.

5. Beaujeu (1973), xxvi-xxvii, following Regen (1971) in his chapter on 'the concept of *potestas*' (24-83), points out that Apuleius substitutes the hierarchy of highest god–visible gods–daemons for the Greek text's distinction between transcendent god and that god's power at work in the universe. See also Beaujeu, 117-18, Harrison (2000), 176-7, Moreschini (1978), 128-32 = (1966), 105-6; and (1976), 204-6, and Gersh (1986), 1.273-80. Apuleius also alters the Greek text by adding both citations of Roman writers (Beaujeu, 113-16) and first person accounts of phenomena (Beaujeu, 116-17). Finally Apuleius inserts a long passage on the winds from Favorinus' account (*DM* 318-21), which we know from Aulus Gellius (*Noctes Atticae* 2.22.3-29). See Beaujeu, 321-3.

6. Hijmans (1987), 437-8, provides a useful table comparing the attributes of the highest god as they appear in *DP* 190-1, *Apol.* 64, *DDS* 124, and *DM* 342ff.

7. I accept the transposition proposed by Beaujeu, which he defends at (1973), 255-6. He is followed by Moreschini (1991), 92. For a defence of the reading of the MSS., see Gersh (1986), 1.287-90.

8. Alcinous discusses these three principles (ἀρχαί, 162.21; cf. 163.10-11 and 164.6) in chapters 8-10 of his *Didaskalikos*. As Göransson (143-4) notes, however, he does so in the reverse order of Apuleius and with certain additions. Thus, Apuleius is not dependent on Alcinous, but is following a common handbook tradition in which these three principles are also laid out. For the trifold division in other authors, see Beaujeu (1973), 254-6, Moreschini (1978), 69-70 = (1966), 31-3, and Gersh (1986), 1.244-6, who lists sixteen sources including Alcinous; for a twofold division in Diogenes Laertius, see Gersh (1.244 n. 99).

9. For the epithets in Apuleius, see Hijmans (1987), 437-8, and Gersh (1986), 1.269-72. For the use of the epithets in other writers, see Beaujeu (1973), 256-7, and especially Moreschini (1978), 71-3 = (1966) 31-3; cf. (1978), 199. Van den Broek (58-67) links the terms *beatus et beatificus* and ἀδάμαστον to Gnostic and magical texts.

10. Van den Broek (1982), 57, notes that the Greek equivalents of *incorporeus, unus, beatus, indictus, innominabilis,* and the Greek terms ἀπερίμετρος (which is a hapax), ἀόρατον, and ἀδάμαστον do not appear in Plato's writings. Although this is true, as is his statement that Apuleius' list is 'typically Middle Platonic' (57), it is nonetheless true that all of the words on the list are derivable from Plato's philosophy.

11. θεὸν εὑρεῖν τε ἔργον, εὑρόντα τε εἰς πολλοὺς ἐκφέρειν ἀδύνατον. 'God' is a substitute for Plato's 'the maker and father of this universe', and Plato's text concludes with 'impossible to *tell to everybody*', *Tim.* 28c3-5.

12. Scholars are perplexed by the use of *caelestis* here. Beaujeu (1973), 257 n. 5, thinks it has 'sans doute ici un sens assez vague' and opposes it to 'terrestre'. Dillon (1977), 312-13, thinks that Apuleius is 'using the epithet 'heavenly' loosely here.' Hijmans (1987), 438, agrees with Beaujeu and adds that 'Apuleius usually employs the word as a general qualification, rather than one referring to a specific aspect of the cosmic order.' As we shall see, there is a more philosophical reason underlying its usage here. Moreschini (1978), 71-3 = (1966) 32-3, discusses eleven of the fourteen epithets and their appearances in other writers but strangely omits *caelestis*, along with ἀόρατον and ἀδάμαστον.

3. Apuleius on the Platonic gods

13. *Quem patrem et architectum huius divini orbis superius ostendimus* (204); cf. *genitor rerumque omnium exstructor* (190). There are similar expressions in *Apol.* 64 (*mundi opifex*), *DDS* 124 (*omnium rerum dominator atque auctor*), and *DM* 342 (*de rectore quippe omnium*) and 343 (*sospitator quidem ille <et> genitor est omnium*). See also *DP* 205-6, where 'the highest and most exalted (*exsuperantissimi*) of all the gods' (*summus exsuperantissimusque deorum omnium*) fulfils the role of the Platonic Demiurge by arranging the visible gods in the cosmos and handing over the rest of creation to them.

14. *Tim.* 27d-28b. Beaujeu (1973), 260, cites Plato's *Tim.* 37bc and *Phd.* 65f. and 78f. The editors suggest that the two οὐσίαι which the Demiurge blends to make the soul at *Tim.* 35a1-3 also lie behind this distinction.

15. There are echoes in this passage of *Rep.* 474b-80a and of 509d-11e (the Divided Line), especially with its stress on the kinds of cognition involved at each level: first substances are perceived by the mind and really exist, while secondary substances are 'judged by sensible and irrational opinion.' The echoes continue later in *DP* 194.

16. Moreschini (1978), 100 and n. 60 = (1966), 69-70 and n. 140. In his brief remarks on 193, Moreschini without comment reduces the four kinds of substances to three: 'Dio, le idee, l'anima', leaving *mens* out of the picture, perhaps subsuming it under the heading 'god', (1978), 79 = (1966), 42.

17. (1986), 1.252-64; this is based on the rather dubious grammatical argument that the connector *-que* functions in a way different from *et* in this sentence (253, n. 119). Thus in the list *primum deum esse et mentem formasque rerum et animam* 'mind' and 'Forms' are more closely linked together by *-que* than are the three items (god, mind/Forms, and soul) by the two occurrences of *et*. One could as well argue that the conjunction *et* closely binds 'god' and 'mind,' on the one hand, and 'Forms' and 'soul,' on the other, and that *-que* links the two closely related pairs. Given Apuleius' rhetorical propensities, I would argue that he uses *-que* as a form of *variatio*, avoiding a triple occurrence of *et*, and that all four items in the series have equal weight.

18. Dillon (1977), 328.

19. τὸ μὲν δὴ τιμιώτατον καὶ μέγιστον ἀγαθόν, 27.1, 179.36; *bonorum igitur alia eximia ac prima*, *DP* 220. On the passage, see Dillon (1993), 165-7. For the similarity in the way both Apuleius and Alcinous handle secondary goods, see 167-8. Dillon (168), like Göransson (1995), 161, thinks both authors are following a common text at this point.

20. Göransson (1995), 160, n. 2. He cites Beaujeu (1973), 281-2, who also transcribes the passage from Alcinous and links its meaning both to the *Republic* passage on the Good and to the *Laws* 631d5, where all the human goods have an eye 'toward the leader, intellect (εἰς τὸν ἡγεμόνα νοῦν)'.

21. For the accusation that Apuleius makes errors in his translation of the Περὶ Κόσμου, see Beaujeu (1973), xi-xv; Hijmans (1987), 399-406. Hijmans (406) concludes: 'it is now quite clear that many of the mistakes can be attributed to the state of the text in the manuscripts of the Greek words he was dealing with, that other divergences are deliberate interpretations ... whereas others again may be due to lack of knowledge in a particular field.' As an example of this lack of knowledge, Hijmans (406 n. 30) cites geographical knowledge. Thus, on an area as important as the highest god and intellect, one would not expect a mistranslation on Apuleius' part.

22. See Beaujeu (1973), 173; Harrison (2000), 23.

23. It should be noted as well that the words of Alcinous are not all that clear.

It is quite possible to take the τε καί as connective rather than as epexegetical. In this case, Apuleius may in fact be interpreting the source correctly and Alcinous incorrectly.

24. See Apuleius' *Apol.* 64.4, where he quotes from Plato's *Phdr.* 247c: τὸν ὑπερουράνιον τόπον. Apuleius is thus implying that the highest god is supracosmic and bases that doctrine on the Platonic text.

25. I agree with Göransson (1995), 146 and n. 1, that Apuleius 'seems unaware of the doctrine of the Ideas as the thoughts of God'. Thus the Forms are fully separate from the highest god, just indeed as they are in the *Timaeus* itself.

26. 'He [i.e. Plato] names three classes of gods, of which the first is that one and only highest, hypercosmic (*ultramundanus*), incorporeal, whom we have shown above the father and maker of this divine world. Another class is that which the stars hold and other divinities, which we call "heavenly". They hold a third whom the ancient Romans call *medioximi*, as it is in their account, but in place and power they are inferior to the greater gods but certainly superior to the nature of human beings' (204-5). For the term *medioximus*, which is cited as Apuleian by Servius, see Beaujeu (1973), 271-2.

27. See above, n. 5.

28. See also *DDS* 128, where Apuleius refers to Plato (*Symp.* 203a2) for the doctrine that god does not mix with humankind: *nam, ut idem Plato ait, 'nullus deus miscetur hominibus', sed hoc praecipuum eorum sublimitatis specimen est, quod nulla adtrectatione nostra contaminantur*. Cf. Beaujeu (1973), 212-14.

29. In *DDS* 115, Apuleius notes that we should judge what is highest, intermediate, and lowest not only by separation of place but also by worthiness of nature (*non modo loci disclusione verum etiam naturae dignitate*). This tenet holds good in the *DM* as well.

30. Beaujeu (1973), 330 n. 6. So too Gersh (1986), 1.278-9, and Hijmans (1987), 445. Apuleius himself (*DM* 350-1) says that god dispenses his powers to 'the Sun, Moon, and all the heaven'. Hijmans (445) notes that the passage 'adds some further precision in its insistence that it is not the creator himself who looks after creation, but that he delegates his *potestates* to the visible gods.' For the importance of this passage to Apuleius' reworking of the Περὶ Κόσμου, see Beaujeu (1973), 331-2. For the Sun, Moon, and other planets in *Flor.* 10, see Gersh (1986), 1.282 n. 222.

31. For significance of Apuleius' addition of the words *et per se et per alios* to the original Greek text, see Beaujeu (1973), 331 n. 3.

32. *DM* 351. The movement is imparted from the highest to the next proximate, and so on.

33. See also *DDS* 123, where it is said that the highest god cannot be spoken of 'because of the incredible and ineffable excess of his majesty' (*maiestatis incredibili quadam nimietate et ineffabili*).

34. For *in solio residat altissimo*, see *DM* 343: *in arduis arcibus habere solium consecratum*, also said of the highest god.

35. The Greek text simply reads: ἡ θεία φύσις ἀπό τινος ἁπλῆς κινήσεως τοῦ πρώτου τὴν δύναμιν εἰς τὰ συνεχῆ δίδωσι (398b20-2). The first god from a simple motion in himself provides power to those after him, but the author does not say how this is done.

36. Xenophanes was of importance as well to Ammonius, the teacher of another Middle Platonist, Plutarch; see Tarrant (2000), 174 with 246 n. 41. Plutarch discusses his teacher's view on the sharp dichotomy between the upper world and this lower world of flux in the *E at Delphi* 391e-394c.

37. See also fr. 12, where Mind is 'mixed with nothing but was itself alone with itself'. On the concept of Mind in Anaxagoras, see Kirk, Raven, and Schofield (1983), 362-5; Guthrie (1965), 272-9.

38. See *OLD* 2b, which cites *Apollo salutiferus* in *L'Année Épigraphique* 20.37.

39. It will be recalled that at *DM* 343, Apuleius called the Demiurge *sospitator quidem ille <et> genitor est omnium*, thus again combining the religious (*sospitator*) and philosophical/demiurgic (*genitor*) aspects of the god.

40. See *Flor.* 16.38 and Augustine *Ep.* 138.19. Apuleius was most probably a priest of the imperial cult in the province of Africa. See Harrison (2000), 8.

41. The division appears in several Apuleian writings. In *DP* 1.204, there are four classes of souls: the visible gods ('Sun, Moon, and other stars') are made from fire; daemons made from air; mortal creatures from earth and water, both πεζός and χερσαῖος. For these two Greek terms, I accept the emendation of Floridus, adopted by Moreschini (1991), 101. Beaujeu (1973), 269-70, suggests ἔγγειος and ἐπίγειος, from *Rep.* 546a, but (as Moreschini notes) it is more likely that Apuleius is following the *Timaeus* here. The threefold division appears also in *DP* 204-5 and *DM* 343, as we have seen. Cf. *DP* 205-6 and *DDS* 116-67. The source of the doctrine is *Epinomis* 984d-985c.

42. Hijmans (442) attempts to find a reference to these invisible gods in *DP* 204: *aliud genus est quale astra habent ceteraque numina, quos caelicolas nominamus.* Beaujeu too (204 n. 6) claims that 'même distinction entre les dieux astraux et les autres dans le *De d. S.*, 121'. However, the distinction that Apuleius is drawing is not between celestial and invisible gods but rather between two sorts of celestial gods. This would appear to be Apuleius' interpretation of *Tim.* 41a3-5, 'all gods who go about visibly and who appear to the extent that they are willing'. Who these gods are that 'show themselves as they will' is unclear. Later, Iamblichus and Proclus identify them with sublunar gods, but Apuleius need not think so. The point is that they are somehow on a par with the celestial gods in that they are in the cosmos and ethereal.

43. Trapp (1990), and for Galen see Rocca's contribution to this volume.

44. Gersh (1986), 1.306 n. 331, cites this text in combination with *DDS* 121, and at 305 n. 325 connects it with the *Phaedrus*. Beaujeu (1973), 311 n. 2, also refers to *Phdr.* 247b8. Neither considers the consequences for Apuleius' doctrine of the invisible gods.

45. Cf. *Apol.* 64, where Apuleius employs both 'τὸ ὑπερουράνιον τόπον' and 'οὐρανου νώτῳ' in relation to the highest god. The context suggests that the highest god exists above the 'back of heaven' in the 'supracelestial place'. Thus, the invisible gods share this place with him.

46. There are more than these twelve: *ceterique id genus, quorum nomina quidem sunt nostris auribus iam diu cognita (DDS* 122).

47. Apuleius unfortunately includes Vesta, who according to Plato remained at home (*Phdr.* 247a1-2). This is probably an oversight of Apuleius, caused in part by the attraction of using Ennius' lines.

48. Both Gersh (1986), 1.307-8, and Hijmans (1987), 441 with n. 188, observe that Apuleius uses the names of invisible gods also for visible gods (Jupiter, Venus, Mercury, Mars, Apollo, Juno; see Gersh 1.307 n. 335) and for daemons (Minerva appearing to Achilles, *DDS* 145). As both scholars say, this affords evidence that Apuleius conceived of the higher gods as presenting lowers aspects of themselves under the same name (so-called σειραί). The evidence is, *pace* Gersh, too scanty to allow a definite conclusion. But it presents an intriguing possibility and an early anticipation of a Neoplatonic doctrine. It should be noted also that such a chain of divinities dependent ultimately on the highest god is another way in which a religious philosopher can allow for the highest god's simultaneous transcendence and immanence. God is at work in the universe through directly dependent intermediaries. Gersh (1.307 n. 336) would seem to allow the highest god to be manifest in the sphere of the fixed stars, but there is no good reason to delimit his power so.

'Plato will tell you':
Galen's use of the *Phaedrus* in *De Placitis Hippocratis et Platonis* IX

Julius Rocca

> When many of the Platonists themselves have held views contrary to Plato's words, how could anyone be surprised at the other philosophers who do not know how to separate what is plausible but untrue from unshakeable truth?
> *De Placitis Hippocratis et Platonis.*[1]

i. Plato in Galen's world

Albinus the Platonist is mentioned once by Galen in his extant writings.[2] Yet there is no doubt that this philosopher exerted an influence on Galen both at an important period in his remarkably extensive and thorough education and throughout his career as a doctor. Galen was headed for a philosophical career from the age of fifteen and received instruction from representatives of all four schools.[3] Philosophy was part of his intellectual make-up and infused his work as a practising physician. Indeed, as he tells it, he arrived in Rome with the reputation as a philosopher, not a doctor.[4] Galen spent the bulk of his professional life in Rome, a city whose intellectual life was set in large measure by the Second Sophistic, when 'the study of Plato was promoted vigorously'.[5] The influence of Albinus can be judged not only by the number of (mostly lost) works on Plato and Platonism which Galen composed, but in the laudatory yet critical way in which Galen read, interpreted, and used Platonic dialogues.[6] If it is true that 'Albinus belonged to the era when Platonic texts were documents regularly used in the teaching of Platonic philosophy',[7] then such an approach to Plato is clearly discernible in Galen, where Plato is used primarily, but not solely, for purposes of instruction.[8] But instruction in what? It also should be noted that although Galen regarded himself as a philosopher, he was no Platonist and was not interested in teaching the philosophy of any school. Yet clearly there was something akin to a fundamental appeal in Plato's writings, which drew the attention of this second-century physician/philosopher. The purpose of this paper is simply to illustrate Galen's use of parts of one dialogue, the *Phaedrus*, in book IX of his *De Placitis Hippocratis et Platonis*. In so doing, it is hoped to cast light on Galen as a reader of Plato, one who 'thought of his relation to Plato as direct, not mediated by the Platonists'.[9] Yet Galen must also have felt that his use of Plato reflected a doctrinal orthodoxy as practised by Albinus, and that such an orthodoxy would be understood and appreciated by his audience as readers themselves. Galen's use of the *Phaedrus* also shows a familiarity and sureness which contrasts with how it is often interpreted today.[10] In so doing, I will concentrate more on what Galen is saying about Plato than on the secondary literature on the *Phaedrus*.[11] Finally, Galen's use of the *Phaedrus* may provide corroborating evidence as to how Plato was read by others in the second century AD and for what purposes.

ii. Plato and instruction in the *PHP*

Few works were more formally entrenched in the 'cultural syllabus' of Hellenic *paideia* by the second century AD than Plato's *Phaedrus*. 'Its rich range of subject-matter – love, the soul, beauty, human destiny, the cosmos, rhetoric, dialectic, teaching, and writing – combined with its literary and stylistic brilliance, made it an object of intense and sustained interest to rhetors and philosophers alike.'[12] Galen quotes from it no fewer than ten times.[13] Seven of these citations (in order, 262a5-7, 262a9-b1, 261e6-262c3, 263a2-d1, 265c8-e3, 271c10-272b2, 273d6-e4), which Galen uses to promote his ideas of instruction,[14] are found in book IX of his magisterial work on medical philosophy, *De Placitis Hippocratis et Platonis* (hereafter, *PHP*).

This text, which according to the medieval Arabic tradition included a tenth book that has not survived, ranks with *De Usu Partium* as one of Galen's greatest works.[15] It is bold in intent, as its title indicates. The underlying theme is not only to discuss the *doctrines* of Hippocrates and Plato, Galen's medical and philosophical mentors and exemplars, but, more sweepingly, to put forward that these doctrines should be read as complementary.[16] The aim of this constructed concordance is to prove that Plato's tripartite soul and Hippocratic notions on the powers that govern us can not only be reconciled but may be scientifically established. Hippocrates and Plato form part of a broad picture of an extensive debate on the hegemony of the rational soul, and are used to endorse Galen's conception of encephalocentrism.[17] In the first six books of *PHP*, Galen employs Platonic soul tripartition first and foremost as a means to provide him with the philosophic underpinning of soul tripartition, to which he supplies the necessary anatomical and physiological argumentation, which is detailed in *De Anatomicis Administrationibus* and *De Usu Partium*. For Galen, the student, in order to become a good physician, must be properly trained in being able to distinguish between opinion and truth. The notion of instruction is the subtext that runs through *PHP* and, under the rubric of distinguishing between similars and the art of rhetoric, forms the theme of book IX, where the seven citations from the *Phaedrus* are to be found. In what follows, these will be examined not only for how they serve Galen's didactic purposes, but for the ways in which Galen is engaging in the *Phaedrus* as a reader himself.

iii. Earlier citations in book IX

Galen begins book IX by stating that the purpose of the *PHP* was to examine the points of agreement between Hippocrates and Plato, and that he has already dealt with those topics of major concern for medicine and philosophy. Now he must deal with those that remain. One of these is how to distinguish properly between similars. In this, Hippocrates and Plato can help us, for although they themselves differ in their approach and the examples used, their methodology was the same, using respectively examples from medicine and philosophy. In this way, these two disciplines can contribute to a methodology Galen employs to train the physician. This method of instruction begins with two citations from the *Phaedrus* (262c5-7 and 262a9-b1). In the first, Galen states that Hippocrates spoke generally concerning those similarities (*homoiotêtes*) 'that mislead and perplex even the good physician', and Galen links this to Plato's statement that if one wishes to deceive another and not himself be misled, he must 'know accurately the similarity and difference in things'.[18] In the second citation (*Phdr.* 262a9-b1), which follows immediately from the above, Galen states that:

> Plato will tell you how to succeed in this when he says: 'Can a person who lacks knowledge of the truth about a thing discern in other things any similarity, great or small, to the thing he is ignorant of? – He cannot.' But first listen to me as I describe clearly and concisely how a person might discover the truth about each matter that comes under investigation; and when you have stored what you hear in your memory, then go to the passages from these men.[19]

Like Plato, Galen will describe clearly and concisely how to determine the truth (*alêtheia*) of the matter under investigation. The means of acquiring knowledge of the truth is as important to Galen as it is to Plato, albeit not in the strict metaphysical sense of the latter. For Galen, the truth in matters concerning the function of the body and the *hêgemonikon* of the soul is attained by rigorous training using the method of apodeictic proof.[20] As will be seen, Galen's doctrinal reading of the *Phaedrus* carries the message that this was also Plato's intention. The above two citations, which Galen cites in the more extended quotation from the *Phaedrus* at *PHP* pp. 546.30-548.13 De Lacy; V. 729-30 K, are used to present Plato to his audience not only with authority, but with immediacy and even intimacy. The language Galen employs to preface these quotes underscores this: Plato is presented as the teacher instructing us by the spoken word. Moreover, immediately after the second citation, Galen, as quoted above, utilizes this immediacy to reinforce his own claims to authority in the subject: we must listen to Galen as we have just listened to Plato and retain these words in our *memory* (*mnêmê*). Then, and only then, should we turn to the written word of Plato (and of Hippocrates). This pedagogic approach is as good an illustration as any of 'the *Phaedrus*' potential as an object of classicizing *mimesis*' in the second century AD.[21] What counts for Galen, as it would have for Platonists and Sophists of this era, is his use of such passages drawn from established authorities for teaching purposes.[22] This is well brought out in Galen's next citation from the *Phaedrus* (261e6-262c5), where, according to Galen, Plato instructs us in the correct training for accurately distinguishing the similarity and difference in things. In so doing, we will be able to distinguish truth from opinion, and, as Plato has Socrates conclude:

> Then, my friend, the man who does not know the truth but has been on the hunt for opinions will, it appears, make a ridiculous and artless display of the art of speaking.[23]

Galen prefaces the beginning of the citation by instructing us to listen to what Plato has to say because it is Plato who will provide us with the requisite training. Galen's expressiveness calls to mind one of his sophistic peers, Aelius Aristides, whose 'self-assertive reuse of the *Phaedrus* in support of his own values and pieties as a sophist'[24] reflects a familiarity with Plato that Galen would appreciate if not quite approve.[25] But unlike Aristides, who is arguably more concerned with 'Setting Plato against Plato',[26] Galen provides an image not only of a Plato in direct communication with us, his receptive audience and pupils, but of a Galen confident enough to maintain that these citations from the *Phaedrus* represent unambiguous Platonic doctrine. However, in order to do this, Galen must present the citation in such a way as to offer a more forceful, certain account of what is being discussed.[27]

This becomes clear in the next passage (*Phdr.* 263a2-d1), where Galen continues the above argument, first by again emphasizing the point of agreement between Hippocrates and Plato, and then by providing a context in which Plato is read with what amounts to a Galenic certainty in expression, and a forcefulness when it comes to differentiating between opinion and truth. It is the right sort of training and instruction which makes such a differentiation possible, since, 'as Hippocrates said, some things are very easily known, others not, the beginning must be made from the things most easily known, which have also been agreed to by all men because of their clarity.'[28] Galen then goes on to state that Plato also held the same view, and proceeds to cite *Phdr.* 263a2-d1. This passage discusses rhetoric as a subject in which proficiency can be attained, and he who would be a master of rhetoric 'must first have investigated these things methodically and must have learned some distinguishing mark of each class, the class of things about which the majority of men are

52

necessarily at variance, and the class about which they are not.'[29] The passage ends with an allusion to love, and whether it belongs to the class of disputed or undisputed things. Galen interprets the citation that discusses rhetoric in the following way:

> This passage in the *Phaedrus* was written as [Plato] was teaching [us] that what falls clearly under the natural criteria (*ta phusika kritêria*) is never in dispute, but dispute arises about the things that fall under these criteria not at all or obscurely. And we must train ourselves for the latter sort by distinguishing the similarities in things. For some things are so related to each other in terms of the similarities or the diversity of what is in them that they are similar in one respect, different in another. And the expert must be capable of distinguishing such things, so that he can determine accurately and quickly whether they are similar to each other or dissimilar.[30]

Plato, however, has said nothing about the 'natural criteria'. The concept is first noted at the beginning of book IX, where Galen states that the possession of natural criteria allows us to distinguish between similarity and dissimilarity and division and collection.[31] The possession of natural criteria is an essential prerequisite for a proficient or 'technical criterion' (*technikon kritêrion*).[32] To Galen, nature has endowed human beings with a double gift: the criteria themselves, and our 'untaught trust' (*to pisteuein adidaktôs*) in those criteria.[33] The natural criteria consist of the faculties of sense perception (*aisthêsis*). How well they are used is determined by training and judgement (*diakrisis*).[34] The information obtained from one's senses is reliable, but must also be subject to discrimination and verification, which is why Galen also refers to the criteria as comprising sense-perception (*aisthêsis*) and *understanding* (*gnômê*).[35] Galen's methodology relies on accepting the evidence available through sense-perception, thanks to these natural criteria, which in turn enable discrimination and interpretation of the evidence by the employment of the technical criterion.

Clearly then, the technical criterion is not only dependent on the natural criteria, but must also be taught. This is why Galen does not follow up his citation of *Phdr.* 263a2-d1 with an overt criticism of rhetoric.[36] It is not as if he is endorsing rhetoric in and of itself as a path to knowledge. Rather, the point Galen attempts to make is that the expert (*technitês*)[37] or master of a skill (*technê*) is someone who has learnt the correct method and is able to distinguish 'the similarities in things'. Galen's definition implies not so much approval of the *art* of rhetoric, but an acceptance that, if correctly instructed, a rhetorician can be acknowledged a master of his particular craft, even if that expertise is ultimately persuasive and not demonstrative. The notion that a skill can be correctly taught is Galen's aim, and this probably reflects Middle Platonic thinking.[38]

53

iv. The final citations

The final three citations from the *Phaedrus* appear almost continuously in two sequential pages in *PHP*, and deal with the method of division. Throughout, Galen provides his own interpretation of what he believes represents Platonic doctrine. In the first, Galen cites *Phdr.* 265c8-e3 in order to show that:

> ... the theory of division and synthesis is most necessary for the construction of the arts, and he [Plato] prescribes a two-fold exercise in it: a descent from the first and most general class to the units that no longer admit of division, by way of the intervening differentiae, from which ... the definitions of the species are constructed; then a return, by synthesis, from the lowest species, which are many in number, up to the first genus. The path is the same for both, but the journey is two-fold, as it begins from one or the other of the two ends and passes to the remaining one.[39]

Galen presents once more Plato as a teacher, training us in the method of division. This stress on instruction allows Galen to focus his argument clearly on 'the art of rhetoric', for this too can be correctly taught. Galen's largest citation of the *Phaedrus* (271c10-272b2 at *PHP* p. 568.5-22 De Lacy; V.755-6 K) follows immediately from the above and is designed to show that Plato and Galen are in accord as far as instruction in the art of rhetoric is concerned. For Galen ends the citation by claiming that:

> This is what (Plato) said about rhetoric here, as he instructed us how best to construct the art by the use of a method, not by experience and familiarity, as most men do.[40]

However, the thrust of the Socratic argument is that rhetoric, even if mastered, is insufficient (and always will be) for the seeker after truth. But Galen's reading concentrates rather on mastering a skill *per se*. Galen would therefore certainly agree that there is the 'presence of a true art of rhetoric'[41] in this part of the *Phaedrus*, even if apparently denied by Plato. Galen's reading, however, allows him to determine that Plato is implying that an art or skill can be properly taught by a method. It cannot be left to mere experience. Galen's final citation (*Phdr.* 273d6-e4) leaves us in no doubt that his reading of the *Phaedrus* is very much concerned with what it has to say about an attainable *technê*:

> And he made another statement further on ... which he summarised in these words: 'Therefore if you have anything else to say about the art of discourse, I would gladly listen; if not, we shall be persuaded by the account that we have just now given, that if a person does not enumerate the natures of those who will hear him and is unable to divide things by classes and to include each thing individually under a single form, he will never have the skill in discourse that man is capable of.'[42]

4. 'Plato will tell you'

Galen endorses the art of rhetoric as a 'skill in discourse', provided, as earlier stated in his citing of *Phaedrus* 271c-272b, that it is taught by the use of a method and not by 'experience and familiarity'.[43] For Galen, these, whether taken singly or together, cannot be of any use in correct instruction. They are haphazard precisely because they provide an incomplete methodology divorced from formal instruction or training.[44] One's natural abilities are not enough: although they form an essential starting point one must, like the masters of rhetoric, practise repeatedly and conscientiously until proficiency – true skill – is gained.[45]

Galen's endorsement of rhetoric as an art or skill correctly taught and practised may profitably be compared to Alcinous' discussion of the complete orator, whose skill can be called the science of speaking well.[46] A not dissimilar approach may also be seen in Hermogenes of Tarsus, a figure of some standing in the Second Sophistic and much admired by Marcus Aurelius.[47] In *On Forms of Style*, Hermogenes states that there are two ways to improve one's style. The first is by merely imitating the ancients. This is unlikely to succeed as it relies on experience and familiarity. The better way is to possess knowledge of the forms of style themselves.[48] This is 'surely a reference to the "scientific" rhetoric projected in the *Phaedrus*'.[49] It also shows that Galen's way of reading this interpretation from the *Phaedrus* was most likely widespread and accepted. The science of speaking well was extremely important to Galen. Like others, he built his career in Rome upon it, and the success of his public demonstrations of anatomical and physiological prowess required in significant measure a willing employment of those rhetorical skills he ostensibly demoted and despised.[50]

v. Conclusion

In order to obtain proficiency in medicine or philosophy in the second century AD, mere paraphrasing an authority was not enough. Galen clearly felt the need to cite substantially from Plato in order to support his arguments, even when those arguments, on first inspection, do not appear to follow from *our* reading of the dialogues in question. In the case of the *Phaedrus*, as with the other dialogues he uses, Galen was not citing Plato merely to score points or to display his erudition (although elements of such an approach are certainly present). Galen not only possessed a profound knowledge of Plato's works, but also knew that his audience would be familiar with them. It is not suggested that sophists such as Aelius Aristides and Hermogenes, and writers such as Maximus, directly influenced Galen's own reading of Plato. But their reading seems to have reflected an accepted, perhaps even orthodox way of reading the dialogues for what they could provide in terms of doctrine. As far as the citations from the *Phaedrus* are concerned, Galen is not using them entirely in the same way as his teacher Albinus, that is, for the teaching of Platonic philosophy.[51] However, one way he is using the *Phaedrus*, which Albinus would have recognized, is *analogously*. Galen employs the discussion of similars and differences, together with that of rhetoric, to show that a mastery of these is possible by training in the correct method.[52] By extension, one can be properly trained as a doctor provided the correct method is employed. For Galen, the *Phaedrus* shows that the concept of a training methodology is valid and thereby renders legitimate the notion of instruction by an adept.

But for all that, Galen also believed – as a physician who was also a philosopher – that Plato was speaking *directly* to him, and that he is taking from Plato fundamental, unmediated truths that can be applied to the art and science of medicine. 'Plato will tell you', as Galen instructs his readers. Provided of course you are prepared to listen. This paper has sought to outline how Galen read parts of one Platonic dialogue, how he interpreted it, and, in passing, whether others may have done so in a broadly similar way. It is more than time to examine in detail how Galen reads Plato. It is to be hoped that not only will this shed further light on Galen as a philosopher and on his relationships with past and contemporaneous Platonists, but that his citations may also reveal that there were (and indeed are) different ways of reading Plato than those to which time and scholastic habit have given custom.

Notes

1. 600.25-9 De Lacy; V. 795 K, trans. De Lacy 601. All citations from this text are taken from the edition and translation of De Lacy (1978-84). This and other works of the Galenic Corpus are cited in accordance with the critical editions of the *CMG* series (where they exist) as well as by volume and page number of Kühn (1821-33), (= K).

2. In *De Libris Propriis*, XIX. 19 K, Galen states that he travelled to Smyrna to study under him.

3. Cf. *De Lib Propriis*. XIX. 39-40 K; *Ord. Lib. Propr.* XIX. 59-60 K.

4. This reputation was stated by Eudemus, the Peripatetic philosopher whose illness is a focal point for Galen's prognostic skills in *De Praenotione*. Eudemus had thought Galen proficient 'only in philosophical theory' (*Galeni De Praenotione* [= Nutton (1979)], p. 76, 26-9; XIV. 608 K). Eudemus probably instructed Galen in philosophy in Pergamum and Galen refers to him explicitly as his teacher (*Praecogn*. p. 82, 12 Nutton; XIV. 613 K).

5. De Lacy, 'Plato and the Intellectual Life of the Second Century AD', in Bowersock (1974), 5.

6. The lost Platonist works include: *The Platonist Sect; To Those Whose Opinion on the Forms differs from that of Plato; Plato's Logical Theory; Analogical Procedures in the Philebus; The Parts and Faculties of the Soul.* There was also a synopsis of the dialogues in eight volumes. Cf. *Lib. Propr.* XIX. 46 K.

7. Tarrant (2000a), 7.

8. One can suppose that the lost summary of Platonic Dialogues was just such an instructional handbook.

9. De Lacy (1972), 29.

4. 'Plato will tell you'

10. 'The problems which confront readers of Plato in general are particularly acute in the interpretation of the *Phaedrus*.' Rutherford (1995), 241. Rutherford in a sense echoes Galen's implicit task as a reader when he states that 'the *Phaedrus*, for all its humour and playfulness, does have something to say, and that it is the interpreter's task to elucidate a text, rather than to celebrate its impenetrability.' ibid., 242.

11. See for example Rossetti (1992).

12. Trapp (1990), 141.

13. Apart from the seven in *PHP*, Galen cites *Phdr.* 270c-d in: *De Methodus Medendi* XI. 13-14 K; *De Compositione Medicamentorum per Genera* XIII. 594 K; *In Hippocratis De Natura Hominis Comment.* CMG V 9, 1 p. 54 Mewaldt. At first glance, it seems odd that Galen does not quote this passage in *PHP*. After all, it deals with the method of division, which Plato seemingly ascribes to Hippocrates. However, although it provides Galen with an example of Hippocrates and Plato in accord, it does not give Plato's own views on division and synthesis, which is what Galen needs in book IX of *PHP*.

14. Trapp (1990), 165, states that these seven passages are concerned with 'rhetorical and dialectical technique'. This is true as far as it goes but there is more at work here, as will be shown.

15. 'In no other work can this academic superiority of Galen be seen so well as in *PHP*, in its range and accuracy of quotation, its insistence upon proper methods of debate and its desire to synthesise medicine and philosophy.' V. Nutton, 'Review of *PHP* Books I-IV', *Medical History*, 24 (1980), 98-100, 99.

16. Galen holds that Plato himself 'took his most important doctrines from Hippocrates.' De Lacy (1972), 37.

17. See Rocca (2003), ch. 1.

18. *planas kai diaporias kai tois agathois iatrous parechei*: *PHP* 540.16-17 De Lacy; V. 721 K; trans. De Lacy, 541.

19. *PHP* 540.18-23 De Lacy; V. 721-2 K; trans. De Lacy, 541.

20. Cf. *PHP* 110.8-9 De Lacy; V. 220 K; 480.7-8 De Lacy; V. 648 K. Cf. Rocca (2003), 50-8. Cf. De Lacy (1972), 35 n. 25.

21. Trapp (1990), 141.

22. On Galen's students and his education programme see Mansfeld (1994), 119ff., 167-73.

23. *PHP* 548.11-13 De Lacy; V. 730 K. The entire citation is on 546.30-548.13 De Lacy; V. 729-30 K. This passage is also alluded to in *PHP* 584.32-4 De Lacy; V. 776 K.

24. Trapp (1990), 166.

25. Galen nevertheless seems to have held Aelius in great respect (cf. *In Platonis Timaeum Commentaria Fragmenta*, CMG Suppl. I, Leipzig-Berlin [1934], 33 Kahle). Similarly, the rhetor Herodes Atticus is called by Galen 'the most able orator of our time' (*De Optimo Medico Cognoscendo*, CMG Suppl. Or. IV, Berlin [1988], p. 113.15-6 Iskandar).

26. Trapp (1990), 166.

27. Galen might be subtly altering the thrust of the argument put by Socrates in order to highlight Galen's own importance on the need to discriminate between opinion and truth for his own pedagogic purposes. For Socrates to say, as Galen seems to have him say (at *PHP* 548.9 De Lacy; V. 730 K), 'by his art' rather than 'by the art' (the usual rendering), carries the implication that his particular art has gone astray in this instance, not that there is a problem with the art in terms of its methodology. Thus, properly trained, the student will not make mistakes 'by his art' because he will be using the correct art. If this reading is correct, then Galen is here subtly altering the Socratic criticism of rhetoric, replacing it with a more Aristotelian reading which admits of a true (*qua* epistemic) method of rhetorical discourse.

28. *PHP* 548.14-16 De Lacy; V. 730 K; trans. De Lacy 549.

29. *PHP* 548.25-7 De Lacy; V. 731 K; trans. De Lacy 549.

30. *PHP* 548.34-550.7 De Lacy; V. 732 K; trans. De Lacy 549, 551.

31. *PHP* 542.7-20 De Lacy; V. 722-3 K.

32. *PHP* 542.7 De Lacy; V. 722 K. Not 'scientific' criterion as De Lacy translates. Strictly, *technê* refers to a skill or expertise which may differ in degree; *epistêmê* refers to a body of knowledge from which a skill may be derived. Galen seeks to emphasize the practical nature of the criterion used for obtaining knowledge, in contrast to the theoretical concerns of philosophers.

33. *PHP* 544.10-12 De Lacy; V. 725 K. At *PHP* 482.21-6; De Lacy; V. 652 K, Galen describes the 'firm belief' of those who, properly trained in the logical method, acknowledge as correct the arguments of Hippocrates and Plato concerning the *hêgemonikon* of the rational soul.

34. Galen's own programme of education was quite demanding. In *De Constitutione Artis Medicae* I. 244 K, the would-be physician must possess certain moral, social, and intellectual qualities in order to qualify for instruction at Galen's hands. Cf. Mansfeld (1994), 119ff., 167-73.

35. *PHP* 542.27-30 De Lacy; V. 724 K. Galen's separation of what is apparent to the senses and to the intellect is in keeping with Fourth Academy teaching. Cf. Tarrant (1985), 109 and 168 n. 35.

36. For examples of where he does, see Pearcy (1998).

37. The word can also mean 'deceiver'; a Socratic thrust Galen must perforce ignore.

38. Maximus of Tyre, active in the reign of Commodus, whose *Dialexeis* are infused with Middle Platonism, regarded the rhetorician as the practitioner of a true craft (20.3). Cf. Tarrant (2000a), 134-5.

39. 566.18-26 De Lacy; V. 753-4 K; trans. De Lacy, 567 (the citation from *Phdr.* 265c8-e3 is at 566.26-568.2 De Lacy; V. 754 K).

40. 568.22-4 De Lacy; V. 756 K; trans. De Lacy, 569.

41. Tarrant (2000a), 135.

42. 568.25-31 De Lacy; V. 756-7 K; trans. De Lacy, 569.

43. On Galen's scientific methodology see G.E.R. Lloyd, 'Theories and Practices of Demonstration in Galen', in M. Frede and G. Striker (eds), *Rationality in Greek Thought*, Oxford (1996) 255-77. See also Rocca, op. cit., above n. 17, 50-8.

44. Galen uses a similar line of argument against his two principal medical opponents, the Empiricists and Methodists.

45. Cf. *PHP* 550.8-552.2 De Lacy; V. 732-4 K. For Galen, this proficiency is not the same as the set of skills needed for scientific demonstration. Cf. Rocca (2003), 54-6.

46. *Didaskalikos* 6.8 = p. 12, Dillon (1993), cf. commentary p. 84.

47. Cf. *CHCL* 1. 314-7.

48. 213-14, Rabe. Cited in De Lacy (1974), 8.

49. De Lacy (1974), 9. There are echoes of a similar approach in Olympiodorus, for whom: 'The true rhetoric of the *Phaedrus* ... was true because of the scientific approach that it took towards the achievement of persuasion.' Tarrant (2000a), with references.

50. Cf. von Staden (1995), 47-66.

51. Cf. Tarrant (2000a), 7.

52. Whether Galen is entirely following Albinus' distinction between two grades of Platonic doctrine remains unclear. However, his approach bears some resemblance to the 'likeness-producing doctrines' employed by Albinus. Cf. Tarrant (2000a), 199, with references.

5

Platonists on the origin of evil

John Phillips

When ancient Platonists turned their attention to the question of the primary cause of evil, three candidates came to mind: matter, soul, and body. In *Enneads* I.8, his treatise on evil, Plotinus attempts to eliminate from consideration two of these three possibilities.

> The nature of bodies (*sômatôn physis*), inasmuch as it shares in matter, would be an evil that is not primary. For [bodies] have a sort of form that is not true (*eidos ti ouk alêthinon*) and are deprived of life and destroy each other and their motion is disorderly (*phora te par' autôn ataktos*) and they are impediments to soul's activity and in their incessant flowing they escape being, being a secondary evil (*deuteron kakon*).   I.8.4.1-4

> Soul is not in itself evil nor is it entirely evil. But what is the evil soul? It is as he [Plato] says, 'those who are enslaved to that part in which the soul's sinfulness naturally arises', which is to say, the irrational form of soul that accepts evil, such as lack of measure, excess, and deficiency, from which come licentiousness, cowardice, and the rest of soul's sinfulness ...   I.8.6-11

So the evil that attaches to the nature of bodies and to soul is only secondary and arises through their contact with matter, which for Plotinus is primary evil. However, like many of his Platonist predecessors, Plotinus was faced with the problem of explaining how matter, which lacked all quality and was absolute deficiency, could be the cause of evil in soul and body. In this passage, as was often the case in earlier Platonism, the solution lay in invoking the words of Plato himself who, these Platonists felt, dealt specifically with this issue in various dialogues. My aim in this paper is to determine what role Plotinus' reading of Plato played in his theory of matter and its participation in the generation of evil in the world. Along the way, we shall learn more about his place within the Platonist tradition and what reaction his interpretation of Plato provoked among later Platonists, particularly Proclus.

i. Matter and soul

I would like first to discuss the second section of the passage from I.8.4 quoted above, where Plotinus deals with the corruption of soul by matter.

He locates soul's evil in the irrational soul, identifying it with Plato's reference in *Phaedrus* to the part of the soul in which evil naturally occurs (256b2-3). Yet Plotinus makes it clear that this is the part of the soul that 'receives' evil from its association with matter, to which, to be sure, it is 'inclined' (one wonders immediately how much of soul's inclination toward matter is due to the admixture of matter itself and how much to soul's natural receptivity of evil). Nonetheless, it is most important for Plotinus, perhaps in order to distance himself from the evil World-Soul of Plutarch and Atticus, to stress that evil is an external addition to soul, as it is to body.

Here, as in much of the latter half of his treatise, Plotinus is concerned with the rich tradition of debate regarding soul's relationship to evil, and, as with the question of the body's connection with evil, much of the discussion centred on exegesis of various texts of Plato. Plotinus' principal opposition in this debate comes from two doctrines, each of which he treats in some detail. Both doctrines take over the Stoic *aporia* with which Platonists well before Plotinus' time were forced to deal: If matter possesses no qualities, how can it be evil?[1] And if matter is not evil, then must not the evil in soul be primary and part of its nature, rather than something accidental to it? The first theory, according to which evil is privation or the absence of good, in the soul, Plotinus addresses in I.8.11. Although there is much that could be said about this discussion, I want to concentrate on a second theory that Plotinus treats at length in I.8.

This theory asserts that evil is a weakness (*astheneia*) of the soul. Plotinus cites various states that exhibit a lack of moral and emotional steadfastness as possible examples of this. We must ascertain the cause of this weakness, which, he states, may or may not be the same as what brings about weakness in the body, i.e. matter. As a matter of fact, he continues, psychic weakness occurs only in souls that have contact with matter, the higher, undescended soul remaining pure and unhampered by the constraints of activity in the physical world. At this point Plotinus again quotes from *Phaedrus* to corroborate his notion that weakness is a phenomenon limited to souls that have already descended and is itself a byproduct of the descent.

Before analysing the doctrinal context for Plotinus' comments here, let us first take up briefly another passage in the *Enneads* where Plotinus parries a different attempt by a rival school to foist the blame for evil on soul's nature. In this case the text comes from II.9 and his opponents are the Gnostics. In II.9.10 he summarizes a Gnostic myth of creation and then proceeds to ridicule it by pointing up its many incongruities. I want here to concentrate on his criticisms presented in chapter 12 of that treatise, which establish two important truths regarding the role of the soul in the generation of the universe. There soul is said to descend in order to illuminate the darkness, which is matter. This descent, which both Plotinus and these Gnostics agree is necessary, must be in accordance with soul's nature, for if it is not, then evil originates in (or is co-eternal with, or is perhaps caused by) the intelligible world, and is then introduced into the universe by soul in its descent. Secondly, the ultimate responsibility for all of creation, including matter if indeed it is created, resides in what he calls here the 'first principles'. Expression of the second tenet, of course, is intended to counter the Gnostic dualism according to which soul descends to illuminate a pre-existing darkness, but it serves as well to contradict the major dualistic systems of Platonism insofar as one of the possible interpretations of the Gnostic myth outlined here, i.e. that soul's descent opposes its own nature, results in a cosmic condition that is in its general contours equivalent to what is found in Middle Platonism: evil is introduced into matter from the outside during the process of creation, and the ungenerated pre-cosmic soul is directly to blame.[2] In each of these dualistic systems evil in whatever its manifestation is a divine and eternal principle. Hence we begin to see the foundation for Plotinus' interpretation of the *Phaedrus* passage in I.8.14: a proper reading of Plato requires us to deny that soul descends because of some weakness inherent to it, that is to say, some weakness that makes it act against its nature, and this denial allows us to escape the same untenable dualism that he here ascribes to the Gnostics.

A closer look at I.8.14, however, will reveal that Plotinus' own theory of evil is hardly pure of dualistic features. What Plato's account of soul's descent into the world demonstrates, Plotinus argues there, is that weakness comes to soul as an accretion only after its descent; its presence to soul will not be a removal of something it already possesses; it is, rather, the presence of something different from soul, just as the body takes in phlegm or bile. This foreign addition is, of course, matter with which the descended soul comes into contact while remaining essentially separate from it. To explain the nature of this contact Plotinus resorts to a number of vivid metaphors: when matter is present to soul it 'begs' and 'troubles' soul in its desire to enter it; matter 'lays itself out under' soul and is thereby illumined by it, although it cannot get hold of the origin of the light. Having thus gained entrance to soul, matter darkens its light and provides soul the opportunity to generate through it. 'Thus matter is responsible for weakness in soul and responsible for its wickedness' (I.8.14.49f.).

But this interpretation of *Phaedrus* had its opponents among the later Neoplatonists, whose treatment of evil was more strictly monistic. In chapter 33 of his treatise on evil (*De Subsistentia Malorum*), which may well be a direct response to *Enneads* I.8.14 (the chapter is part of a sizeable portion of the treatise devoted to a refutation of Plotinus' claim that matter is absolute evil), Proclus presents an interpretation of the descent passage of *Phaedrus* that is fundamentally at odds with that of Plotinus.[3] Here, in a much more detailed consideration of the passage than what Plotinus gives us, Proclus demonstrates that according to everything that Plato says there – one of the horses strives to pull the chariot downwards in advance of its actual descent – soul possessed its weakness before its contact with matter.[4] Thus matter is not the cause of soul's descent; soul itself is responsible. If Proclus is indeed reacting specifically to I.8.14, then there is here the implied criticism that Plotinus is much too selective in his reading of Plato, concentrating exclusively on those souls that continue to follow Zeus and maintain their upward vision. The very fact that some souls deviate from this course is proof that, in Plato's view, they, at least, already possess evil.[5] Plato thereby indisputably shows that matter cannot be the cause of soul's weakness; rather, it must be intrinsic to soul. Thus matter is not primary evil.

In his critique Proclus invokes a question that is as central to his theory of evil as it was to that of Plotinus, one that arises inevitably out of this debate over the exegesis of *Phaedrus*: how can matter, which is completely without quality and so completely unable to act, be said to be the cause of anything? In asking this he may well have been thinking of Plotinus' description at the end of I.8.14 of how soul gains its weakness from matter – how, we recall, matter 'begs' and seemingly tempts soul to come down to it. Proclus refers to this notion as matter's 'seduction' of soul and is appropriately wary of it. For, as he amply argues, if matter does exert a kind of attraction upon soul, then there are two possible views of soul's own role in its descent: either, despite this attraction, it descends through its own 'power and impotence', in which case its descent is a matter of deliberate choice rising from its intrinsic weakness, or soul succumbs to the blandishments of matter and is drawn down to the physical world, in which case we would be forced to admit that soul possesses neither self-movement nor free choice; that is, the Platonic soul would cease to be what it is.

The target of Proclus' critique, the idea that the soul can be seduced by matter, an image taken from *Phaedo* (79c6-8), was popular in the post-classical schools, especially among certain dualistic Platonists who, although insisting that matter possessed no qualities, claimed nonetheless that matter fulfilled some sort of active function in the creation of the world. Plotinus was certainly familiar with this tradition and, like Proclus, rejected it. The dualists' claim that matter is some sort of power that resists the beneficent work of divine Providence is a favourite target for Plotinus. Matter is absolute evil, but it is at the same time absolute deficiency, a mere 'decorated corpse' that always remains unchanged whenever form is present in it, but never alive or thinking (II.4.5.15). But he does outside of I.8 occasionally speak of matter as if it possessed a will of its own, although it is almost always the Peripatetic expression of matter's 'desire' for form or the Good,[6] and he more than once makes it clear that he is employing a metaphor. Perhaps his most emphatic statement in this regard comes in a late treatise (VI.7.28) where he asks an intriguing question: If matter had a will, would it wish to become form exclusively (i.e. exclusive of its own nature as matter)? His answer is twofold. First of all, we must not take literally any language that imputes desire to matter. Moreover, even if such attribution were possible, it would be self-contradictory to suppose that matter, if it is absolute evil, could will to become form, for, since form is good, matter would be wishing to cease to be what it is.

But if Proclus is responding to what he perceived as manifest inconsistency in Plotinus' theory of evil, he had good reason to do so. Despite what he says elsewhere, we are reminded that in I.8.14 Plotinus comes close to depicting matter as a seductive power in something other than a purely figurative sense. As well, there are a number of passages where he describes what I would characterize as a certain predisposition on the part of the descending soul to succumb to the attraction of matter. A number of these passages contain apparently conflicting statements regarding the cause or causes of soul's descent into the physical world. We discover what look to be competing statements, on the one hand that soul is sent into this world by God to create, establish order, and preserve what it has generated (IV.8.1-3), and on the other that descent is a matter of soul's wilful separation from the intelligible world in an act of self-assertion (V.1.1.1ff.; IV.7.13.1ff.).[7] Related to these are the incongruous claims that descent is an inclination (*neusis*) of the soul (I.1.12; I.8.4.20) and that it is not (II.9.4); that, on the one hand, this inclination is a spontaneous urge and not a matter of deliberate choice (IV.3.3.13; IV.8.5.27)[8] and, on the other, that it is the result of reflection (V.1.5.1ff.). It will be worthwhile here to contrast specifically Plotinus' commentary on *Phaedrus* 246c in IV.8.4 (*On the Descent of the Soul into Bodies*) with what we have seen in I.8.14. In the former passage the 'moulting' of soul's wings is due to a voluntary act of separation from the intelligible arising out of a power (*dynamis*) directed toward the world below, and it is specifically said to be the cause of soul's descent (line 37); no mention is made of the determinative role that, according to I.8, matter is supposed to play in this process. And we should note that in this early treatise Plotinus distinguishes between two kinds of sin, one related to the cause of descent and the other to the evil that soul accomplishes after it descends (IV.8.5.17ff.). This statement would seem to bring him into agreement with a number of earlier Platonists (Numenius, Cronius, and Harpocration) who claimed that there is evil in the descent itself, quite apart from what happens after soul descends, which is where Plotinus limits soul's evil in I.8.[9]

Such is the inconstancy in Plotinus' treatment of the source of evil, a lack of uniformity that was noted as early as Iamblichus, who, in his treatise *On the Soul*, has Plotinus endorsing two opposing theories concerning soul's responsibility for evil, including him both among those philosophers who grounded evil in some fault in the rational soul itself that causes it to descend (due to soul's 'first otherness' or 'differentiation')[10] and among those who associated evil with causes external to the rational soul, to external 'accretions', which is the argument of I.8.4 (due to nature and the irrational life).[11] We might look at Plotinus' problem, if indeed it is a problem, as one that is unavoidable for any commentator on Plato. Plotinus admits that Plato himself gives various reasons for soul's descent (IV.8.3.6f.), although in the same breath he clarifies that there is no inconsistency in these differing accounts.[12] And Plotinus is by no means the only Platonist who betrayed ambivalence when it came to the soul's participation in the generation of evil.[13]

Still, it is the more positive reading of *Phaedrus* that in the end held sway in Plotinus' mind, so that we see him arguing forcefully in I.8 and other treatises that the higher soul is completely free from sin;[14] that sin is an addition to soul that takes place after its descent;[15] that the lower soul that enters matter is merely 'receptive' of evil rather than already infected by it (I.8.4.12ff.); that soul's inclination (*neusis*) to descend is not itself a sin (I.1.12.24ff.); and that soul would not have descended if there had not been darkness already there for it to illuminate (I.1.12.25ff).[16]

But if Plotinus can say that the lower soul is somehow 'receptive' of evil, then perhaps the differences between Plotinus and Proclus on the subject of evil are really simply matters of degree rather than of substance. There may, then, be merit in the solution to this problem proposed by Denis O'Brien some thirty years ago.[17] To quote O'Brien, 'It appears ... that matter and weakness in the soul are part causes of evil in the soul. They are never singly but only jointly a sufficient cause' (1971, 139). He arrives at this conclusion as a means of bringing coherence to a theory of evil that holds, on the one hand, that soul's descent would not be evil were it not for the presence of matter (the point made repeatedly in I.8) and, on the other, that, as O'Brien puts it, ' ... the presence of matter is not in itself sufficient to account for evil in the soul' (1971, 139). So, in O'Brien's thinking, soul's weakness will be a sufficient condition of sin, but not a causally sufficient condition. However, the presence of matter *is not* a sufficient *condition* of sin. That is to say, while matter is evil in itself and so provides the occasion for sin even when the soul is not weak enough to fall prey to its attraction, sin will not occur unless and until soul becomes sufficiently weak to succumb. Matter is thus the cause of soul's weakness, although not a sole and sufficient cause and never a sufficient condition for sin (1971, 140-1). O'Brien makes it clear that by refusing to accept the possibility that soul can sin without the presence of matter, Plotinus was compromising his conception of evil, leaving himself open to the charge that his matter is a principle independent of the Good. And this is precisely the indictment made by Platonists who followed him, among them Proclus.

ii. Matter and the nature of bodies

Let us now turn to Plotinus' treatment in I.8.4.1-4 of the influence that matter exerts over the 'nature of bodies', where again he alludes (here indirectly) to Plato. Bodies, he says, possess forms, but these forms are not 'true' forms. Now, it is clear that the nature to which he is referring is a pre-corporeal nature from which complete forms have been abstracted, for these bodies do not have true form and their disorderly motion opposes soul and the order that it brings to the body. So what exactly are these illegitimate forms? There can be little doubt that Plotinus is speaking of the unarticulated elements of *Timaeus* 52d1-53b9. There Plato describes the pre-cosmic chaos to which God brings order in the creation of the universe. Before the process of creation begins, these adumbrations of the elements (Plato calls them mere 'traces' (*ichnê*) of themselves), which already possess motion, are brought into contact with the 'nurse of becoming', which later Platonists rather naturally took to be a reference to Aristotle's primary matter. 'Matter', then, 'receives' the elements and is thereupon shaken and disturbed by them; but matter also reciprocates, in turn imparting its inherent instability to the elements. This mixture and its resulting disturbance Platonists identified with the disorderly motion (*horaton ... kinoumenon plêmmelôs kai ataktôs*) described in 30a. That matter gives as good as it gets in the generation of the pre-cosmic chaos exercised many of Plato's interpreters, who took to heart the often repeated objection that matter, being entirely without quality, could hardly itself produce change in something else.[18]

One who was not so exercised was Numenius, who identified matter with Plato's disorderly motion and, thus, with the Necessity that opposed Reason; but, then, his matter possessed a soul and so its own source of motion. Most, of course, saw fit to separate soul from matter, although in many cases they did not specify the origin of the disorderly motion, an omission that Aristotle finds in Plato's own account.[19] Exceptions to this rule are Plutarch and Atticus, who attributed the disorderly motion to the evil World-Soul of *Laws* 896aff., which combines with matter to form the *akosmia*, the state of chaos on which God then imposes order. For Plutarch, who saw the creation of the world as a temporal event, the *akosmia* that Plato describes in *Timaeus* 30a and 52dff. is a kind of proto-genesis that precedes the true creation. Nonetheless, we do find in Plutarch that matter, while completely devoid of qualities and by no means possessing self-motion, is not entirely passive in these two stages of generation, but contributes something of its own nature to the process. Similar views of the role of matter are found in other sources.[20] In none of these accounts is matter made out to be an efficient cause of evil; still, although motion is imparted by the traces of the elements, the disorderliness of the motion is the responsibility of matter itself and is 'given' to the mixture by matter by virtue of the instability that Plato ascribes to it as an intrinsic trait in *Timaeus* 52dff.[21] Clearly Plotinus is in agreement with this tradition. For, while in all likelihood he ascribed the source of the motion of the *physis sômatôn* to the incomplete forms, he leaves no doubt that the disorderliness of the motion – that is to say, its evil – is due to matter itself.[22]

For a fuller picture of Plotinus' reading of Plato on this matter, we shall need to examine several other texts that flesh out his interpretation. Perhaps most important is III.9.3.8-17, where he asserts that soul undergoes two approaches or descents (*prosbolai*). During the first of these descents soul creates an image (*eidôlon*) of itself that is indefinite and irrational; in its second *prosbolê* it 'gives shape' to this image. Exactly what sort of creative activity the soul is engaged in during these two approaches (*prosbolai*) or descents is not clear.[23] Certainly the fact that soul undergoes a kind of double descent is remarkable, and if we are going to arrive at some understanding of Plotinus' meaning here, we shall need to make a more accurate accounting of it.

Consideration of two additional passages, II.3.1647-54 and I.8.7.1-8, will shed light on this one. The first of these passages makes it clear that in the creation of a single, harmonious universe there are two, hypothetically discrete processes of becoming, one involving soul directly in the production of good things and the other described as matter's production of what is worse through the 'disturbance' that is visited upon it by the 'preceding principles'. Whatever these principles are, they are distinguished from the *logoi* that create what is good and they somehow come 'before' these *logoi*.[24] When soul comes to the disturbance caused by the initial *logoi* and matter, it no longer creates, but simply forces order on disorder toward the formation of a unified whole.

The second passage makes the same distinction, although here the production of what is worse is identified with the 'Necessity' of the *Timaeus* and is due to the 'ancient nature', an allusion to the myth of the *Statesman* where Plato describes the period of pre-cosmic disorder (*ataxia*) brought about by the dominant corporeal element (*sômatoeides*). In the *Statesman* myth as well as in the *Enneads*, once order is imposed, all that is good comes from the divine creator and imposer of order, while all that is evil derives from the 'ancient nature' that survives in the generated cosmos. Now, it was by this time a standard feature of Platonic exegesis to link closely the pre-cosmic disorderly motion of the *Timaeus* to the pre-cosmic disorder of the corporeal element in the *Statesman*.[25] The same thinking, I suggest, is behind this and the other *Enneads* passages under discussion here. The generation of evil in the world comes from what Plato mythically describes as the disorderly motion or 'disturbance' (*seismos*) caused by the mixture of matter and traces of the elements or forms. Plotinus, then, in principle agreed with those exegetes who saw in the process of creation three discrete stages of matter: matter in and of itself, matter combined with the traces (sometimes called 'potencies') of the forms, and, lastly, matter combined with the true forms. Thus the production of 'what is worse' described in the passages we are considering now comes not from primary matter, but from the mixture of matter as the substratum with the incomplete forms – what Plotinus refers to elsewhere as the 'traces' (*ichnê*) of soul[26] – so that the 'foregoing *logoi*' that soul apparently produces and sends forth first are the Plotinian equivalent of Plato's traces of the elements in the *Timaeus*. And this stage of matter corresponds both to the result of soul's initial *prosbolê* in III.9.3 and to the *physis sômatôn* of I.8.4.1-6.

To repeat, the 'traces' of the higher soul that come down to the corporeal nature are the *logoi* or forming principles of things. Elsewhere Plotinus describes them as the 'outshining' (*eklampsis*) of both Intellect and the higher soul. Soul produces them as images of itself[27] and they descend in increasingly weaker creative activity.[28] In their higher phases they are alive and rational, carrying with them traces (*ichnê*) of what they will produce when they join with matter (III.6.18.24ff.). In their lowest phase, however, as they approach matter, they have become irrational, lack definition (III.9.3.10ff.), produce what is lifeless insofar as they are no longer real forms of soul (III.4.1.1ff.); they are, in short, mere phantasms that are themselves dead and have no power to create (cf. III.8.2.30ff.), the 'untrue coming to the untrue' (III.6.13.34). As complete indefiniteness, they must be 'perfected' (*teleioumenon*), taking on true form, before they can generate bodies (III.4.1.1ff.). It is at this lowest phase of creation that evil arises, not out of bodies themselves, but from the nature of bodies – or, more specifically, from this nature's disorderly motion – that precedes fully formed bodies. While it is clear that, at the point when the incomplete forms enter matter, the motion that results is provided by the *logoi* insofar as they are remnants of soul, it is equally clear from I.8.4 and 7 that the disorderliness of the motion, and thus the evil, are due to matter. But it is important to note that Plotinus thereby adopts the orthodox Platonic view that the evil that is produced is nothing more than a lack of order, and therefore, by implication, not a principle that actively opposes the Good. Plotinus says as much in I.8.8: matter controls the forms that enter it, not as a power like that of a form that controls its opposite (hot, for example, dominating cold), but as shapelessness opposing shape and formlessness opposing form. So it is that in the description of the descent of soul in VI.4.15 the disturbance of the *physis sômatos* is referred to, not as a force or power of the body, but as its weakness (*astheneia*), the same term that he, and Proclus after him, employ to depict the evil that attaches to the soul (cf. III.6.6).

What we have here, I believe, are elements of the first Neoplatonic reading of Plato's disorderly motion. In certain formal respects, as well, this reading draws from the exegetical tradition of Middle Platonism, as, for example, Plutarch's distinction, mentioned earlier, between the proto-generation that brings about the pre-cosmic *akosmia* and the creation of the ordered cosmos. And if we look to post-Plotinian Platonism, we find close parallels to a similarly hypothetical division of the process of demi-urgic creation recognized by Proclus and associated by him with Porphyry and Iamblichus, where the 'initial' stage is a corporeal (*sômatourgikê*) generation when bodies with their disorderly motion come to be, followed 'later' by an ordering (*kosmêtikê*) generation during which fully rational forms are imposed on these bodies.[29] But in its specific formulation Plotinus' reading contains much that is new and transformative of the tradition, particularly with respect to the role played by the soul. Here there is one universe made up of things that are constituted in two ways, one through the guidance of soul and the forming principles, so that what is produced is 'better', and the other through matter and the 'untrue' forms that disturb it, so that what is produced is 'worse', due to the resulting disorderly motion. In Plato's cosmic order, of course, the better governs the worse. So, while some parts of the universe contain evil, the whole is unified and good.

For Plotinus, then, Plato's treatment of the disorderly motion connects the origin of evil not only with the creation of the cosmos, but also with an account of the descent of the soul that goes beyond the question of soul's 'audacity'. Yet even in this, as in his consideration of the evil in the soul, Plotinus gives to matter an active role – both in its 'seductive' power over the soul during its descent and in its production of disorder in the motion of the pre-cosmic corporeal nature – that, strictly speaking, it should not have. And he did so by appropriating Middle Platonic interpretations of Plato and reassessing them in starkly novel ways. The result is a theory of evil that categorically rejects any form of dualism while at the same time accepting and exploiting a number of its exegetical principles. But, as Proclus demonstrates, the Plotinian exegesis invited a more conservative reading to challenge it, one that construed the dialogues as not only providing a more coherent theory of matter, but also preserving the autonomy of the soul. As O'Brien observes, Proclus as well as other later Platonists realized that Plotinus' embrace of features of the old dualism of two independent and co-eternal principles was the 'Achilles' heel' of his theory of evil. Yet we must certainly admire a philosopher whose original and resourceful approach to the texts of Plato stands in such bold relief to the comparatively staid Platonism that preceded and followed him.

Notes

1. Cf. I.8.10.1: *Apoios de ousa pôs kakê*;

2. Although for the Gnostics this soul is not primarily responsible, nor is there evidence here at least of a Gnostic appeal to Plato's evil World-Soul of *Laws* 896a.

3. Cf. also ch. 49. The *Phaedrus* passage was something of a *locus classicus* for arguments concerning soul's responsibility for its own sinfulness; cf. Plutarch *De An. Procr.* 1026f and Iamblichus ap. Proclus *In Tim.* III 334.4ff.

4. Cf. also *Pl. Th.* I 18.85ff.: the *parhypostasis* of evils comes not from power, but from weakness (*astheneia*) of beings that receive the illumination of the gods; cf. 86.15f. and *In Tim.* I 380.24ff.

F.P. Hager's ([1962], 99) suggestion that ch. 33 refers only to soul's 'precondition' to evil is irrelevant if evil for Proclus is a weakness, impotence, or absence of Good: this 'precondition' to commit sin just is soul's evil. As Plotinus says at

5. Platonists on the origin of evil

I.8.5.14f., great deficiency is the possibility of falling into evil and is itself already evil.

5. And Proclus might even have construed this as Plato's repudiation of the possibility of an undescended soul.

6. Cf. III.6.11.32 and 14.9f.; VI.7.25.25; also note the very interesting comment at II.4.3.8 that soul seeks form as the 'matter' of Intellect.

7. Although in the latter passage soul in its separation is inspired by the beauty and order of Intellect.

8. IV.8.5 argues that there is no conflict in these two explanations, for both are true.

9. Cf. *De Abstin.* IV 20.17ff. Nauck and see Hager (1962), 84.

10. Cf. V.1.1.

11. ap. Stobaeum *Ecl.* I 375.2ff. (Wachsmuth).

12. Cf. IV.8.5, where he argues for this in detail.

13. Sources tell us that Numenius held both that evil is an external accretion to soul (fr. 43 des Places and cf. Calcidius ch. 298) and that soul can be infected with moral perversity before its embodiment (fr. 49). And Porphyry maintained a number of conflicting positions regarding the source of evil during his career. See *Sent.* 30 and cf. 37; *De Abstin.* I 30 (matter is the ground of evil); *De Antro Nymph.* 5 (matter opposes Providence); yet also see *Sent.* 20 (matter is absolute non-being) and *Ad Marc.* 29 and cf. *Sent.* 32 (soul is cause). Cf. Hager (1962), 93 on Porphyry's inconsistency.

14. I.1.9-12 and VI.2.22.30ff.

15. Cf. II.3.8.14f. and 11.

16. Indeed, that there is an undescended, higher soul is for Plotinus sufficient proof against the concept, found in Plutarch and Atticus, of a soul evil in itself, for insofar as one part of soul is entirely free from evil, it cannot be the case that soul *per se* is evil (cf. IV.7.10).

See also II.9.3.17ff. where Plotinus argues, against the dualism of the Gnostics, that soul cannot be separated from matter. Of course, qualification is due on the last idea: matter does not pre-exist descent as a co-eternal first principle; cf. II.9.12 against the Gnostics and dualists.

17. (1971), 113-46.

18. See, for example, Plutarch of *De An. Procr.* 1015ab, p. 150 Hubert.

19. *Met.* 1071b 31ff. and cf. *De Caelo* 280a 5ff. and 300b 16ff. On this see Baltes (1978), 156, n. 276.

20. Cf. Alcinous *Didask.* 12.2 and 13.3 and Calcidius *In Tim.* ch. 352, the latter likely following a Middle Platonic source.

21. Essentially the same interpretation occurs in Alcinous (*Didask.* 12.2 and 13.3 and in Calcidius (ch. 352). Some regard this ambivalence regarding matter's participation in the generation of the world as characteristic of Middle Platonic exegesis of Plato; cf. Den Boeft (1970), 86f. and van Winden (1959), 233-42.

22. In support of my reading of I.8.4.1-6, I might add that the use of the phrase *phora ataktôs* to refer to the *horaton* is attested already in Plutarch (*De An. Procr.* 1017a). Also, from their readings of the *Timaeus* both Porphyry (ap. John Philoponus *De Aet. Mun.* 14.546.17ff.) and Proclus (*In Tim.* I 383.1-22; 389.5ff.; 394.9ff.; *Pl. Th.* I 11.9ff.; *In Parm.* 1045.26ff.; *De Subs. Mal.* chs 55 and 58) speak of a *physis* that bears a strong similarity to Plotinus' *physis sômatôn*. See also Dodds (1963), 209, Baltes (1978), 155ff. and Erler (1978), 187.

23. O'Brien (at, among other places, [1971], 127ff.) maintains that when soul produces an image of itself during its first approach it is creating matter. In this second descent, then, soul brings form to matter, this being the primary function of its movement away from the intelligible world. Although there is no space here to explain why, I will say that I disagree with this interpretation.

24. They are closely connected if not identified with the perceptive or vegetative soul.

25. Cf. Plutarch *De An. Procr.* 1014bc; 1015de; 1017ab, and Proclus, *In Tim.* I 389.5ff.

26. Cf. VI.4.15-16, where Plotinus describes the coming-to-be of a living being, which occurs when only a trace (*ichnos*) of soul, to be distinguished from a full part of soul, enters the nature of body (*physis sômatos*), which itself is not completely without soul, but is in a state of confusion and disorder, pummelled by blows from outside itself. Hermeias (*In Phaedr.* 102.21ff.) employs the phrase *ichnos psychês* to describe the irrational soul, which is also termed irrational life and the mortal form of soul. Erler (1978), 125, n. 1, compares this passage with Proclus' description of Plato's *horaton* in *Timaeus* 30a as possessing both *ichnê* of the forms and a disorderly motion. But perhaps a more appropriate source of comparison would be Plotinus. On the notion that soul cannot enter a completely soulless body, see Blumenthal (1971b), 63. He notes that the level of soul that initially enters the body must be the *phytikon*.

27. IV.3.10.38ff.; VI.4.16. These passages are sufficient evidence against O'Brien's claim that the image that soul produces in III.9.3 is primary matter.

28. On the different orders of *logoi* cf. III.3.1.1ff.

29. *In Tim.* I 383.1-22.

The *species infima* as the infinite:
Timaeus 39e7-9, *Parmenides* 144b4-c1 and
Philebus 16e1-2 in Plotinus, *Ennead* VI.2.22

Atsushi Sumi

I have argued before against the widespread view that Plotinus could not find any *locus classicus* in Plato's writings for the identity of intellect and intelligible. Careful reading of the *Enneads* shows that *Phdr.* 247d7-e1, quoted in V.8.4.52-6, is the *locus classicus*.[1] Here Plotinus affirms that Plato left us to investigate and discover the hidden meaning of the *Phaedrus* phrase, if we claim to be worthy of our name as philosophers.[2] According to Wallis, Plotinus' treatment of Plato in V.8.4.52-6 suggests that he regards him as 'an intentional propounder of enigmas leading us to seek the truth for ourselves'.[3] Gatti suggests that Plotinus 'considered Plato to be a philosopher who posed problems or aporias that often did not have definitive solutions'.[4]

The extent of Plotinus' debt to Plato – whether he considers himself to be simply Plato's disciple or an autonomous thinker – is beyond the scope of this paper.[5] But the following point should be unanimously accepted: in V.1.8.10-14 Plotinus characterizes himself as an interpreter of Plato's *unstated* thought. As Atkinson explains, the interpreter's role is 'to recover the hidden meaning from Plato's philosophy'.[6] Thus Plotinus' exegesis of Plato is indeed regarded as 'philosophical' and 'metaphysical,' but viewed critically, if not pejoratively, as 'decidedly unhistorical'.[7] The best-known example of his 'philosophical' reading would be the doxographical chapter V.1.8, and his exegesis of *Phdr.* 247d7-e1 in V.8.4 would be its most radical case.

In this paper I will explicate the *ne plus ultra* of Plotinus' philosophical reading of Plato in VI.2.22. Here Plotinus treats together *Timaeus* 31b1 and 39e7-9, *Parmenides* 144b4-c1 and *Philebus* 16e1-2, viewing the former two texts as Platonic riddles. This complicated situation makes the interpretation of the key passage in lines 11-23 extremely difficult.[8] Hence translations of that passage differ widely. Then I suggest some necessary modifications to Armstrong's translation, and clarify this extreme case of Plotinus' reading of Platonic enigmas, so that our inquiry must proceed rather like a running commentary. The basic text used in this paper is the minor edition (H-S^2) by Henry and Schwyzer. Several translations in

European languages are referred to, where 'the German translators' collectively stand for Harder, Beutler and Theiler. Before our careful analysis of the key passage, we must review the related context.

i. The related context and the first riddle of *Timaeus* 39e7-9

In VI.2 Plotinus deals with the genera of real being in Plato's *Sophist*. Problems about their identity are concluded in VI.2.18. VI.2.19 raises a new question about how species are engendered from the primary genera – Being, Movement, Rest, Sameness and Otherness (19.10-12). It is a requirement for any solution to this problem that it must not let each genus disappear into its species and lose its own pure and unmingled essence (19.12-17).[9]

A further difficulty is raised in 19.18-23. While Plotinus claims that Intellect is composed of all the primary genera, he considers the genus of Being to be prior to all the members of the noetic world as species and parts, including Intellect.[10] In other words, the paradox arises that Intellect seems at the same time both prior and subsequent to all entities. Plotinus tries to resolve this difficulty, relating Intellect to the genera in VI.2.20, and to the rest of the intelligible realm in VI.2.21.[11]

Referring to passages of the *Timaeus*, Plotinus states that quality, quantity, number and figure derive from, and along with, the primary genera to be altogether included in Intellect. Intellect is said to be 'a complete living being' (ζῷον παντελές, 31b1) and 'that which is a living being' (ὅ ἐστι ζῷον, 39e8) in 21.56-8.[12] It is in this context dealing with the derivation of the subsequent entities from the primary genera, that Plotinus, at the beginning of VI.2.22, points out that these passages of the *Timaeus* (31b1 and 39e7-9) are somewhat enigmatic:

> And Plato speaks riddlingly (ἠνιγμένως) of 'the way in which Intellect sees the Ideas being in (ἐνούσας) the complete living being [observing] of what kind (οἶαι) they are and how many (ὅσαι) they are'.
> 22.1-3, trans. Armstrong, adapted

Plotinus is haunted by the passage from the *Timaeus* which once annoyed him in III.9.1. After this remark he mentions that Intellect not only sees the Forms better when it looks to what precedes itself, but also sees that it sees (22.3-7),[13] and reconfirms that Intellect as one-many makes many individual intellects as a necessary consequence of its multiplicity (22.7-11).[14] Then comes the key text which calls for serious consideration.

Consideration of the context reminds us of the following three points. First, Plotinus is addressing the resolution of the riddle about the passage of the *Timaeus*. In the section preceding the text in question (22.3-11), this enigma is not touched yet. Second, Plotinus' mind is consistently occupied by the requirement (set in 19.12-17) that in the derivation of species from genera, each genus must not disappear into its species in such a way as to lose its own pure and unmingled essence.[15] Finally, we are told in 21.1-6 that we have to see how all things coming from the whole Intellect are present in (ἔνι) it, because the problem of how the whole Intellect, while remaining one in its definition, produces the partial entities is the same problem as the problem of how the subsequent species proceed from the primary genera. Unless this point is kept in mind, we cannot understand how the articulation, described in the key text, from the genus to the ultimate species makes a contribution to the solution of the riddle, mentioned in 22.1-3, about the whole Intellect's contemplation of the Forms present in itself. Without attending to these three points, we cannot adequately construe the following key text.

ii. Apprehension of specific form

But in general it is not possible to apprehend the numerical one and the individual; for what you apprehend is specific form; for it is without matter.
22.11-13, trans. Armstrong, adapted

Only a slight adaptation is necessary here. Three points deserve mention. First, Harder, Bréhier and Cilento insert 'im Geist', 'en elle [sc. l'intelligence]' and 'nello Spirito' respectively into the second sentence. This phrase does not occur in the text, but its insertion is justified by the preceding statement that the Forms are seen better in Intellect (22.4-5).

Second, the phrase 'the numerical one' is originally found in *Categories* 1b6-7, and refers to the sensible particular composed of form and matter, e.g. the individual man and the individual horse. Although Plotinus' allusion to the *Categories* for the characterization of the sensible particular as the individual seems abrupt, it appears to be well calculated. This point will be considered in the next section dealing with the riddle in the *Parmenides*. The final problem, concerning the subject of ἄνευ ὕλης in 22.13, will not influence the analysis of the wider text.[16]

iii. The second riddle of *Parmenides* 144b4-c1

So Plato makes this cryptic remark also, that 'real being is cut up to infinity.' For as long as the generation (or derivation), from genera for instance, proceeds to another species, the species is not yet infinite; for the species is limited by the species which have been generated.
22.13-16, trans. Armstrong, adapted

I here try to reconstruct the laconic ἕως-clause in 22.15 by having recourse to the verb γεννᾶν in 22.16. Before the first riddle of *Tim.* 39e7-9 is resolved, another riddle (αἰνιττόμενος) from *Parm.* 144b4-c1 is introduced.[17] The obscurity of the key text as a whole seems to be due in no small measure to the complication of these two enigmas. As mentioned above,[18] Plotinus usually construes the deduction from the second hypothesis in the so-called second part of the *Parmenides* as referring to Intellect, which is one-many, and *Parm.* 144b4-c1 is included in this deduction. The phrase εἰς ἄπειρα in 22.14 paraphrases ἀπέραντα in 144c1. The verb κατακερματίζειν in 22.14, originally from *Parm.* 144b4-5, appears also in 12.10, where the genus is said to be as a whole immanent in each of its species without being cut up. Related to 22.11-12, the citation of *Parm.* 144b4-c1 is supposed to make the reader perplexed enough to ask the following question: if we do not apprehend the individual or that which cannot be divided in Intellect and at the same time real being in the intelligible world is cut up to infinity, then what do we ever apprehend there? This seems to be the reason why this citation is characterized as a riddle. Hence the infinite division of real being must not be literally understood. The resolution of the enigma begins in 22.15 and is brought to a conclusion in 22.16-19.

In light of γὰρ in 22.16, the subject of ἄπειρον in 22.15 is the same as that of περατοῦται in 22.16.[19] Their common subject is εἶδος in 22.13.[20] The focus in the present passage is definitely the species apprehended by Intellect. The binary μὲν and δ' in 22.15-16 seem to signal the contrast between the species in general and the ultimate species, that is, the species which is divided into its lower species and the one which is not further divided. Strictly speaking, the subject in question is particularized as the species-in-general except for the ultimate species.

There are four related problems to be considered. First, is it possible to read anything else as the subject of ἄπειρον? It would seem to be difficult.[21] Second, although Bréhier does not translate ἄλλο in ἄλλο εἶδος in 22.15, it seems to be important in distinguishing 'another species' from εἶδος in 22.13.[22] The plural τοῖς γεννηθεῖσιν εἴδεσι in 22.16[23] refers to ἄλλο εἶδος so that 'another species' cannot be the subject of περατοῦται – for it is totally inconceivable that 'another species' is limited by itself in the plural. 'Another species' seems to mean 'a species lower than the species in question'. Third, οἷον in 22.15 indicates that the theme of the sentence in question is not the generative process from the genera to their proximately lower species. It implies instead that the process from a given species to 'another species' is a downward movement from the upper to the lower as it starts from the genera. Therefore the 'limitation' in 22.16 is that of the species by its proximately lower species. Finally, we may examine other readings for the subject of περατοῦται. Although Armstrong and the German translators take 'the division' and 'der Vorgang' respectively as the subject, no counterpart is found in the text.[24] Even if this reading were possible, it would be difficult to consider 'the limited division' and 'the unlimited ultimate species' to form such a balanced contrast as is signalled by μὲν and δέ.

iv. The *species infima* as the infinite

But the ultimate species which is not divided into species is infinite (rather than limited).

22.16-17, trans. Armstrong, adapted

The ultimate species, having no lower species into which it may be divided, is not limited by any lower species and therefore is infinite. On the contrary, all the species except for the ultimate ones are limited by each of their proximately lower species and therefore each such intermediate species is not infinite. Thus the genuine contrast between 'the limited species in general' and 'the infinite ultimate species' is signalled by μέν and δέ in 22.15-16. At this point the second riddle of the infinite division of real being is half resolved. The phrase εἰς ἄπειρα in the *Parmenides* cannot be taken literally; it means 'to the infinite ultimate species'. Since the ultimate species which are the objects of Intellect's apprehension are known as τὸ εἶδος ἄτομον or *species infima*, they are indivisible.

The indivisibility of the ultimate species is also mentioned in VI.2 (2.8; 2.12; 2.33). Readers of the *Enneads* here notice that this passage from the *Parmenides* presents a riddle. We notice this by seeing that the phrase εἰς ἄπειρα is related to the indivisibility of Intellect's object of apprehension – in spite of the statement in 22.11-12 that we do not apprehend the individual or the indivisible in the noetic world. But if ἄπειρα here simply implied the infinity of the ultimate species, then this riddle would be superficial. Hence Plotinus' reference to the *Categories* in 22.11-12 seems to be a subplot of his own devising. Is the generic Form, then, really 'cut up' as its species are derived from it? This question is eventually answered in 22.19-20.

Here two problems need to be discussed. The first concerns the meaning of μᾶλλον in 22.17. Taking it as 'rather', we consider μᾶλλον ἄπειρον to be an elliptical form of μᾶλλον ἄπειρον ἢ οὐ περατοῦται. Armstrong, Cilento and the German translators take μᾶλλον ἄπειρον as the comparative. But neither the comparative nor the superlative of ἄπειρος is conceivable. We can also easily understand this from the usage of the English adjective 'infinite', which allows of no comparison.[25]

The second problem concerns the notions of limit and infinity. The lower species and its proximately upper species are the active and the passive relata respectively in the relation of limitation, so that limit is attributed to the latter. On the other hand, the ultimate species cannot be a passive relatum in this relation and is 'infinite' because of the absence of limit from it. Infinity is originally the notion attributed intrinsically to the hyper-ontic activity like the One or non-being like matter. It is seldom conceived in any relation and the present notion is exceptional in the *Enneads*.

The uniqueness of limit and infinity here must be explained. Armstrong elucidates the unlimitedness in terms of one constant life of the All, which is the work of Zeus or the cosmic soul, described in IV.4.9.13-18 as follows:

> ... this is the sense of τὸ ἀδιάστατον, complete and simultaneous unity, the state proper to eternal and non-spatial spiritual being in which there is absence of limit by division in the sense that one part is not here and another there, one does not exist now and another then. This sense of course applies to the lower Hypostases, and not to the absolutely partless One. It is applied both to the Divine Intellect and to Soul.[26]

This notion and the infinity in question share the root meaning of 'absence of limit by division' which Plotinus seems to have in mind in the present passage. Whereas the former notion is intrinsically attributed to the intelligible world as a whole, the latter is conceived with regard to the ultimate species as an individual member of that world in the schematic relation of genus and species. Furthermore, the former is closely connected to all- or mutual inclusiveness and eternity of Intellect in Plotinus' metaphysics.[27] On the other hand, even though the reason why the latter is appealed to becomes clear in VI.2.22.19-20, it is hardly significant in his doctrine of the noetic world. This seems to be the peculiarity of the infinity of the ultimate species.[28]

The infinity of the ultimate species constitutes the halfway point toward the complete resolution of the second riddle of the *Parmenides*. Since infinity is originally a negative notion which is given a meaning solely as a negation or privation of limit, we need to ask what situation the limitation of the upper species by its proximately lower species ever indicates. It is apparent that the limitation in the former's extension is not described here, because the present context does not deal with either the extension or intension of a concept. The present theme definitely concerns the articulation of the intelligible world in terms of the genus-species scheme, so that the limitation in question must concern the being of the specific Form, inseparable from its essence.[29] Then what does this mean? We are told in 12.11-14 that the genus, remaining in itself, is as a whole immanent in the species which participate in it.[30] The 'immanence' certainly implies that the relation between the genus and the participating species is *internal* to the latter. In other words, the genus is somehow built into the structure of the species that shares in it.

On the other hand, the limitation of the upper species by its proximately lower species is characterized as a relation between the active and the passive in actuality as defined in *Metaphys.* 1021a14-19. In reducing the opposite notions of activity and passivity to one, Plotinus dismisses passivity as movement proceeding into other things (VI.1.19.21-6). Insofar as the limitation of the upper species by its proximately lower species proceeds into the former, the relation of limitation in question is internal with regard to the former, so that we are forced to conclude that the lower species may be somehow immanent in the upper species limited by it. If this situation of limitation were applied to the entire realm of Forms, the species would be immanent not only in all the upper species but in all the genera, insofar as the latter are immediately participated in by the former. This supposed immanence of the lower species in the upper Form is prone to infringe on the pure and unmingled nature of the genera in the sense different from the remark made in VI.2.19.12-17.

Thus two deadlocks await us. First, the notions of limit and infinity are abandoned altogether in order to defend the pure nature of each generic Form. Second, the limitation invites the situation of the immanence of the lower species in the upper, which is unavoidably incompatible with the immanence of genus in species. Although the limitation in question must be conceptualized in such a way that it can steer a clear course between this Scylla and this Charybdis, no clue to the solution is found in the present passage. There remains a way out which dismisses the 'limitation' as a mere *façon de parler*. But to do so leads to an evasion of the resolution of the second riddle of the *Parmenides*.[31]

v. Plotinus on the dialectical method in the *Philebus*

This is the meaning of 'at this point to let them go into the infinite and say goodbye to them'.

22.17-19, trans. Armstrong

No emendation is necessary here. The quotation is from *Phlb.* 16e1-2, where the dialectical method is explained in relation to the one-many problem. It is obvious that 'the infinite' indicates the ultimate species. Here it becomes fully clear that Plotinus takes εἰς ἄπειρα in the *Parmenides* as εἰς τὸ ἄπειρον.

Phlb. 16c-17a is normally construed such that 'we are told not to "apply the character of unlimitedness" to our plurality' until we have reached the extreme point at which Limit ceases to be applicable, i.e. until we reach the *infimae species*,[32] or the division ends by dispensing with the unlimited after it reaches the ultimate species.[33] Plotinus' interpretation is quite different from these views, which make the ultimate species *distinct* from infinity. Whereas the scheme of one, many and infinity is usually taken to mean genera, species and particulars respectively,[34] Plotinus associates this infinity with the ultimate species. (In spite of the characterization of Intellect as 'one-many' in 22.7-11, such a problem of one and many as is posed in the *Philebus* is not discussed in the present passage.) Plotinus' unique exegesis seems to be based on two points. First, he seems to understand the connection of plurality and infinity (ἄπειρος ... πλήθει, 17b4; ἄπειρον ... πλῆθος, 17e3) such that it does not mean quantitative unlimitedness, but the plurality of the ultimate species and the absence of proximately lower species' limitation from them.[35] Second, he seems to take the referent of τῶν ἀεὶ λεγομένων εἶναι (16c9) consisting of one and many as Forms and soul; he attributes infinity to the latter in 22.22-3.[36]

Porphyry does not abide by Plotinus' exegesis of the *Philebus* and is relatively close to Plato's modern readers. He applies the scheme of one, many and infinite to ten most generic Aristotelian categories, numerically finite *infimae species* and quantitatively unlimited particulars (*Isagoge* 6.11-16, Busse).[37]

The present passage from the *Philebus* is not treated as a riddle. We are perhaps allowed to call it a partial 'solution' to the second riddle of the *Parmenides*, insofar as the phrase εἰς τὸ ἄπειρον – which refers to the infinity of the ultimate species – clarifies the cryptic phrase εἰς ἄπειρα. Plotinus' elucidation of *Phlb.* 16e1-2 seems to reach to 22.23, if it is not included in the lacuna supposed in 22.24-5.

vi. The first and the second riddles resolved

But as far as the ultimate species are on their own, they are infinite; but as soon as they are comprehended by the one they now arrive at number.
22.19-20, trans. Armstrong, adapted

The German translators, Bréhier and Cilento read 'the individual (τὸ ἄτομον)' in 22.12 as the common subject of ἄπειρα and ἔρχεται. But it is quite difficult to do so, because 'the individual' is not apprehended in the noetic world. The fact that the aorist participle περιληφθέντα in 22.20 is a neuter plural indicates that the ultimate species in the plural τὰ ἔσχατα εἴδη are the common subject of both.[38] This aorist tense seems to imply the logical priority of the 'comprehension by the one' to the 'arrival at number'. The advantage of this proposed reading is of course the straightforwardness that no change in the subject occurs from 22.16-17. Since ἀλλ' in 22.19 signals an opposition to 22.16-17, the same subject must be taken over in the present passage.

Judging by ἐπ' αὐτοῖς, we are not allowed to see the contrast signalled by μέν and δέ as that between the absolute and the relative viewpoints. The sentence 'as far as the ultimate species are on their own' does not mean that they are abstracted from their relations to all other Forms. The viewpoint of 'division to species' in 22.17 is, rather, retained here. From this viewpoint, the ultimate species do not have lower species into which they may be divided and by which they may be limited, and so are infinite. In other words, the absoluteness meant by ἐπ' αὐτοῖς is a consequence from the situation that the one relatum which must be considered relatively is paradoxically considered in isolation because of the absence of another relatum. Therefore the contrast in question is that between (i) the case in which the ultimate species are abstracted from their relations to the upper Form represented by 'the comprehending one' and (ii) the case in which the ultimate species are considered with these relations.

6. The species infima as the infinite

Then what is 'the comprehending one'? Bréhier alone clarifies it by supplementing 'l'unité' with 'd'un genre'. In VI.2, however, no privileged status is given to the genus of Being; the sole exception is 19.18-23 where the aporia is posed. In the present treatise the primary genera number four, including Sameness and Otherness (19.1; 21.2). Therefore it seems most consistent to take 'the comprehending one' as the unity of 'one Intellect (εἷς νοῦς)' in 22.10, namely the whole Intellect.[39]

The final sentence 'the ultimate species now arrive at number' is of the utmost importance. Then what does it mean to 'arrive at number'? A passage from another treatise dealing with the hypostatization of intelligible objects in connection with number helps our inquiry.

> If then beings are not as many as they are just casually, number which pre-exists is a cause of their being so many: that is, it was when number already existed that the things which come to be participated in the 'so many' and each one of them participated in 'one,' so that it might be one.
>
> VI.6.10.12-15, trans. Armstrong, adapted

From this passage we can understand that the total number of the ultimate species is finite and is counted 'so many'. Each of them is one entity discrete and different from every other. From this, moreover, it is concluded that the total number of intelligible objects is finitely many and each of the Forms, generic or specific, is one entity, discrete and different from the others.[40] In VI.2 too, it is noted that each intelligible entity, separate from others, is what it is, and all of them again are in one (21.54-5). The locution 'to be embraced by the one' is replaced with 'to participate in the one (τοῦ ἓν μετέσχεν)' in the above quotation. Both the finiteness of the total number of Forms and the discreteness of each of them are exclusively referable to their being embraced by the unity of the whole Intellect. On the other hand, infinite multiplicity is a total falling away from unity (VI.6.1.1-8).[41] But it would be rash to say that the unity of the whole Intellect is responsible for internal relatedness among Forms, which is, in our present treatise, crystalized into the immanence of genus in species.

At this point the two Platonic riddles are eventually resolved. The first riddle of *Tim.* 31b1 and 39e7-9 is read in three ways. First, the Forms immanent in the whole Intellect are identical with the complete living being which that Intellect sees. As a result of the Forms being immanent in the whole Intellect, the finitely many Forms embraced by its unity become objects of contemplation. If the Forms were outside Intellect, they could not participate in the latter's unity and so should be infinitely many. Second, following from the first resolution, the reason why Intellect sees *how many* the Forms are is that the Forms inside it are thus *finitely plural.* Finally, the reason why Intellect sees *of what kind* the Forms are is that the individual essences of the Forms to be seen are exhaustively unfolded when the articulation from the genera arrives at the ultimate species.

81

Plotinus seems to believe that the all-inclusiveness of the complete living being needs to be systematically related to the articulation of the intelligible world by means of the genus-species scheme, which is able to explain the exhaustive realization of the individual essences of Forms included in the living being. However, this doctrine is based on the tacit assumption that all the so-called qualitative or adjectival Forms are deployed in the articulation as differentiae.[42]

In the second riddle of *Parm.* 144b4-c1 matters are slightly different. First of all, the hidden meaning of this section is that the genera are divided down to the ultimate species, which are 'infinite'. In the articulation of the noetic world toward the ultimate species, neither genus nor species is literally 'cut up' and disappears. Here we need to remember the remark in 19.12-17 that each of the primary genera must not disappear in its species in the process of derivation of the species from the genera. If the total number of Forms were infinitely many, the one would be absent from the intelligible world. This absence would mean not only that the unity is absent from the entire noetic cosmos but that each of the Forms can no longer be one individual Form, so that the genera eventually disappear. The one protects the genera from disappearing and losing their individual essences, pure and unmingled, and ensures that the Forms are finitely many by being seen inside the whole Intellect and embraced by its oneness. In short, Plotinus here entertains a coherent logical nexus, interweaving (i) Intellect as one-many, (ii) the immanence of the Forms in Intellect, (iii) the immersion of the entire intelligible world in the unity of the whole Intellect, (iv) the finite plurality of the Forms and (v) the individual unity (or 'not to disappear') of each Form, including the generic ones. But the deduction from the second hypothesis in the *Parmenides*, which is the *locus classicus* of (i), and 'the infinite' in the passage of the *Philebus* dealing with the one-many problem are *prima facie* incompatible with (iv), so that the coherence of the logical nexus may be compromised. We can suppose that Plotinus, in his exegesis of the *Philebus*, appeals to his unique notion of the infinity attributed to the ultimate species to the point where he abandons the Aristotelian notion of limit[43] in an attempt to avoid incoherence.

Finally, Blumenthal takes the present passage as indicating Plotinus' rejection of the Forms of individuals.[44] Indeed the fact that no Form limits the ultimate species rules out Forms of individuals. But insofar as the context does not require Plotinus to deal with the Forms of individuals, it is not helpful to refer to them in relation to the present passage.

vii. The last part of the soul as the infinite

So then Intellect holds the soul which comes after it, so that the soul, too, is in number down to her last part, but her last part is already infinite altogether.

22.20-3, trans. Armstrong, adapted

6. The species infima as the infinite

The conjunction οὖν in 22.20 indicates that the contrast signalled by μὲν and δέ resumes that between 'infinity' and 'arrival at number by virtue of the unity's embracement'. While the soul is embraced by the unity of the whole Intellect (via an individual intellect preceding herself), and arrives at number, her last part or Nature,[45] having no subsequent entity, is infinite, just as the ultimate species is not limited by anything. The notion of ἄπειρον in 22.23 is the same as that of ἄπειρον in 22.17 or ἄπειρα in 22.19. Beutler and Theiler comment on the present passage: 'the soul in her lowest part disappears to infinity.'[46] But this note overlooks the force of οὖν.

The soul herself is identified with number in V.1.5.9. In VI.6.16.42-6, too, a similar idea is found in relation to *Tim.* 36e6-37a1; the number of soul is a real being in the sense that the soul is a real being. In IV.3.8.22-4, furthermore, we are told that each of the souls, which are real beings identified with numbers, is numerically one and individual. Therefore the statement that 'the soul is in number' means that she as well as the Form is an individual entity different from others of her kind.[47]

The last part of the soul is 'infinite altogether' (ἄπειρον παντάπασι), but one does not need to ask whether or not the ultimate species can similarly be called 'altogether infinite'; for it is impossible to compare one infinite entity with another in respect of infinity. On the other hand, one ought to ask whether or not the ultimate species is limited by the soul subsequent to itself, and, if it is somehow limited, how it is so. But the infinity of the soul's last part primarily indicates that *Phlb.* 16e1-2 still influences the ensuing passage down to 22.23. 'The infinite' in the *Philebus* even includes the soul's last part, which implies that Plotinus regards not only the Forms but the soul as the referents of 'things that are ever said to be' in 16c9.[48]

A difficult passage including a lacuna follows the present section. As suggested by H-S[1], the referent of νοῦς ... ὁ τοιοῦτος in 22.23 is an intellect which holds the soul subsequent to itself (22.20-1), namely an individual intellect identical with one of the ultimate species. It reappears in 22.27 as the plural οἱ ἄλλοι νοῖ.

viii. Epilogue

Plotinus' exposition of the genera in the intelligible world in VI.2 ends with the following remark: 'We have explained the way in which we think about real being and how it might accord with the thought of Plato' (VI.3.1.1-2, trans. Armstrong, adapted). 'The way in which we think about real being' seems to cover not only Plotinus' systematization of the 'greatest genera' of *Sophist* 254d-257a but his reading of the riddles of the *Timaeus* and the *Parmenides* with the clue from the *Philebus* in VI.2.22. Plotinus' 'original' reading of those texts, as Wallis points out,[49] is only made possible by an assumption of *Plato's authority*. But our inquiry does not simply result in either the harmony of originality and authority, or the subordination of the former to the latter.

The analysis of Plotinus' 'original' reading of Plato requires both 'philosophical' endeavour and philological sensitivity from ourselves. A literal reading of the *Enneads* can hardly explain to us how Plotinus actually tackles the Platonic riddles with 'a great deal of circumspection' (II.9.14.42). He writes the key text as if to urge us to excavate from it the logical nexus that we have explained. His exegesis of the Platonic enigmas itself constitutes yet another complex 'riddle'. In short, Plotinus' reading of Plato is, in its *ne plus ultra*, so 'philosophical' as to stimulate the philosophical spirit of readers of the *Enneads* themselves. It acts as a kind of *protreptikos logos* to the intermediate or advanced level of his philosophy. Interestingly, this stimulation is witnessed by Porphyry's report that Eustochius acquired the character of a genuine philosopher by devoting himself to Plotinus' thought alone (*VPlot.* 7.10-12). Fully engaging with Plotinus' position, including his response to Plato, can lead one to challenge aspects of his system.[50] Hence we may conclude our inquiry by parodying the remark in V.8.4.54-5: Plotinus left us to justify our adventure, if we claim to be worthy of our name as philosophers.

Notes

1. Sumi (1997), and (2002a), 67-8, n. 50.
2. Gatti (1996), 21, refers to Charrue's observation that the Plotinian reading of Plato is heuristic.
3. Wallis (1972), 17.
4. Gatti (1996), 20.
5. For the list of the supporters of the two views, see Gatti (1996), 18.
6. Atkinson (1983), 191.
7. Gatti (1996), 21-2. As Wallis points out (1972), 23, nevertheless, the case in which we cannot treat Plotinus' reading of Plato as totally worthless is his refutation of the Stoicizing exegesis of *Phlb.* 30a-b as making individual souls parts of the cosmic soul in IV.3.7.
8. Blumenthal (1971a), 127, and Bréhier (1924-8), 1:44, are aware of this complicated situation, but I cannot agree with Bréhier that Plotinus here substitutes the notion of the chain of being for the abstract idea of logical hierarchy. Furthermore, Armstrong's (1966-88) synopsis of the chapter (6:10) reads: 'Exegesis of *Timaeus* 39E in terms of this doctrine [of Intellect's all-inclusiveness], with confirmatory texts from the *Parmenides* and *Philebus*.' But *Parm.* 144b4-c1 is not 'confirmatory', but as enigmatic as *Tim.* 39e7-9.
9. This problem is already posed in 2.19-27. The expression 'genera of being' is Plotinus' coinage. It is neither Platonic nor Aristotelian. See Evangeliou (1982), 76.
10. With Beutler and H-S[1] we delete νοῦν εἶναι in 19.20.
11. For the analysis of VI.2.20 in terms of this difficulty see Gurtler (1988a), 31-9; also (1988b). But I cannot agree with his reading of 20.21-2 (1988b), 9.
12. For the details of this reference, see Sumi (1997), 410 n. 26.
13. One should not posit Intellect seeing *and Intellect seeing that it sees* on the

basis of this remark. Plotinus rejects such bifurcation (II.9.1.33-57). Knowing and knowing-that-one-is-knowing are mutually implicative (Gerson [2002], 113-14). The bifurcation of Intellect is a doctrine of the Gnostics, supported by their own reading of *Tim.* 39e7-9 (6.16-24). For the historical background of this doctrine, see Armstrong (1966-88), 2:226-7, n. 1. For the view that Plotinus' early writings are influenced by or akin to Numenius' theory of double intellect, see Armstrong (1966-88), 5:146, n. 1; Dodds (1960), 19-20; Rist (1967), 42-4. For objections to this view, see Bussanich (1988), 18-20; Sumi (1993), 204 n. 1.

14. The status of Intellect as 'one and many' or 'one-many' is mentioned repeatedly in the *Enneads*, and in VI.2 the second chapter is designed for its elucidation. The secondary One, which is 'one-many', and identified with Intellect in V.1.8.25-6, has its origin in *Parm.* 142b-155e. 'One-many' derives from τὸ 'ὸν ἓν πολλά. On the grammar of these phrases in Plato and in Plotinus see Atkinson (1983), 197.

15. For an essentially similar problem see *Phlb.* 15b2-4, where we meet the problem of how to divide one Form into many without compromising not only the unity of that one generic monad but that of each of many divided monads. See Sumi (1993), 54 n. 63; Dancy (1984). For a parallel see Sumi (2002b), 266, n. 92.

16. H-S^2 suggests ὁ νοῦς. In light of γὰρ in 22.13, however, it would be straightforward to regard ὁ τι ἂν λάβῃς in 22.12 as the subject, as in Armstrong's translation. The universal quantification in the German translation 'denn alles, was man immer erfassen mag, ist Art' is unnecessary, and so is the limitation of the object in Bréhier's translation 'on ne peut y sasir que des espèces' and Cilento's 'al più, quel che potrai cogliere non è che forma'. In particular, the phrase 'al più' in the latter is misleading. While the suggestion in H-S^2 is attractive, it is necessary to insert the phrase 'in the (whole) Intellect' into the first and the second sentences, in order to make the context smooth. In this respect the suggestion is at a disadvantage. In Bréhier's translation 'puisque tout y est sans matière', its subject is not found in the text. Cilento's translation 'poiche la materia viesula affatto' is slightly free, adumbrating the subject. In 8.3-5, where Plotinus deals with Intellect's knowing and positing of three primary genera, 'being' of the intelligible world, namely the objective side of intellection, is said to be without matter. This point would somewhat, if not definitely, support our reading.

17. ἠνιγμένως in 22.1 is the adverbial form of αἰνίττεσθαι used here. For the use of these words for Plato, see I.6.6.3, IV.2.2.49, IV.3.2.6 and VI.9.9.31.

18. See note 14.

19. Armstrong alone takes ἄπειρον as the predicate. The German translators read the sentence οὔπω ἄπειρον: 'Liegt noch kein Unendliches vor'. Bréhier and Cilento translate it respectively, 'il n'y a pas encore d'infinité', and 'non c'è ancora l'infinito'. But, since ἄπειρον is not accompanied with any article, this sentence cannot be taken as describing the non-existence of something.

20. Only Sleeman and Pollet (1980), 118, relate ἄπειρον in 22.15-18 to εἶδος.

21. The genitive γένους in 22.15 is not central to the argument. Nor can the feminine οὐσίαν in 22.14 be the subject. Since τὴν οὐσίαν is the term in the Platonic riddle, to say that real being is not yet infinite does not lead to the solution of it. Again, ἄλλο εἶδος in 22.15 cannot be a candidate for the subject, because the phrase εἰς ἄλλο εἶδος is the paraphrase of εἰς ἄπειρα in the citation and so it is contradictory to say that another species is not yet infinite.

22. Cilento's translation reads 'una nuova specie'. But we cannot understand why another species is 'new'. Instead of 'la divisióne' he here uses the term 'il frazionamento', which reminds us of κατακερματίζειν. Since it is really postulated that the generic Form is not 'cut up', this Italian term tends to be misleading.

23. The German translation 'die Arten, die aus der Klasse erzeugt sind' is misleading. Here the relation of the generated species to their proximately upper species is in focus, but not so is their relation to the genus.

24. In Bréhier's translation, 'on trouve des bornes dans les espèces qui sont engendrées', and Cilento's, 'che s'incontra sempre il limito delle forme via via generate', the limit is attributed to 'the species which have been generated'. But the text does not allow of this reading. If this reading were adopted, the limited species which have been generated would be contrasted with the infinite ultimate species. But no real contrast can be constituted by them, because the ultimate species, also, are 'the species which have been generated' in the final phase of eidetic derivation from the genera, and each of them limits its proximately upper species.

25. The same objection is applicable to Bréhier's translation 'près de l'infini'; besides ἄπειρον is not accompanied with any article. Bussanich, also, reads the predicate as the comparative (1988), 170.

26. Armstrong (1955), 52. Since Plotinus does not attribute infinity to the One on its duration-less or interval-less nature, Armstrong's remark is correct. The One is once called ἀδιάστατος in VI.8.17.21-2. For the application of the adjective ἀδιάστατος to Intellect, see III.7.6.34-6; V.8.9.19-21; VI.4.13.5-6; VI.5.5.7; 11.1-2.

27. See Sumi (1985), 41-3; Heiser (1991).

28. The infinity attributed to the ultimate species abrogates the definition of limit in *Metaph.* 1022a4-5 as the last point (τὸ ἔσχατον) of a thing beyond which no part of it is. According to Aristotle's definition, infinity should be placed outside the ultimate species, which is the extremity of the realm of Forms.

29. For the inner identity of what a thing is and the fact that a thing is in the intelligible world, see Corrigan (1996), 113.

30. The usage of μετέχειν here is the same as that applied to the interrelations of Forms in the *Sophist*, on which see Cornford (1955), 255-6.

31. The objection will be raised that Plotinus' criticism of Aristotle's theory of categories in VI.1 may not apply to the present issue in VI.2.22. Our tentative reply is that in VI.2.16.10-12 Plotinus subsumes activity and passivity in the noetic realm into the genus of Movement, though they do not constitute the primary genera; again, in V.9.10.8-9, he accepts 'actions and affections which are according to nature' in the intelligible world. It is beyond my present scope to explain how it is possible to reconcile the passivity in the noetic world with the impassibility of intelligible entities (III.6.6) and Plato's own refusal to apply the alleged criterion of being, which is the capacity of activity and passivity, to real being in *Soph.* 248d10-e4. Nevertheless some interpreters try to read something positive from Plotinus' reduction of activity and passivity to movement. Evangeliou ([1987], 159 n. 10; cf. [1988], 171) views this reduction as the principal modification of Aristotle's theory, which should be considered to be Platonic; Wagner (2002), 39-40, considers the Plotinian reduction in terms of the scheme of conceptual dualities pertaining to natural reality.

One may also object that the supposed immanence of the lower species in the upper may not be inconsistent with the immanence of genus in species because these two modes of immanence can jointly entail the mutual inclusiveness of intelligible beings. But this objection is refutable since the mutual inclusiveness is definitely due to the All-things-are-in-all-things principle. For this principle, see Bréhier (1958), 94; Armstrong, 'Plotinus', in Armstrong (1967), 245. If one further objects that the two modes of immanence may be more fundamental than the All-things-are-in-all-things principle and justify it so that the latter no longer be called a 'principle', we answer that no evidence is given for such an interpretation in the text of V.8.4 and V.9.10, where Plotinus describes the mutually embracing nature of each member of the intelligible world.

32. Hackforth (1945), 24, n. 1.

33. Benitez (1989), 54-5.

34. Benitez (1989), 55, 57; Hackforth (1945), 25-6; Ross (1951), 131-2; Taylor (1926), 412; Teloh (1981), 181-2. But Shiner (1974), 40, claims that since the division ends with the ultimate species, the πολλὰ ἄπειρα (16d6) cannot be particulars. As Benitez points out (1989), 40, this view is confusing.

35. For the original sense of infinity as infinite plurality, see Hackforth (1945), 24 n. 1. Damascius, in his note on *Phlb.* 16c10-e2, states that 'at the extremity of each Form there appears infinite plurality' (*Lectures on the Philebus*, trans. Westerink, 63.1). Although this statement is somewhat near to Plotinus', the literal interpretation of the connection of infinity and plurality marks their decisive divergence. In addition, Syrianus reports that Amelius, the disciple of Plotinus, believed in the infinite number of Forms (*In Met.* 147.1-6 Kroll). For the philosophical import of Amelius' innovaton, see Sumi (2000b), 242.

36. For various views about the referent of 'things that are ever said to be' and the critical examination of them, see Benitez (1989), 39-42.

37. Ammonius, in his note on this passage of the *Isagoge*, erroneously ascribes the infinity to the repeated production by specific differentiae (*In Porphyrii Isagogen* 85.1-4, Busse).

38. Since the neuter plural governs a singular verb, ἔρχεται is not grammatically incorrect. Although Armstrong simply refers to the common subject as 'they', it may be natural to regard the referent of 'they' as the ultimate species in the plural. In light of the plural ἄπειρα in 22.19, the aorist participle in question turns out to be the neuter plural nominative.

39. If the sentence 'many Forms, different from one another, are embraced from without by one Form' in *Soph.* 253d7-8, as Cornford construes it (1955), 267, describes the fact that specific Forms are embraced by the generic one, then τῷ δὲ ἑνὶ περιληφθέντα in 22.19-20 can be reminiscent of *Soph.* 253d7-8. For an objection to Cornford's view see Sayre (1969), 178 n. 39.

40. Furthermore, the view that the locution 'to arrive at number' indicates the finiteness of the total of Forms is justified by the thesis that there is no such a number as is called unlimited since unlimitedness clashes with number (VI.6.2.1-7; 17.1-3). For the numerical finiteness of intelligible objects in Plotinus, see Sumi (2002b), 264-5, n. 84.

41. When, as discussed in V.5.1.41-6, intelligible objects are finitely plural and exist being mutually isolated outside Intellect, one may ask whether or not this disjunctive multiplicity can be viewed as infinite because of its departure from unity; for finitely many objects which are not internally related with each other are somewhat conceivable. But, when the intelligible objects exist outside Intellect, the former are outside the latter's unity, so that the total number of the former cannot be fixed and so finitely many. The indirect argument for the presence of the intelligible objects in Intellect by a *reductio ad absurdum* in this passage can be explicated from this viewpoint; the disjunctive multiplicity cannot be finite plurality in Plotinus. For the detailed analysis of the passage in question, see Sumi (1993) 106; (1997), 415-16.

Furthermore, Martin (1982), 15, regards the entity Intellect as a fusion consisting of the disjunction of intelligible objects represented by the 'nondenumerably infinite' individual constants. But this misses the present point and the logic has no basis in Plotinus' metaphysics.

42. The all-embracing nature of the complete living being in the *Timaeus* is not so extensive as Plotinus entertains. See Cornford (1937), 42. In explicating the structure of the world of Forms in accordance with the genus-species scheme from *Soph.* 253d, Cornford (1955), 271-2, believes that such a complex nature of the generic Form 'Animal' that he instances is supported by the all-inclusiveness of the living being in *Tim.* 30a and 39e. But this view does not assure us that in Plotinus the articulation of the intelligible world in accordance with the genus-species scheme is confined to such an extension of the all-inclusiveness of the living being as is originally conceived in the *Timaeus*. See also Sumi (1997), 408, n. 18.

43. See n. 28.

44. Blumenthal (1971b), 127; Trouillard (1955), 76, expresses a similar view, though different in nuance.

45. Nature is designated 'an image of Intellect' and 'the last part of soul' in IV.4.13.3-4. Also in VI.2.22, the lower part of soul is called 'an image of soul' (line 33).

46. Beutler and Theiler (1960-7), 4b, 480.

47. For the status of the soul as number, see also III.6.1.31 and VI.5.9.13-14. For the finite plurality of souls, see V.7.1.17-18.

48. In VI.2.1.28-30 Plotinus delineates being, discussed thematically in this treatise, by stating that Plato indicates its immutability by prefixing ἀεὶ to it. From this statement we can suppose that Plotinus might take ἀεὶ of τῶν ἀεὶ λεγομένων εἶναι in *Phlb.* 16c9 with εἶναι rather than λεγομένων by considering the possibility of Plato's own avoidance of the hiatus. Striker (1970), 22, takes ἀεὶ with εἶναι. But Benitez rejects this reading on the ground of the parallel between τῶν ἀεὶ λεγομένων εἶναι and τῶν λεγομένων ἀεὶ in 15d5 (*Forms*, 40). In quoting 16c9-10 Damascius leaves out εἶναι (*Lectures on the Philebus* 62.9-11, Westerink). Volkmann-Schuluck (1966, 94-5) rightly associates Plotinus' treatment of the Platonic notion of immutable being in VI.2.1 with his definition of the notion in III.7.6.

49. Wallis (1972), 23; see also Gatti (1996), 17; Evangeliou (1987), 147.

50. See Sumi (2002b); in particular note my claim that 'If the Psyche were not an individualization of the creative One, Forms would eternally remain isolated from one another' (250). This claim that the conjunctive togetherness of disjunctive multiplicity can still be infinite plurality is a bold challenge to the Plotinian position that the disjunctive multiplicity cannot be finite plurality. For the creative One as a departure from classical theism see Ford (2002), 215.

The doctrine of the degrees of virtues in the Neoplatonists: an analysis of Porphyry's *Sentence* 32, its antecedents, and its heritage[1]

Luc Brisson, translated by Michael Chase

In Ancient Greece, one can speak of the virtues of the eyes, of the ears, or of horses. In all these uses, the term *aretê* is used not only to designate a function – seeing for the eyes, hearing for the ears, or running for horses – but above all to indicate optimal realization, or the excellence of that function. In the current use of the term, *aretê* designates the most accomplished thing man does, and this implies determining the objective end he must seek to obtain. Thinkers in Greece were unanimous in their view that the subjective end sought by every human being was *eudaimonia*, happiness. The happy person lives well, because he realizes his humanity and his individuality fully and objectively. This is why we cannot speak of virtue without setting forth a definition of man, even implicitly: and this is the point at which Platonism, Aristotelianism, and Stoicism diverge.

i. Plato

Plato takes up this use of *aretê*, but understands it in terms of his own definition of a living being[2] as a soul that moves a body. Henceforth *aretê* must be defined according to the principle of this action, i.e. the human soul, understood as the source of all spontaneous motion in man, physical as well as psychic. Moreover, like Socrates before him, Plato demands that man's *aretê* be defined on the basis of reflection and knowledge, as the capacity to determine the end of action and to choose the means to achieve it. Such are the features that characterize *aretê*, which is also translated by 'excellence', to express the idea of optimal accomplishment in man. More precisely, this accomplishment takes place in what is best in man, that is to say his soul, particularly when it uses its highest faculty, intellect (*nous*), which makes him like a god.[3] In this context, human good, on which virtue depends, designates an internal way of being, that consists in the harmony established in the soul between its various constituent parts – reason (*nous*), spirit (*thymos*), and desire (*epithymia*) – and their respective functions ; and here reason must always occupy the first place.

In the *Republic*, Plato insists that this harmony in an individual human soul can be brought about only in the context of a political organization that is itself structured as a function of the soul's constituent parts. In the ideal city, power must be wielded by wise men – the philosophers chosen from a group of warriors selected for their courage – and supplied by a group of producers who should practise moderation. The same moderation must, of course, also be practised by the warriors and the philosophers, in order to maintain justice in the city. Here we find the four cardinal virtues that must be practised in order to realize excellence and happiness in the soul and in the city: wisdom, courage, moderation, and justice. Plato was subsequently to maintain this position, although he modified the modalities of its application, particularly in the *Laws*.

ii. Aristotle

In Aristotle, practical philosophy is clearly distinguished from theoretical philosophy, insofar as its goal is not so much to seek the truth, and to know it, as to have an effect on action. Ethics and politics form the two great domains of practical philosophy. Ethics seem to be definitely subordinated to politics, insofar as political life is the best condition in which to realize the education of pleasure and pain, without which there can be no acquisition of that virtue that is sought by both ethics and politics. To live under good laws is the best way to anchor within oneself the habits that will lead to virtue. The realization of virtue, and, in general, public happiness, therefore depend upon the legislator.

For Aristotle, as for Plato, the initial axiom is that each human being wants to be happy. *Eudaimonia* represents the ultimate goal of all actions, so long as they are rational. Ethics must, above all, raise the question of knowing exactly in what this happiness consists, how to achieve it, and how to form that human moral character that is the principle of the actions that aim to attain this goal. In this sense, the moral philosophies of Plato and of Aristotle represent two forms of that eudaimonism that was so characteristic of ancient thought: the individual accedes to morality at the same time as he seeks his own happiness. Yet what distinguishes the ethics of Plato from those of Aristotle is the insistence with which Aristotle defines the domain of ethics as that of human affairs, which are contingent, and not susceptible of demonstration.

The excellences of practical rationality that Aristotle identifies with ethical virtues belong to this realm of behaviour. The ethical virtues ensure the realization of moral character when they are transformed into habitual and almost natural ways of being, cultivated from childhood on. Man's proper and distinctive function is activity in conformity with the intellect, which alone can impose a measure upon the passions. Human virtue consists in the excellence of this activity. Such a choice must be apparent in every particular detail of human life. The most characteristic sign of virtuous or excellent conduct in a moral agent is aptitude for preferring the good. Virtue can thus be defined as a constant disposition from which virtuous action is born, which action in turn maintains the disposition. This disposition is neither natural nor innate; indeed, natural dispositions are not as such the object of either praise or blame. Thus, virtue, which is susceptible of moral evaluation, must be considered as an acquired disposition. Yet it is genuinely virtue only when it is exercized in the same way as an innate disposition, without any effort, and with the pleasure that is proper to it. In short, the virtues are dispositions that depend on deliberate choice, as well as on pleasures and pains; they concern the intellect as much as the character.

iii. The Stoics

Like all schools at the time, Stoicism admits as a basic principle that all human action is oriented ultimately by one subjective end, in view of which everything else is only a means or a partial end, itself sought as a means; and this end is *eudaimonia*. To know how to achieve happiness with certainty, we must know in what it consists; this is why each soul is characterized and differentiated by the particular formulation it gives of man's objective end (*telos* or *skopos*).[4]

In Stoicism, the *telos* is not itself virtue. The Stoics maintain that virtue is sufficient for happiness, but they do not confuse it with happiness, of which it is at the same time constitutive and generative. According to Zeno, the supreme end must be to 'live in accordance' (*homologoumenôs zên*).[5] This truncated formula means to live in conformity with a unique and consistent rational law established in the soul. For both psychological and moral reasons, Chrysippus, and with him the most consistent Stoics,[6] adopt a monistic conception of the soul. Its guiding principle, the *hêgemonikon*, is itself psychologically affected and morally compromised by the passions. These may be defined both as errors in judgement – that is, unjustified assents to faulty impressions concerning what is good or bad – and as excessive impulses, or tendencies to act precipitously, as a function of such false judgements. Therapies for the passions thus do not consist in modifying them, or canalizing their energy for the benefit of a reason they have left intact, but in extirpating them completely, so as to purify reason of the intrinsic perversion they have inflicted upon it.

Whoever achieves this result may be called a 'sage' (*spoudaios*), as opposed to 'ordinary people' (*phauloi*). Yet the Stoic sage, however perfect he may be, remains a man. He has a body, and because of this he remains subject to physiological reflexes of which he is not master. Moreover, despite the radical gulf it establishes between sages and non-sages, the Stoic conception does not deny moral progress (*prokopê*), nor does it render vain such techniques of moral education as advice, admonitions, precepts adapted to individual situations, and guidance of the conscience. Once he reaches the final point he can attain, the person making progress accomplishes, without exception, all the duties (*kathêkonta*); that is, everything that needs to be done. In sages, the *kathêkonta* become right actions (*kathorthômata*), since they have their source in the perfection of his inner disposition.

iv. Plotinus

With Plotinus, everything changes. The point is no longer to propose a new definition of virtue, but to find a synthesis of all those that had been proposed so far. We thus witness the birth of the theme of degrees of virtue,[7] which was to be enriched down to the end of Antiquity, and was prolonged throughout the Greek and Latin Middle Ages, in both the Eastern and the Western Empire.[8] Plotinus must have written his treatise *On the Virtues* (*Enn.* I.2 [19])[9] around 260, given its place in the chronological order of his works. In that treatise, we find a distinction between three kinds of virtues: civic, purificatory, and contemplative, placed in relation with the four cardinal virtues mentioned in Plato: prudence, courage, moderation, and justice. In fact, civic, purificatory, and contemplative virtues are related to the doctrine of virtue developed by Aristotle, the Stoics, and Plato. They are the result of the combined exegesis of *Republic* IV 427e-444e on the four cardinal virtues in the soul and in the city, of the *Phaedo* (67b) on purification, and of *Theaetetus* 176a-b on assimilation to god. In fact, the purificatory virtues may be practised on two different levels.

The soul must first realize that it was produced by the intellect. At the highest level, therefore, purification means for the soul to return completely to its principle. Virtue, which is identical with the soul's recovered excellence, consists in becoming similar to the divine, since the intellect is the closest divine reality to the soul. However, although there is only this one path for the soul, we must also say that it contains this possibility within itself, and needs no mediator. The first level is that of liberation from corporeal passions, whereas the higher level implies the soul's conversion towards the intellect, which contains the Forms that are the models of the virtues.

The models of the virtues, that is, their Forms, are mentioned, but without being considered as virtues in the proper sense of the term. Porphyry was to make them virtues in the full sense, thereby opening the door for the multiplication of the 'degrees of virtues'. Plotinus himself, despite the fact that he supplied Porphyry with the conceptual foundations that enabled him to postulate this fourth degree of virtues, clearly affirms the following: 'Virtue is the *proprium* of the soul, it does not pertain to the intellect nor to the principle that is beyond the intellect' (*Enn.* I.2.3). Plotinus thus goes no farther than the level of the incarnate soul.

v. Porphyry

Porphyry's most extensive discussion of the virtues occurs in *Sentence* 32.[10] In keeping with the problematics discussed above, and following Plotinus, Porphyry shows how the ethical positions defended by Aristotelianism, Stoicism, and Platonism mesh with one another to form a kind of system. Plotinus and Porphyry thus refer not to Plato, Aristotle, or any particular Stoic, but to the representatives of the Platonic, Aristotelian, and Stoic schools. Plotinus, and following him Porphyry, thus take their place within a polemical context in which school tradition is a deciding factor. Here, in other words, Plato, Aristotle, and the Stoics are considered only through an interpretative filter.

Thus, the four 'cardinal' virtues: justice, wisdom, courage, and temperance, which come directly from the *Republic* – find themselves stripped of the political garb they wore in the *Republic*. This is the case even for the civic virtues, where their definition is completely general, and presents no relation to a specific sort of city that includes the three functional groups of philosophers, warriors, and producers.[11] Nevertheless, the first group of virtues concerns the community.

The civic virtues: definitions

Porphyry begins by mentioning the civic (*politikai*) virtues, those of the citizen, which correspond to those emphasized by an Aristotelian interpretation of Plato's *Republic*:

> The civic virtues, based as they are in the imposition of a measure upon the passions (*metriopatheiai*), consist in following and going along with the process of reasoning relative to our duty (*kathêkontos*) in the field of practical action; hence, since they have regard to a community of action which avoids doing harm to one's neighbors, they are called 'civic' by reason of their concern with gregariousness and community. They are as follows: [practical] wisdom, relative to the reasoning element [in the soul], courage, relative to the spirited element, moderation, which consists in the agreement and harmony of the affective element with reason, and justice, consisting, for each of the elements in the soul, in its performance of its proper role with respect to ruling and being ruled.
>
> *Sentence* 32, p. 23.4-12 Lamberz = 32.6-14, trans. Dillon

In this passage, we encounter Platonic and Stoic elements that make it apparent that the Aristotle we find evoked here is not the historical Aristotle.

The civic virtues: interpretation

The civic virtues concern action (*praxis*) and activity (*energeia*), and that which is in conformity with nature (*kata physin*), understood in the Stoic sense of a rational law. They imply a rational appreciation of duty in this area: *ta kathêkonta* is a term of the Stoic technical vocabulary for 'duty'. In other words, these are virtues that concern the soul which must live in a body.

More generally, these virtues have the goal of making life in a group possible. The groups in question are groups of living beings, not necessarily human, as is implied by the expression 'civic' (*politikê*), which refers to the city-state, but also to animals that live in herds; this is implied by the expressions 'gregariousness' (*synagelasmos*) and 'community' (*koinônia*).[12] The question thus arises whether the civic virtues might not also pertain to animals. Finally, we may note that these virtues are presented in an exclusively negative light. They are to enable the members of a group to live together without harming one another.

To attain the goal of community life, the civic virtues impose a measure on the passions. The term *metriopatheia* designates the operation that consists in imposing a measure on the passions, which pertain to the irrational, by orienting them towards actions carried out in the realm of things in conformity with nature. They thereby imitate the demiurge, who, in the *Timaeus*, imposes measure on necessity, considered as an errant cause given over to the irrational. We should note that, probably in the second half of the second century AD, Diogenes Laertius (V 31) opposes *metriopathês* to *apathês*, which designates the Stoic ethical ideal. Yet the term *metriopatheia* does not appear in Aristotle, and this absence lets us understand that Porphyry is talking about Aristotelianism[13] as it was perceived at his time, and not about Aristotelian texts read independently of the context of their reception. In short, the civic virtues set mortal man in order, and assign limits to his irrationality.

At this level, the soul is still turned away from its true being, because it is oriented towards the body and the city. Since the goal of the civic virtues is to lead a human life in conformity with nature, with regard to the virtues proper to mankind, they could not be appropriate for a god. This is why the person who practises these virtues is here qualified as a sage (*spoudaios*) – a Stoic term. Nevertheless, one is surprised to note that the definitions of the four cardinal virtues given by way of illustration concern inner life, not political life; all the links established by Plato in the *Republic* between the soul and the city have disappeared.

Purificatory virtues: definitions

In this world, the soul suffers from two evils: union with inferior things, and the excessive character of this union. Whereas the civic virtues cure us of excess, the purificatory (*kathartikai*) virtues enable us to reduce the soul's union with inferior realities to a minimum. We here find ourselves within a Stoic context:

7. The doctrine of the degrees of virtues in the Neoplatonists

The virtues, on the other hand, of the person who is making progress towards the state of contemplation (*theôrêtikou*) consist in detaching oneself from the things down here below; hence these are also termed 'purifications' (*katharseis*), being seen as consisting in abstention from actions in concert with the body, and from participating in the passions that affect it. For without doubt these virtues are those of a soul which is in the process of abstracting itself [from the body] in the direction of true being, whereas the civic virtues are concerned with the imposition of order on man in his mortal state – the civic virtues, we should specify, are precursors of the purifications; for it is only after one has been set in order in accordance with them that one can abstract oneself from performing any act in concert primarily with the body. For this reason, at the purificatory level, wisdom consists in the soul's not sharing any opinions with the body, but acting on its own, and this is perfected by the pure exercise of the intellect; moderation is the result of taking care not to assent to any of the passions; courage is not being afraid to depart from the body, as if one were falling into some void of not-being; and justice is the result of reason and intellect dominating the soul, with nothing to oppose them. In brief, the disposition characteristic of the civic virtues is to be seen as the imposition of measure on the passions, since it has as its aim living a human life in accordance with nature, while the disposition that results from the contemplative virtues (*kata tas theôrêtikas*) is manifested in total detachment from the passions, which has as its aim assimilation to god.

Sentence 32, pp. 24.1-25.9 Lamberz = 32.15-32, trans. Dillon

We note that the purificatory virtues present a twofold aspect: negative to be sure, for they enable detachment from all that is corporeal, but also positive, insofar as they enable a return from dispersion towards unity. The mention of 'assimilation to god', a Platonic theme taken up and reinterpreted by the Stoics, constitutes a sign of the fact that we are in a context that is not historical, but theoretical.

The purificatory virtues: interpretation

The purificatory virtues consist in detaching oneself from the things down here below, in abstaining from actions performed with the body, and in refusing to share its passions: thus, they are identical with purification. They belong to the soul that is distancing itself from the body in order to head towards true being; that is, towards the intelligible. We thus have here the idea of a progression (*prokopê*) towards contemplation of the intelligible. The purificatory virtues are virtues of the human soul; that is, of the soul united to a body. Their acquisition takes place in this life, and their objective is to rid the soul completely of those passions which, up until this point, have received only a measure. And their goal is assimilation to god, a Platonic formula.

The disposition that corresponds to these virtues is impassibility (*apatheia*). At this second level, the soul, not content with imposing a measure and a limit on passions, undertakes to free itself completely of them. It

95

does this by detaching the soul, as far as possible, from the body. Of course, such liberation is on the level of judgement, and does not lead to real impassibility. Only death could lead to total impassibility, which would be equivalent to total liberation. Now, there is a paradox here, for in order to contemplate, one must be alive. This is why he who practises the virtues can only progress towards this state of virtue, and this progress earns him the name of *daimôn*, a being situated between human beings, qualified as *spoudaios* when they practise the civic virtues, and the divinity (*theos*), to whom he who pratices the contemplative virtues is assimilated.

Some of the cardinal virtues are interesting. Just as the soul's purity is the consequence of its separation from the soul, so purity of the intellect is the consequence of its separation from the soul. Moreover, the definition of courage recalls the theme of philosophy as a preparation for death in the *Phaedo*. Such a concept of philosophy leads directly to the Platonic ideal of assimilation to god.[14] This is the only place in the *Sentence* where Porphyry alludes to this ideal – an ideal we encounter throughout Plotinus' treatise *On the Virtues* (*Enn.* I.2).

Nevertheless, a twofold question arises, which Porphyry attempts to answer at the end of *Sentence* 32:

> We ought therefore to direct our attention most of all to the purificatory virtues, basing ourselves on the reflection that the attainment of these is possible in this life, and that it is through these that an ascent may be made to the more august levels. We must therefore consider up to what point and in what degree it is possible to receive purification; for it involves, after all, separation from the body and from the irrational motion provoked by the passions. We must state how this would come about, and up to what point. For a start, it is as it were the foundation and underpinning of purification to recognize that one is a soul bound down in an alien entity of a quite distinct nature. In the second place, taking one's start from this conviction, one should gather oneself together from the body even, as it were, in a local sense, but at any rate adopting an attitude of complete disaffection with respect to the body.
>
> *Sentence* 32, pp. 31.9-32.9 Lamberz = 32.95-106, trans. Dillon

Thus, impassibility cannot be complete in man, for, at least in this world, one must have a body in order to contemplate.[15] We cannot rid ourselves completely of fear and aggressiveness, which can be considered as warning signs, or as natural reactions in the face of imminent danger, to face such danger or to escape it. Likewise, we cannot completely eliminate pleasure and pain. Pleasure is associated with a whole series of natural acts, which are absolutely necessary to ensure the survival of the individual, and eventually even that of the species. Porphyry recommends that we undergo this pleasure without sharing it with the body. As far as pain is concerned, Porphyry advises us to put up with it, up to the point where suffering risks constituting an obstacle to action. We must then try to eliminate it, or at least assuage it.

7. The doctrine of the degrees of virtues in the Neoplatonists

With regard to the lust for food, drink, and sexual pleasure, it must be considered to be relative to the body. This implies that the soul as such must not share in them in any way; it must separate itself from the body that feels them, as if it were a foreign reality. In this perspective, it is better to speak of detachment from passions than of impassibility.

The contemplative virtues: definition

For a Platonist, purification must not be sought for itself, but in order to make contemplation (*theôria*) possible; the practitioner of purification is therefore called *theôrêtikos*.[16] In Porphyry,[17] however, these virtues have no name of their own:

> It is requisite, then, that, once purified, the soul unite itself with what has engendered it; and in consequence the virtue that is proper to it after its conversion consists in the acquaintance and knowledge of being, not because it does not possess it in itself, but it is not capable of seeing what is within itself without the cooperation of what is superior to it. There is therefore another class of virtues, a third one, after the purificatory and the civic, which are those of the soul as it is exercising intellection (*noerôs tês psychês energousês*).[18] [At this level], wisdom, both theoretical and practical, consists in the contemplation of the contents of intellect; justice is the fulfilling [by each of the parts of the soul] of the role proper to it in following upon intellect and directing its activity towards intellect; and courage is detachment from the passions through which the soul assimilates itself to that towards which it turns its gaze, which is itself free from passions. And, naturally, all these are reciprocally implicated, as are the earlier ones also.
> *Sentence* 32, pp. 27.3-28.5 Lamberz = 32.51-62, trans. Dillon

In fact, Porphyry speaks of two degrees of contemplation: that of the person making progress towards contemplation, and that of the person already established in contemplation, whose soul is exercizing intellection. The term Porphyry uses to designate the virtues of the first level, *theôrêtikai*, was to be used by the later Neoplatonists to designate the virtues of the second level, with the first-level virtues being qualified as *kathartikai*.

The exercise of contemplation constitutes the fulfilment of the process of purification. This, moreover, is what Porphyry declares in the *De Abstinentia*: 'Our goal is to obtain the contemplation of being. When this is obtained, it realizes, within the limits of our possibilities, the union of nature between contemplator and contemplated' (I 29.3). Yet these few lines take us further, as we shall see.

The contemplative virtues: interpretation

Whereas the civic virtues deliver the soul from the first form of evil, that is, the excess of passions, the purificatory virtues deliver the soul from the second form of evil: the soul's unificaton with inferior things. While the

97

civic virtues regulate our relations with the things here below, the purificatory virtues put an end to such relations.

The contemplative virtues (*theôrêtikai*) are those of the person who is already a contemplative, and whose soul henceforth contemplates the intelligible. Unlike the preceding virtues, which involved effort and progress, the contemplative virtues are at rest. They are the virtues of the soul that acts in the mode of the intellect. Indeed, the soul knows what is in itself only by turning towards the intellect. The soul possesses within itself a knowledge which it must somehow recall in the process of reminiscence. Even before taking up this third kind of virtue, Porphyry had already stated that the disposition (*diathesis*) that derives from the contemplative virtues is manifested in the absence of passions, since its goal is assimilation to god. The objective of these virtues is that one should act without even the necessity of thinking about detaching oneself from the passions.

He who succeeds in acting only according to these virtues is a god (*theos*). With these virtues, the process of purification is brought to its full achievement. The soul that is completely turned towards the intellect no longer knows any *pathos*, and gives itself completely over to contemplation. For a Platonist, it is indispensable that the virtues be brought to this level, since it consecrates the re-discovered unity between the soul and the intellect. In this way, the ideal of assimilation to god is realized.

Once he reaches the end of his description of the contemplative virtues, Porphyry adds: 'naturally, all these are reciprocally implicated, as are the earlier ones also.' This doctrinal point, which he takes over from Plotinus, constituted a crucial aspect of Stoic doctrine. Because of 'reciprocal implication' (*antakolouthia*), the virtues are interdependent with one another in such a way that he who possesses one of them possesses them all. Such 'reciprocal implication' holds not only for the three kinds of virtues we have just seen, but also for the fourth.

The paradigmatic virtues: definition

By means of the purificatory virtues, the soul that has been purified unites itself with that which engendered it – that is, with the intellect – which is indissociable from the intelligible, and this union follows upon the soul's conversion towards its principle. Yet in this union, the soul is no longer a soul: it coincides with the intellect. Hence the particularly ambiguous status of the paradigmatic virtues:

> The fourth group (*genos*) of virtues is that of the paradigmatic (*paradeigmatikai*), which are, as we have agreed, actually to be found in the intellect, seeing as they are superior to those of the soul, and are the paradigms of these, the virtues of the soul being their likenesses. At this level, intellect is that in which the paradigms enjoy a simultaneous existence:[19] what counts

as practical wisdom is scientific knowledge, while theoretical wisdom is the intellect in the act of knowing; moderation becomes self-concentration; performance of its proper act [= justice] is just the performing [by the intellect] of its proper act; courage is self-identity, and remaining purely on its own through the superabundance of its power.

Sentence 32, pp. 28.6-29.8 Lamberz = 32.63-70, trans. Dillon

We have here an example of a distortion by Porphyry of Plotinus' text. Porphyry writes 'The fourth group of virtues is that of the paradigmatic', whereas Plotinus had been much more prudent, and wrote: 'These virtues in the soul, too, imply one another reciprocally, in the same way as the exemplars (so to call them) there in intellect which are prior to virtue' (*ta pro tês aretês [hai] en nôi ta hôsper paradeigmata*) (Plotinus, *Enn.* I.2.19.7.1-3, trans. Armstrong). In other words, it was Porphyry who made the models of the virtues, virtues in the full sense of the term, calling them paradigmatic virtues. I shall try to explain these enigmatic few lines.

The paradigmatic virtues: interpretation

The paradigmatic virtues are the virtues of the intellect, insofar as it is intellect, separate from the soul. They are precisely those virtues that are situated within the intellect, that is, intelligibles, or Forms. Superior to the virtues of the soul, they are the models of which the virtues of the soul are the images. Because of this, we can no longer really speak of them as virtues, since virtues are dispositions of the soul, whereas we now find ourselves at the level of the intellect and the intelligible. Instead of paradigmatic virtues, it would be better to speak of virtue-models, or even of models of virtues.

Paradigmatic virtues may be interpreted in three different ways. (1) There are the virtues of the soul that identifies itself with the intellect (as will be seen in Damascius). (2) There are the theurgical virtues, as is the view of Olympiodorus – an interpretation perhaps suggested by Porphyry.[20] (3) There are *the* divine virtues. Here, we reach a level that is no longer that of the human being, defined as the provisional union of a soul with a body, but that of the divine. The argument for this is as follows: if the intellect that contains the intelligible paradigms of all that exists can only be the intellect, then we are inevitably forced to believe, as do Macrobius and Marinus, that the paradigmatic virtues are no longer virtues of a human being, but of god. These virtues go hand in hand with the essence of the intellect.[21]

vi. Iamblichus, Proclus, and Damascius

In a lost work entitled *On the Virtues*, mentioned by Damascius in his *Commentary on the Phaedo* (I. 138-51, pp. 84-93 Westerink), Iamblichus[22] enriched the list of virtues by adding two new levels of virtue before the political virtues – the natural virtues and the moral virtues – in the context of the reading order of Plato's dialogues, which he established:[23]

> First among virtues are the natural virtues, which we have in common with the animals and which are inextricably linked with the bodily temperament and frequently clash with each other; either they belong mainly to the animate body or they are reflexes of reason when not impeded by temperamental disorder, or they may be due to routine acquired in a previous life. ... Above them are the ethical virtues, which we acquire by habituation and by a sort of true opinion. They are the virtues of well-bred children and are also found in certain animals. Being beyond the influence of temperament they do not clash with each other.
>
> Damascius, *Commentary on the Phaedo* I. 138-9, pp. 84-5 Westerink.

After these come the civic, purificatory, and contemplative virtues. Above and beyond the paradigmatic virtues established by Porphyry, Iamblichus added the hieratic virtues, to preserve divine initiative as far as union with the divine is concerned, by means of rites that allowed the soul to obtain union with the divine:

> Paradigmatic virtues are those of the soul when it no longer contemplates the intelligence [contemplation involving separateness], but has already reached the state of being by participation the intelligence that is the paradigm of all things; therefore these virtues too are called 'paradigmatic', inasmuch as virtues belong primarily to intelligence itself. This category is added by Iamblichus.
>
> Lastly, there are the hieratic virtues, which belong to the godlike part of the soul; they correspond to all the categories mentioned above, with the one difference that while the others concern being, these concern the One. This kind, too, has been outlined by Iamblichus, and discussed more explicitly by the School of Proclus.
>
> Damascius, *Commentary on the Phaedo* I. 143-4, pp. 86-9 Westerink

How can we explain Iamblichus' innovation if, as we have seen, the level of paradigmatic virtues had already been added by Porphyry as the fourth degree of virtues? Either Iamblichus gave a philosophical justification to Porphyry's addition, or he did not make a clear distinction between paradigmatic and hieratic virtues.[24] Alternatively, it may have been Proclus who clarified this distinction between paradigmatic and hieratic virtues, so as to provide a basis for the search for a systematic accord between philosophy and theology. We should note that the term 'hieratic' remains rather vague. In any case, the list of degrees of virtue accepted by Iamblichus was taken up in the School of Athens, and particularly by Proclus.

vii. Marinus and Olympiodorus

It is, moreover, around the theme of the degrees of virtue that Marinus structured his *Life of Proclus*:[25]

7. The doctrine of the degrees of virtues in the Neoplatonists

First of all, then, after having divided the virtues according to their various groups (*kata genê*) into virtues that are natural [dealt with at 3-6], moral [7-13], civic [14-17], virtues which are above these, that is, purificatory [18-21], contemplative [22-5], and the virtues that are called theurgical [26-33], to say nothing of those that are still higher, since they are henceforth beyond the human condition, we shall begin ...

Marinus, *Life of Proclus*, 3

We should note two things in this inventory which, as far as the level of the contemplative virtues, remains the same as that which Damascius attributes to Iamblichus. The paradigmatic virtues are not mentioned, whereas the virtues Iamblichus qualified as 'hieratic' are called 'theurgical' by Marinus. It seems, in fact, that, in Marinus, the paradigmatic virtues have become virtues that are 'beyond the human condition'. To explain this, we might adduce the interpretation of the paradigmatic virtues mentioned above. If the paradigmatic virtues are intelligibles, and if the intellect that contains the intelligible forms of all things can only be the divine intellect, it follows that the paradigmatic virtues are no longer human, but divine virtues. Moreover, the theurgical virtues that replace the hieratic virtues mentioned by Iamblichus are not situated only within intellective activity,[26] but also within ritual practice.[27] In this perspective, theology (whose most accomplished expression is to be found in the *Chaldaean Oracles*) becomes the summit of philosophy, which must seek harmony with it.

We find a similar classification in Olympiodorus,[28] who however identifies the paradigmatic virtues and the theurgical virtues:

There are, indeed, also paradigmatic virtues (*paradeigmatikai aretai*); for just as our eye, when illuminated by the sunlight, is at first different from the source of the light, as its recipient, but is afterwards somehow united with it and joined to it, and becomes as it were one with it and 'sun-like', so our soul is at first illuminated by intellect (*hypo nou*), and its actions are directed by the contemplative virtues (*theorêtikas aretas*), but afterwards it becomes in a way identical with the source of the illumination and acts in union with the One (*henoeidôs energei kata tas paradeigmatikas aretas*) in conformity with the paradigmatic virtues. The object of philosophy is to make us intellect (*noun*), that of theurgy to unite us with the intelligible realities (*tois noêtois*), so as to conform our activity to paradigms (*energein paradeigmatikôs*).

Olympiodorus, *In Phd.* 8.2.12-20, pp. 117-18 Westerink.

This identification of the paradigmatic virtues with the theurgical virtues in fact brings us back to Porphyry's *Sentence* 32,[29] and proposes a reasonable interpretation of the passage there on the paradigmatic virtues.

viii. Psellus and the East, Macrobius and the West

Psellus[30] takes up a doctrine of the degrees of virtue that seems very close to that set forth by Marinus: there are virtues that are natural, moral, political, purificatory, contemplative, theurgical, and higher than the theurgical virtues.

Finally, through the intermediary of Macrobius, this doctrine was passed on to the Scholastics,[31] Alexander of Hales, and Thomas Aquinas. We should note, however, that Macrobius attributes to Plotinus the doctrine of the degrees of virtue in Porphyry, and that he situates the paradigmatic virtues within the divine.[32]

The Neoplatonists, who, with the natural and moral virtues, wished to take even animals into consideration, thus sought, within the metaphysical system that was peculiar to them, an accord not only between the ethical doctrines of the various philosophical schools – Plato, Aristotle, and the Stoics – but also between philosophy and theology. To the civic and purificatory virtues, which concern the soul linked to a body, they added the contemplative virtues, which – in one way or another – concern the intellect, and the paradigmatic virtues, which are situated within the intelligible. They also mention the theurgical or hieratic virtues, which enable union with divinity through the intermediary of rites.

As they broadened the domain of virtue in this way, the Neoplatonists encountered two problems. The passage from the purificatory virtues to the contemplative virtues could not take place without difficulty, as we can tell from the oscillations of Porphyry's vocabulary. Moreover, it seems that the question was also raised of whether all these virtues pertained only to the human soul in its relations with the body (which man shares with the animals), with other human beings, the intelligible, and even the One. Indeed, everything indicates that some Neoplatonists, among whom was Marinus, wished to escape from this framework, particularly by interpreting the paradigmatic virtues as divine virtues, and not only human ones.

Thus, we encounter once again the idea that philosophy is a way of life,[33] even for a Platonist philosopher who wonders about the excellence of his own activity, when he uses his intellect to contemplate the intelligible, and when he takes an interest in sacred doctrines or rituals. We can thus understand why Porphyry and Marinus describe their masters Plotinus and Proclus as having practised virtue at all its degrees.

Notes

1. While I was preparing this text, I was able to read the article by Dirk Baltzly published in this volume. Our two contributions seem to me to be complementary.

2. 'What is called "living being", is this whole combination of a soul and a body' (*Phaedrus* 246c5).

3. By the contemplation of the intelligible, a soul succeeds in assimilating itself

7. The doctrine of the degrees of virtues in the Neoplatonists

to god: 'This is what the life of the gods is like. Let us move on to the other souls. That which is best, because it follows the god and tries to resemble him ...' (*Phaedrus*, 247e-248a). In Plato, we find the theme of assimilation to god in seven different passages, in five different contexts:

(a) in an epistemological context, the soul assimilates itself to an object of knowledge, which is divine (*Phaedo* 79d, *Phaedrus* 248a).
(b) in a mythological context, the god to whom one assimilates oneself is a god of traditional religion (*Republic* X 613a, *Laws* VI 716a).
(c) in a cosmological context, the god in question is the universe (*Timaeus* 90a).
(d) in an ethical context, assimilation to god is an invitation to live a just life (*Theaetetus* 176e).
(e) in an ethical and political context (*Republic* VI 500a), which enables the *Theaetetus* passage to be understood, by replacing it within a wider context.

On all these passages, see Merki (1952).
4. All the philosophical schools of Antiquity touched upon this theme. For an inventory drawn up on the basis of doxographies, see Festugière (1953), 261.
5. *SVF*, II.127 = Plutarch, *De Stoic. Repugn.* 10.1035f. Another version of the Stoic formula gives the adverb (*homologoumenôs*) the complement *têi physei*; the formula now becomes 'living according to nature'. For Cleanthes, the nature in question is common nature; that of the entire universe, which corresponds to the nature of man (*SVF* III.16 = Stobaeus, *Ecl.* II.77.16W). In short, the principle in accordance with which we must live is simultaneously the nature of the whole, and the particular nature of man, since they are ultimately the same.
6. *SVF* III, 12 = Galen, *PHP* V.6.
7. The expression 'degrees of virtues' is a fabrication of historians of philosophy. The Neoplatonists use terminology that is much more vague: *genos* (Porphyry, *Sentence* 32, p. 298 Lamberz = 32.71; Marinus, *Life of Proclus* 3.1) and *eidos* (*Sentence* 32, p. 28.6 = 32.63). However, since the groups of virtues they discuss are hierarchized, we are, it seems to me, authorized to speak of degrees of virtues.
8. There is now a recent overview in the Introduction to Marinus' *Life of Proclus* (Saffrey et al., 2001), lxix-xcviii. The authors give an inventory of the passages concerning this doctrine from Plotinus to Eustratius of Nicaea (pp. lxx-lxxi), and a comparative table (Porphyry, Marinus, Damascius, Olympiodorus, and Psellus, p. lxxxii).
9. See now the annotated French translation of Flamand (2003).
10. The Greek title of the *Sententiae* (*aphormai pros ta noêta*) remains as enigmatic as its nature. Is it a commentary on the *Enneads*, or simply a series of reflections on Plotinus' masterwork? In any case, in this work, which must have been composed at the end of the third century AD, we find a long passage, *Sentence* 32, which presents itself as a reflection on Plotinus' treatise *On the Virtues* (*Enn.* I.2.19). There is an excellent edition of the *Sentences*, edited by E. Lamberz. Our CNRS team (UPR 76) has published a French translation of the *Sentences*, with copious annotation (see Brisson [2005]). This work contains the previously unpublished English translation by John Dillon used here.
11. Perhaps the interest Plato shows in the concrete change of the city where he lived was no longer appropriate in the Empire, where the frequent overthrow of Emperors did not entail a brutal modification of social and political structures. In Plotinus' lifetime, seventeen Emperors succeeded one another, for an average

duration of reign of a little more than four years. On this subject, see Brisson et al. (1982-92), vol. 1, 127-39.

12. The term *synagelasmos* is rare, and refers to life in a herd. In the *De Abstinentia* (III 11), Porphyry gives the life of ants and bees as an example of this type of life. However, we can perceive here an allusion to the myth of the *Statesman*: under the reign of Kronos, men lived like animals, in herds, under the protection of secondary divinities.

13. Like I. Hadot (1978, 150-8), I see an Aristotelian influence in the notion of *metriopatheia*. We should note, however, that the term *metriopatheia* as such, which is attested since Philo (see Lilla 1971, 99-106), can hardly be considered a technical term of Aristotelian vocabulary. On this subject, see also Dillon (1983).

14. See note 3.

15. In order to contemplate it is neither sufficient nor permissible simply to get rid of one's body; thus, suicide is condemned in *Sentence* 9.

16. Indeed, the contemplative virtues (*theôrêtikai*) coincide with the purificatory virtues (*kathartikai*), as we can see by re-reading the lines (*Sentence* 32, pp. 24.1-25.9 Lamberz), which have just been cited.

17. See, for instance, *Sentence* 32, pp. 24.1-25.9 Lamberz, quoted above.

18. This is why Psellus calls them 'intellective' (*noerai*). On the oscillation in Psellus' terminology regarding this degree of virtues, see Saffrey et al. (2001), p. lxxxix, n. 1.

19. As is the case for all intelligible realities, which are 'together' (*hama*).

20. The person who possesses them is called 'father of the gods' (*theôn patêr*, *Sent.* 32, p. 31.8 Lamberz = 32.98), a phrase some have wished to understand on the basis of the *Chaldaean Oracles*. It is hard to interpret this expression, but if we take 'father' in a scholarly sense, as meaning 'master', we might think of a master who trains his disciples to contemplate the intelligible, or the Forms. This, however, brings us back to the first interpretation.

21. On this subject, see Festugière (1969).

22. See Dillon (1987), 902-4.

23. For the Neoplatonists, natural virtues, which are innate, are alluded to in *Republic* (VII 518d-519a), whereas moral virtues, which come from habit, are alluded to in *Laws* (I-II, VII 788a-VIII 842a). Plato deals with civic virtues at *Republic* IV, 434d-445b, with purificatory virtues in the *Phaedo*, and with contemplative virtues in the *Theaetetus* (173c-177c).

24. This is the explanation given by L.G. Westerink, in his note to Olympiodorus, *In Phaed.* 8.2-3. It is also possible that Damascius had only a second-hand knowledge of the *Sentences*, perhaps through Iamblichus.

25. Porphyry had already proceeded in the same way in his *Life of Plotinus*; on this subject, see Brisson et al. (1982-92) vol. 2, 1-29.

26. For instance, the reading of and commentary on the *Chaldaean Oracles* and the Orphic poems (*Life of Proclus* 26-7).

27. That is, theurgical rites, miracles, and familiarity with the gods (*Life of Proclus* 28-33).

28. *Commentary on the Phaedo* 8.3.3, pp. 117-21 Westerink.

29. We should note the parallel between *henoeidôs energei kata tas paradeigmatikas aretas* and *energein paradeigmatikôs* in Marinus, on the one hand, and *noerôs tês psychês energousês* and *ho energôn kata tas paradeigmatikas aretas* in Porphyry, on the other hand.

30. *De Omnifaria Doctrina* 66-74.

31. As is explained by Van Lieshout (1926).

7. The doctrine of the degrees of virtues in the Neoplatonists

32. 'The fourth type comprises the virtues that are present in the divine Mind itself, the *nous*, from the pattern of which all the other virtues are derived. For if we believe that there are ideas of other things in the Mind, then with much greater assurance must we believe that there are ideas of the virtues' (*In Somn. Scip.* VIII, 10).

33. P. Hadot (1995).

8

The mathematics of justice

Hayden W. Ausland

In the *Laws* Plato contrasts proportional equality with democratic equality. The latter is simple equality; by proportional equality the just varies quantitatively in accordance with a given claimant's merit. The idea was fundamental already in Homer and Hesiod, and flowers in the political discourse of classical Athens, where Thucydides' Pericles argues that a proportional equality is the ruling principle of the Athenian regime. Later on, recalling the ancestral polity, Isocrates will explain how that nominal democracy still observed an equality that distributed a suitable allotment of honor or access to privilege in accordance with a ratio reflecting the recipient's worth.[1]

In the *Gorgias*, Socrates attributes a 'geometric' equality to some unnamed 'wise men'. Evidently suggested is one part of a formal theory of three mathematical means – arithmetic, geometric, and harmonic. Plato embeds these same means mythically in the Pythagorean generation of the World-Soul in the *Timaeus* and by implication in Socrates' musical harmonization of the individual soul in the *Republic*.[2] By the terms of the connection running through the trilogy these form with the *Critias*, the same theory should inform the best polity, the polity that is perfectly just. The three means were shortly to be brought to bear on the political question of the best regime.[3] This and other such uses, however, involve not only two, but three kinds of equality. A problem is thus to see how all of them might likewise be involved in an account of justice.

A mathematical solution of the problem of justice is already implicit in the pre-philosophical tradition, but a full treatment along such lines is found only in the works of Plato's associates, pupils, and later readers and interpreters.[4] What follows is a preliminary study of some key features of, and possible origins for, the later, developed tradition.

i. Arithmetic and geometric equality

In the fifth book of the *Nicomachean Ethics*, Aristotle explains that, while justice as equality is not itself a mean in the way the other moral virtues are, it occurs in kinds that regard various mathematically expressible means. The geometric mean is a principle for distributive justice; the arithmetic, for corrective justice. Aristotle evidently has in view the

Hayden W. Ausland

mathematical theory of at least two of the three basic means. But he also mentions another species of justice regarding a further kind of proportion, associating these with an obscure 'Pythagorean' saying that justice involves reciprocation of some kind. This third kind of justice exhibits affinities with both the other kinds, but is simply identical with neither. Its special office is to preserve the community for the sake of whose initial organization, and subsequent maintenance, they respectively function.[5] Among modern interpreters, no interpretation of this third, reciprocal justice has been agreed upon.[6]

The geometric and arithmetic principles referred to by Aristotle in explanation of what is just in distribution and correction again represent two of the three basic means mentioned before. These means of ancient Greek number theory may be expressed in modern fashion as follows (a and c standing for extremes, and b for a mean):

mean:	arithmetic	geometric	harmonic/subcontrary
modern formula:	$a - (= a + c / 2) - c$	$a - (= \sqrt{ac}) - c$	$a - (= 2ac / a + c) - c$
ancient root(s):	2 4 6	2 4 8	2 3 6 3 4 6

Their ancient representation was quite different. They are set forth in various standard ancient mathematical works, but it is in a musical context that we find them explained by Plato's friend, the Pythagorean Archytas of Tarentum.[7] According to this tradition the arithmetic represents the mean between two extremes with respect to their absolute difference: the excess by which the greater extreme exceeds the mean is numerically or *quantitatively* equal to the deficiency by which the lesser extreme is exceeded by the same mean (e.g. using the root numbers, 6–4 = 2 and 4–2 = 2). And the *difference* is in either case the same. With the geometric mean it is otherwise, for the differences are unequal. But here there is still an equality discernable of another kind, since the difference in either case reflects proportionately or *qualitatively* the original inequality of the extreme terms (e.g. using the root numbers, 8–4 = 4, which is to the extreme 8 as 4–2 is to the mean 4). Here the *ratios* are equal.

This forms the mathematical basis for the two equalities distinguished by the orator Isocrates as (1) giving each one the same and (2) giving each what it merits, respectively. It is in a slightly different way also the basis for Aristotle's distinction between distributive and corrective justice. The absolute quantities of the extreme terms must be conceived of as standing for the merits of the men or classes to whom goods are to be accorded. These goods are distributed 'equally' in either instance; in the one, however, their equality is absolute and without respect to the differing worths of the different parties, i.e. what is to be equalized is represented by the *numerical difference* between the two extremes. In the case of geometric equality differing worths are respected, so that in mathematical terms it is now the *ratios* that are to be equalized. Viewed as principles of equality, the arithmetic and geometric means in a way complement each other. In assigning equal amounts to either extreme, the arithmetic mean fails to achieve the rational equality that the geometric does. But the latter, in so doing, assigns amounts that are in absolute terms unequal. The equality aimed at by institutions embodying a principle of arithmetic proportion is visible in assignments of the same to each member of the community. The kind of equality aimed at by those reflecting a geometric principle will consist in assignments that observe an equality in relation to the several parties' greater or lesser worths. Isocrates speaks of proportional equality as the old way, and simple equality as the new. Aristotle speaks as if both have practical application, but clearly regards the geometrical principle as the prior, assigning to it the prior, *distributive* task, and to the arithmetic a secondary, *corrective* one: a numerical correction of an imbalance founded upon an initially proportional distribution will tend to preserve that distribution's original character (or perhaps its developed implications).

ii. A third kind of equality

A question arises as to what practical relevance there may be to the third, the harmonic or 'subcontrary', mean. Mathematically, it produces neither kind of equality that the others do, but rather an equality that combines features of these. The numerical differences between the extremes and the mean are, to be sure, not equal (as with the arithmetic mean) and neither are the ratios of these differences to the extremes (as they are with the geometric mean). But the differences are equal when they are regarded as *parts* of the extremes (e.g. using the second of the two roots, 6–4 is one third of the extreme and greater term 6 and 4–3 is likewise one third of the extreme and lesser term 3). While the arithmetic mean assigned equal amounts, but lesser ratios, and the geometric assigned unequal amounts but equal ratios, the harmonic assigns unequal ratios and unequal amounts, but these amounts are still equal *if regarded as parts of the extremes.*

The inequalities of the ratios occasioned by both the arithmetic and harmonic means, when viewed against the equality of ratios assigned by the geometric mean, stand opposite each other: the former assigns a greater ratio to the lesser extreme, and a lesser to the greater; the latter assigns a greater ratio to the greater, and a lesser to the lesser. The geometric is in this sense the *intermediate* case, assigning equal ratios to both. The way in which the harmonic mean figures in relation to the other two means seems to have occasioned its early designation as the mean 'subcontrary' to the arithmetic.[8] Regarded in the terms of the ratios they generate, the three kinds of mean taken together thus constitute a kind of meta-proportion in which the arithmetic and harmonic form kinds of extremes with the geometric functioning as their mean.[9]

mean:	arithmetic	geometric	harmonic/subcontrary
assignment of ratios to extremes	greater to lesser and lesser to greater	same to same	lesser to lesser and greater to greater

The arithmetic and harmonic (and so by implication, also the geometric) means figure in the construction of the World-Soul in the *Timaeus* in a related form that Nicomachus, in concluding his *Introduction to Arithmetic*, will call the 'most perfect proportion', which is a 'three dimensional' one in four terms such that the extremes are mediated by two means – one arithmetic and one harmonic. Thus as 12 is to 9, so is 8 to 6 (viz., as 4 is to 3) – with 9 forming the arithmetic, and 8 the harmonic, mean between 12 and 6. Nicomachus says that this proportion is especially important to musical theory and that it is most authoritatively called 'concord' (*harmonia*).[10]

The political applications of the other two means have been outlined, and we have seen that Isocrates and Aristotle seem to restrict their discussions to two opposed kinds of equality, which seem in turn to represent applications of these two, namely the arithmetic and geometric principles. What does there remain for the third? Or is it politically irrelevant? Following for a moment Aristotle, we may postulate that in application to questions of distribution the arithmetic principle is unjust, whereas the geometric is just. Likewise, in cases requiring the restoration of a balance lost, the geometric yields to the arithmetic.

But in what connection or on what terms, then, could the harmonic principle be said to be just? From the standpoint of the simple equality aimed at with the arithmetic principle of justice, a harmonic principle would appear to constitute an even grosser injustice than would the proportionate justice achieved with the geometric principle. The party of greater merit would receive not only a numerically greater *amount*, but even a greater *proportion* of goods. Yet in mathematical terms, it is exactly this quality in virtue of which the harmonic mean has a claim to inclusion in the greater scheme of all three. How can something seemingly so unjust be part of a picture of justice? As a start to answering this question we may observe that the reason given for the harmonic mean's having been originally called 'subcontrary' is the way in which it 'reciprocates' (*antipeponthei*) with the arithmetic.[11]

This is potentially significant in view of the problem of the Pythagorean, 'reciprocal' principle added to the other two by Aristotle in *EN* 5.[12] It is more than likely that this definition is (or at least was by the Pythagore-

110

ans) intended also in a mathematical sense. Aristotle illustrates by saying that the result of one man's striking another, for instance, will differ according as the striker or one struck may hold a political office.[13] He also alludes to the differences between appropriate punishments for voluntary vs involuntary infractions. We might thus at first think that this principle has a legal use in fixing corrective punishments according to a geometric proportion reflecting such considerations as the respective ranks of the parties to a battery, or the involuntary character of otherwise criminal acts.[14] But Aristotle speaks as if the reciprocation is meant more broadly, assigning it a use in communal transactions (*en tais koinôniais allakti-kais*). So one possibility must be that what Aristotle terms 'reciprocal' in some way is or involves the third principle of harmonic proportion that is required as a member of the greater proportion formed by it together with the arithmetic and geometric means. But why should this have been referred to as 'what reciprocates *with something other*' (*to antipeponthos allôi*)? And why does Aristotle say that those who follow the Pythagorean teaching hold that this is *simply* just (*haplôs dikaion*)? At least the second feature suggests that this account of what is just was intended as being of more universal validity than one extreme of a balanced triad would be. In order for it both to play a role within the schema of proportions that define what is just, and also to be defined as what is just simply, what is reciprocal in this sense would have to function mathematically both as a member and as a defining principle of the scheme of three taken together. Is there any way in which the harmonic mean can accomplish this?

Ancient writers note the way it combines the principles represented by the other two means.[15] But this itself involves an interesting further dimension as well, which elucidates a key connection between the *Timaeus* and the *Republic*. The paradigm case illustrating the coincidence of the three classical means is the musical scale comprising the fundamental notes called the *hypatê* (1st/*do*), *mesê* (4th/*fa*), the *paramesê* (5th/*so*), and the *nêtê* (octave/*Do*). These notes – named from corresponding strings of the lyre – were assigned absolute numerical quantities (corresponding to the lengths of differing strings producing them at the same degree of tension) of 6, 8, 9, and 12, respectively. These are just the terms of Nicomachus' 'most perfect proportion'.[16] The ratio of the octave to the first (the *dia pason*) is thus double (2:1); that of the fifth to the first (the *dia pente*) is three halves 3:2), and that of the fourth to the first (the *dia tettaron*) four thirds (4:3). The interval between the *mesê* and *paramesê* was defined by the *tonaion* (tonal) ratio (9:8). Given that the ratio of the *mesê* to the *nêtê* was 4:3 and that of the *paramesê* to the *hypatê* 3:2, the *mesê* thus constituted the harmonic mean, and the *paramesê* the arithmetic mean, between the extremes of the *nêtê* and *hypatê*. The geometric mean is represented by no note within the simple octave, but it is present in the *nêtê* itself within a system of two octaves (6 : 12 :: 12 : 24). If these octaves are represented as each including just one of the two other means, then we have a system including all three means, with the geometric mean flanking the other two:

24	octave (b)	*DO* (*nêtê*)		
18	4th	*Fa* (*mesê*)	4:3	(harmonic mean)
12	octave (a)	*Do* (*nêtê/hypatê*)	2:1	(geometric mean)
8	5th	*so* (*paramesê*)	3:2	(arithmetic mean)
6	1st	*do* (*hypatê*)		

Is there in any way connected with this musical fact also a mathematical affinity between the greater harmony among the three means and the harmonic proportion that produces only one of them in its specific application? Iamblichus speaks of a sense in which there is: he says that the harmonic mean is so called because one may see in it 'seminally the ratios in a concord' (*spermatikôs tous en harmonia logous*).[17] There are two roots for the harmonic proportion: 2-3-6 and 3-4-6. In the second root, the three terms fall into ratios corresponding to the fourth (4:3), the fifth (6:4), and the octave (6:3). This is one sense in which the harmonic mean even in its special application embodies a principle like the one comprehending the greater whole it forms with the other two basic means, and does so in a way like the general structure of the octave within which only one note represents a harmonic mean. This fact might begin to account for the Pythagoreans' speaking of what is just as 'simply' reciprocation in a pregnant mathematical sense. It may to us seem strange that a definition of justice should be framed in terms ambiguous for an ordinary practical usage on the one hand (requital in the sense of the *lex talionis*) and a mathematical phenomenon on the other. Yet it is quite characteristic of the Pythagoreans Aristotle mentions to have sought a mathematical accounting of moral phenomena.[18]

iii. Three kinds of soul and three kinds of justice

In Plato's extended definitional dialogue on justice, Socrates nowhere develops an explicitly mathematical account even of the partial sort that we find in Aristotle, mentioning geometrical equality only to criticize degenerate democracy after the fashion of an orator like Isocrates. But Plato does employ the theory of the three means psychologically in different ways in both the *Timaeus* and the *Republic*, and he does so in each dialogue with their roles in the musical scale firmly in view. Thus it is with just such a structure that Plato compares the soul in book IV of the *Republic* (443d5-e1), where he has Socrates compare the relations among the rational, spirited, and desiring parts of the human soul to those among the first, fourth, and octave of a concord. In this comparison, the spirited part of the soul appears as the harmonic mean between the other two. But

8. The mathematics of justice

this psychological application[19] is only one of a number of argumentative or imaginative structures that are framed in analogous triads throughout the *Republic*. Of these the most important for the present question is the series of Socrates' three interlocutors' attempts to define justice in the first book.

Republic I: Three insufficient definitions of justice

[Cephalus]	[Polemarchus]	[Thrasymachus]
to tell the truth and to return what one has received (331d2f.)	to render what is fitting to each (332c2)	what benefits the stronger party (338c2)

Each of these understandings of justice has a certain natural appeal; and the second (if not in Polemarchus' own version, at least in Socrates' interpretation of Polemarchus' quotation from Simonides) anticipates the subsequently traditional definition of justice.[20] But does any of them have anything to do with Pythagorean mathematical theory? Pythagoras himself is reported as having identified justice as a quadratic number (*arithmos isakis isos*).[21] If he did, he must have kept back precisely which number he intended, since one view arose that it was the square of the first even number two (i.e. 4), and another that it was the square of the first odd number three (i.e. 9).[22] The second account accords with the table of opposites preserved by Aristotle and better fits with a complicated, much later attested, but reportedly Pythagorean definition of justice as 'a power of rendering what is equal and fitting comprehended by the mean of an odd square number'.[23]

Iamblichus explains this definition with reference to the pentad. By his account, the ratio of justice (*logos tês dikaiosynês*) according to an arithmetic analogy is evident in the mean of the number 9 (the first square of an odd root). This mean is 5, as is seen when the number 9 is set out as the terminus of a row of the numbers from 1 to 9. The middle number, 5, will divide both the numbers that, as inside of it, have 'less than is fitting' (*elatton ê prosêkon echontas*), and those beyond it, which 'have more' (*pleonektountas*). It will do this inasmuch as the greater numbers come always closer to 9, while those coming closer to one are always less. Now what 'is fitting to each in accordance with the ratio of equality' (*prosêkei te hekastôi kata ge ton tês isotêtos logon*) is a ninth of the sum of the entire series (i.e. 45 divided by 9 = 5), which is reflected *per se* solely through the mean between greater and lesser (i.e. the central member 5), since justice, like other virtues, is itself nothing other than a mean. For this reason, the first number (1) is deficient by that quantity by which the last (9) is in excess and thus at variance with what is fitting (*para to kathêkon hyperechei … kai pleonektei*), with the same going for 8 in relation to 2, 7 to 3, and 6 to 4. Number 5, which is in the central position, is deficient and in

113

excess equally, i.e. not at all, and functions as the scale's fulcrum. Among the various properties that these greater and lesser numbers exhibit in relation to one another, the role of 5 as a uniquely central number serves as a kind of technical rule by which to equalize them all with one another. Taking the fifth number (counting back from 9), and giving it to one, the most extreme injustice will be made right as the one most injured and the one injuring most will be equalized (*isothesontai*). Now 4 is the fifth number back from 9 (viz. in the shortened series 87654), which, when taken from 8 and added to 3, equalizes these. Taking the fifth number back from 6 likewise, which is one, from 6, and adding it to 4, causes these to be equal. And the same even goes for the canonic number 5 (viz. 5-0 = 5), which thus will be equal to itself.[24]

Iamblichus' corrective equalizations are on their face based upon an arithmetic principle. But the language he uses also suggests that it is important to the justice of these corrections that they through taking and awarding 'render what is equal and fitting' and further, that they do so by taking from and giving to different parties according to an analogical standard. This standard is taken to be a member generically the same as the parties involved, but distinguished specifically from them by its lack of any excess or deficiency. The language he uses is primarily that of taking and giving back with a view to achieving an arithmetic equality, and in this way answers to Cephalus' 'definition' of justice in *Republic* I (... *ha an labêi tis apodidonai*, 331d2f.). It also reflects the sense in which Polemarchus' developed definition of what is just as rendering each what is due (*to prosêkon hekastôi apodidonai*, 332c2) is offered to substantiate, while modifying, Cephalus' definition. Can it carry a further sense appropriate to the harmonic principle, or even to the terms of Thrasymachus' definition?

Iamblichus outlines, but defers closer consideration of an additional, 'natural' way in which the Pythagorean definition of justice may be understood, a way that involves contemplating a more elaborate figure in three dimensions that will exhibit a reciprocal kind of proportion.[25] However his bare sketch is to be understood, one difference made clear is that receiving what is due no longer results in simple equality in all cases – some parties still get more and some less. This seeming injustice is apparently what is to be dispelled by the fact that these numerical inequalities are still seen to be rational in reference to a kind of analogical reciprocation (*kata tina analogon antipeponthesin*). Thus it is unnecessary to speculate about the mathematical details of this further construction of 'a power for rendering what is equal and fitting' in order to see that it is in several respects compatible with the principle of harmonic, in its role as subcontrary to arithmetic, proportion.[26] Just as the arithmetic mean made numerical equalization intelligible, so this application is intended to account for what, although when they are seen arithmetically are inequalities, are nevertheless the results of a proportion observable at a higher level through the construction of a mathematical solid.[27] The equality implied evidently resides in some kind of proportional reciprocation, but as with Aristotle earlier, justice as a complex kind of mathematical reciprocity seems for now left at the level of suggestion.[28]

One might at this point feel inclined to wonder what any of this has to do with Plato. Some have wondered whether Plato himself was so very informed about contemporary advances in mathematics[29] and modern scholars instinctively doubt that Plato himself intends such arcane allusions in a 'philosophically serious' way (i.e. in the way a 'Neo'-Pythagorean presumably would).[30] The possibility raises, among other problems, the spectre of a socially exclusive 'esoteric' reading of the dialogues – a matter for the consideration of which great scholarly care is required on any hypothesis, but especially when relying upon Pythagorean sources of doubtful authorship and date. One firm clue is provided by the *Gorgias*, in which Socrates alleges that Callicles neglects geometry, and geometrical equality, by preferring 'to have more' (*pleonexia*, 508a7). The doctrine that one stronger or better should have more emerges as a mark of Thrasymachus' justice, with which Callicles seems in substantial sympathy. Neither Socrates nor Thrasymachus ever develops a mathematical account of it in the way Iamblichus might, but a curious passage in *Republic* I suggests that something of the kind underlies a constructive understanding of justice as the advantage of the stronger. When Thrasymachus asks Socrates what *he* thinks justice is, he cautions him against answering as usual, by saying 'the beneficial' or the like. Socrates shortly offers an arithmetical comparison in protest: it is as if Thrasymachus has asked him what twelve is but will not allow him to answer that it is 2 times 6, or 3 times 4, or 6 times 2, or 4 times 3.[31] Why has Plato chosen this example? Socrates hints at an answer by mentioning four ways in which 12 is an oblong number, while omitting mention of its significant status as the first pentagonal number beyond the limiting quantity of the pentad itself. To say what 12 is in a way reflecting this requires a formal viewpoint transcending simpler arithmetical operations of the kind he lists.[32] What is more, 12 (as we have seen) is the number assigned to the octave. The factors Socrates lists are exhaustive but they also form either arithmetic or harmonic proportions when grouped into various possible triads. They will not by themselves form a geometric proportion. But all three means are embraced first within a double octave where the octave, itself forming the geometrical mean, is the number 12. Understanding what 12 is may mean ignoring its factors, and instead viewing it against a larger background within which it emerges as a central figure. The problem of justice is analogously complex, Socrates seems to suggest.

Cephalus' definition resembles justice on a principle of arithmetic proportion, while Polemarchus' definition reinterprets his father's definition on a principle of geometric proportion; perhaps, without realizing it fully, Thrasymachus evokes a third definition based upon a principle of harmonic proportion. It is no wonder that it should offend ordinary egalitarian sensibilities. But, if Socrates' own dialectical teaching on justice is to correct each of these while making sense of all, then it will have to subsume all three in some way. His teaching on the musical structure of the soul in book 4 paves the way for this, since it is within the concord of three formed according to the harmonic mean that each member will 'mind its own business'.[33]

iv. Archytas on political justice

What of a recognizably political application of justice in the *Republic*? When Plato has the Athenian Stranger appeal to proportional equality in the *Laws*, it is for the purpose of recommending an 'intermediate' regime combining what he calls democracy and monarchy. In Hellenistic times and onwards there was a significant incidence of this theme. Of the several passages that explain it in terms of a theory of proportions, some fragments of a lost work *On Law and Justice* attributed to Archytas are most relevant to the political considerations special to Plato's *Republic*. Whether they are of Archytas' own composition has been doubted, but they at least embody a potentially fruitful ancient interpretation of Plato.[34]

Archytas says that law bears the same relation to soul and life that attunement (*harmonia*) does to hearing and voice: just as law educates the soul and constitutes a man's life, so attunement makes hearing cognitive and voice in agreement. He claims that every community (*koinônia*) consists of a ruling element, one that is ruled, and law – which can be either written or unwritten. The happiness of the community depends upon the law's expression at every level. Actions derive from ruling, being ruled, or thirdly mastery (*kratein*). Rule is properly of the stronger (*kreissôn*), and the weaker is ruled, but both master. The rational element of the soul rules; the irrational is ruled, but they both master the passions. The harmony (*synarmoga*) of both is the source of virtue, which leads the soul to a state of quietude.[35] It is requisite, he says, that a law that is perfect do three things: it must (1) follow nature, (2) respect what is practically possible, and (3) conduce to the good of the political community. The first it accomplishes by imitating what is just by nature. This is 'what is analogous and what is fitting to each in accordance with each one's worth'.[36] The second requirement is met when the law possesses 'a harmony in relation to those for whom it is legislated', since many are not of sufficient ability to receive what is by nature, or primarily, good, but only what is relative to themselves, and possible, as, for example, when men who are sick or diseased receive medical attention.[37] The third is met, if the law is not monarchical (or even privately beneficial), but beneficial to the community and pertains throughout all things. Before describing how this is to be achieved, Archytas mentions a practical difficulty: different human souls can no more receive the same virtue than every soil the same

116

fruits. For this reason what is just is partly aristocratic, partly democratic, and partly oligarchic. Archytas explains the distinction between these principles in terms of the three mathematical means: the harmonic is the principle of the aristocratic regime, the geometric of the democratic,[38] and the arithmetic of the oligarchical (or tyrannical).[39] These are the political varieties of what is just, Archytas explains, so that the best polity and city will be composed out of the three kinds, mixing features taken from each, for '... law must not only be good and noble, but also reciprocate (*antipeponthenai*) with its parts, for this is strong and sure; by 'reciprocate' I mean for it both to rule and be ruled in respect of the same rule'.[40] When Archytas says that law must 'reciprocate with its parts', he alludes to the greater proportion that the three means constitute together – a proportion seen as ruling its members, which are in this case also seen as ruling their own subordinate terms. The best law and city is thus like a higher proportion compounded out of the three basic means.[41]

This political doctrine of a complex harmony is developed against the triple background of the three goals Archytas set out for law. It must (1) be just naturally by rendering each its due; but it must also (2) respect the necessity posed it by human frailty. Finally, it can (3) actually foster a self-sufficient city that contains within itself the cause of its own preservation or security. Giving various further prescriptions concerning the scale of goods to be observed, he concludes that the optimal arrangement will render the whole city self-sufficient, since it will contain within itself the principle of its own security.[42] Stressing the importance of freedom in the sense of self-control, Archytas concludes:

> Law must therefore deeply penetrate the habits and activities of the citizens; for it will make the citizens self-sufficient and will distribute what is merited and due to each; for so too does the sun as it is carried through the zodiac distribute the fitting portion of generation, growth, and livelihood to all the things on the earth, providing the salutary combination of the seasons as a kind of *eunomia*.[43]

v. The idea of the good

Points of comparison with Plato's *Republic* surface throughout these fragments,[44] but outlining a single key instance must serve to close this study. Archytas' comparison of law to the sun reminds us of another mimetic triad in the *Republic* – the three comparisons with which Socrates tries to explain the idea of the good to Glaucon. These comparisons themselves form a triad with the analogy of the sun and the image of the cave as extremes flanking the divided line in between them. The divided line is itself a mathematical construction of a continuous quantity divided into segments according to a geometrical proportion. Since its two central segments are necessarily equal, they can be construed as differing kinds (rather than degrees) of clarity vis à vis the same sunlit world that we all inhabit, whether we are oriented toward the upper world of ideas, or bound to the lower one of idolatry.[45] To be more specific, when placed parallel to one another, the schemata for the two extreme images exhibit the ambiguity of the terms 'sun' and 'visible things' that they both employ:

```
(sun analogy): visibles : sun :: intelligibles : good
(cave image): shadows : fire :: daylight visibles : sun
```

But if the same two comparisons are brought into contact in the way suggested in the relations present in the construction of the divided line, they stand revealed as extremes which it binds together as a kind of mean:

```
(sun analogy):                          visibles : sun :: intelligibles : good
                                        _____|_____
                                        :: thought :        intellect
(divided line):         [images]    [things]          [ideas]
                        imagination : conviction ::
                        _____|_____|
(cave image):       shadows : fire :: visibles : sun
```

The cave is an image of the sunlit world of opinion from the perspective of the intellectual world of ideas. The world of ideas, in turn, is a projection from the sunlit world on the analogy of its relationship to a real cave. The divided line mediates the two extremes by bringing them together in a continuous, geometrical proportion.[46]

Socrates offers Glaucon these three comparisons rather than a full account of the good. In Pythagorean terms, this action itself seems to be one of justice, for, although his fuller discussion of the mathematics of justice has been lost to us, Iamblichus has characteristically placed a protreptic illustration of the principle at work in the introductory first book of the same work,[47] where he credits Pythagoras with having treated his hearers differently according as they were more or less naturally fit to receive his teachings. His account uses much of the same terminology.[48] It emerges, therefore, as perhaps no accident that ancient discussion of the mathematics of justice sometimes speaks only of two kinds of equality, but at other times either names or implies a third, for the extent to which this third kind of equality may be clearly presented is itself a consideration for political justice. It has from time to time been recognized that attempts to define justice by Cephalus and Polemarchus that are seemingly 'rejected' in book 1 in fact play a constructive role in the subsequent books.[49] But these men sing only two parts of a three-part harmony. Examination of the

118

mathematical theory underlying their partial attempts shows, among other things, why any role to be played by Thrasymachus' definition must be less obvious, since it is best presented as something utterly to be rejected if it is to play an effective role in a political sequel.[50]

On the assumption that *On Law and Justice* preserves something of the thought of Archytas, Plato may have suggested such an approach to his friend, Archytas may have suggested it to his, or they may have developed it in concert. Alternatively, it may reflect only a later interpretation from the tradition that comes to sight most clearly in Iamblichus' use of Nicomachus' kind of Pythagoreanism. It would be interesting to know which of these is so, but not everything hangs on the question, since modern readers acquainted with the theory of three means and the role they play in the accounts of Plato's later readers can at least see and so begin to consider the possibility and implications of such a dimension to Plato's own political teaching.

Notes

1. *Laws* 756e9-758a2. Cf. Homer, *Iliad* 9.318-20 (cf. Lysias 31.25); Hesiod, *Theogony* 71-4; Solon fr. 34.7-9 and 36.18-20 West; Thucydides 2.37.1; Plato, *Menexenus* 238b7-9a4 and *Republic* 558c3-8; Isocrates, *Areopagiticus* 21f. and 60. For the interpretation of Solon's poetical statements of the theme, see L'Homme-Wery (1996), 146f. On the two equalities more generally, see Harvey (1965).

2. *Gorgias* 507e6-508a8. See Theon Smyrn., *Exposit.*, 116.3-7 Hiller; Nicomachus, *Intr. Arithm.* 122.11-14 Hoche; and Iamblichus, *In Nicom.* 100.19-25 Pistelli. Cf. *Timaeus* 36a2-5 with *Epinomis* 991a4-7. For explanations of the role of these means in the formation of Timaeus' World-Soul, see Plutarch, *De An. Procr.* 15 (1019b-e) and *De Musica* 22; Nicomachus, *Harm. Ench.* 8; Aristid. Quintil., *De Musica* 3.5; and Proclus, *In Tim.* III 171.19-173.4. On the way the three means bind the World-Soul together, see Proclus, *In Tim.* II 198.29-200.21. For the geometrical mean used in the fabrication of the World-Body (31c2-32a7); see Proclus, *In Tim.* II 18.22-23.8. For the musical organization of the soul at *Republic* 443d5-e1, see Ptolemy, *Harm.* 95.28-98.4 and Aristid. Quintil., *De Musica* 3.8.

3. The three types of regime distinguished by the mid-fifth century were combined at the latest in Plato's *Laws* in a theory of the mixed politeia. For these as correlative expressions of the three means, see Aristid. Quintil., *De Musica* 3.8 and Boethius, *Instit. Arithm.* 2.45. Delatte (1948) argues that the theory originates with the Pythagoreans. Bleichen (1979) plausibly contends that the political classification originates in real political struggles, which, of course, need not exclude a Pythagorean influence (see Ryffel, 1949). Aalders' rather categorical skepticism (1968, 23) is to be controlled accordingly.

4. Commenting on *Gorg.* 508a6 Dodds holds Isocrates' expression at *Areopagiticus* 21f. unmathematical, but cf. *Nicocles* 14f. and Aristotle's related attribution to Solon at *Athenaion Politeia* (7.3).

5. Aristotle, *EN* 5.5, 1132b31-4.

6. English discussion gets under way with Monroe (1854). Subsequent controversy remains unresolved, but Gill (1998) includes no contribution on this problem.

7. B2 D.-K., the oldest extant treatment. Cf. Nicomachus, *Intr. Arithm.* 2.22-7

Hayden W. Ausland

(122.11-140.13 Hoche); Theon Smyrn. *Exposit.* 106.12-7.14 and 113.9-19.15 Hiller; Iamblichus, *In Nicom.*, 100.15-113.16 Pistelli; and Boethius, *Instit. Arithm.* 2.41-50 (138.26-164.13 Friedlein). Cf. Olympiodorus *In Gorg.* 182.1-183.4 Westerink; cf. Scholium ad Plat. *Gorg.* 508a [168.1-14 Greene]). See further Taylor (1816), chapters 24-9.

8. See Iamblichus, *In Nicom.* 100.25-101.1 and 110.17-11.26; cf. Philolaus A24 D.-K., and other texts cited in note 9. Burkert (1972, 440f. with nn. 83 and 87) finds an origin for both names in musical theory.

9. See Nicomachus, *Intro. Arithm.* 2.23.6 and 2.25.2; Boethius, *Instit. Arithm.* 2.47; Iamblichus, *In Nicom.* 100.25-101.1 and 110.17-111.26. Cf. Aristotle fr. 47 Rose (ap. Plut. *De Musica* 23). Pappus later produced a construction of the three means together, on which see Heath (1921), 2, 363-5. In the light of this construction, Brown (1975) makes a case for this feature having originally not only characterized, but defined, the third kind of mean.

10. Nicom., *Intr. Arith.* 2.29. Cf. id., *Harm. Ench.* 6 and Boethius, *Instit. Arithm.* 2.54. On the Pythagorean character of the proportion and on Plato's use of it at *Timaeus* 36a-b, see Iamblichus, *In Nicom.* 118.19-119.13 and cf. Nicom., *Harm. Ench.* 8. See further Heath (1921), 1.86, and Michel (1950), 395-7.

11. See Iamblichus, *In Nicom.* 100.25-101.1 and 110.25f.; cf. Nicomachus, *Intro. Arith.* 2.23.6, 2.25.2f.; and Boethius, *Inst. Arithm.* 2.47.

12. ὡρίζοντο γὰρ ἁπλῶς τὸ δίκαιον τὸ ἀντιπεπονθὸς ἄλλῳ (Aristotle, *EN* 5.5, 1132b22f.).

13. *EN* 5.5, 1132b28-31. Cf. Plato, *Laws* 876e-882c; Demosthenes, *Meid.* 32-3; and Arist., *Problemata* 29 passim (especially 29.14, 952b28-34). Isocrates explains the larger political implications in cases of mayhem at *Loch.* 15-18 (19-22 exhibits a merely apparent discrepancy).

14. For Dike interpreted as the harmonic mean, see note 43.

15. See Aristid. Quintil., *De Musica* 3.5; Boethius, *Instit. Arithm.* 2.48.

16. See van der Waerden (1943), 181-7.

17. Iamblichus, *In Nicom.* 108.13-15.

18. See Arist. *Metaph.* A5 985b29f. and M4 1078b23. For the mathematical usage, see Mugler (1958), 66f. For Pythagorean doxography running along the same lines, see Delatte (1922), 57-60. On the Pythagorean conception of justice in particular, see Klein (1968), 65.

19. Plato elsewhere has Socrates consider a seemingly Pythagorean view that the soul is something like the attunement or concord (ἁρμονία) of the strings of a lyre (*Phaedo* 85e3ff.). In a lost work quoted by Plutarch Aristotle (fr. 47 Rose [25 Ross]) speaks of the octave itself as a concord. The Pythagoreans seem to have spoken similarly; see Philolaus B6 D.-K. Interestingly, in the *Phaedo* Socrates' concluding objection to the harmony-theory is that it fails to account adequately for moral responsibility (*Phaedo* 94a8-95a3). By rejecting the idea that a soul is an attunement, Socrates by no means precludes that it can have an attunement and that its moral status is to be understood accordingly.

20. *iustitia est constans et perpetua voluntas ius suum cuique tribuens* (Ulpian, liber 1 *Regul.*; *Dig.* 1 1; *De Iust. et Iure* 10 pr.; *Inst.* 1 pr; Justinian. *Inst.* 1 1; cf. Thomas Aquinas, *Summa Theologica* 2.2 q. 58 a. 1.). Antecedent variants are found in Plato, *Def.* 411d8-e2 (δικαιοσύνη ... ἕξις διανεμετικὴ τοῦ κατ' ἀξίαν ἑκάστῳ), the Stoics in Stob., *Ecl.* II 59.9f. (δικαιοσύνη ἐπιστήμη ἀπονεμητικὴ τῆς ἀξίας ἑκάστῳ), Cicero, *De Inv.* 2.53.160 (*iustitia est habitus animi, communi utilitate conservata, suam cuique tribuens dignitatem*), and [Cicero] *Ad Herr.* 3.23 (*iustitia est aequitas ius unicuique re tribuens pro dignitate cuiusque*). Compare

120

8. The mathematics of justice

Republic 332b9-c4. For the historical development, see Senn (1927), 1-54, and cf. Westrup (1939), 9-15 and 34-42.

21. Aristotle, *Mag. Mor.* A1.6 1182a11-14; Alex. Aphr. *In Metaph.*, 38.11f.; Macrobius, *In Somn. Scip.*, 1.5.17.

22. See Alex. Aphr., *In Metaph.* 38.10-16 (some say 4; others say 9) and 741.5-6 (the number 5). See Anatolius apud *Theol. Arithm.* 29.6-10 (the number 4); Macrobius, *In Somn. Scip.*, 1.5.17 and Martianus Capella 7.740 (the number 8); Iambl., *In Nicom.* 16.11-20.6 [cf. *Theol. Arithm.* 35.6-40.9.] (the number 5, as mean of the number 9); Asclepius, *In Metaph.* 34.17-22, 35.34-5, 36.1 and 65.17-22 (the number 5).

23. δύναμις ἀποδόσεως τοῦ ἴσου καὶ προσήκοντος ἐμπεριεχομένη ἀριθμοῦ τετραγώνου περισσοῦ μεσότητι, preserved in Iamblichus, *In Nicom.* 16.15-18 and in *Theol. Arithm.* 37.1-4. Cf. the related formulations in Iamblichus, *Protr.* 118.1-3, *Comm. Sci.* 61.1-3, and Anatolius, *De Dec.* 31.22-3.

24. *In Nicom.* 18.2-21. The same scheme is set out with some differences at *Theol. Arithm.* 37.10ff.

25. *In Nicom.* 19.21-20.6.

26. It is not fully clear what Iamblichus intends with his preserved remarks, but they suggest, as competing with (a) arithmetic correction, (b) a principle of rendering and receiving what is due (cf. ἀπειληφότων τὸ ἐπιβάλλον 20.1 with τοῦ ἴσου καὶ ἐπιβάλλοντος ἀποδοτικοί earlier), which also once more (c) observes an analogical standard in assigning things to different parties, only this time in reciprocation (compare 20.3f. with 18.5-7). For the asymmetric political relation between the arithmetic and harmonic means, see Proclus, *In Tim.* II 226.29-227.26. For the more general importance of stereometry in Plato's ethics and politics, see Klein (1965), 191-202.

27. Cf. Michael Psellus' echo of the definition Aristotle attributes to Pythagoras: ἡ δὲ δικαιοσύνη δύναμις ἀνταποδόσεως τοῦ ἴσου καὶ προσήκοντος ἐμπεριέχεται ἀριθμοῦ τετραγώνου περισσοῦ μεσότητι. See O'Meara (1989), 224f. and cf. 75 for Iamblichus' reliance more generally on Aristotle's discussion of justice. The ancients, of course, had access to a number of Aristotelian works now lost.

28. Iamblichus may well have resumed the topic in the lost seventh part of his larger work *On Pythagoreanism*, in which he treated ethical matters, including the single virtues, in mathematical terms. See O'Meara (1989), 30-5, 73-5, and 86-91.

29. For a flat denial that Plato participated in fourth-century mathematical advances, see Frank (1923). For the opposite case, see Mugler (1948). For an answer dissociating the *Republic*'s dialectic from mathematics, cf. Cherniss (1951). Cherniss' outlook rests on a conventional interpretation of the divided line, and persists in O'Meara (1989), 22.

30. See O'Meara (1989) 20 n. 44 and cf. the interesting remarks in Jones (1923), 272-6. Adam (1891), 21f. and 75f. finds the geometrical mean (and therewith the elements of the other two) within the famously obscure 'number' of *Republic* VIII. In discussing geometric proportion, Nicomachus mentions the passage, promising to elaborate on another occasion. In commenting on Nicomachus, Asclepius (β 57-73 [68 col. 1 Tarán]) says a little more, associating the passage with *Timaeus* 31b4ff. For the obscure manner in which Plato employs complicated mathematical imagery in his dialogues, and the critical value of ancient technical treatments in trying to understand them, see Toeplitz (1933), 288f. n. 5.

31. *Republic* 336c6-d4 and 337b1-4.

32. See Klein (1985), 46f., and cf. note 22.

33. Cf. Sophocles' musical image for his earlier subjection to passions at *Republic* 329c7f.

34. Arguments for authenticity in Delatte (1922), 71-124. Arguments against: Aalders (1968), 14-23; cf. Bertelli (1962-3), 196-9. Further references in Thesleff (1961), 34f., who himself strikes a middle path, holding that *On Law and Justice* at least comes early in an artificial literary tradition that Archytas himself may have inaugurated. See Thesleff (1961), 92f. and 103, and id. (1962), 35. See further a discussion in Thesleff and Burkert (1971), especially Thesleff's concessions on p. 60 and his proposed compromise at 82-4. Although the work seems unnoticed by anyone before Stobaeus, since Delatte's defence of it and Thesleff's examination of the genre, many doubters are inclined to place it at least well before the time of Nicomachus. The question of its authenticity is largely immaterial to the present study.

35. Fr. 1 Thesleff.

36. τὸ ἀνάλογον καὶ τὸ ἐπιβάλλον ἑκάστῳ κατὰ τὴν ἑκάστου ἀξίαν.

37. Fr. 2 Thesleff.

38. Archytas anticipates (or pseudo-Archytas echoes) a long Hellenistic–Roman tradition in which 'Democracy' becomes a polite term for the rule of monarchs over feckless vestiges of democractic or republican institutions. See Langstadt (1937), 349-64, and cf. Goodenough (1938), 86ff. For a reconsideration of the Archytean fragments in this light, see Goodenough (1928), 59-64. According to Langstadt and Goodenough the ideal implied remains that of Plato; Aalders thus misses an important point in holding this feature a sign of inauthenticity (1968), 13f.; persisting in id. (1975), 29 and n. 101.

39. Fr. 3 Thesleff.

40. δεῖ τοίνυν τὸν νόμον μὴ μόνον ἀγαθὸν καὶ καλὸν ἦμεν, ἀλλὰ καὶ ἀντιπεπονθέναι τοῖς αὑτῶ μερέεσσιν· οὗτος γὰρ ἰσχυρὸς καὶ βέβαιος· τὸ δ' ἀντιπεπονθέναι λέγω αὐτῶ καὶ ἄρχεν καὶ ἄρχεσθαι τὰν αὐτὰν ἀρχάν.

41. Cf. Proclus, *In Tim.* II 220.19-221.4. The idea approximates to a system of checks and balances: '*ita compositum, ut suis sive reipublicae partibus singulis aliquid opponat.*' (Gesner). Offering no explanation, Gruppe held the use of ἀντιπεπονθέναι a sign of inept forgery (1840, 91), but see the explanation in Delatte (1922), 113f. and cf. id. (1948). Delatte (1922, 259) supposes that the concern with checks and balances reflects the politics of Tarentum during Archytas' own times. See note 3 and also Minar (1942), 90-2 and 111-13.

42. Fr. 3 Thesleff, cont. Cf. Plato, *Republic* 433b7-c3 and 443e5f.

43. τὸν νόμον ὧν ἐν τοῖς ἔθεσι καὶ τοῖς ἐπιτηδεύμασι τῶν πολιτῶν ἐγχρῴζεσθαι δεῖ· τοὺς γὰρ πολίτας αὐταρκέας θήσει καὶ διανεμεῖτὸ κατ' ἀξίαν ἑκάστῳ καὶ τὸ ἐπιβάλλον· οὕτω γὰρ καὶ ὁ ἅλιος φερόμενος διῳ τῶ ζοφόρῳ διανέμει τοῖς ἐπὶ γᾶς πᾶσι καὶ γενέσιος καὶ τροφᾶς καὶ βιοτᾶς τὰν ποθάκουσαν μοῖραν, οἷον εὐνομίαν τὰν εὐκρασίαν τᾶν ὡρῶν παρασκευαξάμενος. The identification of geometric equality that renders each its due as eunomia recalls the tradition of Solon. See note 1, with Solon fr. 4.32-9 West. A more distant background yet is seen in all three *Horai* of Hesiod (*Theogony* 902). Proclus holds the three means, as principles of psychic organization, also images of these three daughters of Themis: geometric of Eunomia, harmonic of Dike, and arithmetic of Eirene (*In Tim.* II 198.14-29).

44. Morrison (1956) sees no reason to doubt the authenticity of the Archytean fragments, concluding that '[it] is this theory which Plato takes over in the Republic, where much of Pythagorean practice is also reflected.' (155) He seems to mean this rather differently, however. Cf. id. (1958), 198-218, where Morrison observes that 'the bond of unity in the *Republic* is the harmonic *isotes*' – as distinct from the geometric proportion forming the basis of the social and physical order in the *Gorgias* (213f.). Morrison notices some important points of contact with the

Republic's teaching on temperance, but may have confounded the general and special roles of the harmonic principle. For more exact exploration of Archytas' mathematical influence on Plato's philosophy, see Barker (1978) and (1994).

45. Cf. Klein (1965), 119 n. 27 with Wieland (1982), 209-15.

46. In his public lecture on the good, Plato spoke – tiringly to most – mainly of mathematics. (Aristox., *Harm*. II, 30.10-32.9 Meibom) In the *Republic*, Socrates characterizes a synoptic stage of mathematical education at which the promising dialectician reveals himself or herself as such by grasping rationally how the several disciplines are interrelated. (cf. 531c9-d5 with 537b8-c8). See Tarán (1975), 337, commenting on *Epinomis* 990e1-991a1. Socrates has just before compared undialectical rulers to irrational lines (534d3-6; cf. Eucl., *Elem*. 10, Def. 3); it is possibly relevant here that Pappus credited Theateteus with having originated the theory of irrational lines antecedent to Euclid's treatment in *Elem*. 10, since he seems to have accomplished this using the three basic means as a heuristic device. See David (2002), 52ff. The precise form of the development of the theory of irrationals before Eucl., *Elem*. 10 is a matter of some debate; see Michel (1950), 455-81. For Theaetetus' approach, see Heath (1921), I, 209-12. See also Pappus' own remarks in his commentary on Eucl. *Elem*. 10 , where he associates the triad of means with the soul's ability to grasp irrationals in virtue of the ratios arising within it. (I 9.13, 71f. and 76f. Thomson-Junge – quoted in E.S. Stamatis' Teubner edition of Euclid, *Elem*. 10, xxvf.)

47. See O'Meara (1989), 40.

48. *Vit. Pyth*. 18. Cf. Proclus, *In Tim*. I 22.5-23.2.

49. See Jahns (1850), 25f.

50. See Aulus Gellius, *NA* 10.22.

A historical cycle of hermeneutics in Proclus' *Platonic Theology*

Tim Buckley

Gadamer's hermeneutical imagination returned again and again to the Platonic dialogues. It is fitting then that in a volume of papers treating later Platonic interpretation of the dialogues we touch on an important aspect of Gadamer's thought: the necessary dependence of a text's meaning on historical distance.[1]

Without claiming for the fifth-century Neoplatonist Proclus the status of a progenitor of modern hermeneutics, we can find much that is considered and apparently new in his framing of interpretive problems. Of course, there is nothing to be gained from making inflated claims on Proclus' behalf. If his *Platonic Theology* can be shown to argue the necessary historical dependency of a Platonic text's meaning, it must be admitted that this argument is self-serving and circumscribed, and allows only that historical changes in interpretation will culminate in his own pre-eminent rectitude as a reader of Plato.

Proclus envisaged himself as standing at the apex of a hermeneutical cycle. This cycle is interesting to us for two reasons. The first reason is that it appears to be based on the movement of the *periphora* in the great myth of the *Phaedrus*. The result of this conflation is that Proclus and his forebears are as it were inscribed into the great myth, and subject and object in this interpretive model become aspects of a single complex. The second reason is that Proclus' selection of certain forebears to illustrate this cycle can tell us much about the nature of his hermeneutical thinking; as indeed do his notable omissions.

The proem of Proclus' *Platonic Theology* sets out the relation between Plato and the higher beings, and between Plato and his followers – people whom we would call Neoplatonists (I 5.6ff.). In so doing it presents Proclus' hermeneutical horizon, both with regard to the texts of Plato and the exegesis of these texts by Proclus' forebears. The forebears he mentions are not only linked through a rough chronology from the time of Plotinus up until Syrianus, but are also select philosophers who meet in a divine choir, and have reached a state of ecstatic revelry through Plato's texts (I 6.16-7.1). To provide an appropriate context for this picturesque idea, it is necessary to detail several elements of the proem.[1]

Proclus states his belief that Plato's philosophy first came to appearance by the grace of higher beings, and that it reveals to engendered souls the higher truths – to the extent that it is permitted that these be revealed (I 5.6ff.). His statements recall those passages of the *Phaedrus* that describe the trains of the gods, and the souls who follow in them (248a-c, 253a). A quick look at the apparatus of Saffrey and Westerink's edition reveals that the proem leans more heavily on the *Phaedrus* than any other dialogue – and on the myth in which these images appear above all. This reliance will engage our attention presently.

Regarding those engendered souls to whom divine wisdom is revealed Proclus makes several provisions. In the briefest span these set out the metaphysical laws and resultant historical conditions under which Platonism had come into being, withered or occulted itself, and subsequently revived (I 5.8-16). They are:

(1) That whatever knowledge engendered souls have of higher things is mediated through Plato (I 6.2);
(2) That these souls are a minority, for the greater readership has had hidden from it the true meaning of the texts of Plato (I 5.12-16, 6.7-10);
(3) That the hermeneutical possibilities of the texts alter according to an established temporal cycle (I 5.16, 6.10-13);
(4) That figures whom we would call Neoplatonists are the beneficiaries of a (propitious stage of this cycle (I 6.10-11).

All of these points must be taken as providing a framework, within which we are to make sense of Proclus' list of initiates. But different parts of the framework point us in different directions. On the one hand points (1) and (2) taken together suggest that it is the fidelity of interpretation that rewards certain philosophers with initiation. On the other hand points (3) and (4) taken together suggest that it is the propitiousness of a particular stage of a 'cosmic/hermeneutical cycle' which helps to account for their membership. This is a bald statement of the two directions, and Proclus does not state them as incompatible. But a bald statement suits us at present, for it allows us to bring to the foreground problems presented by both aspects of this hermeneutical model.

First, with regard to fidelity to the texts of Plato, and the scarcity of those who truly comprehend his meaning (*Rep.* VI 496a11-b1, esp. c5-7; *Phd.* 69c), we should consider the following difficulty. Of those Bacchants listed by Proclus – Plotinus, Amelius, Porphyry, Iamblichus, Theodorus and Syrianus – the first and last are treated with particular honour, as respectively originating and bringing to perfection the latter-day Platonic tradition (I 6.19, 7.1-8). If the interstitial members of the list are honoured to a lesser degree, certainly no mention is made of differences or rivalries: the impression is of a general excellence and rare sympathy with the texts of Plato. But when we look at this list of exegetes more closely we encounter a problem.[3] We know from Porphyry himself and from Proclus' *In Timaeum* that Plotinus' students, Porphyry and Amelius, were often at variance.[4] As for the relation between Porphyry and Iamblichus, it can be likened to the influence exerted by Plato on Aristotle, in that it is most visible in the form of criticism rather than imitation.[5] And it has been suggested that Iamblichus and Theodorus were the heads of rival schools or factions of the new Platonism.[6] How then is Proclus able to award a general honour for faithful exegesis to philosophers who seem to have been at each other's throat over their differences?

Again, when we look at this list of exegetes in the context of the *Parmenides* there is a problem. Parts of Proclus' *In Parmenidem* can give one the impression that the history of later thought was a series of partial solutions or lemmata to the *Parmenides*, culminating in Syrianus' eventual solution of the text (*In Parm.* 1061-4; cf. Saffrey [1984a], 2-8). The lemmata to which I refer are of course those of the second section of the dialogue – the hypotheses, their number and meaning. In Proclus' conspectus of the various interpretations proposed by these figures, divergences in the meaning and even the number of hypotheses are prominent, and Proclus uses these divergences to catalogue the excesses and defects of almost all his predecessors, leaving aside of course the always-right Syrianus (*In Parm.* 1052-64; Saffrey and Westerink [1968-97, vol. 1, 1968], lxxv-lxxxix). How can figures lauded as revellers, as the few that penetrated the secrets of Plato's texts, be so consistently wrong?[7]

Second, with regard to the propitiousness of a historical/hermeneutical cycle, we face the problem that philosophers who seem to have blossomed in this environment – one thinks particularly of Plutarch of Athens – are not named by Proclus. Although he makes provision for there being more members of this select group than are enumerated in the proem (I 6.23-7.1), this failure to mention Plutarch is particularly mystifying. The sequence of names seems designed to manifest a historical development from the time of Plotinus to Proclus' own age, and it is disconcerting that an essential figure in this development is passed over (Saffrey and Westerink [1968-97, vol. 1, 1968], xlvii). On top of this we recall that for his preliminary studies in the Academy Proclus was in the charge of Plutarch, studying Aristotle's *De Anima* and the *Phaedo* with him (*Vita Procli* 21.15-17). Less immediately disconcerting, but puzzling nonetheless, is the passing over of the 'philosopher of Rhodes', so important to Proclus' historical picture of the elucidation of the *Parmenides*' hypotheses.[8] Even as Proclus condemns the schema of 'the philosopher of Rhodes' for not having soul as its central element, he notes its elegance and understanding (*In Parm.* 1058.2-3). Taken together in the context of the interpretation of the *Parmenides*, these apparent rebuffs are positively enigmatic, for it is obvious that the contribution of both philosophers brought about significant improvements (to Proclus' mind) to the understanding of this most important text.[9]

Having adverted to the problems posed by Proclus' proem, we shall look for answers to two questions. First, why does Proclus mention certain figures (i.e. the four philosophers named between Plotinus and Syrianus)? And second, why does Proclus omit certain figures (notably Plutarch of Athens)? I believe that reasonable, if not exhaustive, answers to these questions can be obtained by paying heed to the way in which Proclus' history of hermeneutics is fitted to the great myth of the *Phaedrus*.

The *Phaedrus* myth is germane to Proclus' hermeneutical model for two reasons:

(1) It can show in broad terms how to read the *epopteia* of initiates described by Proclus;
(2) Its tensions and conflicts match those of the hermeneutical model that is built around these initiates.

(1) Though terms of Bacchic celebration do not occur in the *Phaedrus* myth proper, words associated with initiation into the mysteries are frequent.[10] Proclus seizes on these in his lengthy discussion of the myth in book IV of the *Platonic Theology*, and it is through them that we may begin to form a picture of his understanding of the myth. Curiously for Proclus, discussion of the myth's initiation-theme does not involve too many propositions of the type '*x* means *y*' (a notable and otiose example is IV 30.24-31.1). In seeking an explanation for this fact, we should pay close attention to Proclus' statements of methodology at I.17-23. Here he distinguishes the various modes in which Platonic dialogues treat of theological matters. The first of the four modes discussed is that of the *Phaedrus*, a theology that is delivered of ecstatic and divine madness. This divinely inspired mode (I 18.10) speaks directly of divine matters, without interposed symbols or veiled language (I 20.13-19).[11] The basis for this claim may be found in the myth itself at 249c4-d3: in that mythic sphere the soul approaches those things that make a god divine, and if only it can recall and see once more that primal scene, it will pour forth in divine madness all that it has known.

If one suspects that the theme of initiation has been exaggerated by Proclus, it is worth considering Plutarch's statement that both Plato and Aristotle referred to the immediate and simple apprehension of intellect as *epopteia*.[12] Whether Proclus knew of these ideas from Plutarch or from some other source is beyond our knowledge, but there is a remarkable fit between Proclus' declared methodology and this evidence for the use and function of myth in the Old Academy.[13]

Regarded in this light the *Phaedrus* myth can tell us a good deal about the apparent *epopteia* of initiates in Proclus' proem to the *Platonic Theology*, and can guide our reading of that initiation. Two details of the myth are particularly valuable for this purpose: the inscription within it of the philosopher, and the anamnesis that the myth in part describes, but which also seems to be the fuel that drives the whole thing.

Metaphor and allegory are Platonic commonplaces, but it is unusual for Plato's metaphors to be too hermetic or self-effacing: even where there may be controversy over the tenor of a particular metaphor, its status is generally patent (e.g. the Divided Line and Cave). But in the case of the *Phaedrus* myth it is not at all clear which elements are metaphorical. As Hackforth notes in discussing the myth, though a few elements lend themselves to interpretation (such as the charioteer and his steeds), 'there is much in the present section and in the pages which follow that cannot be so translated, and that Plato does not intend to be translated'.[14] One such untranslatable is the idea of the philosopher as one who has seen in a discarnate existence that which truly is, and secures access to the memory of that vision once incarnate. The details Plato builds up are fantastical, but it is difficult to see the description in its entirety as metaphorical – Plato does indeed seem to have taken metempsychotic recollection very seriously. And in line with these exigencies (of which Hackforth is as much sensible as Proclus), Proclus largely eschews allegory and accepts the myth as literal truth, albeit of an inspired sort (I 17.25-18.12). It is true that as Hackforth is able to elucidate isolated parts of the myth, Proclus is able to draw into his discussion of the noetic and the noeric the cosmic *periphora*, and the vault or arch that bears up the heavens (IV 59-65); and the nectar and ambrosia of the gods are interpreted as dual aspect of *pronoia* (IV 46-7). But the soul's vision and path are treated as literal truth, and Proclus restates rather than reframes this part of the myth (IV 76.22-78.4).

As the myth is read literally in the *Platonic Theology*, and the philosopher's way is taken as truth, the conclusion must be drawn that Proclus saw himself and his predecessors not just as readers of the myth, but also actors in its drama. If one identifies oneself and one's predecessors as true philosophers and initiates, as Proclus does (IV 77.9-19, 69.6-15; I 6.24), the myth must speak to one almost as an *ad hominem* argument.[15]

It seems otiose to say that Proclus' ideal reader of the *Phaedrus* is the philosopher; but if we understand 'philosopher' to mean someone who has seen the realm of true being and even now has recollection of that realm, there is some sense in regarding the *Phaedrus* as a test-case of interpretation. It addresses itself to one who understands what is said by virtue of the fact that he is implicated in it. This knowledge does not arise out of one's deductive capacities, or one's knowledge of the Platonic corpus (though these things may derive from or reflect the true source of one's knowledge). And so it may be that the myth had particular value for Proclus as a way of distinguishing the true initiate from the orthodox but profane follower. We shall test this hypothesis presently.

(2) As well as providing a possible test by which to make judgements concerning the inclusion or exclusion of certain philosophers, the myth has

a specific bearing on the hermeneutical framework detailed at the outset of this essay. The framework exhibits a tension between individual achievement and broader hermeneutical environment, which reflects the interweaving of individual effort and cosmic *periphora* in the myth (cf. IV 59.4-14). There are points of intersection where the soul's striving is successful and borne up by the *periphora* (247b5-c2), but also points when for all its efforts there is no reward, and where in fact the centrifuge seems to push it down (248a6-8). Significant too is the *periphora* as a cyclical measure, and the extraordinary lengths of time an unsuccessful soul must wait outside the cycle (248e-249a). We have noted that the *periphora* is for Proclus one of the few tractable elements of the *Phaedrus* myth. As it turns out, it provides the latent structure for his Bacchic procession.

Plotinus is a new beginning for Proclus, and Proclus describes the renewed philosophy as being carried out by true initiates whose lives were in keeping with holy mystagogy: most importantly, the efforts of Plotinus' and succeeding generations went as far as their hermeneutical horizon would allow (I 6.10-13). Taken together with *In Parmenidem* 1052-64, this last statement helps us to overcome a problem posed by the many differences and errors Proclus detected among these earlier Platonists. These need not reflect a lesser vision of true being, but rather a less conducive or receptive environment in which to disseminate this vision. Plotinus seems to mark the horizon of a new cycle, but not its zenith, and therefore it is not surprising if later philosophers, not necessarily more cognizant of the true vision, achieve greater accuracy and success. In fact Proclus imagines the cycle continuing on well beyond his death (I 7.11-14), presumably reaching a peak before inevitably sinking away at the far horizon. As for the sniping and differences of opinion, these are subsumed as easily into Proclus' history of philosophy as Plato's winged hooligans are integrated into the myth of being (248a6-b3). But out of both sets of scrums must come souls that can indeed push their heads above and see or recall that which truly is (248a1-3).

So Proclus' list of names is a shorthand way of mapping out the topography of the *Phaedrus* myth onto the *Platonic Theology*. The *periphora* of the myth is projected onto the previous generations of Platonists, from Plotinus through to his own time. The names serve as markers of stages of an interpretative cycle. This seems particularly to hold for those paired philosophers who had displayed all the enmity and competition that the *Phaedrus* myth would lead us to expect of winged souls clamouring over the same piece of territory. Thus philosophical differences that arose at various stages of the post-Plotinian tradition are correlated with conflict in the myth over parts of the *periphora*. The confidence that Proclus everywhere displays concerning Syrianus' and his own formulations of Platonism indicate that he imagined himself to be riding a crest of this interpretative cycle. As a minor point I would suggest that the eventual decline implied after this zenith aligns well with Proclus' perception of Christianity as heralding in some kind of dark age.[16] But the cyclical nature of the interpretative framework also allows for a measure of optimism, in that the nadir as well will pass, and there is therefore good reason for leaving one's interpretations to those to come (I. 7.11-14).

*

We return now to problems posed by the list. How has our discussion of the myth helped us to understand the absence of certain philosophers (Plutarch) and the inclusion of others (Porphyry and Amelius, Iamblichus and Theodorus)? And in light of the discussion so far, to what extent can we give reasons for inclusion or exclusion in terms of the *Phaedrus* myth?

The easiest matter to deal with is the inclusion of Iamblichus and Theodorus. They are mentioned together in book IV precisely for their perception of the true nature of the 'subcelestial vault' (*hypouranios hapsis*, IV 69.1-15). In fact, in this passage these two figures are linked directly to Plato, as indeed is Syrianus (IV 69.9). What is of relevance is that Iamblichus and Theodorus do not give a metaphorical interpretation to the subcelestial vault (which would be at odds with Proclus' reticence to take the great myth as metaphor); rather, they draw fine distinctions between different parts of the myth's topography – the subcelestial vault, the *periphora*, and the supercelestial area (IV 68.23-69.8). In this way Iamblichus and Theodorus present themselves as true philosophers, souls that have raised their heads briefly into the supercelestial field.

So we have here a very good fit with the kind of interpretation that Proclus regards as necessary to the *Phaedrus* myth: the literal apprehension (albeit in a higher than rational mode) of an inspired discourse. We may note that this need not conflict with other points that have been made – that the two are treated as a pair, that they were perhaps rivals, that they mark a certain stage in Proclus' history of hermeneutics. As we have noted, the two come together at the same point on the *periphora*, and their rivalry may have been to Proclus' mind as much a matter of winged beings in struggle as philosophers vying on earth.

The second problem in order of difficulty is Plutarch. Regarding his exclusion from the list, one can construct from the *Vita Procli* a possible dissent between him and Syrianus regarding the separability of the 'head' and the 'body' (*Vita Procli* 21.22-36), indicating some difference in their interpretation of *Phdr.* 248a2-3.

The story goes that Plutarch, a grandfatherly figure to Proclus, pleaded with him to relax his strict vegetarian regimen. Plutarch's argument was that the body should be the soul's help. Proclus demurred, whereupon Syrianus entered the argument and told Plutarch that it would be far better for one such as Proclus to follow his inclination even if he should die (that is, untether body and soul) in the process. Of the two views of how soul and body should interact, the first precludes the epoptic separation, and implies ignorance of that moment at which the charioteer raises his head above the heavens. Just as the *Phaedrus* myth describes the *literal* separation of the head from the body in initiation into true being (separated as they are by the different realms they inhabit), and as a mystery initiation described by Proclus in this connection (the burial of the entire body, leaving only the head exposed) describes a *symbolic* separation (Saffrey and Westerink [1968-97, vol. 4, 1981], 135-6, on IV 30.17-20), so the separation of mind from body was the organizing principal of a life that celebrated a mystagogy of philosophy.

If we understand the anecdote to describe some deficiency in Plutarch's interpretation of the great myth, we can understand why he would be excluded from the proem – and indeed why Proclus would seem to have attached some importance to the story (*Vita Procli* 21.32). One would guess, if the full weight of the hermeneutical model of *Platonic Theology* is to be applied, that Plutarch was the beneficiary of a benign part of the historical cycle, but that he did not raise himself up quite as high or for as long to glimpse to the realm of true being.

The most intractable problem is that posed by the inclusion of Porphyry and Amelius. One can understand why they should be included in the list, insofar as they come at a propitious stage of the interpretive cycle, and are 'recipients' (I 6.20) from Plotinus' circle of a recovered Platonism – redactors and editors and propagandists. But we can find no specific statement in Proclus' works that acknowledges their peculiar *epopteia*. Worse, there is no indication that Porphyry wrote a commentary on the *Phaedrus*.[17] The idea that most later Platonists derived their ideas of Plotinus through Porphyry may be of some help,[18] but then we have the even greater problem of Amelius to face.

There may be clues to be found in the references to these figures elsewhere in Proclus' writings. The *Parmenides* commentary is not much help in this regard, discussing the views of both philosophers only within the compass of the *Parmenides* itself, and certain longstanding debates concerning the forms fuelled by that dialogue. Much more promising is a passage in the *Timaeus* commentary detailing Porphyry's exegesis of *Tim.* 23e2-4, which explicitly links it to the cycles of *Phdr.* 248d-e (*In Tim.* I 147.6-30). It is noteworthy *first* that his views are quoted at length, *second* that Proclus seems to assent to Porphyry's interpretation despite a counter-argument posed by Iamblichus (*In Tim.* 147.24-148.3 etc.), and *third*, that Porphyry's use of the *Phaedrus* myth is consonant with the principles laid down in the *Platonic Theology*. This is the kind of indication we need that Proclus saw more in Porphyry than an editor of Plotinus' writings, but again we are left with the problem of Amelius.

Despite these shortcomings, I would say that whereas previously I had assumed that the *Parmenides* held the key to this list, I now believe (*pace* Saffrey and Westerink [1968-97, vol. 1, 1968], 131) the *Phaedrus* to be the crux. I had previously supposed that the hermeneutical model of the

9. A historical cycle of hermeneutics in Proclus' Platonic Theology

Platonic Theology was linked to the gradual explication of the hypotheses of the *Parmenides*, from the time of Plotinus through to Syrianus and Proclus. Despite the obvious lacunae of Proclus' estimation of Porphyry and Amelius, I now believe that the *Phaedrus'* inspired mode serves as a test by which Proclus estimates the worth of his predecessors, and as a force that gives historical shape to these estimations. I would add that whereas previously I had believed that the hermeneutical model of the *Platonic Theology* held good as a general picture of Proclus' interpretative ideas, I now believe that it holds largely for the *Platonic Theology* itself, and cannot be mechanically applied to other works. And yet, one cannot avoid the fact that one is more likely to hear from Plutarch of Chaeronea than from Plutarch of Athens in the *Timaeus* commentary, and that Plotinus rarely walks abroad in Proclus' works without Porphyry or Amelius in his company.[19]

Notes

1. Gadamer (1960), 289.
2. Cf. Saffrey and Westerink (1968-97, vol. 1, 1968), 131, on an analogous potted history in Augustine's *Contra Academicos* III, xvii.37-xix.42.
3. The word exegete is Proclus' (I 6.16). For the idea of Plotinus as an exegete, cf. *Enn.* V.1.10-14, Gatti (1996), 17, P. Hadot (1963), 14.
4. Larsen (1974) 2-4, 6-7; Dillon (ed.) (1973), 10. Bidez (1913), 46, with reference to *In Tim.* II 300.24; Porphyry's *Vita Plotini* portrays an essentially friendly if competitive, and at times strained, relationship (e.g. 7.6-8 and 21.17-18).
5. Note however that Kroll (1916), 645, states that Porphyry had exerted 'keinen entscheidenden Einfluß'.
6. Dillon (ed.) (1973), 14, on Julian, *Epistle* 12; Fowden (1982), 44; Bidez (1913), 39.
7. A striking example of the same phenomenon appears at *Plat. Theol.* IV 69.6-25, where Theodorus is praised as divinely inspired and promptly refuted.
8. This point does not hold if one accepts that the Rhodian and Theodorus of Asinus are one and the same: cf. Saffrey (1984b), 65-76. Against this view cf. Dillon (1973), 387, who has two objections: (1) we have no evidence that Theodorus was Rhodian; (2) what we know of Theodorus' metaphysics is incompatible with what we have in the *In Parm.*
9. *In Parm.* 1061.13-20. On the importance of the *Parmenides* for the definition (and self-definition) of Neoplatonism, cf. Dodds (1928), 129-43; Rist (1962), 389; Dörrie (1976), 524; Whittaker (1969a), 96 (n. 5 citing Merlan [1970], 94); Merlan (1968), 105, 196; Whittaker (1969b), 109-25.
10. While terms of Bacchic ecstasy describe poetic madness (245a2) and philosophical love (253a6), the term does not occur in those passages that deal directly with the soul's cosmic travails. Metaphors of initiation and revelry occur at 249c7-8, 250b6, 250b8-c5, 250e1 251a2, 252d1, 252e1. It must be pointed out that alternative forms of Bacchic activity are to be found in the dialogues: *Ion.* 533e-534c (proposing that Bacchic madness grows out of divine patronage of the poet); *Phaedo* 69d1 (using *bakkhoi* to express the paucity of true initiates in philosophy); and *Republic* VIII 560d-e (a conspicuously negative depiction, focusing on the ingressive, even invasive, nature of Bacchics as evidenced both in myth and in ritual).

11. Note however that for Proclus *synthemata* do play a part in the structuring and nature of some entities that the myth encompasses (IV 41.12-14).

12. Ross (1955), 23 = *Eudemus* fr. 10, and 84 *Peri Philosophias* fr. 15b (Psellus), and ad loc. Bos (1995), 64. P. Hadot (1968), 127-8, discusses related but lesser claims made by Theon of Smyrna, Clement and Origen.

13. *Vita Procli* 21.15-17 mentions that Plutarch taught Proclus the *Phaedo* and Aristotle's *De Anima*. My feeling is that the latter text may well be the *Eudemus* – which would seem a more suitably propaedeutic text, and which, at least according to Bos' reconstruction, would fit well with Proclus' notion of *epopteia*. Clearly this is not the place to settle this question.

14. Hackforth (1952), 72.

15. Further evidence of Proclus' conception of himself as a Bacchant can be found at *Plat. Theol.* III 23.83.15, *Hymn* III l.11, and *Vita Procli* 38.24-5.

16. Saffrey (1975), 553-63; Athanassiadi (1993), 1, 6-7.

17. Sodano (1966), 195, P. Hadot (1968), 180-1, Beutler (1953), 279-81.

18. E.g. Courcelle (1969), 282-3.

19. See Dillon's article in this volume; also Tarrant (2004).

10

Proclus as a reader of Plato's *Timaeus*

John J. Cleary

Introduction

From our 'superior' modern perspective, on the one hand, it appears that Proclus carries far too much Neoplatonic baggage into his interpretation of Plato's *Timaeus*, but, on the other hand, from an ancient perspective he may be taken as accurately reflecting one tradition of interpretation whose legitimacy cannot be dismissed, since it can be traced back to the early Academy. Given our historical distance from Proclus, it is relatively easy to identify his interpretive presuppositions, though our own prejudices remain largely hidden from us. In this respect, Proclus might well serve as an object lesson with regard to the necessary hermeneutical situation of any reader of ancient texts; namely, that there is no such thing as an interpretation that is completely free of all presuppositions. So, as readers of Plato, we should strive to become aware of our own presuppositions as we are engaged in a dialogical conversation with the text.

In this paper, however, I will try to identify some of the hermeneutical assumptions that guided Proclus in his reading of Plato's *Timaeus*, while exploring how these assumptions are related to a central philosophical problem in the dialogue. For instance, in the third section of my paper, I will pay some attention to the traditional Platonic question of whether or not the sensible universe is generated, which is reformulated by Proclus in Neoplatonic terms as whether or not the universe is self-constituted. Even though such a question seems incidental to the dialogue itself, by highlighting the problem Proclus is obviously continuing an ancient tradition of reading Plato's *Timaeus* that had begun already within the early Academy with the dispute between Aristotle and Xenocrates as to whether Plato held the sensible universe to be eternal or rather temporally generated.[1]

In his attempt to interpret Plato's *Timaeus*, therefore, it was inevitable that Proclus should deal with the philosophical question of whether or not the sensible cosmos is generated. Within that dialogue, the character named Timaeus had argued that the sensible cosmos belongs in the class of things that are generated, so that it must have a demiurgic cause, yet he had insisted that the cosmos remains perpetually in existence because of the good will of that divine craftsman. Such apparently conflicting claims led to an interpretive crux within the early Academy when Aristotle

135

took Plato literally to be saying that the sensible cosmos is generated and so perishable, whereas Xenocrates and Crantor took him to be speaking metaphorically for the sake of explication, just as one does in talking about the construction of eternal geometrical objects.[2] For Proclus, however, the problem is resolved by placing the sensible cosmos within the Neoplatonic hierarchy of causes that descends from the transcendent One through the intelligible realm and into the sensible realm.[3] More specifically, he reformulates the problem in terms of the question of whether or not the sensible cosmos is self-constituted. Since it is not, according to him, then there must be some other higher cause on which it depends, and so Proclus undertakes the task of relating it to a hierarchy of causes that culminates in the One.[4]

i. Proclus' principles of interpretation

From our hermeneutical perspective Proclus' commentary appears deceptively like an 'open book' because he gives us so much information in his Prologue as to how he proposes to read Plato's *Timaeus*. For instance, he declares the literary genre or character of the dialogue to be a Pythagorean/Socratic inquiry into causes, which is not only physical but also theological in character. According to Proclus, the *skopos* or purpose of the *Timaeus* is to discuss the most perfect achievements[5] of natural science and to pay attention to the principal causes of nature; cf. *In Tim.* I 1.17-24. Obviously, however, Proclus has imported into his interpretation an Aristotelian understanding of the causes and of their history in Greek physiological speculation.[6] Thus, for instance, he says that the material cause is to be found already among the natural philosophers (I 2.11-15), while the enmattered formal cause is discussed in Aristotle's *Physics* (I 2.15-20). However, he thinks that proper efficient causes, along with paradigmatic and final causes, can be found only in the Pythagoreans or in Plato (I 2.29-3.5). Within the context of such a historical review, Proclus criticizes Aristotle's notion of efficient cause as falling short of the genuine efficient cause which is truly efficacious (*drasterion*). By contrast, according to Proclus, Plato uses the accessory causes (*synaitiai*) to serve merely as instruments of generation for the primordial causes (*tas protourgous aitias*); i.e. the efficient, the paradigmatic, and the final causes. For that reason, as Proclus explains, Plato established outside the universe a demiurgic Intellect or Intelligible cause within which the universe pre-exists as a model, as well as the Good which is the pre-established object of desire for the creative intellect; cf. *In Tim.* I 3.4-7.[7]

In relation to Proclus' initial discussion of the *skopos* of Plato's *Timaeus,* we should notice several important points. Despite what Plato may have said about a 'likely story', Proclus considers the Platonic physics to be exact (*akribeia*) and this means that it can be set out deductively from first principles, as Proclus himself tried to do for Aristotle's treatise on motion in his *Elements of Physics*. Thus he regards the first part of the *Timaeus* as being concerned with the true causes of the cosmos (i.e. the transcendent, efficient, and final causes), whereas the latter part of the dialogue, dealing with the Receptacle and embodied forms, is seen as belonging to Presocratic and Aristotelian types of physical inquiry. Consequently, Proclus holds that part of the purpose (*skopos*) of the *Timaeus* is to study the primary causes of the universe, ascending through the hypercosmic deities from the Demiurge (Intellective) to the living Intelligible, and ultimately to the One. It is within the context of such a *skopos* for the *Timaeus* that we should understand Proclus' question about the self-constitution of the universe, given that there is no such question in Plato's text.[8] Similarly, Proclus pursues in great detail the question about the identity (and triadic constitution) of the Demiurge, which Plato had left vague and open-ended.

We can see how these preoccupations influence the *divisio textus* for the *Timaeus* given by Proclus at *In Tim.* I 4.6-6.16. He refers back to the target (*skopos*) being aimed at (*stochazesthai*) in Plato's *Timaeus*; namely, to show that the cosmos is a god, endowed with a soul and an intellect, and having characteristics produced by a demiurgic intellect, which makes it a copy of the model in the Living Intellect with the participation of the Good. Assuming this to be the purpose of the *Timaeus*, Proclus outlines the following division of the text:

(a) the order of the universe is made visible through images;
(b) in the middle, the whole creation of the cosmos is presented;
(c) finally, the partial works and last achievements of the demiurges are presented.

Under the second (b) division, Proclus discusses Plato's teaching about the demiurgic or efficient cause of the universe, as well as about the paradigmatic and final causes. He takes this section to be an inquiry into causes, and hence to be exact, despite what Plato says about the *Timaeus* being an *eikos logos*.

In this way, Proclus treats the 'hypotheses' (27d5-28b5) and 'demonstrations' (28b5-29d5) as presuppositions or assumptions (I 4.28; I 8.26-8) of Plato's treatise about the demiurgic ordering of the whole universe.[9] For him this inquiry has a status superior to that of physics, since it deals with the higher principles; and so it is partly theology. Thus he emphasizes Plato's separation of *Timaeus* 27d5-29d5 from the rest of the dialogue, by considering it almost as if it were a self-contained treatise on causes.[10] Subsequently, he treats the creation of the body and soul of the universe as a production of the universal Demiurge, before the task of creating mankind is handed over to the secondary (and particular) demiurges. In general, therefore, I agree with Alain Lernould (2001, 73) when he claims that Proclus' division of the text of the *Timaeus* conforms very well with Proclus' own plan for his commentary. First there is the Proemion or

Prelude in which the Hypotheses and Demonstrations are discussed. Then there is a discussion of the creation of the universe and its parts through the action of the universal and particular demiurges, which takes up most of the extant commentary by Proclus. Finally comes the topic of the last achievement of the particular demiurges in shaping the matter of the cosmos to suit the immanent forms, which is projected for the latter (non-extant) part of the commentary on the *Timaeus*.

Subsequently (*In Tim.* I 7.17ff.), when specifying the genre (*eidos*) or character of the dialogue, Proclus reports as universally accepted that Plato was inspired by a book from Timaeus the Locrian.[11] He also takes as agreed, by those familiar with Plato's writings, that the character (*ethos*) of the dialogue is Socratic; namely, as displaying *philanthropia* and as giving proofs. So, within this dialogue, Plato combines the spirit of Socrates with that of the Pythagoreans.[12] According to Proclus, the dialogue adopts from the Pythagoreans their sublimity of spirit, their intellectuality, their inspiration, their tendency to make everything depend on the intelligible, to define everything by numbers, to express things through symbols, and to prove things mystically in an elevated tone. On the other hand, the dialogue adopts from Socrates his conviviality, his good spirit, the tendency to give proofs, the capacity to grasp reality through images, his ethical character, and all such things. Therefore the dialogue itself is solemn, holy, and it deduces from above (*anôthen*) all its conclusions from first principles (*apo tôn prôtistôn archôn* – I 8.2-3), while it mixes the apophantic with the demonstrative (*apodeiktikon*). Furthermore, he claims that the dialogue presents for consideration natural things, not only physically but also from a theological perspective (*In Tim.* I 8.4ff.). By way of justification for this latter claim, Proclus argues that Nature herself can guide the corporeal on the right lines only insofar as she herself is dependent on the gods and is permeated by their inspiration. Nature neither possesses fully the quality of the divine nor is she completely deprived of divine properties, as she is illuminated (*proslampesthai*) by the gods. In addition, given that it is appropriate to assimilate the discourse to the realities which it interprets, as Timaeus says (*Tim.* 29b), then it is also proper (*prepon*) that the dialogue have not only a physical but also a theological character in imitation of Nature (*mimoumenon tên physin*), which it studies.

If one had any doubts about the hermeneutical orientation of Proclus' commentary, they should be laid to rest by his digression on the notion of physis; cf. *In Tim.* I 9.31ff. Since the *Timaeus* sets out to examine Nature, it would be proper to know what is nature (*tis hê physis*) and from what it proceeds (*pothen proeisi*) and how far (*mechri tinos*) it extends its productions. Proclus now gives a typical Aristotelian review of predecessors on the use of the term *physis*, which is clearly inspired by Aristotle's survey in *Physics* II. For instance, Proclus refers to Antiphon giving the name *physis* to matter (*hylê*), and to Aristotle who gave the same name to form (*eidos*) in many places (*Phy.* II.1, 193a28), while others gave the name to the whole (*to holon*), as Plato reports in the *Laws* (X 892b), where the name is applied to naturally produced things. Others gave the name *physis* to natural powers or qualities such as heavy/light, density/fineness, like some Peripatetics and older natural philosophers. Again others called 'nature' the artifice of the divine (*technê theou*), while others called it soul (*psychê*).

By contrast, according to Proclus, Plato refuses to give the name *physis* in its primary sense (*prôtôs*) to matter or to the enmattered form or to body (*sôma*) or to natural powers. Yet he also hesitates to call soul itself nature, though (again according to Proclus) he gives us the most correct teaching on nature by placing it in the middle between soul and the bodily powers because, on the one hand, it (nature) is inferior to soul by virtue of being dispersed through bodies and not returning to itself (*mê epistrephei eis hautên*); whereas, on the other hand, it is superior to what comes after it by virtue of containing the creative seeds (*logoi*) of everything and by virtue of generating living things. According to the common notions (*koinai ennoiai*), one must distinguish between nature (*physis*), according to nature (*kata physin*), and by nature (*têi physei*). Since the product of art is different from the art itself, Nature is no less different from the intellective soul (*psychê noêra*, *In Tim.* I 10.24). For Nature belongs to bodies, since it plunges into body and is inseparable (*achôristos*) from it, whereas soul is separate (*chôristos*) and is rooted (*hidrytai*) in itself, while simultaneously belonging to another. On the one hand, soul does participate in another thing (body) but, on the other hand, it does not veer (*neuein*) towards the participant, so that it belongs to itself, just as the father of the soul is not participated but belongs uniquely to himself.

Eventually (*In Tim.* I 12.26ff.), as a result of this discussion, Proclus provides a summary definition of 'nature' according to Plato; namely, an incorporeal essence (*ousia asômatos*), which is inseparable from bodies (*achôristos sômatôn*), which has in itself the creative principles (*logoi*) of bodies, and which is incapable of looking back to itself (*eis heautên horan*).[13] According to Proclus, it is clear from this definition in what way the dialogue, which discusses the making of the whole cosmos, is 'physical' (*physikos*). But notice that he is careful to retain the theological dimension of 'higher' causes throughout his discussion of nature.

At this point (I 13.1ff.), Proclus makes some revealing classificatory remarks. According to him, the whole of philosophy is divided into a theory of intelligibles (*peri tôn noêtôn*) and a theory of encosmic beings (*peri tôn enkosmiôn*), since the cosmos is double (*ditton*); i.e. the intelligible (*noêtos*) and the sensible (*aisthêtos*), as Plato himself says (*Tim.* 30c9). But the *Parmenides* contains the treatise on intelligibles, while the *Timaeus* deals with encosmic beings; the first dialogue teaches us about all the divine classes of being, while the latter deals with all the procession (*proodos*) of encosmic beings. Yet the *Parmenides* does not completely neglect the theory of beings within the universe, nor does the *Timaeus* neglect the theory of intelligibles because the sensibles are in the intelligibles paradigmatically (*paradigmatikôs*), while the intelligibles are in the sensibles iconically (*eikonikôs*).

Still, the *Timaeus* is more concerned with the physical domain (*peri to physikon*), whereas the *Parmenides* is concerned with the theological domain (*peri to theologikon*), in conformity with the persons after whom these dialogues are named. For, according to Proclus, the historical Timaeus had already written a physical treatise concerning the universe (*gramma peri tês tou pantos ... physeôs* – I 13.13-14), just as the historical Parmenides had already written a treatise about real being (*peri tôn ontôs ontôn*). Thus, according to Proclus, Iamblichus was correct in saying that the whole philosophy of Plato is contained in the two eponymous dialogues, given that everything which concerns the encosmic beings and the hypercosmic beings is to be found completed in these dialogues, and there is no class of beings which is left unexplored.

Significantly, Proclus claims (*In Tim.* I 13.20) that there is a deep similarity between the modes of presentation in the *Timaeus* and in the *Parmenides*; for just as Timaeus traces the cause of things in the universe back (*anagei*) to the Demiurge, so also Parmenides makes the procession (*proodos*) of all things depend on the One (*exaptei tou henos*). In other words, the *Timaeus* shows how everything participates in the providence of the Demiurge, while the *Parmenides* shows how everything participates in the completely unitary essence. In addition, just as Timaeus considers encosmic beings in the mode of images before engaging in the science of Nature, similarly Parmenides makes an inquiry into immaterial forms prior to engaging in theology. Just as in the *Timaeus* it was necessary first to practise by means of discussion of the best political regime before ascending to grasp the universe, so also in the *Parmenides* it was necessary to exercise one's mind with the challenging difficulties about the Forms before ascending to the mystical contemplation of the Henads.

One thing that may appear odd to us as modern readers of Plato's *Timaeus* is the rather sharp distinction which Proclus tries to make between Platonic and Aristotelian senses of cause. What is particularly striking is his describing as *synaitiai* such forms and matter as are embodied in the sensible universe, since in his physics Aristotle treats form and matter are causes in the full sense. Despite Aristotle's report that Plato separated the Forms, one might even conclude that the Platonic causes are not much different from the Aristotelian. Hence we may find rather strained the emphasis which Proclus puts on the higher 'theological' status of the Platonic causes, such as efficient, paradigmatic and final causes which are integral to the role of the creative Demiurge. But, once again, I think this emphasis must be understood within the context of a Neoplatonic hierarchy of causes, which represents a substantive development beyond the thinking of both Plato and Aristotle. One must also take account of Proclus' typical Neoplatonic attempt to reconcile the Platonic and Aristotelian doctrines of causality by treating the former as theological and the latter as physical. For instance, in his *Commentary on the Parmenides* (841.26), Proclus conceives of Platonic Forms as being both paradigmatic and creative, thereby combining the notion of a creative Demiurge with Aristotle's notion of the divine as a final cause.

ii. Interlude on prayer

Perhaps the most revealing glimpse of Proclus' tendency to treat Plato's *Timaeus* as a treatise on the first principles of nature is given through his peculiar interpretation of the passage where Timaeus invokes the gods to aid him in the project which he is about to undertake. What seems to us like a conventional invocation on the part of Timaeus is seized upon by Proclus as an opportunity for a longish excursus (*In Tim.* II 206.26-214.12) on the cosmological significance of prayer. He proposes (207.21ff.) to examine the essence (*ousia*) of prayer and its perfection, along with its origin within souls. Consistent with his general approach to the *Timaeus,* Proclus gives the following (208.23ff.) noteworthy justification of prayer: since we are part of the whole (*tou holou*), it is proper to pray because it is through conversion (*epistrophê*) to the whole that we obtain salvation (*sôtêria*). Such a justification is subsequently (209.9ff.) clarified in terms of the following starting-point: all beings are progeny of the gods, and they remain rooted in the gods. Thus the One is everywhere, insofar as each thing takes its existence from the gods, and while everything proceeds from the gods yet it remains rooted in them. Here Proclus is invoking the 'wondrous way' (*thaumaston*) in which effects both proceed from their causes, and also remain in them.

In fact, the typical Proclean triad of remaining, procession, and return is being invoked here (210.2ff.) to clarify the function of prayer in the *Timaeus*. When things have proceeded, they must also return; thereby following the triadic motion that brings them to perfection when they are enveloped by the gods and the primary henads. Thus, all things both remain in and return to the gods; so that they receive from Nature (*para tês physeôs* – 210.18) powers and characteristics corresponding to the essences of the gods. According to Proclus (210.27ff.), this explains why the soul has the double character of 'remaining' (*menein*) and of 'reverting' (*epistrephein*); namely, according to the One it is rooted in the gods, whereas according to intellect it has the capacity to revert to them. But it is the activity of prayer which realizes this capacity for reversion to the gods within the soul. In fact, the ultimate goal of prayer for Proclus is the complete union of the soul with the divine, when the one of the soul and the one of the divine constitute a single activity. But, on the way to this goal, several stages must first be reached through prayer; e.g. knowledge of classes of the divine, being at home with (*oikeiôsis*) the divine, contact with the divine, immediate proximity to the divine, and finally mystical union with the divine.[14]

Subsequently (*In Tim.* II 217.24-6), Proclus refers back to the invocation of the gods by Timaeus as evidence in support of his own contention that natural philosophy is a kind of theology because natural things have a divine aspect insofar as they are generated by the gods. This claim is made within the context of his general discussion (217.18ff.) of the different aspects under which one might consider the universe; namely, as corporeal, as participating in both the whole soul and the particular souls, or as having intellect. Indeed, it is the general principle that the word 'logos' can be said in many ways, which he explicitly (218.13) adopts from his teacher Syrianus, that enables Proclus to address a puzzle arising from the text of the *Timaeus*: namely, Plato's use of the word *pêi* at 27c4. Proclus is concerned with this small point of textual exegesis mainly because it has a direct bearing on what he takes to be the central problem of the dialogue; i.e. whether or not the sensible cosmos is generated. For instance, Proclus reports (219.10ff.) that for Albinus the cosmos is eternal in a way (*pêi aei ôn*) or, as Proclus explains, in a way generated but in another way ungenerated. Thus Albinus belongs among the older interpreters (218.1ff.) who take the particle *pêi* in this double way.[15] Having considered and rejected some interpretations of previous exegetes like Iamblichus, Proclus concludes that *pêi* does not refer directly to the universe itself but rather to different ways of speaking about it; namely, either intellectually (*noêrôs*), or scientifically (*epistêmonikôs*), or didactically (*didaskalikôs*).

iii. The Demiurge as efficient cause of the sensible cosmos

However, it is with regard to the principal 'hypothesis' of the *Timaeus* that we can see the full consequences of Proclus' hermeneutical assumptions about the dialogue. Firstly, as the starting-point of the whole inquiry, he identifies the leading question of whether the sensible cosmos is generated or ungenerated. Before giving his own answer to the question, he reviews in a typical Aristotelian manner the answers given by some previous commentators, which are reflected in particular readings of the text of the *Timaeus*. On the one hand, there is Albinus who interprets the question of whether the universe is generated as being about whether it has a more ultimate cause.[16] On the other hand, Porphyry and Iamblichus take the question to express a standard aporia as to whether or not the sensible universe is generated. In fact, according to Proclus, the correct answer to this question is of the greatest importance for the whole science of physics. Beginning from this starting-point (*ek tês hypotheseôs*), he thinks we can discern the character of the universe according to its essence (*ousia*) and powers (*dynameis*), as will become clear later (*In Tim.* I 227ff.). So he makes the following preliminary statement (219.28-31): 'Let us say that the discourse about the universe is undertaken for the sake of instruction (*didaskalias heneka*),[17] beginning from the hypothesis of whether the universe is generated or ungenerated, and from this starting-point drawing out all the other things as consequences.'

Now let us consider some of Proclus' comments (*In Tim.* I 258.8ff.) on Plato's axiom at *Timaeus* 28a: 'Everything which is generated must be generated by some cause'. Proclus takes Plato to be proceeding according to the geometrical method of assuming basic axioms, having already set down his definitions. In other words, after defining 'what is being' (*ti to on*), and 'what is generated' (*ti to gignomenon*), Plato posits (*prostithesi*) other common notions (*koinai ennoiai*); i.e. that everything which is generated comes to be from some cause, and that it is impossible for something to come to be, unless it is generated from some cause, and that the product is beautiful if it is created according to an eternal paradigm. Proclus insists that Plato is not referring here (*Tim.* 27d5) to his method of division, but is rather making distinctions between his basic principles; cf. *In Tim.* I 226.22-9.

Proclus (258.23-6) adopts an Aristotelian analysis when he distinguishes between one proposition as a middle term (*hôs meson*) and the other as conclusion (*hôs symperasma*); the first is most evident, while the latter is less evident and less clear. Thus Proclus analyses the whole argument in terms of a categorical syllogism:

Premise 1: It is impossible for anything generated to be generated without a cause;
Premise 2: But everything for which it is impossible to be generated without a cause is necessarily generated from some cause;
Conclusion: Therefore, everything generated is necessarily generated by some cause.

In reflecting on the ontological reason why the middle term in this syllogism is clearer than the conclusion, Proclus suggests (259.19ff.) that it is easy to understand how, if something generated is separated from its cause, then it will lack power and force (*adynaton esti kai asthenes*), since it cannot conserve itself (*heauto sôzein*), nor is it maintained through itself (*mêd' hyph' heautou synechomenon*). Since it does not contain within itself the cause of its conservation and coherence, it is clear that, if it is separated from that cause, it will be reduced by itself to impotence (*hôs adynaton*) and will tend to disperse into non-being. For Proclus (259.24-7) what this shows is that any generated being cannot come into being without a cause, because if it came into being it did so through the action of a producer (*hypo tinos gignetai poiountos*). In support of his interpretation, Proclus cites the *Philebus* (26e2-4, 27a1ff.) where Plato posits a producer (*to poioun*) for that which is produced or generated. But this producer must either be a self-producer or be produced by something else. If it is produced by itself then it is a being which is eternal.

In another of his revealing digressions, Proclus (*In Tim.* I 260.19-261.1)

143

discusses the metaphysical implications of Plato's concept of *aition*. By means of the term 'cause' (*aition*), Plato reveals the unique character (*henoeidê*) of the demiurgic principle, in the sense that the name 'cause' indicates that which produces (*to demiourgikon*) and not simply that which sustains (*to hypostatikon*) another thing. Notice that in insisting upon the singularity of the efficient cause here (cf. also 262.2), presumably in order to distinguish it from the formal and final causes, Proclus seems to imply that the term 'cause' belongs most properly to efficient causality.

This implication becomes explicit when Proclus subsequently (261.1ff.) considers the different senses of 'cause' according to Aristotle, which he presumes that every exegete of Plato would have in mind. By contrast with Aristotle's four causes, Plato espouses three senses of cause and of accessory cause (*synaitia*). However, while acknowledging these different senses of cause in Plato and Aristotle, Proclus insists that for Plato the efficient cause is most strictly a cause, and so Proclus remarks (261.23-5) on his talk about a 'certain cause' (*aitiou tinos*) being responsible for generation. He insists that Plato has in mind the efficient cause when he talks about the intellect of the universe (*ho nous tou pantos*) and the soul and nature.[18] Even though there is a multiplicity of effects and of causes, there is not a plurality of efficient causes for a particular effect, and hence Plato is correct to talk about a 'certain cause' because a particular effect is always created by a certain cause, and not by all of them.

As is well known, Proclus' own interpretation of Plato's question of whether or not the sensible cosmos is generated, rests on a long tradition of distinguishing between different senses of 'generated'.[19] There is no need for me to rehearse these distinctions here, though I do want to draw attention to Proclus' (*In Tim.* I 293.6-294.28) own way of resolving the apparent contradiction involved in Plato saying that the sensible cosmos is generated and yet never perishes. For Proclus (293.15-20) there is a crucial distinction to be made between the cosmos being imperishable in the temporal sense of lasting throughout all time,[20] and being perishable in the sense of being incapable of conserving itself in existence. It is in the latter sense that the sensible cosmos is perishable, precisely because it is corporeal.[21]

It may be worthwhile for us to dwell somewhat on Proclus' argument for this conclusion, while also paying some attention to the language in which it is couched. He claims that no body has the capacity to generate itself or to preserve itself in existence. First he argues that every generator is an efficient cause, and that every efficient cause is incorporeal (*pan de to poioun asômaton esti*, 293.24). By way of justification for this rather unaristotelian conclusion, Proclus argues that, even if the mover is a body, it creates something by means of incorporeal forces (*dynamesin asômatois*). Therefore, every generator is incorporeal, and everything which has the capacity for conserving something also produces the double effect of unity and indissolubility. Thus, everything which produces such an effect is itself indivisible (*ameres*). Therefore, Proclus concludes that, whatever has the capacity for preserving itself (*to heautou synektikon*) cannot be a body because holding together (*to synechein*) does not belong to body, which is divisible insofar as it is a body.

Although he is quite clearly drawing on Aristotle's *Physics* for some of his claims about body, Proclus explicitly appeals to Plato's *Sophist* (246a7-c2) where the view of the materialists that everything is bodily is critically examined. On this basis Proclus argues that what holds bodies together is something indivisible (*to synechon ameres, In Tim.* I 294.1); so that, even if what is conserved is corporeal (as in the case of the sensible cosmos), it is not the body which conserves itself but rather something incorporeal that preserves it. Thus, using an emphatic *anankê*, Proclus concludes that, necessarily, whatever conserves itself is indivisible (*ameres einai to hyp' heautou synechomenon* – 294.2-3). Terminologically, what is noteworthy about this whole argument is that Proclus does not use the familiar contraries of *authypostaton* and *anhypostaton* with reference to the mode of being of the sensible cosmos. The first of these terms is only briefly mentioned earlier (*In Tim.* I 277.8-32) in an ostensible historical reference[22] to Crantor and the Academic view that the sensible cosmos is not self-generated or self-constituted (*ouk onta autogonon oude authypostaton* – I 277.9-10).[23] Significantly, however, Proclus declares (I 277.14-15) what he takes to be the Academic interpretation of the *Timaeus* to be the most true.

So, when Plato describes the sensible cosmos as something which is generated, this is taken by Proclus to mean that it has a cause other than itself and, therefore, that it does not belong among those higher beings which are self-constituted. For further clarification of this notion in Proclus, we might perhaps refer to his *Elements of Theology*, Proposition 40, which states that everything which proceeds from another cause is subordinate to principles which get their substance from themselves and have a self-constituted existence.[24] This notion may be further clarified through Proposition 42, which states that everything which is self-constituted is capable of reversion upon itself. But Proposition 44 states that everything which is capable of reversion upon itself in respect of its activity is also reverted upon itself in respect of its existence. However, we know from Propositions 15 and 16 that self-reversion is characteristic of incorporeal entities, so that we may infer that it does not belong to corporeal things like the sensible cosmos. This inference is confirmed by Propositions 45 and 46, which taken together state that everything which is self-constituted is ungenerated (*agenêton*) and imperishable (*aphtharton*). This is further confirmed by Proposition 47, which states that everything which is self-constituted is without parts and simple. Thus, as Proposition 49 claims, everything which is self-constituted is eternal. Conversely, as Proposition 48 makes clear, everything that is not eternal either is composite or has its subsistence in another.

Such propositions about the self-constitution of the cosmos only make sense within a Neoplatonic hierarchy of being, given that Proclus' intention is to establish the inferior position of the sensible cosmos within that schema, and thereby establish the necessity of higher explanatory principles such as Forms and Intellect. In his *Parmenides* commentary (*In Parm.* 786-7), for instance, the argument has the typical structure of a *reductio ad absurdum*: If this sensible cosmos were self-constituted, many absurd results would follow. For whatever is self-constituted must be without parts, since everything that creates and everything that generates is altogether incorporeal. Proclus claims that even bodies themselves produce their effects by means of incorporeal powers; e.g. fire produces heat (by hotness). Assuming that whatever creates must be incorporeal, and since in a self-constituted thing it is the same thing that creates and is created, then the self-constituted thing must be altogether without parts. But the physical cosmos does not have such a character, since every body is divisible in every way; and so the cosmos is not self-constituted.

Within this passage in the *Parmenides* commentary, Proclus goes on to argue that the cosmos is not self-activating, in contrast to self-constituting things which are self-generating, and so naturally able to act on themselves. In effect, the argument is that the cosmos is not self-moving, since it is corporeal. Thus the cosmos derives its being from some other cause which is higher. But this leads Proclus to raise a related question about whether this cause acts by rational choice, or whether it produces the universe by its very being. If it acts by deliberate choice, its action will be unstable and variable; so that the resulting cosmos would be perishable.[25] Judging from Plato's account of the creative activity of the Demiurge in the *Timaeus*, one might think that he accepted this implication about the perishability of the cosmos, even if it never actually perishes; cf. *Tim.* 41a-b. But Proclus claims that, since the cosmos is sempiternal, what creates it must do so by its very being or essence (*autôi tôi einai*).[26] In fact, Proclus says (*In Parm.* 787.1), everything which acts by deliberate choice necessarily has some creative activity that it exercises by its very being; e.g. our soul does many things by choice but it gives life to the body by virtue of its very essence. In this argument he is appealing to a general principle of Proclean metaphysics (cf. *ET* Prop. 57); namely, if the power of creating by its very essence extends more widely than creating by deliberate choice, then it flows from some higher cause. Proclus explains that such creative activity is effortless, and is also characteristic of the divine.[27]

These parallels from *Elements of Theology* and the *Commentary on Plato's Parmenides* provide some of the metaphysical reasons[28] as to why Proclus holds that the sensible cosmos is not self-constituted but rather depends for its subsistence on the Demiurge as an external cause of its existence. However, this conclusion is also clear from his commentary on the *Timaeus,* which argues in terms of the efficient causality of the Demiurge with respect to the sensible cosmos as a product.

Conclusion

Thus, once again, I find myself in agreement with Alain Lernould (2001, 159) about Proclus' guiding idea in his explication of *Timaeus* 27d6; namely, that the sensible cosmos is generated according to its essence (*kat' ousian*). Proclus' interpretation of Plato's distinction between eternal and generated being is guided by the idea that the universe is generated in this double sense: (1) that it does not have in itself the principle of its own existence (*anhypostaton*) – by contrast with beings that are self-constituted (*authypostaton*); (2) and that it has its essence in time, even if it lasts throughout all time. These two meanings of the 'generation' of the cosmos are contained in this single thesis that the cosmos is generated according to its essence. This thesis results from Proclus' application to the sensible cosmos of the first hypothesis of the *Timaeus*. Thus, in the first part of his interpretation, Proclus devotes his efforts to distinguishing the cosmos which is always (*aei*) generated, insofar as it is sensible, not only from intelligible being, which is always (*aei*) eternal, but also from soul, which is intermediate between sensible and intelligible being.

I think it is clear that Proclus is conscious of standing at the end of a long tradition of interpreting Plato's *Timaeus* that goes right back to the early Academy, and obviously this tradition dominates his whole interpretation of the dialogue. For instance, he feels obliged to adopt a solution to the old problem of whether or not the sensible universe is generated, and his answer to this question influences the way in which he reads Plato's *Timaeus*. Significantly enough for our knowledge of that whole tradition, the question takes up so much space in Proclus' commentary that it has become the major source for scholars who want to discover the views of obscure Middle Platonists or even of better known Neoplatonists on this and related questions. For instance, he reports the minority Platonic view of Plutarch and Atticus, who took Plato literally as saying that the sensible cosmos is temporally generated. By contrast, Proclus refuses to take such talk of generation literally, arguing that the ontological dependence of the sensible universe on the creative Demiurge does not involve creation in time. Having adopted a solution to the traditional problem, Proclus proceeds to read the whole dialogue in this light, while criticizing alternative readings based on different solutions. In this way, Proclus continues the long tradition of reading Plato's *Timaeus* in the light of a particular solution to the leading metaphysical question about the relationship between the sensible universe and a creative Demiurge.

Notes

1. See Aristotle, *De Caelo* 279b32ff., Xenocrates, frs 153-8 and 163 Isnardi, Speusippus, frs 41 and 72 Tarán. Plutarch and Atticus seem to be in the minority among Platonists in claiming that Plato held the sensible universe to be temporally generated; cf. Proclus, *In Tim.* I 276.30ff. According to Baltes (1976, I, 22), Xenocrates probably argued for the eternity of the sensible world from the eternality of the World-Soul, while reinterpreting Plato's temporal talk as being for the sake of explanation; cf. *In Tim.* I 395.1-10.

2. The typical formulae associated with this view are *didaskalias* (or *theôrias*) *charin* and *saphêneias* (or *theôrias*) *heneka,* which Theophrastus reported with reference to the Academy, according to Philoponus; cf. *Aet.* VI.8.145.20ff.; VI.8.148.7ff.; VI.21.188.9ff.; VI.27.220.22ff.

3. See Plotinus *Enn.* II.9.3.1-14; VI.1.6.37ff.

4. In this respect, Proclus seems to accept the monism of Plotinus in taking the One to be the single and ultimate cause of all things, including matter; cf. *In Tim.* I 370.13-371.8. By contrast, for instance, Atticus is rather unorthodox in treating pre-cosmic matter as independent of any divine cause; cf. *In Tim.* I 283.27-285.7; 384.2.

5. In our email correspondence, Carlos Steel has informed me that *horoi* is often used by Proclus to refer to whatever provides perfection, measure or structure; cf. *In Remp.* I 247.24; *In Tim.* II 194.10.

6. Alain Lernould has suggested to me through email correspondence that Proclus' tendency to reconcile Plato and Aristotle is consistent with the Pythagorean tradition of cultivating friendship as part of the effort to reunite ourselves with the divine; cf. Iamblichus, *Life of Pythagoras,* sections 229 and 240.

7. According to Proclus, it is the presence of the Good in the demiurgic intellect that enables it to be creative and productive; cf. *In Tim.* I 361.6-16. Thus, within the divine Demiurge, the triad of efficient, paradigmatic, and final causality is a manifestation of the creative power of the Good or the One; cf. *In Tim.* I 363.9-364.23; 368.15ff., 388.9-28.

8. In some written comments on an earlier draft, David Runia has pointed out that the question of whether the cosmos is self-constituted is hardly extraneous to the concerns of the dialogue, especially if we broaden the perspective with a reference to *Laws* X, where the question of whether the cosmos is by design, by nature or by chance is discussed. See also Runia (1997) where he argues that the Proemium of the *Timaeus* should be treated as a dialectical exercise, beginning from hypotheses, like that found in Plato's *Phaedrus* as a prelude to a mythical discourse.

9. See also *In Tim.* I 235.32-238.5 for a detailed discussion by Proclus of this topic.

10. David Runia has pointed out to me that Proclus is following the lead of Plato in making this separation of the Proemium from the rest of the dialogue. See also Runia (1997).

11. It is an interesting hermeneutical question (which I cannot discuss here) as to why the Middle Platonic tradition felt it necessary to invent a work, *Peri physios kosmô kai psychas,* which was written in Doric and attributed to Timaeus of Locrus. Perhaps it was an indirect appeal to the authority of Pythagoras, since Aetius (II 4.1) reports as the view of Pythagoras that the cosmos is *genêtos kat' epinoian,* which looks very like the view of Xenocrates and Crantor, who may themselves have appealed to the authority of Pythagoras; cf. Baltes (1976, I, 94-6).

12. This remark seems to imply for Proclus that the *Timeaus* dialogue combines the scientific character of both mathematics and dialectic, with the latter being the higher science which proves the hypotheses of mathematics; cf. *In Eucl.* 42.16; *In Parm.* 986.29

13. See also *In Tim.* I 11.9-19 for a preliminary account of nature, according to Proclus.

14. See Dillon (2002, 288-90) for a brief account of the different stages of prayer, according to Proclus, that lead the human soul towards mystical union with the divine.

15. Plutarch (*Procr. An.* 9.1016d) has a similar double intepretation of *pêi*, and this seems to be part of the tradition of taking 'generation' in many different senses; cf. *In Tim.* I 340.25.

16. We should notice the significance of Albinus as foreshadowing Proclus' own more elaborate solution. In the *Didaskalikos* (14.3, 169.26ff), once confidently claimed for Albinus, it is argued that Plato's talk of the 'generation' of the cosmos should not be taken literally but rather as saying that it is always in generation, and so is in need of some higher cause for its existence. In other words, the cosmos is not self-subsistent but rather dependent on some higher cause such as a continually creative god; cf. Baltes (1976, I, 96ff.).

17. Although the implicit reference to the view of Xenocrates and Cantor is unmistakable in the language, yet Proclus is rather following Iamblichus in taking Plato's talk of 'generation' in the Timaeus as 'theoretical' or hypothetical.

18. Proclus later (*In Tim.* I 267.4) castigates Aristotle for departing from the authentic Platonic teaching when he traces the so-called 'upward tension' towards the unmoved mover, without tracing the downward chain of causal dependence.

19. For some of these senses of 'generated' in Taurus and Porphyry, see Philoponus, *Aet.* VI.8.145.7-147.25, 148.7ff.; VI.10.154.6ff.; VI.23.193.25ff.; VI.25, 200.10ff.; VI.27.223.8-19.

20. With respect to things which exist in time, Proclus distinguishes elsewhere (*ET* Prop. 55) between those which have a perpetual duration (*aei chronon*) and those which have a dated existence in a part of time (*en merei chronou*). Obviously, it is in the first sense that the sensible cosmos exists in time.

21. For Neoplatonists like Proclus, the fact that the cosmos is sensible and corporeal does not imply that it must have a temporal beginning but rather having such qualities implies lack of unity or simplicity, lack of independence or, more specifically, dependence on a higher cause; cf. Simplicius, *In De Caelo* 299.22.

22. Whittaker (1975) has shown convincingly that Crantor could not have used the term *authypostaton*, whose use Dillon (1973, 303) dates as late as Iamblichus. Whittaker also points out that no usage of *autogonos* can be reliably dated before Porphyry. According to Whittaker, Proclus mistakenly attributes to Crantor what was historically a Middle Platonic response to the Stoic thesis that the cosmos is self-caused. However, as Lernould (2001, 244 n. 40) notes, Proclus is contrasting Crantor, not with the Stoics, but with Plutarch and Atticus, who both interpret the *Timaeus* discussion of generation in a strong temporal sense.

23. At *In Tim.* I 232.12ff. Proclus elaborates on the contrast between *authypostaton* and *anhypostaton* in terms of the superiority in being of what is self-constituted over what is dependent on an external cause for its existence. But, given that he accepts the Plotinian monistic system in which everything depends on the One as an ultimate cause, it is unclear how there can be such self-constituted or independent things; cf. *Enn.* IV.8.6.1-28.

24. The argument in Proposition 40 seems to depend on that of Proposition 9 that whatever is self-sufficient (*autarkes*), either with respect to being (*kat'ousian*) or activity (*kat'energeian*), is superior (*kreitton*) to anything that is dependent on another as the cause of its completeness.

25. Cf. Plotinus, *Enn.* III.2, for a similar rejection as inappropriate of talk about the Demiurge planning or choosing to create the sensible cosmos, since there must be an eternal product of an eternally active cause. According to Plotinus (II.9.7.1ff.), the cosmos is a natural image (*physei eikôn*) of an eternal Paradigm, and the eternity of the copy follows from the eternity of the paradigm; cf. *Enn.* V.8.12.17-26, Proclus, *In Parm.* 824.28ff., 911.1ff., 1129.15ff. This orthodox Neoplatonic argument is also used by Proclus in Argument II of his *On the Eternity of the World*.

26. Cf. Trouillard (1958) for a classic elucidation of this Neoplatonic notion of causality. In his criticism of Atticus for accepting the temporal generation of the cosmos, Proclus argues that, since the Demiurge is eternally creative, the universe must be sempiternal and coextensive with the whole of time; cf. *In Tim.* I 366.20-5 and 367-8 passim.

27. A corollary of *ET* 34 states that all things proceed from intelligence (*nous*), since it is an object of desire for all things. Thus, according to Proclus, it is from intelligence that the whole world-order (*kosmos*) is derived, even though the latter is sempiternal. Perhaps this represents another attempt to reconcile Plato's talk of the 'generation' of a cosmos in the *Timaeus* with the Academic tradition that the world-order is eternal. If the procession is logical rather than temporal, intelligence can proceed eternally and be eternally reverted, while still remaining steadfast in its own place in the cosmos.

28. I accept that Proclus' commentary on the *Timaeus* is temporally prior in composition to his *Elements of Theology,* but this does not prevent us from using the latter to clarify the former. Indeed, in her written comments on my conference paper, M. Martijn has plausibly suggested to me that many of the metaphysical principles formulated in *ET* may have been provoked by interpretative difficulties arising from apparent inconsistencies in the *Timaeus* commentary.

The *eikôs mythos* in Proclus' commentary on the *Timaeus*[1]

Marije Martijn

In the very first sentence of his commentary on the *Timaeus*, as well as on several other occasions, Proclus tells us that this dialogue in its entirety concerns the science of nature.[2] Now since nature itself has a divine aspect, he continues, and, since Plato himself tells us that a *logos* should be likened to its subject matter, it is only fitting that the *Timaeus* combines the science of nature with theology.[3] In his commentary, Proclus seems to be rather keen on drawing our attention to the fact that Platonic physics transcend the banal level of the sensible world, e.g. by repeatedly comparing Plato's method to that of a geometer. My aim in this paper is to show that this divine aspect of nature, combined with Neoplatonic hermeneutics, accounts for Proclus' treatment of the famous *eikôs mythos* passage in the Proemium of the *Timaeus*.

This paper consists of three parts. Part 1 contains a discussion of formal aspects of Proclus' treatment of the Proemium of the *Timaeus*. How does the commentator go about the task of elucidating the text on which he is commenting? The main focus is on the division of the text into *lemmata*, and on one exegetical technique involved in that division: the distinction within the discussion of the lemmas of Plato's text between *theôria* (general theory) and *lexis* (terms). One thing that stands out in the distribution of the exegesis is Proclus' relatively meagre treatment – compared to contemporary commentators – of Timaeus' remarks about the *eikôs mythos*. Part 2 is a description of this *eikôs mythos* as presented by Timaeus, of the modern debate and of Proclus' interpretation thereof. In Part 3, finally, the role of theology in physics and of the Neoplatonist principle of *heis skopos* as accounting for Proclus' 'lack of interest' in the *eikôs mythos* will be considered.

Some known facts to begin with: a brief summary of the contents of the Proemium. Unlike Proclus, in the Proemium I do not include the summary of the *Republic* or the *Atlantis* story.[4] I refer to what Socrates himself calls the *prooimion*: *Timaeus* 27c-29d, which contains what we might call the foundation of Timaeus' entire exposition of the coming into being of the universe. After some preliminaries, i.e. the invocation of the gods and the exhortation of the audience, Timaeus lays down three ontological or metaphysical and epistemological principles (27d5-28b2), and applies them to the universe – as the sum of the objects of perception (28b2-29b3). After this he formulates yet another principle, one we might call, using a term coined reluctantly by Runia, 'logological', which he applies to his account of the universe.[5] This principle concerns the textual[6] consequences of the epistemological difference between being and *genesis*, in other words, the *eikôs mythos* (29b3-d3).

i. Exegetical strategy in the *In Timaeum*

As Iamblichus prescribed, the curriculum of every student of the Neoplatonic school in Athens at that time contained, as the second and highest cycle of his education, two subjects: physics and theology. For physics the philosopher-to-be studied the *Timaeus*, as the summit of all enquiry about the encosmic.[7] Traces of this 'Sitz im Leben' remain both in the commentary's content and in its composition and style, for example in the frequent use of doxographic material. However, the best illustration of the origin of the commentary in classroom exegesis is to be found in its most formal characteristics: the standard structure a teacher applied to the text to be discussed and commented upon in his lectures. The text is divided into lemmas, consisting of one or several lines that would then be treated in *theôria* and *lexis*.[8]

Proclus treats the Proemium in 27 lemmata, the exegesis of which is of varying length. Let us examine them in a graph.[9]

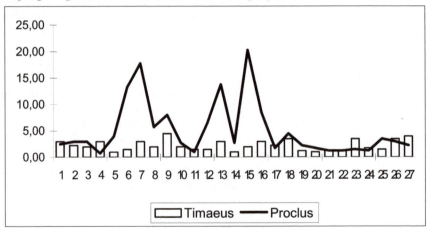

Graph 1 – *divisio textus*

This graph shows the number of lines each lemma consists of (columns) and the corresponding number of pages Proclus spends on that lemma (line). What jumps at us immediately is, of course, the enormous peaks in the line: these refer to the discussion of (lemma 6) 27d6-28a1, being and becoming; (lemma 7) 28a1-4, the definition of being and becoming by our modes of cognition; (lemma 13) 28b7-c2, the question if the universe has a beginning (in time); and (lemma 15) 28c3-5, the nature of the demiurge; other well-treated subjects are (lemma 9) 28a6-b2, the dependency relation between the model used by a creator and the quality of his product; and (lemma 16) 28c5-29a2, the question what kind of model the demiurge used for the creation of the universe. It is also quite clear from this graph that after the application of the principles, from 29b2 onwards, when the great metaphysical questions have been answered, and all that is left is the *eikôs mythos* or 'logology', Proclus 'loses interest', so to speak. I will return to this point later.

Another compositional feature of the commentary is the traditional division of the exegesis into *lexis* and *theôria*. The principle derives from teaching practice, and in Proclus it comes down to the following:[10] *theôria* (also *ta pragmata*) refers to the general discussion of a lemma and the overall doctrine or theory involved; *lexis* (also *ta kath' ekasta, rhêsis, rhêmata*) refers to the treatment of the wording of a text, the particular problems it evokes, and the logical structure both within the lemma and in connection to the previous one. The order can be both *theôria–lexis* and the inverse, or even a combination.[11] Keeping in mind that it is almost impossible to distinguish when commentators started using words such as *theôria* and *lexis* as 'technical terms',[12] let us take a look in graph 2 (p. 154) at the distribution of *theôria* and *lexis* within Proclus' discussion of the Proemium.

This graph, again, shows the lemmata (x-axis) and the number of pages Proclus spends on them (y-axis), this time split up – where relevant – into *theôria* and *lexis*. The advantage of the use of graphics as opposed to words is their immediacy: the point I want to make concerning the distribution of *theôria* and *lexis* is immediately visible from the graph. Obviously, we should be aware at all times that this immediacy also suggests a simplicity and rigidity in Proclus' application of the division that are not actually there. In fact, he uses the division rather loosely, sometimes explicitly separating the two by formulae, sometimes just following the train of his reasoning. The latter occurs especially towards the end of the Proemium.

One thing that is obvious from the distribution, I think, is that after Timaeus' introductory remarks (i.e. the invocation of the gods and the exhortation of the audience), at the beginning of the Proemium the *lexis* receives at least the same amount of attention as the *theôria*, but once the main terminology has been discussed, *theôria* becomes more important. Finally, towards the end of the Proemium after the great metaphysical questions have been treated (i.e. after lemma 12, *Tim.* 28b6-7), *lexis* and *theôria* tend to merge, or *lexis* is not present at all. This relinquishing of a common exegetical principle in the later lemmata coincides with a decrease in the length of the discussion of these lemmata in general. What stands out most of all, is the relative neglect of all the lemmata that

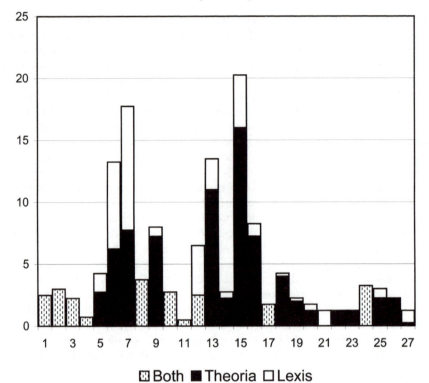

☒ Both ■ Theoria ☐ Lexis

Graph 2 – *theôria* vs *lexis*

concern images (*eikones*): the universe as image of the Forms (17-19), and the text as image of its subject, the *eikôs mythos* (20-7).[13] The brief treatment of the lemmata 17-19 can easily be explained from the fact that we are dealing with the application of the third principle, concerning the formal cause of the universe, which had already gotten a reasonably extensive treatment (lemma 9, 264.10-272.6). The lack of attention to the *eikôs mythos* is, however, an entirely different issue. How are we to explain this stark contrast with the attitude of modern day commentators and scholars, for whom the remark about the status of the cosmology forms one of the most challenging issues of the dialogue?[14] Of course, 'logology' does not come very high in the Neoplatonic metaphysical hierarchy, but surely we would not want to put down the brevity of the treatment to simple lack of interest on Proclus' side?

Another, certainly more interesting possibility is that in the metaphysical lemmata we see traces of the structure and therefore the content of the lectures given by Syrianus. The *lexis–theôria* division – a didactic device – might be a remnant of the method Proclus' teacher used in lecturing on the *Timaeus*. That would mean that, where the division is less present,

Proclus is presenting us with his own interpretation, whereas the passages that are more explicitly divided, that is, the ones dealing with metaphysics, would be nearer to Syrianus' interpretation. An indication for this explanation of the meagre treatment of the second half of the Proemium can be found in the distribution of the doxographic material over the passage: contrary to Proclus' other commentaries, the *Timaeus*-commentary is well known – one might say until recently primarily known – for its wealth of doxographic material. This is a remnant of the commentary's origin in oral exegesis: when discussing a text, students would make use of the existing commentaries. The *In Timaeum* is reported to be Proclus' first commentary (Marinus, *VProc.* 13), so in writing it he may not have had the confidence as a philosopher to venture too far from his teaching ground and boldly state his own interpretation without first mentioning predecessors. Now, if we look at the distribution of the doxographic material we see that it, too, is concentrated around the 'metaphysical' lemmata 6, 7, 13 and 15. Apparently this was generally considered the controversial and interesting material.

Of course, if this interpretation is correct, it implies that – instead of Proclus – Syrianus did not treat the second half of the proemium *in extenso* during his lectures, so the question remains 'why did Syrianus deem it uninteresting?'. It would be difficult, if not impossible, to answer this question, and it would certainly go beyond the scope of this paper. Let me therefore suffice with one indication in Syrianus' own work that seems to support the theory: his commentary on the *Metaphysics* treats only books B, Γ, M and N. Syrianus even explicitly states that he will not discuss everything, since Alexander of Aphrodisias already did that.[15] The reason for this is probably that Syrianus' main aim is not to explain Aristotle's metaphysics, but to refute his criticism of Plato, by explaining how we should interpret the former's erroneous rendering of Plato.[16]

ii. The *eikôs mythos*

In order to explain the abovementioned contrast between Proclus' economical treatment of the *eikôs mythos* remark and the numerous pages that have been devoted to it in contemporary literature on the *Timaeus*, we will have to return to the actual discussion of the *eikôs mythos*.

The contemporary debate[17]

To the modern eye, at the end of the Proemium Timaeus seems to be disqualifying his own exposition before he even starts it: he states that what he is about to tell us about the universe is but a likely story (*eikôs mythos*, 29b3-d3). More precisely: he warns us that we should not expect an exposition about the universe to be entirely consistent and accurate, due to the nature of its subject, the universe, which is an *eikôn* of Being,

155

due to the nature of texts, which may not be incontrovertible and irrefutable, and finally due to human nature. Timaeus' remarks on the status of an account about nature are the subject of extensive discussion in their own right, but above all they have figured in an ongoing debate among Plato's modern-day audience, on the question whether we should read his cosmogony literally or as one great metaphor. In general, those who prefer the latter reading find their foremost clue – or argument – exactly in the *eikôs mythos* remark, that tells them, among others, that Plato never meant the world to have a beginning in time.[18] On the other hand, literalists – as we may call them – try to save their interpretation against the threat of the *eikôs mythos*, for example by claiming that Plato explicitly mentions where his text should not be taken literally, thereby only reaffirming the impression that the text as a whole is a literal account of the cosmos.

Between these two extremes a rainbow of interpretations has been offered, such as the anachronistic reading of the *Timaeus* as verisimilitude, or 'the nearest approximation which can "provisionally" be made to exact truth', and which is subject to perpetual revision;[19] Cornford's reading of the *eikôs mythos* as indicating poetic licence;[20] and Gregory's suggestion that Plato is not presenting us with his cosmological views, but instead challenges his readers to examine their own views.[21]

In the recent surge of interest for the *eikôs mythos* question,[22] apart from readings that fit in the dichotomy sketched above,[23] a certain trend seems to be detectable. In three respects a shift has occurred. First of all, the word *eikôs* is explained quite differently, as expressing the likeliness not so much of the exposition, but of the content of physical theory.[24] Still, the qualification *eikôs* is explicitly given to the text, not to its subject. Considering that this qualification *is* due to the subject matter, I think Zeyl is right to point out that the distinction made is not one between literal and metaphorical, but between consistent and accurate vs less consistent and less accurate, between apodeictic certainty and plausibility. This is an important modification, since it invalidates the *eikôs mythos* remarks as arguments for the 'metaphoricalist' position.

Secondly, more attention is given to the validity expressed in *eikôs* – as opposed to mere limitation. The ontological structure sketched in the Proemium necessitates the likeness of discourse about the universe, but also supports and justifies this discourse.[25]

Finally, in the predominantly literalist scene, the role of science and Plato's scientific method have come to the fore: on the one hand, we find a variant of Zeyl's reading, that Plato means that his cosmology is not a scientific, consistent and irrefutable treatise,[26] or that it is, but only up to the end of the Proemium.[27] On the other hand, Runia suggests that we find in the *Timaeus* an application of the method described in the '*deuteros plous*' of the *Phaedo* (99c6ff), and that *eikôs* refers to the fact that the starting points are provisional.[28] As we will see these three modifications or shifts in the interpretation of the *eikôs mythos*, that is, explaining *eikôs* as referring to the distinction between certainty and plausibility, and to both limitation and validity, and the emphasis on scientific method, all bring us closer to Proclus.

The expectations of the contemporary audience as regards writings about cosmology or science of nature in general are rooted in the modern conception of that science: science of nature is supposed to be a science *par excellence* that requires, if not certainty, at least exactitude. Therefore Plato's qualification of his science of nature as a mere like(li)ness is regarded as a serious issue, with far-reaching consequences for not only the dialogue, but Plato's doctrine about the generation of the universe and physics in general – to the extreme of qualifying the entire cosmology as poetry. For an ancient audience, however, the consequences of the terminology Timaeus uses were not quite so severe.

In general, one could say that from the moment the *Timaeus* was written, the polemics about whether the cosmogony should be taken literally thrived. However, the ancient scholars do not seem to have struggled all that much with the notion that the account is an approximation or an image, but not 'truth'.[29] On the contrary, writers after Plato have borrowed several expressions (*eikotologia*,[30] *kata logon ton eikota*, etc.) from the *Timaeus*, as implying the validity, if within certain limits, of what is said. For example, the expression '*kata logon ton eikota*' implies that something is probable, that it agrees with the facts, however incomplete they may be.[31] So being *eikôs* means being fitting, seeming, probable: it does not imply a negative judgement.

More particularly, in the case of Proclus, it is obvious from his commentary on Timaeus' remarks about the *eikôs mythos* that, if you ask him, they play no part in settling the question about the generation (or not) of the world.[32] Moreover, with regard to the *eikôs mythos* we can safely assume that Proclus sides with the literalists, and as we will see his exegesis of the passage shows remarkable similarities with recent publications on the subject, with respect to the three issues mentioned above.

Proclus' eikôs mythos (337.10-353.29, lemmas 20-7)

As regards Proclus' interpretation of the *eikôs mythos* in the lemmas 20-7, in general one could say that he very explicitly discusses three distinct aspects of the 'likeness' of the likely story: in the nature of words, of the subject matter, and of us humans. Proclus' starting point is that things, thoughts and words are related to each other, and that therefore, after the division of all objects into Being and Becoming, and of our knowledge thereof into understanding and opinion respectively, the third distinction to be made is that regarding *logoi*. Or as he says elsewhere: there is a natural beginning for everything. All things in the universe proceed from the final cause, knowledge as expressed in demonstrations proceeds from the proper hypotheses, and the scientific *logos*, too, starts from a natural beginning. This natural beginning is the distinction regarding the character of the teaching, whether it is certain, unchangeable and exact, or an *eikotologia*, that is, not truth, but belief, and likened to truth. Which of these two it is depends on the subject, because the relation between things, thoughts and words consists in their having the same (ontological, epistemological and 'logological'/truth-) status, i.e. *logoi* are unchanging if they are about Being, and likely if they are about Becoming (337.23-339.2 and 339.5-16).

Proclus proceeds to tell us that this is not a mere rhetorical distinction, as some have it, but also, and foremost, one that is based on a necessary metaphysical relation. Moreover, *logoi* have the same status as their subject, but on top of that they also have the same structure. In the language of Proclus, they *imitate* the demiurge. Just as the principle of the emanation of being pervades everything, so too is the start of the *logoi*, the universal axiom about their character, applied to this text itself (340.16-21), so that it entirely pervades it (339.18-29).[33] Proclus illustrates the metaphysical aspect of the 'likeness' – i.e. the natural relation between *logoi* and their subject matter – with a beautiful hierarchy of *logoi*. Starting with Zeus, a *logos* with regard to the mind of god, passing through soul, a *logos* with regard to the intelligibles, the angelic order, *logos* of the unspeakable of the gods, we reach this *logos*, related to the things, and, as it were, their grandchild, since it is brought to maturity by the cognitions in us that correspond to the things (341.11-21).

This hierarchy at the same time shows that apart from the similarities between *logoi* and subject matter,[34] there exists also a difference, due to the nature of words. *Logoi* are always inferior to their subject. Since a *logos* is cognition made explicit, it proceeds into multitude and has a composite nature, and therefore decreases the unity and indivisibility of the thing (this is, according to Proclus, why Plato speaks of a plural, *logoi*). Related to this inferiority is the important point that, with respect to our knowledge, the scientific account is irrefutable, since we don't have any faculty superior to *epistêmê*, but that with respect to the subject itself it is not irrefutable: it will never be able to capture its nature, or reach its indivisibility. This is why Plato adds 'insofar as possible'. The same goes for our knowledge: whereas it is irrefutable in our souls, it is refuted by *nous*, since only *nous* will express being as it is (342.16-343.15).[35]

The discussion of lemma 25 (344.28-348.7) is slightly longer than the previous ones, mainly because the proportion 'as being is to becoming, so truth is to belief' triggers a discussion of how the notions 'belief' (*pistis*) and 'truth' (*alêtheia*) should be understood in this context. As a parenthesis: remarkably enough, Proclus places *alêtheia* – as used in this context, i.e. truth in the soul – on the same level as *pistis*, being different only with respect to its object and its instrument (cf. 347.20-348.7). Proclus' interpretation of 'belief' is especially interesting, since he suggests that Plato here, as opposed to in the *Republic* perhaps, has in mind a rational belief, which owes its uncertainty only to the fact that it is forced to use perception and imagination. The uncertainty of perception in its turn is due on the one hand to its fallibility and on the other hand to the instability of its objects. In other words: first of all the enmattered is always changing and in flux and therefore it cannot be named with certainty, and does not allow for the universal, immaterial and indivisible, which is what is attached to knowledge; secondly we are forced, in our research, to embrace irrational faculties of knowledge. Now in itself this is limiting enough, but since we are 'seated at the root of the universe' we even use them in a clumsy and erring way, 'filling ourselves with likelinesses'. For example, we are too far away from the heavenly bodies to be able to say anything other than the plausible and approximate about them. If it is possible at all to reach certainty about anything, this can be attained only insofar as the subject partakes in Being, and the only appropriate method is through mathematical demonstrations (346.3-347.2, cf. 351.20-353.11).

The last two lemmas to be treated here (*Tim.* 29c4-7 and 29c7-d3) are, in Proclus' view, mainly about the preparation of the audience, the last component of the Proemium, after the hypotheses and the determination of the character of the exposition (348.13-17, cf. 354.27-355.4). They also serve as a summary of the foregoing. Timaeus, Proclus says, informs us as to how we are expected to receive the following exposition, in two respects: we should be aware first of all that it is not exact, or really about objects of knowledge, but similar to them. Secondly we should be aware that, since the cosmos is composed of both physical powers and intellective and divine beings, the similarity consists in a mixture of belief and truth.[36] Whatever is said about the sensible (as such) contains '*eikotologia*', but what is said about it as originating in the intelligible has a part in the irrefutable and the immutable (348.17-27). The necessity – of approximation – is double: as we have seen, it is caused by both the instability and lack of clarity of the subject, and by our human nature.[37]

To sum up, in the course of Proclus' interpretation, we have encountered three different respects in which an account of the universe is to be called a likely story (*eikotologia*): (1) words are like their subject, in the sense that they reveal its essence, but are also inferior, because of their discursiveness; (2) the universe is full of images, which have a certain likeness to the Forms; (3) because of our human nature we, too, are full of images, or like(li)ness. Moreover, the 'like(li)ness' of *logoi* has two aspects: it is both artificial or logographic and natural or metaphysical. It is important to realise that words have a place in the chain of Being, since they necessarily have an ontological relation, of image and paradigm, with their subject. But the level they are on is variable, depending on their subject and on the job the speaker does. We will come back to this in the next section.

So far, there seems to be no indication whatsoever that Proclus thinks lightly of the *eikôs mythos*, or has a reason not to see the fact that we will never arrive at absolute truth as a problem. However, to the desperate literalist or triumphant 'metaphoricalist' who may ask, 'Then what are we to do?' (τί οὖν φαίη τις ἄν, 353.11) Proclus answers that Plato is right in telling us to be satisfied with what he has to offer, because it is 'second to none'. Observing the mean between irony and boastfulness, Plato calls his account about nature no less likely than that of anyone before him, nor, for that matter, any less likely than the things themselves (353.11-29).[38] According to Proclus, Plato is giving us more than his predecessors, in fact, because he is the only one who not only informs us about the subsidiary causes (matter and form), but also about the proper causes (final, efficient and paradigmatic), and he gives us the most exact (*akribestaton*, I 10.21-2) account of nature.[39] Still, all this does not sound very satisfying to the modern reader. In order to settle the debate about the *eikôs mythos*, without disqualifying Plato's cosmology, a mere relative exactness plus an argument *ad verecundiam* will not do the trick. After all, why should we be satisfied?

iii. Neoplatonic hermeneutics[40] and the principle of *heis skopos*

My proposal is that the answer to this question is to be found in Neoplatonic hermeneutics. We have to be, and can be, satisfied, because in this dialogue, the *skopos* is not just science of nature, but platonic *physiologia*. And the aim of reading the dialogue is not finding the truth about the sense-perceptible universe, but preparing our souls for the contemplation of the Forms. The anonymous Neoplatonist author of an introduction to Platonic philosophy[41] tells us that before reading a text one has to find out what its aim is. After all, he says, Plato himself states that 'there is one way for those who are to take counsel, and that is to know what the counsel is about: otherwise complete failure is inevitable' (Anon. *Prol.* 21.1-9; *Phdr.* 237b7-c3). Moreover, our author continues, referring to another famous passage from the *Phaedrus*, since a well-written dialogue is like a living being, and every living being has one *telos*, every dialogue also has one *telos*, i.e. one *skopos*.[42] These two Phaedrus-references serve as arguments for what Praechter in a 1910 article called 'Die Iamblichische Methode': the principle of *heis skopos*.[43] This principle entails that every Platonic dialogue has one specific and unique subject or aim and that the exegesis of the entire dialogue must be in accordance with this aim: what relates to the forms, *ta noêta, ta paradeigmata, ta hola* should be discussed *theologikôs, paradeigmatikôs, holikôs*, but that which pertains to the sublunar world, *ta physika, eikones, ta merê*, requires an interpretation that is performed *physikôs, eikonikôs, merikôs*. The *skopos*, the aim of the *Timaeus*, Proclus tells us in his Proemium, is the entire *physiologia*, science of nature.[44]

160

On several occasions Proclus refers to this *skopos* explicitly, for example in the discussion of lemma 13 when he rejects Severus' opinion that the world, absolutely speaking, is eternal, but this world here and now does have a beginning (I 289.13-15):

> To this interpretation we will reply as follows: you improperly advance riddles, from myths, into the science of nature (ὅτι τὰ μυθικὰ αἰνίγματα μετάγεις εἰς φυσιολογίαν ὡς οὐκ ἔδει).⁴⁵

And a little further down (I 290.2-4):

> This kind of interpretation should not be accepted in any way, since they are not related to science of nature (φυσικὰς οὐκ οὔσας ἐξηγήσεις).

However, there is more to the *skopos* of the *Timaeus* than meets the eye. To use the words of the anonymous author mentioned before: we should not be satisfied with mere 'science of nature' (μὴ ἁπλῶς περὶ φυσιολογίας) as the *skopos* of the *Timaeus*, because we are dealing with 'science of nature *according to Plato*' (ἡ κατὰ Πλάτωνα φυσιολογία, Anon. *Prol.* 22.22-35). And Proclus, too, tells us on numerous occasions that 'science of nature according to Plato' comes down to a combination of both physics and theology, since nature has a divine aspect insofar as it stems from the gods.⁴⁶ Moreover, 'things, thoughts and words' are by nature related and therefore words should be made appropriate to their subject. A principle that stems from rhetoric, but as we have seen has a parallel or even source in the Proemium of the *Timaeus*. As Proclus himself says in his commentary on lemma 21, the introduction to the discussion of the *eikôs mythos* (I 339.5-22):

> These three are related to each other (συμφυῶς ἀλλήλων), the things, the thoughts and the words ... so some people say that this distinguishing beforehand what the genre of the text is and what the audience should be like belong to the art of writing speeches (λογογραφικόν ἐστι) and that Aristotle, as well as many others of the younger philosophers, tried to emulate this. I however would say that the account imitates the creation itself (μιμεῖται τὴν δημιουργίαν αὐτὴν ὁ λόγος).

The account, then, is a microcosmos, a literary microcosmos, using an expression of Coulter.⁴⁷ Because, Proclus continues, just as creation first produces invisible principles of life, i.e. the World-Soul, and only after that the visible world, so too Timaeus lets the *kosmologia* be preceded by principles. And just as the universe is pervaded by the first principles, so too the *heis skopos* of the *kosmologia* is Platonic science of nature, i.e. a mixture of *ta physika* and *ta noêta*, in the *nomos*⁴⁸ or main part of the dialogue, but especially in the Proemium, that part of the text in which the real, divine causes of the sensible world are de-

161

scribed.[49] We here find a clear juxtaposition of the ontological and artificial likeness of discourse.

Conclusion

The upshot of this is double. First of all, regarding the general question why the *eikôs mythos* receives relatively little attention in the *In Timaeum*: philosophy of language, about words as copies of their subject matter, does not belong to the *skopos* of this dialogue and its exegesis. Rather one would find it in the context of exegesis of the *Cratylus*, for example. Secondly, and more importantly, with regard to the fact that Proclus advocates contentment with a 'mere' likely story: the *Timaeus* is a mixture of physics and theology (as well as, of course, a mixture of *pistis* and *alêtheia*). This *skopos*, which tells us what the aim of a dialogue is, has to be determined by those who embark on its exegesis. And exegesis, for a Neoplatonist philosopher, is a didactic and spiritual process, the *anagôgê* that trains the soul and equips it with the 'attitude' fit for – ultimately – union with the One. The proper order of this process is expressed in Iamblichus' didactic program mentioned above. The reason that science of nature figures so prominently in that curriculum is *exactly because it allows us to examine true being in images.* Or, as Proclus says in the *Platonic Theology*, because in the *Timaeus* we find a very clear example of the mode of exposition that makes use of images.[50] As long as the student of the divine is incapable of contemplating it directly, reading the *Timaeus* will enable him to perceive it in images. First, science of nature shows us true being in appearances, and then mathematics, traditionally the intermediate between our world and that of the Forms, allows us to get acquainted with 'the divine essence' in a more immaterial way (*Theol. Plat.* I 10.25-11.9). Timaeus' *eikôs mythos* remark is not a disqualification of Platonic science of nature; it is a qualification of it as a preparatory kind of science.

As we have seen, all three central issues in the contemporary debate on the *eikôs mythos*, that is, the reference to the distinction between certainty and plausibility, and to both limitation and validity, and the emphasis on science, are all present in Proclus' treatment of the passage, albeit embedded in an entirely different, and for most of us unlikely, ontology. And in the end it is this ontology, that determines a refreshing approach to a text such as the *Timaeus*.

In general, the reading and writing of a text, then, are to be valued not for the final result or the facts (if any) it conveys, but for the impact the process of reading has on the soul of the audience. The text is not just like its subject, but is made to be a profitable image of it by providing physical and mathematical images of the truth. The reader's soul (if appropriately advanced) is able to become like the truth by studying and absorbing these images.[51]

Appendix – *divisio textus* (cf. Festugière 1967, 13-23)

Lemma	*Timaeus*	*In Timaeum*	Summary of content
1	27c1-3	214.17-217.3	The correct start of everything is to call upon the gods
2	27c4-6	217.7-219.31	We are about to enter a discourse on the universe
3	27c6-d1	220.4-222.6	We must call upon the gods
4	27d1-4	222.11-223.2	Exhortation of speaker and audience
5	27d5	223.5-227.3	A distinction should be made
6	27d6-28a1	227.6-240.12	What is *'to on'*, what is *'to gignomenon'*?
7	28a1-4	240.17-258.8	'Definition' by our modes of cognition
8	28a4-6	258.12-264.3	Efficient cause
9	28a6-b2	264.10-272.6	Formal cause
10	28b2-4	272.10-274.32	Name of the cosmos
11	28b4-5	275.3-276.7	Transition to application of principles
12	28b6-7	276.10-282.22	Is the cosmos *'on'* or *'gignomenon'*?
13	28b7-c2	282.27-296.12	Cosmos is *'gignomenon'* (1st principle)
14	28c2-3	296.15-299.9	Cosmos has efficient cause (2nd principle)
15	28c3-5	299.13-319.21	Efficient cause/demiurge is hard to find
16	28c5-29a2	319.26-328.11	Is the formal cause *'on'* or *'gignomenon'*?
17	29a2-4	328.16-330.6	Cosmos is beautiful
18	29a4-b1	330.12-334.27	Formal cause is *'on'*
19	29b1-2	334.30-337.7	Cosmos is an image
20	29b2-3	337.10-339.2	Right start for everything
21	29b3-4	339.5-340.13	A distinction should be made regarding image and model
22	29b4-5	340.16-341.24	Words are related to their subject
23	29b5-c1	342.3-343.15	If subject is *'on'*, words are stable
24	29c1-2	343.18-344.25	If subject is *'gignomenon'*, i.e. image, words are images
25	29c2-3	344.28-348.7	*'On'* is to *'gignomenon'* as truth is to opinion
26	29c4-7	348.13-351.14	Account will not be exact
27	29c7-d3	351.20-353.29	Human shortcomings
(28)	(29d4-6)	(354.5-355.15)	(Socrates' reaction, transition *prooimion – nomos*)

Notes

1. I am grateful to the Netherlands Organization for Scientific Research for their financial support while working on this project, and to Frans de Haas, David Runia, Christoph Helmig, Arianna Betti, Casper de Jonge, Mariska Leunissen, an anonymous referee and the Editors for their valuable comments on different versions of this paper. Any remaining flaws are mine.

2. *In Tim.* I 1.4ff., esp. 17-18.

3. *In Tim.* I 8.4-13, cf. I 217.25-7: οὗ δὴ καὶ ἡ φυσιολογία φαίνεται θεολογία τις οὖσα, διότι καὶ τὰ φύσει συνεστῶτα, καθ᾽ ὅσον ἐκ θεῶν ἀπογεννᾶται, θείαν πως ἔχει τὴν ὕπαρξιν.

4. Proclus uses the word προοίμιον or the plural προοίμια without distinction for both the general introduction to the dialogue, i.e. the summary of the *Republic* plus the Atlantis story (*Tim.* 17a-27c), and Timaeus' Proemium to his own exposition on the universe (27c-29d), as well as their combination (17a-29d). To restrict the scope of this paper even more: Proclus' treatment of the Proemium proper starts at the beginning of his second book, i.e. p. 205. In this paper Proclus' introduction to his discussion of the Proemium, pp. 205.1-214.12, will be left aside, since its character (not lemmatic commentary but a philosophical treatise on the nature and purpose of prayer) makes it unsuitable for this paper.

5. Runia (1997), 110-11: 'Plato aims, as has often been noted before, at a complete integration of *ontology*, *epistemology*, and what we might a little awkwardly call *logology*, that is to say, the determination of the right kind of account for the subject under discussion.'

6. Textual in a very broad sense. The consequences could be e.g. rhetorical or linguistic, depending on the interpretation of the principle.

7. See Siorvanes (1996), 120. See also *In Tim.* I 12.30-13.14, where Proclus states that philosophy as a whole can be divided into physics and theology, each of which is represented in resp. *Timaeus* and *Parmenides*, although both are on the whole, but not exclusively devoted to either area. Lernould (2001) even suggests that Proclus sees the *Timaeus* as theology more than physics.

8. In fact, the text would first be divided into several large *tmêmata* that would in their turn be divided into *praxeis*, units to be read at one session. These *praxeis* would again be cut up into lemmas. The *tmêmata* are large chunks of the entire dialogue and therefore exceed a passage as 'short' as that on the Proemium (150 pages), and since a division into *praxeis* seems to be absent from the commentary, we will start from Proclus' division of the text of the Proemium into lemmas.

9. See Appendix for a table showing the *divisio textus* into lemmata, with a brief description of every lemma.

10. Festugière, to whose very erudite and thorough paper 'Modes de composition des commentaires de Proclus' (1963) this paragraph owes a lot, uses the term *lexis* in a more restricted sense, to apply only to the interpretation of details, single words and expressions. Cf. however lemma 18, if my interpretation thereof is correct.

11. Cf. Festugière (1963), 550-65: 'Ce Commentaire (sur le Timée) donne lieu aux mêmes observations que ci-dessus. On y rencontre sans doute la division entre πράγματα (A) et λέξις (B) dans l'ordre A-B, mais parfois aussi cet ordre est inversé, et le plus souvent fond et forme sont mêlés dans l'exégèse d'un même lemma, Proclus suivant le fil de son raisonnement sans se plier à aucun schème scolaire.' (559); cf. also Segonds (1985, xliv).

12. Every commentator interpreting a centuries-old text is bound to remark on textual problems and general doctrine of that text. However, ancient testimonies do indicate a formalized approach to a Platonic text. For example, Diogenes Laertius (III, 65) remarks that exegesis of Plato's words should consist in three steps, finding out first what the meaning of each of the words is, secondly why Plato says them (for a primary reason or as illustration, to establish doctrine or refute opponents) and finally if what he says is true. On the other hand, modern opinions on when the approach became formal differ: D'Ancona, in a recent article on Syrianus, refers to this principle as the 'modèle aphrodisien', since, she claims, it is in Alexander's work that we first find it applied. D'Ancona argues that after Alexander the model became obsolete, probably until Syrianus started using it again. His pupil Proclus then copied it from him, setting in motion the development of the strict scholastic model as used by e.g. Olympiodorus (D'Anconca [2000b], 325-6; cf. 319). Sharples, however, states that Alexander's commentaries are not formally arranged on the basis of *theôria* and *lexis* (Sharples [1990], 95 and n. 97).

13. Other lemmata that do not receive a lot of attention are 4 (exhortation of speaker and audience), 10 (name of the cosmos), 11 (transition to the application of the principles) and 14 (repetition of the second principle). In the case of the lemmata 4, 10 and 11, we are dealing with a transition of some kind (to the principles, and to the application thereof). In the case of lemma 14 the subject – a repetition of the second principle – allows Proclus to summarily describe the reasons for the necessity of an efficient cause for what has become.

14. Cf. Cornford, who devotes half of his discussion of the Proemium to the *eikôs mythos* ([1937], 28-32), or more recently, Calvo and Brisson (eds) (1997), in which five papers are devoted to the subject. See also Part 2.

15. *In Met.* 54.12-21 <ταῦτα> πειράσεται μὲν ἐν ταύτῃ παραδοῦναι τῇ βιβλίῳ, ἡμεῖς ἱκανῶς ὑπὸ τοῦ φιλοπονωτάτου σαφηνισθεῖσαν Ἀλεξάνδρου πᾶσαν μὲν οὐκ ἐξηγησόμεθα· εἰ δέ που ἡμῖν δοκοίη λέγειν τι πραγματειῶδες ἐξετάσεως πειρασόμεθα κατ' ἐκεῖνο βασανίζειν τό μέρος, τὰ ἄλλα πάντα τοῦ συνεχοῦς ἕνεκα τῆς πραγματείας παραφράζοντες.

16. See D'Ancona (2000a), 212-14.

17. This section highlights different modern interpretations of the *eikôs mythos*, but should not be considered to be an exhaustive discussion.

18. See Baltes (1996), 94-6, and Zeyl (2000), xx-xxv, for an extensive and insightful discussion of this debate. Baltes opts for the metaphorical reading. He does not explicitly play the *eikôs mythos* card, although the argument is present in his reasoning. He refers to Timaeus' repeated stressing of the difficulties involved in understanding what he says, despite the fact that in the *Timaeus*, more than in any other dialogue, the interlocutors are on a more or less equal level. Moreover, it is worth noting here that Baltes mentions Timaeus' statement that it is impossible for the description of the universe to be entirely free of contradiction. Baltes explains this as involving 'dass Timaios sich gelegentlich unscharfer kolloquialer Ausdrucksweise bedient'. Zeyl's reading will be discussed below.

19. Taylor (1928), 59-61; Wright (2000), 14-19; pushed to extremes in Ashbaugh (1988); see also Morgan (2000), 271-81.

20. Cornford (1937), 28-32.

21. Gregory (2000), 241-2. An entirely different approach, which does not fit in this spectrum, is the interpretation of the *Timaeus* as a creation in words. Osborne (1996) considers the 'likeliness' of Timaeus' discourse to lie in the extent to which it succeeds in moulding a world (if I understand her correctly, one that is independent of the material world) to match its paradigm, the Forms. Although this is a very exciting approach, and one that easily relates to Neoplatonic exegesis of the *Timaeus*, unfortunately Osborne's discussion is rather confused and contradictory at times.

22. For example, in 'Interpreting the *Timaeus/Critias*', the Proceedings of IV Symposium Platonicum, five out of thirty-one contributions are to a large extent devoted to the *eikôs mythos*: Runia, Berti, Santa Cruz, Vallejo and Reale.

23. Reale (1997), Vallejo (1997), Dillon (1997).

24. To be fair, this was already pointed out by Tarán (1971, 400-1 n. 104). Tarán does, however, belong to the team of those who read the *Timaeus* as a metaphor ('creation myth'), but this is triggered by the word *mythos*. Throughout the dialogue, we encounter both *eikôs logos* and *eikôs mythos*. I will not go into the question whether they are distinct, since I agree with Vlastos (1965, 382) that *eikôs* is the important word. Cf. however Brisson, who comes up with separate descriptions: 'falsifiable discourse describing the present state of sensible things' (*eikôs logos*) and 'non-falsifiable discourse presenting, in an explanatory model, the state of sensible things before and during their constitution' (*eikôs mythos*) (1998, 129-30).

25. Zeyl (2000), xxxii-xxxiii, Santa Cruz (1997), 133ff., cf. Reale (1997), 152).

26. E.g. Sorabji (1983), 272.

27. Berti (1997), 127, cf. Reale (1997), 152.

28. Runia (1997), 111-12.

29. That is not to say that sceptics did not make use of it for their own purposes, as happened in the case of some uses of the term *eikôs*, as can be seen from Anon. *Proleg.*10; it is significant here, however, that there is no hint that these people had the *Timaeus* specially in mind, and no suggestion that the author is worried by the implications of their argument for this important Platonic text. For a discussion of the role of *eikôs* in the Fourth Academy see Tarrant (1985).

30. This word is not used in the *Timaeus*, but is clearly derived from it. Cf. Theophrastus *Fr.* 51.1.1-3, Philo *Heres* 224.3-7, Stob. *Ecl.* I 283.10-14 etc. Cf. also *eikotologikôs* at *In Tim.* I 340.26, where Gaius and Albinus are said to think that Plato can 'express doctrine' (*dogmatizein*) in this fashion.

31. In Plato: *Tim.* 30b7, 53d5, 55d5, 56b4, 90e8. Cf. Philo, *Plant.* 75.1, *Aet.* 44.2; Plut. *Rom.* 28.10.8; Sext. Emp. *Math.* 9.107.4 etc.

32. See Baltes (1978) for an extensive treatment of Proclus' ideas about the generation of the world.

33. Note that the metaphysical aspect seems to be dynamic, and dependent on the speaker. This is an important statement, which marks a shift with respect to Plato, or at least an opposition with modern interpretations: whereas we would say foremost that it is the fleeting nature of the universe that limits the possibilities of our expositions that have that universe as their subject, Proclus here explicitly says that this exposition, 'as Timaeus himself tells us', is 'made to be like' (*omoioumenos*) the subject. A thorough discussion of writing and reading as creation would require far more space than just this paper, so I will not go into that here.

34. These similarities, Proclus shows, are reflected in similarities between the terminology Plato uses for the things and *logoi* respectively. Cf. I 342.3-16.

35. At this point Proclus rehearses the hierarchy of different faculties of knowledge, from the viewpoint of their relative irrefutability.

36. This point is made very explicitly at I 410.13ff.

37. It is in this context that Proclus explains the use of *mythos*: it indicates the fact that our language is replete with dullness and irrationality, and we need to be forgiving towards human nature (I 353.24-9).

38. This seems to conflict with the earlier statement that *logoi* are always inferior to what they express.

39. Cf. Cleary's paper in this volume. See also Steel (2003).

40. Cf. Coulter (1976), Sheppard (1980).

41. See Westerink's edition with his delightful introduction.

42. Anon. *Prol.* 21.18-25; cf. *Phd.* 264c2-5: ἀλλὰ τόδε γε οἶμαί σε φάναι ἄν, δεῖν πάντα λόγον ὥσπερ ζῷον συνεστάναι σῶμά τι ἔχοντα αὐτὸν αὑτοῦ, ὥστε μήτε ἀκέφαλον εἶναι μήτε ἄπουν, ἀλλὰ μέσα τε ἔχειν καὶ ἄκρα, πρέποντα ἀλλήλοις καὶ τῷ ὅλῳ γεγραμμένα.

43. We find an explicit ascription of this principle to Iamblichus in Elias *In Cat.* 131.10-16: ἀλλ' ὅσον ἐκ τούτων τρεῖς δόξουσιν εἶναι οἱ σκοποί, ὅπερ οὐδ' αὐτῷ Ἰαμβλίχῳ δοκεῖ· ἐν γὰρ τοῖς σκοποῖς τῶν Πλάτωνος διαλόγων παντὸς βιβλίου ἕνα βούλεται εἶναι τὸν σκοπόν. Praechter (1910), 147 = (1973), 207.

44. *In Tim.* I 1.4-4.5, esp. I 1.4-8: Ὅτι μὲν ἡ τοῦ Πλατωνικοῦ Τιμαίου πρόθεσις τῆς ὅλης φυσιολογίας ἀντέχεται καὶ ὡς πρὸς τὴν τοῦ παντὸς ἀνήκει θεωρίαν, ἐξ ἀρχῆς εἰς τέλος τοῦτο πραγματευομένου, τοῖς μὴ παντάπασιν ἐσκοτωμένοις πρὸς τοὺς λόγους ἐναργὲς εἶναί μοι καταφαίνεται. Cf. I 1.18.

45. The interesting question arises, of course, when introducing myths would be proper according to Proclus. Presumably, he would answer that this depends mainly on the kind of myth and the manner in which it is used.

46. Cf. I 9.25-14.3, a digression on φύσις. Cf. also I 204.8-10.

47. Cf. Coulter (1976), 128: 'The special reality of a literary text was a precise analogue, in all significant respects, of the larger reality of the world as a whole, this larger reality being, of course, systematically understood along Neoplatonist lines. The result was that literary texts, for their part, came to be thought of as microcosms endowed with a specifically Neoplatonic metaphysical structure.'

48. I.e. what comes after the Proemium, cf. *Tim.* 29d5-7.

49. Cf. *In Tim.* I 2.1ff., where Proclus distinguishes three different elements of a 'physiologia': from the point of view of (1) matter, (2) form (these two being secondary causes) and (3) real causes (efficient, paradigmatic, final).

50. *Theol. Plat.* I 4, esp. I 4.19.10-11, *dia tón eikonôn*.

51. In a sense even the subject should be 'made alike', i.e. one should not treat any subject, but one that will bring us closer to our ultimate goal, union with the One.

Pathways to purification:
the cathartic virtues in the Neoplatonic
commentary tradition

Dirk Baltzly

i. The cathartic virtues: Plato, Plotinus
and Porphryry

One of the many reasons to study the commentary tradition on Plato is to see how the commentators attempt to systematize Plato's dialogues into a unified philosophical position. They do not entertain anything like the developmentalist approaches to the dialogues that have recently been – more or less – the orthodoxy among contemporary Plato scholars. It is also fascinating to see the way in which the commentators bring Plato's dialogues into conversation with Aristotle's treatises and subsequent developments in philosophy. This is frequently part and parcel of discovering a unified philosophical position for Plato to hold. On the whole, modern readers of the commentary tradition have found value in this too. But there is another tendency in ancient readings of Plato – and particularly in Neoplatonist readings – that has not found so much favour with modern readers. This is the tendency to synthesize Platonism with texts such as the Orphic poems or the *Chaldean Oracles*. The role of theurgy and other forms of ritual in the 'Platonic' account of the soul's return to god is often seen by modern scholars as the final straw in trying to turn Platonism into a religion. We moderns are sure this is an alien accretion grafted on to Plato by the inhabitants of an age less rational than ours or Plato's fifth century BC.

In what follows, I want to consider a particular flash point for these three tendencies in subsequent Platonism – presenting a unified, consistent Platonic doctrine; modernizing it to make it responsive to later philosophical disagreements; and integrating it with sacred texts. Plotinus, Porphyry, Iamblichus and Proclus all seek to make consistent sense of Socrates' remarks on virtue in both the *Phaedo* and the *Republic*. They wish to do so in a way that places them within the framework for discussing *eudaimonia* and virtue that Hellenistic philosophy inherits from Aristotle's *Nicomachean Ethics*. Finally, they seek to understand what they call the cathartic virtues – their version of the gradation of virtue under discussion in the *Phaedo* – in terms of ritual purification, particularly through the Mysteries and through theurgy. I wish to concentrate on this latter point in particular and consider (a) whether Proclus entirely collapses the cathartic virtues into ritual forms of purification and (b) whether Proclus' views on cathartic virtue stand at so great a distance from Plato.

In order to make Plato's dialogues speak to moral philosophy as Aristotle understands it, the commentators find a suitably Platonic *telos* for human life in *Timaeus* and *Theaetetus*: human flourishing consists in 'becoming like god insofar as this is possible'.[1] Setting this up as the *telos* raises immediate and obvious problems for our understanding of the virtues and of god. For, as Aristotle points out, the gods don't need to practise temperance or justice in our sense. They don't need to return deposits or overcome bad appetites (*EN* 1178b7-22). So, the problem is that the middle and Neoplatonist specification of Plato's *telos* leaves the relation between the virtues and the condition of human flourishing pretty mysterious. Call this the 'updating puzzle' since it results from trying to see Plato's dialogues as responsive to what becomes the standard, post-Platonic framework for thinking about moral philosophy.

Here is a second puzzle: what is the relationship between the 'philosophical virtues' discussed in *Phaedo* 67e ff. and the account of the virtues as consisting in the correct relations between the different parts of the soul in *Republic* IV? In the *Phaedo*, the courage and moderation of real philosophers are contrasted with those who practise *aretê dêmotikê kai politikê*. While the latter are courageous through fearing dishonour more than death (68b), those who have philosophical virtue do something else. Unfortunately, it isn't all that clear exactly what that something else is! At the very least we can say that they are *not* courageous through fear and that they recognize that the body is a prison in which we are bound by our own desires (82e). By contrast, courage within a city in the *Republic* is said to be a kind of preservation of *correct belief*. Specifically, it is:

> That preservation of the belief that has been inculcated by the law through education about what things and sorts of things are to be feared.
>
> *Rep.* IV 429c, trans. Grube

Is the kind of courage discussed in the *Republic* passage a fuller specification of the *dêmotikê aretê* mentioned in the *Phaedo*? Or has Plato changed his mind? Or does the *Phaedo* represent a more Socratic account while the *Republic* gives us the view of middle period Plato? Call this 'the interpretive problem about virtue in Plato'. My point here is not to pursue an answer to this question: it is only to say that there is an obvious question here and to note that contemporary scholarly opinion is divided on the matter.

Among Plato's ancient readers, Plotinus was the first we know of to attempt to resolve the interpretive problem about virtue and the updating puzzle with one move.[2] In *Enneads* I.2 he applies an analogy. We do not become like god in the way in which the house that a builder constructs becomes like the one that stands next door. Unlike two houses, we and god are very different kinds of thing. Rather, we become like god in the way that a house may be said to be an imitation of, or like, its plan. There is something in the plan that *corresponds* to the door into the back garden, but it isn't itself a door. Thus, we can become like god through possessing the virtues even though god does not *have* the virtues that we have.

Plotinus also distinguishes two different *levels* of virtue – the civic or constitutional and the cathartic or purificatory. He thinks that the civic virtues are those explained in book IV of the *Republic*. Since these virtues relate to the internal constitution of the entire soul, including the irrational parts of spirit and appetite, they do not make us *like god* (I.2.3, 8-11). We are made *better* by having these virtues since they impose order and measure on our appetites and abolish false opinion. In order to be like god, however, we must undergo purification:

> What then do we mean when we call these other virtues 'purifications' and how are we made like by being purified? Since the soul is evil when it is 'thoroughly mixed' [*Phdo* 66b5] with the body and shares its experiences (*homopathês*) and has all the same opinions (*syndoxazousa*), it will be good and possess virtue when it no longer has the same opinions but acts alone – this is intelligence and wisdom (*noein te kai phronein*) – and does not share the body's experiences – this is self-control – and does not fear departing the body – this is courage – and is ruled by reason and intellect (*logos kai nous*), without opposition – and this is justice. One would not be wrong in calling this state of the soul likeness to god, in which its activity is intellectual and it is free from bodily affections (*apathês*).
>
> I.2.3, 10-21, trans. Armstrong

While the constitutional virtues secure only *metriopatheia*, the purificatory ones secure *apatheia*. This perhaps goes some distance toward explaining why the latter, but not the former, make us like god, since god does not undergo bad appetites or any other affection.

So Plotinus' solution to the interpretive problem and the updating problem work together: First, there are differences between the virtues described in *Phaedo* and in *Republic*. But this is because there are different grades of virtue – not because Plato has changed his mind. Second, the sense in which we become like god in becoming virtuous is *not* the same sense in which one person, say Alcibiades, becomes like another, say Socrates, when the former becomes virtuous. Admittedly, the exact sense in which we become like god is still a bit mysterious. But – third point – the cathartic virtues through which we do this are themselves sufficiently mysterious that it is no longer so odd to say that we are assimilated to god by becoming just, courageous, moderate and wise. At the very least we can say that god is something incorporeal and these virtues also involve some kind of rejection of the body. Furthermore, god is clearly impassive and the cathartic virtues are said to produce this in us. Finally, we can also note that Plotinus' interpretation of Platonic doctrine yields an extra bonus from the point of view of showing how Plato's philosophy is responsive to all the contemporary philosophical concerns. By the time of Plotinus, the ethical goals of *metriopatheia* and *apatheia* have a clear and established sense, and Peripatetics and Stoics had contended about which state was appropriate. By locating both within Plato, and showing that the former are the preliminary steps to the latter, Plotinus can further vindicate Plato's pre-eminence as the most divine and far-seeing of all subsequent philosophers.

Finally, with respect to the question of how purification takes place, Plotinus only suggests that the Mysteries (*hai teletai*) hint at deep truths more properly grasped by philosophy. Thus, in I.6.6 Plotinus remarks that the ancient saying (*ho palaios logos*) that the man who has not been purified will 'lie in the mud in Hades' is just a riddling way of making the point that all the virtues, and wisdom itself, consist in purification.[3] He follows this by examples which show how the cathartic virtues – interpreted as they are in I.2.3 – turn the soul away from the body and to what is beautiful and real. So the Mysteries contain hints at the soul's proper salvation – hints that are fully intelligible only through philosophy.

Plotinus' move is so stunningly successful that it is taken up by subsequent Neoplatonists. In expounding it, however, I believe that Porphyry actually transforms the Plotinian solution quite radically – or at the very least he writes in such a way as to *invite* a transformation of Plotinus' solution. Brisson provides a translation and much more detailed discussion of the content of *Sentences* 32 in his paper in this volume. For my purposes it is sufficient to note that Porphyry adds the theoretic and paradigmatic virtues to Plotinus' civic and purificatory ones. The theoretic virtues are virtues the soul exhibits in relation to *nous*, while the paradigmatic virtues are *of* intellect. Since *nous* is divine, the original puzzle that motivated Plotinus disappears. There is a sense in which god has the virtues and thus it is unproblematic that we become like god by becoming virtuous. The important qualification is that the virtues had by god or *nous* are not the sort of things that involve returning deposits or controlling bad appetites. Yet they are virtues, sufficiently like those we find in humans, for there are continuous gradations between the civic virtues and these paradigmatic virtues of *nous*.

ii. Iamblichus and theurgic virtue

The grades of virtue

Iamblichus further multiplied the gradations of virtues in his *On the Virtues* (ap. Damascium *In Phdo* I 138-51). He includes two lower grades of virtue (natural and ethical) as well as a grade of virtue higher than Porphyry's paradigmatic virtues – the hieratic or priestly virtues.

(i) Natural – held in common with animals and linked to the mixtures of the body. Either they belong to the body, or they are reflexes of reason that are present whenever it is not impeded by some disorder, or they are due to training in a previous life. Cf. *Statesman* 306a; *Laws* VII 807c; 12.963e.

(ii) Ethical – acquired by habituation and right belief. They belong to both reason and the irrational nature. Cf. *Laws* II 653a.

(iii) Civic – these are virtues of reason, but of reason in relation to the irrational part of the soul. They involve reason using these parts of the soul as instruments and their receptivity for such use.

(iv) Purificatory – virtues of reason insofar as it withdraws from relations to other things. It discards the body as instrument and restrains activities that depend on this instrument. The cathartic virtues deliver the soul from genesis. Cf. *Phdo* 69bc.

(v) Theoretic – these exist in the soul when soul has forgotten itself and turned to what is above it, Intellect. They are a kind of mirror image of the civic virtues, since they indicate the soul's activity in relation to something other than itself. Cf. the virtues as discussed in the *Theaetetus*.

(vi) Paradigmatic – virtues exhibited by soul when it is no longer contemplating intellect, but it is established by participation (*kata methexin*) in the intellect which is the paradigm of all things. These virtues are called paradigmatic inasmuch as they belong antecedently (*proêgoumenôs*) to intellect. Damascius credits Iamblichus, not Porphyry, with introducing this level of virtue.

(vii) Hieratic – these exist in the godlike elements of the soul. They are coextensive with all the grades of virtue discussed earlier. However, the hieratic virtues are proper to the One, while the others are concerned with Being.

The Iamblichean virtues are supposed to provide a continuous series and to be the same kind of thing – albeit existing at different levels. Moreover, there is a claim that all these virtues are necessary even to those who would pursue the life of contemplation. The reason is that they are *had by the gods themselves* (ibid. 150). In this way, then, our initial problem is explicitly solved in just the manner intimated through Porphyry's introduction of paradigmatic virtues.

However, the way in which virtue is located among the gods points to a new and potentially problematic element. According to Damascius, the intelligible source of souls and the source of virtues is one and the same – the goddess Rhea-Hecate.[4] This identification places us squarely in the midst of Iamblichus' project of integrating the soteriology of the *Chaldean Oracles* into Platonism.[5] Within the context of the *Oracles*, catharsis takes on a specifically ritual function.[6] According to Iamblichus, *invocations* are able to purify the one who makes the sacrifice from passions, and liberate him from the realm of generation. The soul thus liberated lives a life so completely divine as to not even be counted human (*Myst.* I 12.17-26). The virtues of the soul – and perhaps as well those of the intellect – are inadequate to this task. If it were, divine goods could be present to the soul without such invocations (*Myst.* III 20.26). But this is impossible.[7]

Given the priority that Iamblichus assigns to the hieratic virtues and the forms of catharsis associated with them we might reasonably expect that *the catharsis that really counts is accomplished through ritual.* This philosophical view is likely to have ramification for Iamblichus' interpretation of Platonic texts. Since Iamblichus thinks that this is the truth of the matter when it comes to catharsis and since he thinks that Plato *properly interpreted* is right, we should expect that the somewhat mysterious cathartic virtues discussed in the *Phaedo* will be interpreted in terms of ritualized purifications.

Iamblichus' interpretation of cathartic virtue

We are forced to glean our knowledge of Iamblichus' commentary on the *Phaedo* from remarks in the *Phaedo* commentaries of Olympiodorus and Damascius. Damascius' remarks on philosophy as initiation (*telêtê, Phdo* 69c3-d2) I believe confirm this expectation. They also tend to confirm van den Berg's argument that the Neoplatonists saw the Bacchic and Eleusinian Mysteries as essential to the soul's salvation.[8] In his commentary, Damascius likens the Iamblichean levels of virtue to different stages in mystic initiation. It seems overwhelmingly likely that Damascius has in mind initiation into some Orphic or Bacchic rite – though the Neoplatonists regard Orpheus as the originator of the Eleusinian Mysteries as well – since the dialogue is thought to allude to such *Orpheotelestai.*[9] He interprets Socrates' remarks about the thyrsus bearers in terms of Neoplatonic–Orphic identifications of the Titanic life with enmattered existence. The influence of Iamblichus is witnessed by the fact that Damascius' breakdown of the analogous stages of initiation corresponds neatly with Iamblichus' grades of virtue. The correspondences are shown in the table opposite.

'Systasis' is a term which denotes the presence of a soul to a god that results from the successful performance of theurgic rites. This follows on from the achievement of purification through the previous virtues. Rather than focusing on the theoretic virtues and their connection with systasis, however, Damascius discusses purification at length in the following section. He notes that there are different rites that purify us here and also *ekei* – either 'up there' among the intelligibles or in the underworld. The former purifies our fleshy body, while the latter purifications purify the pneumatic and astral bodies of the soul. Damascius notes that there exists a parallel *anagôgê* through philosophy which also takes place in three phases – phases alluded to in the three thousand-year cycle of the soul's migration in *Phaedrus* 249a. But he insists that the connection with the

Damascius' description of virtue	analogous stage of initiation	Iamblichean virtue
ethical and political virtues	public purification	ethical and political virtues
purification that strips away external accretions	secret purification	purificatory virtues
activity of *theôria* in relation to *dianoêtic* objects	conjunction (*systasis*)	theoretic virtues
integration (*synairesis*) into an indivisible whole	initiation (*myêsis*)	paradigmatic virtues
seeing oneself (*autopsia*) the simple forms	vision (*epopteia*)	hieratic virtues

god achieved by this means is not as exact (*akribês*) as unification achieved by ineffable means – i.e. mystic rites (I 168.13-14). Damascius concludes this section with the famous remark that Porphyry and Plotinus make the philosophical pathway primary while Iamblichus, Syrianus and Proclus stress the hieratic pathway (I 172.1-3).

It is, of course, easy to make too much of this. What is said by Damascius does not entail that Iamblichus and Proclus *utterly abandoned* the pursuit of philosophy as a means by which we may return to the divine. Rather, when considered in its present context, this looks like a disagreement about the relative merits of philosophy or the hieratic arts in the *purification of the soul*. That, after all, is the issue in the text of the *Phaedo* itself.

Robbert van den Berg has argued that Proclus similarly accorded the greatest efficacy to mystic rites in securing the separation of the soul from the body.[10] Such separation is, of course, the role defined for the cathartic virtues. This sort of 'death' – a theme pursued in the *Phaedo* itself – is best achieved through theurgy. I think it is hard to deny that *many* of Proclus' remarks on the cathartic virtues suggest that purificatory ritual is an important aspect of the soul's return to the divine. However, the existence in Damascius' *Phaedo* commentary of another, philosophical form of purification of the soul holds out the promise that we will find traces of this sense of catharsis as well. I claim that this expectation is met. Alongside the catharsis through ritual in Proclus, there are also traces of a doctrine of philosophical purification through the purgation of false opinion.

iii. Cathartic virtues in Proclus

The evidence of Marinus

It seems that the Iamblichean taxonomy of virtues continues to be used in the Athenian school. Proclus' biographer, Marinus, discusses six of the seven, preferring to keep silent about the paradigmatic virtues since these 'transcend the human condition'.[11] About the purificatory virtues, Marinus has this to say:

> Let us now pass to the purificatory virtues, which are a different class beyond the political ones. For the principal task assigned to the latter is to purify the soul in some way, and to enable it to consider human affairs without prejudice, so that it has that likeness to God which is its highest end. ... [T]he purificatory virtues, superior to these [sc. political virtues], separate and liberate them from the truly leaden world of generation, and produce an uncurbed flight from the present world. And it was these that the philosopher pursued throughout the whole of his life.
>
> *Life of Proclus* 18, trans. Edwards

Marinus goes on to illustrate the things that produce separation of the soul by discussing Proclus' enthusiasm for Orphic and Chaldean purifications involving ablutions and the driving off of demons. Chapters 19 to 20 catalogue Proclus' eclectic tastes for religious rites of all sorts. Clearly this is one sense of 'purification' that is connected with the cathartic virtues in Marinus' mind. The consequences of this purification are summed up by Marinus as follows: Proclus' soul gathered itself within itself and all but left his body while still being detained there. He did not merely have the *phronêsis* associated with political virtue, but rather *noêsis* that was moreover *auto kath' hauto* and pure. His soul reverted upon itself and did not believe in accordance with the body. This, together with Marinus' account of Proclus' purified form of moderation, courage and justice coincides with Porphyry's definitions.

This surely makes it sound as if, in Proclus, the stage of purificatory virtue is entirely subsumed in the practice of rituals of purification. But I wish to point out a few discordant notes. These discordant notes cast doubt either on Marinus as a reporter, or on the extent to which Proclus followed Iamblichus entirely on the question of the virtues.

Marinus tells us that Proclus passed on to the next level of virtue easily 'as it were by the steps of initiation'. These will be the theoretic virtues that involve a move from the soul's reversion upon itself to its contemplation of Intellect. Marinus tells us that, upon attaining this level of virtue, Proclus became an eyewitness to the blessed sights up there – the paradigm in the Divine Intellect. He did this not through discursive reasoning but rather through contemplating them by means of simple conceptions (*haplais epibolais*).

This description seems *prima facie* at odds with recent accounts of Proclus' epistemology. Like nearly all subsequent Neoplatonists, Proclus joined in the rejection of Plotinus' undescended soul still present in the intelligible. Steel argues that, for Proclus, the human soul's access to the Forms is always mediated: we contemplate the Forms indirectly through their *logoi* – the innate concepts in the human soul.[12] This is the reason van den Berg thinks theurgy must fill the gap.[13] We are unable to contemplate the Forms since they are utterly separated from our souls. At best we are able to achieve a unification with the Divine Intellect – said to be identified by Proclus with the Demiurge – through theurgy. This unification, van den Berg argues, is mediated by the Leading Gods (*hoi hêgemonikoi theoi*, cf. *Plat. Theol.* VI). The rituals that Marinus tells us Proclus participated in are identified by van den Berg as the basis of the cathartic virtues.[14]

None of this, however, is said *directly* by Marinus. Indeed, quite the contrary. As I said, there is a *prima facie* incompatibility between what Marinus actually says and Steel's view of Proclus' epistemology. For Marinus says that he contemplated the paradigms in the Divine Intellect as an eyewitness (*autoptês*). This suggests a direct, not a mediated, relation through, for example, the Leading Gods. Moreover, *autopsia* corresponds to the *last* stage of initiation and the hieratic virtues in Iamblichus' account above – not the second and third stages corresponding to purificatory and theoretic virtues.

What are we to make of this? Perhaps Marinus correctly reports Proclus' teaching on progress through the virtues and this disagrees with Iamblichus because Proclus deviated from Iamblichus. Or perhaps Marinus is simply confused. In any event, it seems to me that we should not conclude from Marinus' *Life* that Proclus entirely collapsed cathartic virtues into ritual purifications.

Three senses of 'catharsis' in the Alcibiades commentary

Proclus discusses purification at the start of the elenchus of Alcibiades at 106c. The purpose of Socrates' examination of the young man is the removal of 'two-fold ignorance' – the situation in which an agent fails to know something and believes falsely that he does know it. Overcoming such ignorance requires removing obstacles to the recovery of knowledge or recollection. This recovery requires purification, which Proclus says is three-fold. First, there is purification through initiation (*dia telestikês*) discussed in the *Phaedrus*.[15] Second, there is purification through philosophy, which is discussed in the *Phaedo*. The third form of purification takes place 'through this science of philosophical discussion which induces contradiction, exposes disagreement of opinions and delivers us from two-fold ignorance' (*In Alc.* 174.13-14, trans. O'Neill).

The mention of two-fold ignorance and the form of catharsis that overcomes it connects this passage with *Sophist* 229b and ff.[16] In this section of the *Sophist*, the Eleatic Stranger describes the 'noble form of sophistry' that many commentators associate with Socratic questioning. Throughout this passage, the Stranger speaks of this as a kind of purification (*katharmos*). However, the sense of purification that seems relevant here is the *medical one* of purgation – the conceit of false wisdom must be purged before the food of genuine knowledge will do the soul any good (cf.

177

In Alc. 175.10-15 with the similar medical analogy at *Soph.* 230c). However, Proclus immediately then switches to the religious sense of catharsis:

> The purification, then, that precedes all discussion is undertaken for this reason and resembles the purifications of initiatory rites, which, prior to sacred activities, cleanses us from all the defilements (*miasmatôn*) which we contract from birth and prepare us for participation in the divine.
>
> *In Alc.* 175.15-19, trans. O'Neill

The intellectual achievement of being purged of false pretensions to knowledge is assimilated to the ritual purification of those features that the soul acquires in its descent into becoming.

Proclus' remarks here in the *Alcibiades* commentary accord well with his few uses of 'cathartic virtue' in the *Timaeus* commentary:

> ... if someone should pray to the gods, who cut away [the effect of] matter and cause the stains (*kêlidas*) that come from the [process of] birth to vanish, while he himself is engaged in this by means of the purificatory virtues. Such a person would certainly, together with the gods, achieve liberation from the bonds (*desmôn*) of matter.
>
> *In Tim.* I 221.30-222.3

> Therefore only cathartic virtue must be denominated the salvation of souls since it removes and obliterates entirely the enmattered nature and the affections that adhere to us from generation, separates the soul and leads it to the intellect. Cathartic virtues cause the soul to put off the garments which they have donned. For when souls descend to Earth, they receive different garments from the different elements – aerial, watery and earthy – and finally they enter into the dense extension that we discriminate.
>
> *In Tim.* III 297.16-24

> Now toward the removal of these bodies which Plato has made manifest, each of the elements being particularly mentioned by Plato, the philosophical life contributes, just as he said. But in my opinion the life of ritual contributes even more, removing through divine fire all the 'defilements' (*kêlidas*) which arise from generation, as the *Oracles* teach [= *Or. Chald.* 196], and removes all things that are alien which the pneuma and the irrational nature of the soul have drawn along with them.
>
> *In Tim.* III 300.13-20

These passages are all cited as proof texts by van den Berg for his view that ritual and theurgy are the primary means by which Proclus supposed that we achieved our return to the divine. One conclusion to draw is that the ritual sense of catharsis has utterly overwhelmed the medical sense of purgation. The purgation of ignorance now plays little or no role in purifying the soul and making it fit for such contemplation of intellect as human souls are capable of. Before we conclude that the medical sense of catharsis is only vestigial in Proclus, I think we should look more closely at the Alcibiades commentary.

This medical sense of catharsis associated with the removal of ignorance is a frequent theme in the *Alcibiades* commentary. This seems fitting, since the cathartic virtues are the relatively low on Iamblichus taxonomy and the Alcibiades is early in the Iamblichean course of reading. Thus at 152-5, Proclus considers Socrates' assertion that Alcidiades' plans cannot be accomplished without Socrates and the power that he has over the young man and his affairs. Proclus considers that one might object that Socrates here inflames Alcibiades' obvious desire for political power – a thing that is not a genuine good. But Proclus counters that Socrates is only like a good physician. He has diagnosed what is wrong with this patient. The careful soul doctor sees whether he is dealing with someone who suffers from love of pleasure, love of money or love of honour. He then shows him the *pure* form of that which he seeks, which is something other than the *image* of that form that the diseased soul thinks it is pursuing. In Alcibiades' case, he seeks after power. But *dynamis* is only a *phantasm* of that which is the genuine object of desire – capability (*hikanotêtos*). Socrates' first treatment will be to show Alcibiades that he lacks the knowledge to use political power wisely. The catharsis that he undergoes by refutation, which exposes his two-fold ignorance, is only a first step. Proclus again uses a medical analogy. Just as it is sometimes sound medical practice to prescribe dietary treatment of inflammatory diseases rather than a treatment that will expel the bad humours, so too Socrates attacks Alcibiades' two-fold ignorance before attempting to rid his soul of further mistaken notions of what is genuinely good.

In another example, Proclus considers the text of *Alcibiades* 113d ff. Here Socrates shows Alcidiades that he doesn't know what 'the expedient' is any more than he knows what justice is. Alcibiades resists the same sort of argument that Socrates used to establish the previous point. Proclus claims that this is like the situation in which a bodily disease responds on a couple of occasions to one kind of treatment and then does not. This ignorance in Alcibiades' soul will require another form of treatment in order to effect catharsis.

So, in spite of the immediate assimilation of the purgation model of the third form of catharsis to the ritual purification model of the first sort (*dia telestikês*) at *In Alc.* 175.10-19, it seems that Proclus retains an interest in ridding the soul of false opinion. Both are important senses of purification. Let us see how they are linked.

The psychic anatomy of ignorance

I think Proclus gives us an insight into how the type of catharsis associated with refutation is realized in his commentary on *Timaeus* 43d. Here Plato tells us that the inflow of sensation and nutrition in our embodied condition disrupts the rotation of the circles of the Same and the Different within our souls. The rotation of the circle of the Same is blocked, or at least hindered, and the circle of the Different is shaken up (*Tim.* 43d2). Later Plato discusses twisting, fractures, and disruptions, perhaps to both circles. The result is that they are moved irrationally:

> ... being at one time reversed (*antias*), at another oblique (*plagias*) and at another upside down (*hyptias*).
>
> *Tim.* 43e4-5

Proclus turns these remarks into a catalogue of *pathê* and their causes:

> The disturbances of the circles cause the combination of ratios to be moved in opposite ways (*enantias pheresthai*). The breaking (*klaseis*) causes the slanting or oblique motion (*plagias*), and the turnings cause them to be flattened (*hyptias*). And these three affections seen in the case of the rational soul are also seen in the case of the irrational soul in particular. For though the rational soul may at times be in harmony with itself and at times opposed to itself, it is still the case that by a much greater degree it is in conflict with the irrational soul. For the virtues imply one another, the intellectual imply the ethical and the ethical the intellectual.
>
> *In Tim.* III 340.29-341.4

These *pathê* manifest themselves in the rational soul in the following ways:

(1) Opposition (*enantiotêta*) occurs when a better and a worse opinion contend with one another in the soul of a person and the better opinion is not defeated by the worse. When a person assents to a false belief, there must nonetheless be a true belief in the soul which is opposed but not overcome by it. Otherwise Socrates could not have refuted Thrasymachus in accordance with his own beliefs.
(2) The oblique condition (*plêgian thesin*) occurs when two judgements are distorted and one is not able to maintain a coherent position since the judgements say incoherent things. Because rational soul is thus not able to work things out, the judgement gets referred to sensation. The person thus comes to hold a mutually reinforcing set of false beliefs, e.g. pleasure is the good, injustice is wisdom and justice is stupidity.
(3) The flattened (*hyptios*) condition: when the worse opinions entirely dominate the better and the concepts that are projected from within [the rational soul] are dominated by what derives from sensation. In this condition, the better things within the soul are entirely enslaved and become subordinate to what is worse. This person, we may suppose, doesn't care a whit about the content of his beliefs and their consistency at all. He is simply bestial.

It appears that this passage on the *pathê* of the rational soul pertains to the catharsis of wrong opinions as it is described and illustrated in the *Alcibiades* commentary. The person whose rational soul suffers from opposition is salvageable: he can be purified through refutation since there are some true beliefs and inconsistencies with which someone like Socrates can work. The case of the person who suffers from the oblique condition in the rational soul is perhaps less clear – it will depend on whether a skilful psychic surgeon can find any true beliefs that can give him leverage on the interlocking structure of falsehoods. The person whose rational soul is flattened is obviously a write off.

In Proclus' mind the cognitive failings associated with purgation of ignorance are intimately connected with the sense of catharsis in which it ritually cleanses the soul of material accretions. The reason is not hard to seek. The malfunctions of rationality and psychic accretions are linked in Plato's own text in a way that makes specific reference to the anatomy of circles in the soul just outlined:

> ... until he has pulled himself together with the circle of the Same and uniform within him, and dominated by reason the great accretion which later adhered to him from earth, air, fire and water – things tumultuous and irrational – then [when this is done] he might return again to the appearance of his initial and best state.
>
> *Tim.* 42c4-d2

Proclus insists in his commentary on the *Timaeus* passage that by purifying itself from the things that are nearby, it becomes an intellectual flower (cf. *Or. Chald.* frs 1 and 3). The presence of the language of the *Oracles* suggests that the purification he has in mind is accomplished through theurgy. The trick is to move in accordance with the circle of the Same, which is linked to the intellectual life, rather the circle of the different which pertains to generation and opinion.[17] After a confirmation of this from Orpheus (fr. 229 Kern) we get the claim about the importance of cathartic virtue which I have already quoted (*In Tim.* III 297.16-24).

Is that it then? Is van den Berg right to suppose that Proclus thinks we 'pull ourselves together' through ritual acts of purification? I think it is important to distinguish here the real problem with the soul from its antecedent and proximate causes. In the *Timaeus*, what upsets the rotation of the circles of the soul are the motions associated with sensation (43c5) and nutrition (44b1). The Neoplatonists expand these remarks through their notion of the soul's vehicles and the accretions that adhere to these vehicles in the soul's descent into Becoming. But the fact remains that these accretions are *merely obstacles* to the soul's proper functioning. We have been told what results from the presence of these obstacles: inconsistent beliefs (i.e opposed psychic circles), or systematically false beliefs (oblique psychic circles), or failure to worry about truth and consistency at all (the flattened condition). The removal of the 'stains of genera-tion' might be *necessary* for these conditions to be rectified, but there is still the presence of false beliefs to be overcome. Moreover, one must not only cease to hold false and inconsistent beliefs, one must achieve actively embrace the life of contemplation, thus assimilating oneself to the divine objects of *noêsis*.

It may be said that the removal of the material that causes these disturbances to the proper movements of the psychic circles is also a sufficient condition for proper psychic functioning. After all, the vehicles of the encosmic gods give them no trouble and, accordingly, they enjoy a blessed and happy existence. Moreover, Plato himself speaks of the orderly rotation of the psychic circles as *kata physin* (44b). Proclus in his commen-tary on this passage claims that when the obstacles that originate from generation are diminished, then straight away (*euthys*) the soul is led toward a better condition by nature (*In Tim.* III 349.15-19). Thus, you could argue that a return to the natural and unencrusted condition of the psychic vehicles would be sufficient for the happy life. If the life of ritual is able to remove the stains of generation, it alone is sufficient for our salvation.

But I think this will not do. In the passage at *In Tim.* III 349.15-19 Proclus says only that the soul gets *better*: it exhibits order (*taxis*) and reason (*logos*), becomes better able to calculate and is wise (*emphrôn*). Proclus himself immediately relates this to Galen's view that the condition of the soul supervenes on the mixtures of the body. Proclus, of course, rejects this view – whether soul is able to think intellectually (*noein*) does not depend on the body. The body may be an obstacle, but it is not able to produce a life of wisdom (*zoê emphrôn*). As Plato insists, there must be *paideia* (*In Tim.* III 349.21-50.8).

I take the upshot of all this to be that Proclus' position must be just what is says at *In Tim.* III 300.13-20: the life of ritual is *more valuable* than the life of philosophy because without removing 'the stains of generation' our efforts to return to the divine intelligibles and beyond will meet with no success. Cleaning the crud off our psychic vehicles is a necessary, but not sufficient, condition for thinking straight – or rather, thinking perfectly circularly as the World-Soul does!

iv. Conclusion

In this chapter I have attempted to chart the course of the *Phaedo*'s cathartic virtues through some later interpreters of Plato. I have argued against van den Berg that the cathartic virtues in Proclus contain a dual sense. A person achieves the separation of soul from body that is the *telos* of these virtues through ritual acts that expunge the accretions that cling to the soul's vehicles as a result of its descent into becoming. But one also achieves it through the purgation of false opinion. The first makes possible the soul's correct functioning, free of the body's influence. The second capitalizes on these conditions of possibility. I have not ventured to say anything directly about hieratic virtues and whether there exist various higher forms of theurgy that bring about a union between the soul so purified and the intelligible gods, the henads, or even the One. The role of theurgy here is disputed. I only maintain that the cathartic virtues – merely the fourth gradation of virtue, not the final hieratic virtue – involve both cognitive and ritual senses of purification.

Notes

1. See Annas (1999), Sedley (1997), Sedley (1999).

2. There is a solution of sorts to the updating problem in Alcinous, ch. 28. We do become like god through possessing the virtues, but we only become like the encosmic god in this way – not the hypercosmic god who is beyond the virtues. On the question of the relation between the virtues described in *Phaedo* and those in *Republic*, Alcinous probably says that there are virtues that pertain to the rational and irrational parts of the soul (ch. 29) – the text here is corrupt. But in any event, we are not told how this distinction relates to the texts of Plato. See commentary ad loc., Dillon (1999).

3. Plotinus here evokes Orphic teachings via *Phdo* 69c = *Orph*. fr. 6 Kern.

4. *In Phd*. I 151, cf. *Or. Chald*. 51 Majercik and Proclus, *In Tim*. I 208.21-2.

5. Des Places (1984), 2311-13.

6. Cf. Lewy (1956), 177-257, and, more succinctly, Majercik (1989), 21-6.

7. Note that later, when he is discussing the genuine gods who alone are able to provide these divine goods to men (and contrasting them with the works of *daimones*), Iamblichus insists that the recipient of these benefits must be *both* a good man and also purified by ritual (*Myst*. III 31.1).

8. Cf. Proclus, *In Tim*. III 297.8-10 and van den Berg (2003).

9. Saffrey and Westerink (1968-97), VI 150, n. 3.

10. Van den Berg (2000) and (2003).

11. Edwards claims against I. Hadot (1978), 156, that the enumeration of kinds of virtues does not correspond to Damascius *In Phdo* 4-5 (Westerink = Norvin 3). This is true. But surely the relevant text in Damascius is I 138-51. Proclus himself lists the first three of Iamblichus' seven virtues at *In Alc*. 96. He also alludes to the higher forms of virtue. This suggests that Iamblichus' taxonomy of virtues was well established in the subsequent tradition.

12. Steel (1997), 307, cf. *In Parm*. 948.12-38.

13. Van den Berg (2000), 426.

14. Van den Berg (2000), 43.

15. Sheppard (1982) uses Hermias as a source for the views of Syrianus, Proclus' teacher. To the extent that Proclus follows Syrianus – and that is, by Proclus' own admission, quite a considerable extent – we can draw inferences about Proclus' attitude to theurgy from it. Sheppard argues that Proclus recognized three forms of theury: ritual 'white magic'; a form of theurgy that still uses ritual but is capable of raising the soul to the level of the intellectual (*noeros*) but only to the lowest level of the intelligible (*noêtos*); and finally a form that does not employ ritual at all but brings about a union of the 'one in the soul' with the higher intelligibles and the One.

16. Proclus later refers explicitly to this passage from the *Sophist* at 210.5. Cf.

In Alc 8.17 and *Anonymous Prolegomena* 16, p. 211.3-5 (Hermann), cited by O'Neill (1965) ad loc.

17. 'For the revolution of the Same and the Similar conducts the soul toward intellect and the intelligible nature and toward its first and best state. And it is this state itself in virtue of which the soul has wings and joint administration of the whole cosmos together with the gods, being assimilated to the gods themselves' *In Tim.* III 296.23-7.

The transformation of Plato and Aristotle

Richard Sorabji

In Neoplatonism, though not in Aristotelianism, Plato and Aristotle are transformed in a variety of different ways. The transformation is partly driven by a wish to harmonize Plato and Aristotle, but only partly. There is less effort to harmonize the two in some commentators than in others, and on some issues, we shall see, there is less harmonization among our commentators than there was in the Middle Platonism of an earlier period. Further, the transformation of views is driven by other factors too besides harmonization.

Harmonization is most marked in Porphyry and Ammonius. It seems to be least favoured by Syrianus and Proclus. Simplicius says that the good commentator should find Plato and Aristotle in harmony on most points, *In Cat.* 7.23-32. The presumption for a Neoplatonist is that, in case of disharmony, it is Plato who will be right. But even this is reversed by a late commentator, Olympiodorus, who backs Aristotle against Plato on the definition of relatives, *In Cat.* 112.19ff.

As an example of harmonization, Porphyry, on the standard interpretation, defended Aristotle's categories from Plotinus' objections in *Enneads* VI.1-3. Plotinus accepted only four of Aristotle's ten categories for classifying the world perceived by the senses, and that with heavy qualifications. He complained that Aristotle's categories left out the world of intelligible Forms from which the perceptible world derived. Sensible qualities, for example, are only shadows of the activities of intelligible Forms. Porphyry replied, at *In Cat.* 57.7-8, 58.5-7, and 91.19-27, that Aristotle's categories are not meant to be exhaustive. They are only intended to distinguish *words* insofar as they signify things, and words are chiefly used to speak about *sensibles*. For that limited task the categories are to be valued. Porphyry thus made Aristotle's categories for ever acceptable to Platonism. Hereafter, it became increasingly useful to reinforce what I regard as the myth of harmony in the face of Christian charges that pagan philosophers contradicted each other. There was an irony in this, because the harmonization, whose motive was thus partly anti-Christian, finished in the thirteenth century by helping Thomas Aquinas to present Aristotle as safe for Christianity, since the assimilation to Plato had turned Aristotle's God from a thinker into a Creator, and Aristotle's human soul into an immortal one.

There can, however, be more than one approach towards the harmonization of Plato and Aristotle. Lloyd Gerson in this volume offers the most thoroughgoing modern attempt to argue that it is basically correct. If, as I have supposed, it is not, the question arises whether pressure towards a false harmonization would be bad for Philosophy. Having to convince the Christians that Plato and Aristotle agreed with each other on almost everything would surely lead to loss of their wonderful insights. But in fact it gave a distinctive character, interesting in its own right, to Neoplatonism. And, curiously, it led to an even closer reading of the texts of Plato and Aristotle, because their texts had to be read very closely indeed, if one was going to argue that what they really meant was something different from what at first sight might appear. In fact, the pressure to harmonize proved a valuable stimulus to the imagination in the Greek Neoplatonist commentators. They took Plato to postulate a changeless and timeless world of divine Platonic Forms and they had to think out how such a world would relate to the temporal, changing world described by Aristotle.

I should like now to look at some examples of what happened to the views of Plato and Aristotle in Neoplatonism. I shall ask what factors besides harmonization are at work, whether Plato is transformed in the process as much as Aristotle, whether the harmonizations are hostile or friendly to Aristotle, and where the transformations proved important for subsequent Philosophy.

But first a word is needed about methodology. I shall follow the usual practice of the ancient commentators in speaking about what Plato maintained, or held, or insisted on. But the ancient commentators were aware, like the best modern ones, that Plato's works are written as dialogues, so that it can be disputed whether Plato endorses the view he puts into the mouth of a character, even when that character is Socrates. David Sedley has drawn attention to the Emperor Julian objecting to those who discounted certain problematic remarks ascribed to Socrates as being examples of Socratic irony addressed to a particular interlocutor. Julian, *Against the Cynic Heracleius* 24, says:

> It is in any case a flawed method, to scrutinize not what is being said but who the people are who are saying it, and whom their arguments are addressed to.[1]

Ineke Sluiter has pointed out to me that Porphyry's commentaries on Homer have a technical term for solving a question of interpretation by reference to the person being described, *lyesthai ek tou prosôpou*. But this was not the standard practice of the commentators on Plato and Aristotle. Let me now turn to some specimen topics on which Plato and Aristotle were variously interpreted.

It is difficult to harmonize Plato and Aristotle on certain issues concerning rationalism versus empiricism. In the *Theaetetus* 186a-187a, Plato maintains that perception can do practically nothing at all without the aid of reason, and the Middle Platonist, Alcinous, elaborates this view in his *Didaskalikos* ch. 4, to maintain that there would be no perceptual recognition without reason. So far this rejects Aristotle's view that perception is entirely separate from reason and that animals can get along very well by using perception on its own, while completely bereft of reason. But a qualification is that the relevant kind of reason, for Alcinous, is empirically based and manifested in opinions (*doxastikos logos*).

To take another example, Plato holds in the *Phaedo* that our concepts are recollected from a life before our birth and stored in our rational souls. Aristotle, by contrast, argues in the last chapter of his *Posterior Analytics*, 2.19, 100a3-8, that the most rudimentary universal concept of (say) an ox is based on nothing more than many memories of perceived oxen. Moreover, at 100a17-b1, he says that perception is of the universal. How can the very different views of Plato and Aristotle on the role of perception in concept formation be harmonized?

The Platonists go three different ways on the issue. One answer is that we have two kinds of concept. Chapter 4 of the Middle Platonist *Didaskalikos*, already cited, welcomes both Plato's and Aristotle's account of concepts. For the 'doxastic' conception of reason that it invokes is one consisting of concepts empirically gained in Aristotle's manner, and the idea of 'doxastic' reason (*doxastikos logos*) is repeated by a late Neoplatonist, Priscian, *Metaphrasis in Theophrastum* 19.9-13. There are others too who allow that we have both kinds of concept, e.g. Hermeias *In Phdr.* 171.8-25.

A second Platonist move is even bolder, namely the claim that Aristotle himself accepted Plato's recollected concepts alongside his own empirically gained ones. I find this ascribed to Iamblichus and to Plutarch of Athens by 'Philoponus' *In DA 3*, 533.25-35 and 520.1-12, and endorsed by Philoponus *In De Intellectu*, 36-40 Verbeke (*CLCAG*), ms lines 70-43, judging from his talk of knowledge being suppressed by the process of birth.

The third tendency among Platonists came to be the commonest, namely to list Aristotle's empirically based concepts as one type of universal, but to reject them. This tendency is found in Syrianus *In Metaph.* 95.13-17; Proclus *In Eucl.* 50.16-51.9; *In Parm.* 981 and passim; Ammonius *In Isag.* 41.17-20; 42.10-21; Simplicius *In Cat.* 82.35-83.20.

As for perception itself, Priscian repeats that empirically based reason, *doxastikos logos*, is required for perceptual recognition (*Metaphrasis in Theophrastum* 19.9-13). But the late Neoplatonists give a further role to *logos*, now in the sense of a concept. Perceptual recognition cannot occur unless the recollected Platonic concepts are *projected* (*proballein*) from the mind (Priscian 2.26-3.9, and, reporting Iamblichus, 7.11-20) to make the recognition possible. Moreover, though Aristotle says that perception is of the universal, Themistius *In An. Post.* 64.2-9, and Eustratius *In An. Post.* 266.14-29, explain that this is a universal not yet separated from matter, and for Alexander *DA* 85.20-86.6; 87.19-21, Alexander(?) *Mantissa* 108.19-24, and Themistius *In DA* 98.35-99.10, it is intellect that has to separate the universal from matter.

So far, the harmonization concerning the first issue, concepts, has been mixed. There were attempts at harmonization, but another tendency was rejection of Aristotle's account of concepts. On the second issue, perception's independence from reason, rejection of Aristotle has been complete – perceptual recognition cannot occur without reason. But the concept of reason has been modified. In some cases, an empiricist concept of reason has been substituted. In other cases, Plato's insistence on the need for reason has been defended by means of a theory of projecting concepts which goes far beyond Plato.

There is a third issue, also connected with the dependence of perception on reason. How are we aware of our own mental activities? Discussing awareness of our own perceptions, Aristotle says that this is effected by a perceptual faculty, which the commentators take to be the 'common sense', *On Sleep* 455a12-20. But Proclus objects that, besides perception, we also have, and are aware of, reason and different kinds of desire. Surely awareness of all these diverse activities must be assigned to something higher than the common sense, *In Parm.* 957.28-958.11 Cousin. 'Simplicius' *In DA* comes to Aristotle's aid, 187.27-188.35. The common sense can indeed be aware of this great diversity of activities, he says, if we once recognize that human common sense is permeated by reason. This answer is perfectly congenial to the Platonist tradition, which, starting from Plato's *Theaetetus*, regards perception as dependent on reason. But to Aristotle this defence of his reference to the common sense would be anathema. As the great biological taxonomist, he wanted to show that perception was independent of reason and could be used to mark off the animal kingdom. Aristotle loses again in this harmonization.

There is another answer to the question of awareness of our mental activities, which goes beyond both Plato and Aristotle by postulating a special faculty of awarenesss (*to prosektikon*), so 'Philoponus' reports with approval, *In DA 3*, 464.30-465.17; 466.18-29. This seems to me an improvement. The ancient debate on whether perception or reason is responsible for awarenes of our mental activities still continues today.[2] I believe the right answer is that sometimes we need not a further act of perception or reason, but simply *attention* to the perceiving or reasoning we have already performed.

Aristotle does not always lose. Something very unexpected happened in the commentators' discussion of universals. Plato introduced the idea of Forms or Ideas, and these were understood by Aristotle and by other schools in the following centuries to be universals which somehow transcended the physical world and yet explained the acquisition of properties by things in the physical world. This Platonic account of universals was condemned in turn by Aristotle, by the Stoics and by Aristotle's great protagonist, Alexander. Aristotle complained that the changeless Platonic Forms could not act as causes of anything, *Metaph.* 1.9, 991a8-19, and he along with Alexander substituted deflationary accounts of universals. Alexander reduced them to mental constructs, *DA* 90.2-11; *Quaest.* 2.28, 78.18-20, whose practically worthless function is to mark off cases in which a form like *human* happens to be shared by at least two specimens, *Quaest.* 1.11, 23.25-31; *In Top.* 355.18-24, and ap. Boethium *In Isag. (2)* 166.12ff., ed. Brandt, CSEL vol. 48. The form is in itself neither universal nor particular, but when construed as universal, it is a mental construct.

Would we not expect the Neoplatonist commentators to turn against Alexander' deflationary account? It is very surprising, then, to find that the Neoplatonist Porphyry, possibly at *In Cat.* 90, 14-91.7; 75.24-9; 81.16-20, and Boethius expounding Porphyry (Boethius *In Isag. (2)* 166.12ff., ed. Brandt, CSEL vol. 48), seem content with a deflationary account of universals close to the one proposed by Alexander. Indeed, Boethius says in his exegesis of Porphyry that he is following Alexander, so Porphyry may have done the same. What has happened to universals as Platonic Forms? The answer, I believe, is that the Neoplatonists have so emphasized the role of Forms as causes, a role which Aristotle said they could not play, that they are willing to backtrack on the other role of Forms as universals, Simplicius *In Cat.* 82.35-83.20, Proclus *In Parm.* 880.3-11. A Form is not after all something universal and common to all instances, for the instances are too inferior to share the same characteristics in the same sense. If the Form is something common at all, it is common as a cause to all its effects, but not as a common feature. Thus Aristotle loses on the issue of whether Forms can be causes, but he wins on the issue of whether universals are Forms. Here is the comment of Simplicius *In Cat.* 83.10-12:

> For the common cause transcends its effects and is something different from them in all respects. It is common as a cause, but not as a common nature (*koinê physis*).
>
> trans. de Haas, modified

The Aristotelians suffer from a curious distortion of their account of individuals. When Porphyry writes his introduction to Aristotle, the *Isagôgê*, he describes individuals as being unique bundles (*athroismata*) of distinctive qualities (*idiotêtes*) *Isagôgê* 7.16-24, Latin translation by Boethius, ed. Busse, 33.4-7. Why? – for Aristotle believes that the individual consists of matter and form. I conjecture that once again Plato's *Theaetetus* is the ultimate source, although the *athroisma* idea is in the same chapter of Alcinous, *Didaskalikos*, ch. 4. In the *Theaetetus*, the individual Theaetetus is described as consisting of qualities such as a distinctive snubness of nose. The terms 'bundle' (*athroisma*) and 'distinctive' (*idios*) occur earlier in the *Theaetetus* respectively at 157b-c and 154a; 166c. I think Porphyry offers this Platonic view of the individual, because his introduction is for beginners in Philosophy, and he does not yet want to broach the more complex concepts of matter and form, which enter into Aristotle's account of the individual. But because Porphyry wrote this in an introduction to Aristotle, later Neoplatonists, Proclus, ap. Olympiodorum *In Alc. 1*, Westerink, 204.8-12, Simplicius *In Cat.* 83.16-20, and possibly 'Philoponus' *In An. Post.* 2. 437.21-438.2, though they are well aware of Aristotle's belief in matter and form, take it to be a view, if not of Aristotle, at any rate of the Aristotelian school. If so, the Aristotelians' account of individuals has been harmonized with Plato's, this time by a sort of accident of interpretation.

Of my five examples so far, the first three have come from the field of psychology: concepts, perception and self-awareness, the next two from logic and metaphysics: universals and individuals. The following two examples will come from physics. Aristotle disagreed with Plato in postulating a fifth element as constituting the heavens, whereas Plato had been satisfied with one of the standard four elements, namely fire. The commentators offer almost opposite harmonizations, according to whether they are friendly or hostile to Aristotle, and in this regard I would see them as varying more than appears in Lloyd Gerson's account. Proclus, the hostile one, tries to show, in the preface to his commentary on Plato's *Timaeus*, that Plato had already anticipated virtually everything that Aristotle had to say. So when Plato associated the shape of the heavens with the fifth of the five figures that had been shown to be the only possible regular convex solids in geometry, he was anticipating Aristotle's fifth element, *In Tim.* I 6.29-7.2; II 49.29-50.2.[3] The explanation is repeated by Simplicius, *In Cael.* 12.16-27. But Simplicius knows a more friendly method of harmonization, *In Cael.* 85.31-86.7. On this view, Aristotle recognized that the heavens were a particularly pure mixture of the four elements with fire predominating. He spoke as if the result were a fifth element, only to emphasize its divinity in praiseworthy opposition to the sort of view more recently taken by the Christians. On both interpretations Aristotle's view is accommodated, but on the first he comes out an imitator, on the second a hero. Harmonization is not a unitary procedure.

The same hostility is exhibited by Proclus, this time on better grounds, in connection with God's responsibility for the world's existence. Aristotle's God is a thinker, not a creator, and he inspires motion in the universe, but does not provide existence, since the five elements exist independently of him. At best, as pointed out by Iamblichus' pupil Dexippus, *In Cat.* 40.28-1.18, the motion (by producing seasonal rainfall, etc.) gives form and life to some things. But Proclus complains that, on his own principles, Aristotle should have made God responsible for the *existence* of the universe, *In Tim.* I 267.4-268.24 Diehl. Proclus' pupil, Ammonius, effects the harmonization, arguing at book length that this is what Aristotle intended his principles to show, Ammonius ap. Simplicium *In Phys.* 1361.11-1363.12,[4] and Simplicius follows Ammonius. This is the tradition that enabled Thomas Aquinas to harmonize Aristotle's God with Christianity. The argument most relevant here, apparently drawn from Ammonius, is summarized by Simplicius at *In Phys.* 1364.4-8 as follows:

> And if, according to Aristotle, the power of any finite body is itself finite, clearly whether it be a power of moving or a power that produces being, then just as it gets its eternal *motion* from the unmoved cause, so it must receive its eternal *being* as a body from the non-bodily cause.

I should finish with the other harmonization that was crucial for Christian acceptance of Aristotle – the issue of individual immortality. This time, even Plato's views caused some problem. Although he makes Socrates assure his friends in *Phaedo* 115c on the day of his execution that he personally will survive, there is room for worry that the rational soul, which is what Plato regards as the true self, is rather impersonal. On one interpretation, Plato's *First Alcibiades* even recognizes this at 130d. The worry comes to a head when Plotinus discusses those disembodied human souls which have attained the ideal state of identifying themselves with the highest part of the soul or with the Intellect, and whose thoughts have the same content – the Platonic Forms. What is there left to distinguish these souls from each other? Plotinus' analogy is with a theorem in a mathematical system. Each theorem is distinct, but cannot be understood as a theorem, except in terms of the whole system, *Enn.* IV.3.2.49-58; IV.9.5.7-26; VI.2.20.4-23.

But if this preserves some individuality, why should Aristotle agree? He insists from the opening chapter of *On the Soul* that no mental activities, with the possible exception of thinking, can occur apart from a body. The soul turns out to exist only as enforming a living body, so that, presumably, we perish when we die. The special case of thinking is discussed in book 3, chapter 5. Here room is made for a productive intellect to be resident in us. But is this intellect part of us, or, as the greatest defender of Aristotle's school, Alexander, was to say, *DA* 89.9-19, is it rather God resident in us, which offers no immortality to us? Themistius, *In DA* 102.36-103.19, disagreed with Alexander, and made it part of the human soul. But even that leaves a question: is it a soul shared by the human race, as the followers of Averroes were later to say, or is it individual? The idea of an intellect shared by the human race had been applied by Themistius, Philoponus and 'Philoponus' only to the highest of the intellects they ascribed to humans, the productive intellect. Philoponus *In De Intellectu* 49.48-54; 91.40-9, 'Philoponus' *In DA* 3 538.32-539.7 describe it as immortal only through the successsion of mortal individuals. What is new in Averroes' *Long Commentary on Aristotle On the Soul*, and in an earlier letter of his, is that the idea of being immortal only by succession is applied even to the lowest human intellect, the material intellect. It is this that leaves no room for individual human immortality. The shared character of the higher, productive, intellect is described as follows in the commentary *In DA 3* 539.5-7, ascribed to Philoponus:

> That it thinks always we apply not to one intellect in number but to all, just as we say that man lives always, not because of Socrates but because there is always some man living.
>
> trans. Charlton, modified

In his controversy with the Averroists, Thomas Aquinas claimed support from Themistius, who at *In DA* 103.32-104.6, allowed for individual intellects, and hence allowed Thomas to read into Aristotle provision for the immortality of individual human intellects. In this example, immortality of the individual has to be argued for, not only as a view of Aristotle, but also as a view open to a Platonist like Plotinus. So Plato as well as Aristotle have to be subjected to careful reinterpretation, to get the desired result.

The question of individual immortality is one of those selected for discussion in Lloyd Gerson's chapter, and it relates, I believe, to another issue that he discusses, the question of the best life for a human. Because the Socrates of Plato's *Phaedo* believes that after his execution he will continue to philosophize disembodied, he can also believe that the best life for a human is one of pure philosophizing. But if Alexander or Averroes is right, individual humans are, for Aristotle, annihilated at death, and there will never come a time when a human is free of the need to eat, and to engage in social exchange. On my interpretation of Aristotle, then, he never endorses the view which we find in Plato, that the true self for a human is the theoretical intellect. Rather he mentions this view in four places with qualifications, such as 'it is thought', 'if', 'someone might posit' and 'especially'.[5] The exposition in *EN* 10.7 is a thoroughgoing, but dialectical, attempt to put the case in favour of this Platonic view, as indicated by the numerous warning qualifications. In *EN* 10.8, on my view, Aristotle offers the necessary modification. Because humans will always have to eat, the ideal human life will need to practise the social virtues as well as seeking to philosophize. Hence only a comparative claim can be made: the more philosophizing can be included in the life, the happier it will be. Here, admittedly, I am probably in a minority, because I believe the normal view is that Aristotle agrees with Plato on the true self being the intellect. But I may be among the majority in thinking that on most of the other issues canvassed above, Plato and Aristotle did not agree. Lloyd Gerson's support of the Neoplatonist harmonization is therefore particularly interesting.

Let us draw some conclusions. Plato has been reinterpreted as well as Aristotle on perception, on concepts, on the fifth element, on individuals and, most radically, on universals. Only some attempted to harmonize Plato and Aristotle on concepts, and any harmonization on individuals was an unrecognized accident. The forces in play have not only been harmonization. There was also a misinterpretation arising from the reinterpretation of Porphyry's *Isasoge* as an authoritative source for Aristotelian views. And there was a response within Platonism to internal pressures concerning the role of Forms. The more important the causal role, the less defended was the role of Forms as universals. The effect of these changes on Medieval Philosophy was almost as important in the case of universals as in the case of the Creator God and the immortal human soul.

Notes

1. Translated by Sedley in Annas and Rowe (2002), 42.
2. Rosenthal (2002-3); Lycan (2004).
3. See Steel (2003).
4. See Saffrey (1990); Steel (2003).
5. Aristotle *Protrepticus* fr. 6; *EN* 9.4, 1166a16-17; 9.8, 1168b34-1169a3; 10.7, 1178a2-8.

The harmony of Aristotle and Plato according to Neoplatonism

Lloyd P. Gerson

i. The idea of harmony

Aristotle *versus* Plato. For a long time, that is the angle from which the tale has been told, especially to students. Aristotle's philosophy, we are given to understand, was geared to be in fundamental opposition to Plato's.[1] But it was not always thus in the history of philosophy. For example, Diogenes Laertius tells us that Aristotle was Plato's 'most genuine disciple'.[2] And beginning perhaps in the first century BC, we can already observe philosophers claiming the ultimate harmony of Academic and Peripatetic thought. Antiochus of Ascalon is frequently identified as a principal figure in this regard.[3] A similar view is clearly expressed by Cicero.[4] Later in the second century AD, we observe the Platonist Alcinous in his influential 'Handbook of Platonism' simply incorporating what we might reasonably call 'Aristotelian elements' into his account of authentic Platonism.[5] Finally, and most importantly, for a period of about three hundred years, from the middle of the third century AD to the middle of the sixth, Aristotelianism and Platonism were widely viewed and written about as being harmonious philosophical systems.[6] The philosophers who held this view are today usually given the faintly pejorative label 'Neoplatonists'. This paper aims to give a sketch of how the perception of harmony was articulated and defended among Neoplatonists and to what extent it is justified.

Since harmony is a reciprocal relation, the assumption of harmony by Neoplatonists means that Plato's philosophy is interpreted in the light of Aristotle's as well as the other way around. The term 'harmonious' when used of two philosophical positions can, of course, mean many things. Most innocuously, it can mean 'non-contradictory' or simply, 'logically consistent'. There are countless philosophical positions which are uninterestingly harmonious in this sense. Another relatively weak, though significant, sense of 'harmony' underlies the principle 'the enemy of my enemy is my friend'. With the rise of competing philosophical schools in antiquity, a member of one school might be viewed as an ally of members of another school owing to their joint antagonisms.[7] Those who held Aristotelianism to be in harmony with Platonism did not mean merely that their views were not in contradiction with each other or that their views were jointly in opposition to other non-Academic views. The idea of the harmony between Platonism and Aristotelianism that drove the philosophy of our period was somewhat different.

First, the idea rested on a perception of the division of labour. Roughly, it was held that Plato was authoritative for the intelligible world and Aristotle was authoritative for the sensible world.[8] More importantly, it was assumed or argued that the principles upon which their various accounts rested were not merely consistent but consonant as well. What this meant was that Aristotelian principles could be subsumed under the more capacious and, ultimately, true Platonic system in a way roughly analogous to the way that Newtonian mechanics can be subsumed under quantum mechanics or sentential logic can be subsumed under the predicate calculus.[9] Or, to shift to a political example, municipal by-laws or state statutes can be subsumed under federal constitutional law.

Simplicius, one of the most prolific of the ancient commentators and perhaps our most valuable source for the entire commentary tradition, provides in his massive work on *Categories* the fundamental rationale for harmonization.[10] In this work, he expresses an interpretative position that is normative for most of the commentators from Porphyry to the end of the commentary tradition. They reveal several basic points about harmonization.

The Neoplatonists started with the assumption that there was such a thing as Platonism more or less amenable to systemizing. Aristotle's relation to Platonism was neither indisputable nor unambiguous. Nevertheless, on the basis of the textual evidence of the Aristotelian material extant and available to them, they held that Aristotle was in some non-trivial sense an adherent of the principles of this system.

Second, Simplicius gives us one important reason for the occasional appearance of disharmony, namely, that the starting-points of Plato and Aristotle are different. Aristotle starts from nature, that is, the sensible world, and rises to speculation about the intelligible world on the basis of his treatment of nature. By contrast, Plato starts from considerations about the intelligible world and then treats of the natural world on the basis of these. This interpretation of the approaches of Aristotle and Plato is well grounded in the texts of both authors even if it does not represent the totality of their methodologies.[11] Simplicius plainly acknowledges apparent disagreement between Plato and Aristotle. But he thinks it is only apparent – in most matters.[12] The question we need to try to face squarely is how much of this supposed harmony is fact and how much fancy.

The view that the philosophy of Aristotle was in harmony with the philosophy of Plato must be sharply distinguished from the view, held by no one in antiquity, that the philosophy of Aristotle was *identical* with the philosophy of Plato. For example, in Plato's dialogue *Parmenides*, Socrates

196

suggests that Zeno's book states the 'same position' as Parmenides', differing only in that it focuses on an attack on Parmenides' opponents. Zeno acknowledges this identity.[13] The harmony of Aristotle and Plato was not supposed to be like the identity of the philosophy of Zeno and Parmenides. Again, Eusebius famously tells us that Numenius asked rhetorically, 'what is Plato but Moses speaking Attic Greek'.[14] No Neoplatonist supposed that Aristotle was just Plato speaking a Peripatetic 'dialect'.[15]

The harmony of the philosophies of Plato and Aristotle should not be thought necessarily to include the religious aspect of Platonism. One of the significant ways in which Neoplatonism distinguished itself from other forms of Platonism was in its religious practices, especially theurgy and prayer.[16] Iamblichus is the central figure in this regard and for this reason alone deserves to be considered one of the founders of Neoplatonism. The idea that Aristotle's philosophy could be subsumed under Platonism left untouched questions of religious practice. This is entirely understandable, since Aristotle and Peripatetics generally had almost nothing to say about religion. Thus, it should occasion no surprise that a Neoplatonist could regard Aristotle's philosophy as being in harmony with Plato's at the same time as he practised and defended a religious life sharply different from what we could imagine an Aristotelian practising.[17] For example, Proclus' deeply religious way of life did not prevent him from defending harmony where he found it.

The claim that Aristotle and Plato belong to the same school, namely, the Old Academy, should not be understood to entail the identity of the philosophies of Plato and Aristotle for the simple reason that the Neoplatonists, who claimed adherence to this school, differed widely among themselves in regard to specific issues without supposing that one's opponent was thereby an opponent of the school.[18] Nor should we take harmony to indicate some sort of eclecticism or syncretism.[19] Even if these terms have some useful application to various vaguely known philosophers in the period between Plato and Plotinus, they are quite useless in understanding the engagement of Neoplatonism with Aristotle. For one thing, the Neoplatonists did not believe that they were constructing some new philosophy from a supposedly 'neutral' standpoint outside of any commitment to one philosophical school or another. For another, their universally held view that the Platonism to which they adhered was a *comprehensive* system of philosophy precluded the typical motivation of eclectic or syncretic movements. They had no inkling that the terms 'bigger' and 'newer' could be used honorifically in the construction of a philosophical system.

A slightly different way of understanding harmony would see Aristotelianism as a type or version of Platonism. What all versions of Platonism have in common is a shared commitment to a certain set of principles.[20] These principles serve to distinguish Platonism from other philosophical 'schools'. As we shall see, even Plato's own philosophical positions taken together could be viewed as comprising one type of

Platonism, where 'Platonism' is a term practically identical with 'true philosophy'.[21]

We need to make this a bit more precise, since not all of Aristotle's doctrines (on Neoplatonic interpretations) are harmonized with those of Plato (again, on their interpretations) in the same way. There are (1) doctrines of Aristotle that are basically identical with those of Plato; (2) doctrines of Aristotle that are superficially different owing principally to language though they rest on principles that are identical with those held by Plato; (3) doctrines of Aristotle that are different from those of Plato because they rest on an imperfect or incomplete grasp by Aristotle of the correct Platonic principles. Examples of (1) would be the superiority of the contemplative or theoretical life to any other, the immortality of intellect, and the unicity of the first principle of all; of (2) the nature of matter, the role of divine providence, the relative primacy of sensible substance, the immortality of the person, and the rejection of separate Forms; of (3) the identification of the first principle of all with thinking, the completeness of the fourfold schema of causal analysis, and the identification of the first principle of all exclusively as a final cause. Depending on the context, to hold that Aristotle's philosophy is in harmony with Plato's can mean any one of the above, though it is may be doubted whether our Neoplatonic author is always so clear about the precise sense of harmony being employed.

The first concrete indication we possess that Neoplatonists were prepared to argue for the harmony of Aristotle and Plato is contained in a reference in Photius' *Bibliography* to the Neoplatonist Hierocles of Alexandria's statement in his *Commentary on the Golden Verses of Pythagoras* that Ammonius, the teacher of Plotinus, attempted to resolve the conflict between the disciples of Plato and Aristotle, showing that they were in fact 'of one and the same mind' (ἕνα καὶ τὸν αὐτὸν νοῦν).[22] The second indication of an effort to display harmony is found in the *Suda* where it is stated that Porphyry, Plotinus' disciple, produced a work in six books titled 'On Plato and Aristotle Being Adherents of the Same School' (μίαν τὴν αἵρεσιν).[23] We know nothing of this work apart from the title and what we can infer from what Porphyry actually says in the extant works. It seems reasonably clear, however, that a work of such length was attempting to provide a substantial argument, one which was evidently in opposition to at least some prevailing views.[24] It is also perhaps the case that Porphyry is questioning the basis for the traditional division of the 'schools' of ancient philosophy, as found, for example, in Diogenes Laertius.[25]

The principal feature of harmony was identity of principles, as indicated above. But it was universally held by Neoplatonists that Plato had a more profound and accurate grasp of these than did Aristotle. Thus, for example, in countless matters relating to physical nature, Aristotle's preeminence was readily acknowledged. But Aristotle did not, according to the Neoplatonists, possess the correct comprehensive view of all reality.

In particular, he misconceived the first principle of all reality by identifying it with intellect. But in part because he *did* recognize that there was a first principle and that it was separate from and prior to the sensible world, he is legitimately counted as being fundamentally in harmony with Plato.

I should perhaps at this point make explicit what must be obvious, namely, that Neoplatonists held Aristotle's philosophy to be in harmony with *Platonism*, as they understood that. The Neoplatonic view that Plato was the best, but by no means the only, exponent of Platonism will seem ironic only if we forget that for them, our term 'Platonism' would be just equivalent to 'the true philosophy'.[26] Their understanding of Platonism was constructed from evidence that extended beyond the dialogues, including, of course, Aristotle's testimony. The occasions for confusion, mischief, and frustration are many when trying to say what Plato means rather than just what Plato says. The reaction of Harold Cherniss to Aristotle's efforts to say what Plato means is a good example.[27] But Cherniss took Aristotle to task largely because he failed accurately to grasp Plato's meaning. And this is something that one could say only if one grasped that meaning oneself. Inevitably, there were disputes about Plato's meaning. Proclus and Simplicius, just to take two examples, regularly offer long lists of contrary views held by their Neoplatonic predecessors about this or that question. Therefore, one should not be overly surprised if Neoplatonists can call Aristotle a Platonist with a straight face at the same time as they note Aristotle's criticisms of Plato.

Inextricably bound up with Aristotle's account or accounts of Platonism are issues regarding Aristotle's own philosophical positions. If Aristotle was a Platonist, why does he appear to criticize Plato relentlessly? If, on the other hand, he was not a Platonist, why does he say so very many things that seem to be so *echt* Platonic? To begin to grasp this problem, we must realize that the picture is complicated by the existence of Aristotle's dialogues or 'exoteric' writings, albeit largely now available to us only in fragmentary form. These exoteric works do appear to express views that are both easily identifiable as Platonic and also appear to contradict things that are said elsewhere in the so-called 'esoteric' writings, though a minority of scholars have insisted that the exoteric works show no such thing.[28]

Such apparent contradictions naturally elicit various views about a supposed development in Aristotle's thinking.[29] So, we might hypothesize, as Werner Jaeger did, that Aristotle started out as an authentic and loyal Platonist, but that as he then grew intellectually, he moved away from Platonism to a philosophical position that was more or less explicitly anti-Platonic. This general developmentalist hypothesis has been carried forward and applied in the major areas of Aristotle's thought – logic, psychology, ethics, and metaphysics.[30] The basic hypothesis is seldom questioned, even when the details are rejected.[31]

If one follows the Jaegerian hypothesis, then the inconvenient Platonic bits in the works otherwise attributed to the late, anti-Platonic phase have to be explained away. There is considerable scope here for resourcefulness. For example, we discover that a Platonic passage is a 'remnant' of Aristotle's discarded past, something like a permanent food stain on one's shirt that one must simply endure. More typically, we find that such a passage simply indicates the 'background' of the discussion as if Aristotle were just acknowledging the air he was forced to breathe. Sometimes scholars just avert their embarrassed eyes. We also find suggestions of sloppy scissors-and-paste jobs or even of nefarious tampering with the texts by overzealous Platonists. All of these interpretative strategies arise from a common assumption: since the 'mature' Aristotle is obviously opposed to Platonism, any Platonism in the works of his maturity must be there under false pretences. This assumption is so widely and deeply held that it is seldom exposed to scrutiny. But it is still just an assumption for all that.

Nevertheless, it will be insisted that the assumption is well grounded even if its application is occasionally awkward. Aristotle *does* in fact truly and decisively reject Plato's theory of Forms and at least most of the ontological consequences of accepting that theory, including the diminution of the reality of the sensible world. He also rejects the immortality of the soul, arguably the central idea in Plato's ethics and psychology. In short, Aristotle is the determined opponent of what F.M. Cornford aptly termed the 'twin pillars' of Platonism. Given these facts, is it not reasonable to understand Aristotle's supposed Platonism in the 'homonymous' mode? That is, some of the things he says *sound* like Platonism, but they really are not. The words may be the same, but the melody is different.

The Neoplatonists generally followed an opposing assumption: Aristotle was a Platonist from first to last.[32] The feature common to virtually all versions of Platonism is a commitment to what I would call a 'top-down' approach to the entire budget of philosophical problems extant in any particular period. A top-down approach to philosophical problems rejects and a bottom-up approach accepts the claim that the most important and puzzling phenomena we encounter in this world can be explained by seeking the simplest elements out of which these are made. The top-down approach appeals to first or higher or irreducible principles to account for these phenomena. Among these are human personhood, and the personal attribute of freedom, higher cognition, the presence of evil, and the very existence and intelligibility of the world. The top-down approach holds that answers to questions about these phenomena are never going to be satisfactorily given in terms of elementary physical particles from which things 'evolve' or upon which the phenomena 'supervene'. According to Neoplatonism, 'Platonism' is basic 'top-downism' and its only true opponent is 'bottom-upism' represented, for example, by materialists such as the Atomists.[33]

The case for the position that the philosophies of Aristotle and Plato are in harmony is in part cumulative. In the remainder of this paper, I indicate in an indecently peremptory manner five areas in which I think the case for harmony is strongest. I proceed in increasing order of difficulty – or, as some might be inclined to suppose, increasing order of implausibility.

ii. The case for harmony

Categories

It is not particularly difficult to defend the Neoplatonic view that Aristotle's *Categories* – in particular his view of sensible substance and its attributes – is not at odds with the more capacious framework of Platonic metaphysics. Two points stand out in this regard. First, the priority of individual sensible substances both to their accidents and to their species and genera – the secondary substances – cannot plausibly be interpreted to indicate their absolute ontological priority unless one is prepared to discount entirely the evidence of the *exoterica and* the qualified priority of sensible substance elsewhere in the *corpus*, especially in *Metaphysics*.[34] Second, in no way is the Aristotelian universal, thought to be introduced in *Categories* as an antidote to Platonic Forms, in fact a substitute for the explanatory role that Forms play.[35]

Typically, the belief that *Categories* represents a rejection of Platonism is based on the supposition that Aristotle and Plato are offering conflicting explanations of predication. Plato thinks that, in general, if '*x* is *f*' is true where '*x*' stands for some sensible thing and '*f*' stands for an attribute of it, the explanation for this is that *x* participates in a Form of *F*-ness. By contrast, Aristotle's explanation of '*x* is *f*' is supposedly different and incompatible. In fact, when one searches *Categories* for the putative alternative explanation, it becomes clear that though Aristotle has quite a bit to say about statements like '*x* is *f*' and their meaning, he does not in *Categories* regard the statement '*x* is *f*' as needing an explanation in the way that Plato does. So, when Aristotle claims that 'Socrates is white' means that 'white' is present in Socrates, he is not *ipso facto* contradicting the Platonic explanation for the truth of 'Socrates is white', namely, that Socrates participates in the Form of Whiteness.[36]

Aristotle concurs with Plato that, to continue with the example, whiteness is not a white thing and whiteness is to be distinguished from what is predicable of a thing that is in fact white.[37] Things said to be white are named 'paronymously' from whiteness. But Aristotle does not appear to allow that there is any explanatory connection in the paronymy relation between whiteness and white. If this is so, it is easy to understand why whiteness should be identified with a universal. Things are named white from the whiteness that is perceived to be identically present in many. So, one might be tempted to say that paronymy does not explain anything

201

other than a semantic fact, because there is nothing to explain. The problem with Forms is that they seek to explain that which is simply a brute fact, namely, that many things can share what happens to be the same attribute or nature.[38]

It is abundantly clear, however, that this is not Aristotle's view. If there were nothing to explain, then there would be nothing to know. For particulars are unknowable. At this point, it will, of course, be said: what is knowable for Aristotle is the universal.[39] But what is known universally cannot be a universal. This is because 'universal' refers to the way what is known is known, not to what is known. It is because the form that is known is *neither* a particular nor a universal that it can both be known and serve to explain the identity of whatever possesses it.[40] Indeed, it is the form that is the 'substance' of each thing and the cause of its being.[41] Form in this sense is identical with the 'enmattered form' of Platonism. But no substance is a universal.[42] So, Aristotle is in fact committed to the view that form does in some way explain identity in difference because it is neither particular nor universal in itself. There has to be *something* like humanity and whiteness for there to be particular human beings and particular white things.[43]

Proclus gives an acute answer to the question of why a Form of Whiteness is needed in addition to a universal. He is commenting on the passage in *Parmenides* where Parmenides says that if Forms do not exist, then no one will have anything to think about and the power of discussion (τὴν τοῦ διαλέγεσθαι δύναμιν) will be completely destroyed.[44] According to Proclus' interpretation of Plato's theory, the separate Forms are the eternal condition for the possibility of sameness and difference or significant predication in the sensible world. Thus, Platonism is a condition for the possibility of an Aristotelian account of predication.

Ethics

Neoplatonic ethics may be said to take as its guiding slogan the passage from *Theaetetus* wherein Plato recommends 'assimilation to god' as the goal of life.[45] Assimilation to god is identified by Plato with a 'flight from this world'.[46] This passage that encapsulates Platonic ethics for the Neoplatonists has received relatively little attention among contemporary scholars.[47] More precisely, it has received relatively little attention from those trying to understand Platonic ethics. The reason for this is, no doubt, as Julia Annas notes, that a notion of flight from the world seems to be in considerable tension with a view of ethics as requiring engagement with the world.[48] That the Neoplatonists did not perceive any tension is perhaps not a very contentious claim. That they were right in their perception is a quite different matter. And that they were right to suppose that Aristotle's view of ethics was in harmony with their own is, it would seem, highly dubious.

14. The harmony of Aristotle and Plato according to Neoplatonism

The theoretical or philosophical life is understood by Neoplatonists as the 'practice for dying' of *Phaedo*.[49] This involves the 'separation of soul and body'.[50] It is a kind of 'purification' (κάθαρσις).[51] That such purification means more than simply theoretical activity is evident from Socrates' claim that 'in fact, temperance and justice and courage are a sort of purification of these things [i.e. of worldly considerations] and wisdom (φρόνησις) itself a kind of purifying ritual (καθαρμός)'.[52]

Plato himself contrasts the virtues that are a purification with what he calls 'popular or political virtue' (ἡ πολιτικὴ καὶ δημοτικὴ ἀρετή), 'temperance' and 'justice' so called, developed from custom and practice without philosophy and intellect'.[53] The difference between these popular or political virtues and the virtues that purify is that the former do not result in self-transformation. They are entirely behaviour oriented. One who practises these virtues may perform actions for all sorts of motives including those that are *not* ignoble, but these actions are not done as one who is purified would do them.

Plotinus in his treatise *On the Virtues* expresses what became the standard Neoplatonic interpretation of the virtues.[54] The treatise begins with a reflection on the *Theaetetus* passage. Plotinus asks how the practice of virtue can make us like the divine and intelligible reality since there is no virtue there. The divine has no need of virtue because it is perfect.[55] In particular, it has no need of the popular or political virtues, which Plotinus identifies as achievements of an embodied tripartite soul.[56] Likeness to God consists in becoming like eternal intellect, absorbed in the contemplation of eternal reality. All true virtues are understood as advancements towards identification of the person with the activity of a disembodied intellect.

Near the beginning of his *Nicomachean Ethics*, Aristotle declares that the present 'inquiry' (ἡ μέθοδος) is 'political' (πολιτική).[57] Given the identification of ethics as political science, it is not unreasonable that Neoplatonists should assume that the most of the central claims made in both *Nicomachean Ethics* and *Politics* are concerned with the popular and political virtue discussed by Plato in *Phaedo* and *Republic* and not with the purified virtue which constitute the assimilation to the divine.

Book X, chapters 6-8, of *Nicomachean Ethics* announces that after the discussion of the virtues, friendship, and pleasure, it will undertake a discussion of happiness, this being the 'goal of human [activities]' (τέλος τῶν ἀνθρωπίνων).[58] The starting-point of the entire work is the assumption that happiness is the highest good for human being. The highest good turns out to be 'an activity of the soul according to virtue, and if the virtues are many, then according to the best and most complete virtue'.[59] What now remains is a discussion of the best and most perfect virtue.[60] When that is discovered, the question about the best life, taken up in book I, chapters 2-3, and set aside, can be answered.[61] Aristotle proceeds to give a number of reasons why contemplative or theoretical activity is the

Lloyd P. Gerson

highest virtue. According to all these criteria, the political and martial virtues are judged to be inferior.[62] Accordingly, 'this would be the complete (τελεία) happiness of a human being, if extended to a complete (τέλεον) lifetime, for none of the [attributes] of happiness is incomplete (ἀτελές)'.[63]

Aristotle now moves to the crucial reflection on this line of reasoning. As if the main point were not sufficiently clear, he proceeds in the next chapter to consider the life 'according to the other [kind of] virtue'. This is the political life, the life that is happy in a secondary way. There are so many striking similarities between these passages and what Plato says in *Timaeus* and *Theaetetus* about assimilation to god that one cannot help but wonder at the prejudices that have led many either to ignore or to discount them.[64] It is not just the obvious verbal parallels that are so impressive, but the eccentricities of the parallels. Both Plato and Aristotle urge us to try to achieve immortality as much as possible as if that was something both in our power and allowing of degrees. Both urge us to emulate divine life, though the focus of ethics would seem to be our ineluctable humanity. And both urge that the divine life is a contemplative one, specifically removed from 'human affairs'. And both rest what they say upon an assumption that the 'we' of ethical striving is in fact different from a human being.

It would seem that the principal impediment to developing these parallels and drawing together Aristotelian and Platonic ethics as Neoplatonists require is the view that the substance of the above passages from *Nicomachean Ethics* is detachable from the rest of the doctrine of that work. If all the talk about immortalizing and divinizing and contemplating and identifying with a part of ourselves is removable like an unsightly growth on the hard head of the hard body of Aristotle's no nonsense ethics, then it should be done. A touch of developmentalism, excising the offending portions as 'residue' is one way. Trivializing the importance of the passages to the overall doctrine is another.[65] But if the Neoplatonists are correct, this is not possible, since an Aristotelian ethics limited to the discussion of popular and political virtue would be implausibly incomplete.

If one takes the above passages seriously, that is, if one takes them as a part of the ethical doctrine of Aristotle, then the two sorts of lives – the life according to the intellect and the life according to the 'other virtue' – are the lives that are best for 'that which is dominant and better' and for the 'composite'. Everything depends on how we view these two descriptions of a human being. If one takes the 'composite' as primary, then the focus will be on the ethical virtues and practical wisdom. That the nominal bulk of *Nicomachean Ethics* is concerned with these matters, and the related matters of pleasure and friendship, is beyond dispute. The real dispute is whether the life of the composite and its attendant virtues is the best sort of life or whether these virtues are inferior to another sort of virtue and another sort of life.[66] Aristotle in fact tells us exactly what Platonism says: we are ideally intellects.[67] But how we may ask can we be

204

both composites and intellects? The answer to this question is readily given in Platonic terms. The person is not the composite, although the person, when embodied, is a part of the composite. Exhortations to immortalize oneself or to assimilate to the divine are equivalent to exhortations to self-recognition.[68]

The four causes

My third area of putative harmony is in the Neoplatonic treatment of the Aristotelian analysis of the fourfold schema of causality in the framework of a science of nature. Since Aristotle was held by the Neoplatonists to be authoritative for the physical world, there was no large task of showing that here he was in harmony with Plato. There are a number of areas, especially relating to biological science, where Plato was mainly silent and where Aristotle's views were in our period dominant if not unchallenged.[69] The very fact that the Neoplatonic curriculum began with an extensive study of the Aristotle prior to moving on to Plato indicates that the student would hardly be expected to be led astray by imbibing Aristotelian wisdom. Still, an anti-harmonist might well suppose that a deep study of Aristotle's account of the physical world would yield principles in use that, finally, were incompatible or out of tune with Platonism. In fact, Plato's 'two-world' metaphysics, to put it crudely, is not compromised by Aristotle's account of nature.

It is convenient here to focus on Simplicius' statement of how Aristotle's schema of causal analysis compares with Plato's. At the start of his *Commentary on Aristotle's Physics*, he says that among 'principles' (ἀρχαί), Aristotle affirms two 'causes' (αἴτια)?, the 'productive' (τὸ ποιητικόν) and the 'telic' (τὸ τελικόν) and two 'contributory causes' (τὰ συναίτια), the 'form' (τὸ εἶδος) and the 'matter' (ἡ ὕλη). To these, Plato added two more; to the causes he added the 'paradigmatic' (τὸ παραδειγματικόν) and to the contributory causes he added the 'instrumental' (τὸ ὀργανικόν).[70]

Several things are immediately clear from this passage. Most important is the obvious Neoplatonic strategy of incorporating Aristotelian philosophy into the larger Platonic vision.[71] Aristotle's four causes or modes of scientific explanation are 'fitted into' the more comprehensive Platonic scheme. The fit is not entirely straightforward. Aristotle does use the term 'contributory cause' for matter, in the sense of a material condition.[72] Logically, this would make form the other 'co-contributor', though Aristotle does not speak in this way. On the contrary, Aristotle appears to view his four causes as the framework for scientific explanatory adequacy and in no way subordinate to other more fundamental causes.

The basic distinction between cause and contributory cause is clearly made by Plato in *Timaeus*.[73] In this passage, the productive and telic causes, along with a sort of contributory cause that is instrumental, are evident.[74] The paradigmatic cause, namely, Forms (and perhaps the Demiurge itself), are readily supplied from elsewhere in the text.[75] What Aristotle and Simplicius call 'form' is taken to be identical with the 'likenesses' of the paradigmatic Forms, which are imposed on the universe by the Demiurge.[76] This seems to leave the material 'contributory cause' unaccounted for.

Simplicius, along with the Neoplatonists generally, has no doubt at all that Plato has in fact accounted for material causality. For the standard way of referring to the likenesses of Forms is as 'enmattered forms' (ἔνυλα εἴδη).[77] But it is widely if not universally believed that Plato had no concept of matter whatsoever, and that Aristotle's proposed identification of matter with the 'receptacle of becoming' in *Timaeus* or with the principle of the 'great and small' (= indefinite dyad) is a huge mistake.[78] So, a good place to focus seems to be on whether the harmonizing of Aristotle and Plato with respect to a doctrine of material causality has any merit.

The Neoplatonic position can be stated simply as an insistence that there is no explanatory adequacy in the account of images without adducing their paradigmatic causes, that is, without introducing the Forms, the Intellect that contains these, and the first principle of all, the One. For them, an Aristotelian physical explanation has an 'as if' quality, a sort of strategic pretence of adequacy. If you treat flora or fauna or astronomical bodies as if they were basic, then Aristotelian explanations are acceptable. If you recognize that they are not, then those explanations will not be so.[79]

This point is well made by Proclus at the beginning of his commentary on *Timaeus*. Proclus begins by stating that the 'science of nature' (ἡ φυσιολογία) is traditionally divided into parts, the study of matter, the study of form, and, finally, the study of why matter and form are not true causes but only contributory causes whereas the true causes are 'the productive' (τὸ ποιητικόν), 'the paradigmatic' (τὸ παραδειγματικόν), and 'the telic' (τὸ τελικόν). He then turns first to Plato's scientific predecessors, especially Anaxagoras, and then to a contrast between Aristotle's treatment of the causes with Plato's.[80] Proclus' point here is principally the superiority of the Platonic approach to the science of nature to the Aristotelian approach. But he incidentally provides the rational for the harmony between the two. So long as an Aristotelian realizes that physical science cannot be explanatorily exhaustive, its ambit is secure.[81]

There is an important sense in which Aristotle himself acknowledges this point when he sets down the limitation of physical science. In the last book of *Physics*, Aristotle says that nature, taken as a principle of motion, is a hypothesis.[82] To Neoplatonic ears, this sounds like the hypothetical reasoning of Plato's *Republic* that should lead ultimately to an unhypothetical understanding of first principles.[83] The reason why nature is not self-explanatory, even though it be a principle of motion and standstill, is that it is an instrument of motion – a moved mover – and not an unmoved mover. Thus, even if nature always acts for the good by actualizing the potency in anything that exists by nature, nature's so acting is not self-explanatory.[84]

Finally, the two areas which may be felt, with some justice, to be the *fons et origo* of the *disharmony* that I am working to disallow concern the immortality of the soul and the theory of Forms. Surely, here, Aristotle's explicit rejection of immortality and Forms precludes any substantial harmony. Actually, it is in these two areas that claims for harmony between Aristotle and Plato are most interesting and provocative.

The immortality of the soul

The Neoplatonists approached the question of the harmony of Aristotle and Plato in psychological matters in part in the light of assumption that what Aristotle says in the exoteric works is a popular version of what he says in the esoteric works. We have already seen that the grounds for denying this are questionable. The Neoplatonists read the dialogues as committed to the immortality of intellect, which is how they interpreted Plato, based mainly on *Timaeus*.[85] So for them the question is not the harmonization of two opposing views on immortality so much as it was the harmonization of two accounts of how immortal intellect is related to embodied soul.

Aristotle is clear enough at the beginning of *De Anima* that the study of soul belongs to physical science and is distinct from a study of that which is separable from soul, namely, intellect, which belongs to first philosophy.[86] Pseudo-Simplicius in his *Commentary on Aristotle's De Anima* makes the connection between what Aristotle says here and what was said at the beginning of *Parts of Animals*.[87] But the commentator understands that even if there is a separable intellect, still the natural scientist will need to take account of intellectual operations of the soul.[88] In fact, the study of soul belongs between the study of the objects of first philosophy and the non-intellectual entities in nature.[89] As Pseudo-Simplicius aptly remarks, the definition of soul that Aristotle offers at the beginning of book 2 clearly does not apply to this separable intellect.[90] Indeed, as Aristotle himself goes on to argue, a single definition of soul that covered all kinds of soul, though evidently possible, as we have seen, would be useless if we can also give a definition of each different kind of soul.[91] So, it is possible that Aristotle's criticisms of the general definitions of soul given by, among others, Plato, have at least to be considered differently from criticisms of definitions of particular kinds of soul. Part of the problem, of course, is that Plato nowhere gives anything like a definition of the human soul.

The anti-harmonists among contemporary scholars are nothing if not transparent in efforts to sort out the confusion in Aristotle's treatment of separable intellect. One option is simply to dismiss passages in which it occurs as vestigial organs of a defunct Platonism.[92] Another option is to give a 'deflationary' account of separable intellect pressing hard on a functionalist interpretation of cognition in the hylomorphic composite.[93] If, however, we see reason to resist such an account, we shall see that separable intellect inevitably draws Aristotle into the Platonic orbit in his attempt to account for embodied intellectualized activity.[94] If separable intellect were not somehow necessary to account for embodied cognition, then that cognition could be explained functionally, that is, in terms of the material organism's functions. But Aristotle will not do this.

An explicit statement of this particular facet of harmony is made by Pseudo-Simplicius at the end of his commentary on *De Anima*, book 3. The commentator, who holds not merely that Aristotle's doctrine is in harmony with Plato, but that Aristotle is the 'best exegete of Plato', reflects on the meaning of the separability of intellect.[95] This passage is a stellar example of Neoplatonic commentary. It also provides an excellent example of how the harmony between Plato and Aristotle was understood.

Among the salient features of this long passage are (1) the claim that Aristotle's account of the immortality of intellect is substantially the same as Plato's account of the immortality of the soul which in turn is assumed to be the same in *Phaedo* and *Phaedrus*; (2) the association of the immateriality of intellect with self-reflexive cognition. I find the harmonists' assumption especially illuminating here because on its basis the commentator is really trying to appropriate what both Plato and Aristotle offer on the nature of intellect and, equally important, on the nature of personal identity.

Regarding (1), though the Neoplatonists beginning with Plotinus were openly puzzled by many of the things Plato says about the soul, they were generally in agreement that *Timaeus* represents the correct and basic Platonic view, namely, that only intellect is immortal.[96] But intellect is evidently a part of the soul and cannot arise apart from soul.[97] So, the obscurity of the relation between intellect and soul is rooted in Plato's own account. This would not, however, be so much of a puzzle if we could locate the person or self or subject of mental and bodily states unambiguously in either the soul or the intellect. To put the matter in a slightly different way, is the immortality of my intellect the immortality of me and, if it is, in what sense am I identical with an embodied subject? Clearly, Plato does want to say that in some sense, the immortality of my soul, that is, the immortality of the part of my soul that is my intellect, is the immortality of me. But he is far from clear about how the identical subject can both be nothing but a thinker and also the subject of embodied states. Plato's lack of clarity about these matters is undoubtedly to a certain extent responsible for the commentator's confidence that Aristotle is indeed in harmony with Plato. But it is also far from foolish to read Aristotle's words in a way that does make his position harmonious with Plato's.

In (2), the commentator demonstrates how Aristotle can be said without irony to be Plato's greatest exegete. The argument that self-reflexivity is a mark of the immaterial intellect is a large and central theme among

Neoplatonists, especially the later Neoplatonists.[98] It is not made a theme in Aristotle, nor is there a technical term for it, but there are good grounds for interpreting his argument in *De Anima* III, 4-5, as using self-reflexivity to show that intellect is incorporeal. What is striking about the above commentary is the assumption that Aristotle is held to be revealing what is implicit in Plato's argument for the incorporeality and hence immortality of the soul.[99] The point is, roughly that cognition generally requires self-reflexivity (τὸ πρὸς ἑαυτὸν ἐπιστρέφειν) and no body is capable of this.[100] As the latter commentator states it, self-reflexivity is nothing but 'the grasp of one's own actual states' (τὸ τῶν οἰκείων ἐνεργειῶν ἀντιλαμβάνεσθαι). The reason why no body is capable of self-reflexivity is straightforward. If the putative bodily cognizer is in a state of information, then the grasp of that state will, *ex hypothesi*, be a bodily state. One bodily state grasping the state of another body will not be a case of the cognizer 'thinking itself'. It will be a case of one cognizer grasping the state of another cognizer.

It may be objected that construing the identity of the cognizer in this way begs the question. If we assume that the cognizer is a body, then one part of that body can be related to another part of the same body and the body can be 'thinking itself' in a non-problematic fashion. This objection neither is coherent nor is it, more importantly, true to what Aristotle says. Six times in the third book of *De Anima* Aristotle asserts that 'actual knowledge is the same as that which is known'.[101] By this he cannot mean (1) above, that is, that actual knowledge is the same thing as the presence of the form in the intellect, because the presence of the form in the intellect is then still 'somehow in potency' (δυνάμει πως) to actual knowledge.[102] He must mean (2), the unqualified actuality of thinking. But because the intellect in (1) is identical with the form that informs it, the intellect in (2), when it knows, must be the same as the intellect in (1). If it were not, then the form that is in the intellect in (1) would have to inform the intellect in (2), and another intellect would have to be posited to be aware of the presence of form in (2). That is why it is incoherent to suggest that the intellects could be different as they would have to be if cognition were a bodily state or activity. According to this objection, cognition would be a relation – perhaps a representational one – between a cognizer and that which is external to it. But that is precisely the view that Aristotle is opposing.[103]

Forms

This brings me to Aristotle's criticisms of the theory of Forms and, by implication, his metaphysics. Jaeger's developmentalism was in fact inspired principally by the conviction that in metaphysics Aristotle was once a Platonist and then, coming to his senses, an anti-Platonist. Who is to gainsay the great German scholar on this point?

The biggest and seemingly most obvious hurdle for the harmonist is

Aristotle's criticism of Plato's theory of Forms and the alleged implications of that criticism. We have already seen that two of those alleged implications are the reddest of red herrings, namely, the idea that universals are the appropriate Aristotelian substitute for Forms and the idea that sensible substances are the focus of Aristotle's metaphysics. The Neoplatonists, too, were generally aware of the oddness in the claim that the philosopher who rejected the Forms could also be understood to hold views that were in harmony with those of Plato.[104] There are, however, several good reasons why they did not take the rejection of Forms by Aristotle to be the rejection of a fundamental principle of Platonism.[105]

First, a reasonable argument could be made to the effect that Aristotle believed that the unmoved mover's eternal thinking is about eternal intelligible objects (νοητά).[106] These seem to function in a way that the paradigmatic causes that are Forms do, as Alexander of Aphrodisias says in reference to Aristotle's *On the Ideas*. This leads to the second point. The Neoplatonists' view about Forms was built on a reading of all the dialogues, the letters, and Aristotle's testimony. What Aristotle manifestly rejects was to these philosophers something quite different from the picture of Forms that a close reading of all the evidence would show. So, Aristotle, like Plato himself in several places, rejects an inadequate or false theory of Forms, not the true – Platonic – theory.[107]

The basis for the Neoplatonic response to Aristotle's argument is clearly set forth in Asclepius' *Commentary on Aristotle's Metaphysics*.[108] Asclepius takes Aristotle to be railing against a view of Forms which the Neoplatonists have themselves rejected as not Platonic.[109] It is the view that each Form is a self-contained eternal and immutable island of intelligibility. This view is in no way entailed by the fact that each Form is a 'one' over many. Nor is it entailed by the characterization of a Form as 'itself by itself' since this locution indicates the separation of Forms from the sensible world, not their separation from each other or, indeed, from an intellect.[110]

A Form isolated in the way that Asclepius think that both Plato and Aristotle reject would indeed be unable to function as the explanation of identity in difference. How, we may well ask, does refusing to isolate them from an intellect make any difference? The answer is that the intellect, that is, the divine intellect or Demiurge, makes it unnecessary to insist that the separate Form is predicated of those things that participate in the Form's nature. The Demiurge puts intelligibility into the things in the sensible world as images of the divine paradigm. The universality of the Form is not its function; rather it exists universally in the intellect of a knower. Thus, as we have seen earlier, Syrianus distinguishes between the Form existing as an intelligible and the Form existing intellectually, that is in the Demiurge. That is, when the Demiurge thinks a Form, he is thinking it universally.[111] In addition, the identity of Forms with the divine intellect guarantees the immaterial complexity sufficient to be able to make a real distinction between a Form and its nature. To be able to be thought universally, the Form must be really distinct from the object of universal thinking.[112]

The 'separation' of Forms may be understood in four ways: (1) separate from sensibles; (2) separate from each other; (3) separate from an intellect; and (4) separate from a first superordinate principle. Neoplatonists did not suppose that Plato held the Forms to be separate in any way but (1), that is, separate from sensibles, capable of existing independently of them. In this regard, I would hold that their understanding of Forms is superior to that of most contemporary scholars. Generally, Neoplatonists understood Aristotle's criticisms to be levelled at those who took separation in the sense of (1) to entail separation in the other three senses. But is not Aristotle himself committed to rejecting the separation of Forms even just in the sense of (1)?

The brief answer to this question, indirectly given by both Asclepius and Proclus, is 'no' because any anti-nominalist, that is, any realist, such as Aristotle, is committed to the absolute priority of form to form/matter composites. This priority is *not* accounted for by formal causality within the fourfold Aristotelian schema That formal causality explains what a composite is implies the antecedent explanation of the *possibility* of instantiation, namely, the eternal paradigmatic cause.[113]

Asclepius' understanding of the criticism of a Form as a useless 'paradigmatic cause' is indirectly supported by Aristotle's account in book XIII of *Metaphysics* where he says that Forms were adduced in order to provide explanations for 'individuals' (τὰ καθ' ἕκαστα).[114] Asclepius seems justified in insisting that Forms were never intended to provide such explanations and that Aristotle is only criticizing those who thought that they did. That is precisely why there are no Forms of individuals. Even more important from the harmonists' perspective is that the explanations for individuals that Aristotle *does* provide do not preclude or contradict the role of Forms. Indeed, the enmattered form provides the link between the Aristotelian explanations and the Platonic. The enmattered form does what the separate unparticipated Form was never supposed to do. But the enmattered form could not exist if its eternal perfect paradigm did not exist.[115]

A great deal more could be said in regard to all these matters.[116] To a certain extent, Aristotle, from a Neoplatonic perspective, is viewed as a Platonist *malgré lui*. He is viewed in this way owing to his resolute opposition to a 'bottom-up' approach to philosophical explanation. His own approach, like Plato's, is anti-nominalist, anti-materialist, anti-reductionist, anti-Eleatic, and anti-Skeptic. It is not the case, however, that all those who embrace a 'top-down' approach are unqualifiedly Platonist. Those who, like Aristotle, insist incorrectly on the perfect simplicity of immaterial reality, can at best be in harmony with Platonism.

Those who reject the harmony of Aristotelianism with Platonism out of hand do so partly because they are misled by Aristotle's criticisms of Plato and partly, I suspect, because they have a unduly narrow view of what

Lloyd P. Gerson

Platonism is. It is unquestionably correct to insist on their legitimate differences and nothing the harmonists say is intended to deny these. I have been arguing, however, that the longstanding emphasis on the differences, along with the developmentalist theory built on these, has occluded what is at the very least another important part of the story. To read Aristotle as a Platonist (assuming a sufficiently nuanced understanding of Platonism) is to read a philosopher markedly different from the Aristotle generally on offer today.

Notes

1. See, for example, especially Zeller (1923), 475-80, whose influence in this matter as in so much else in the study of ancient philosophy is still felt today. See also, for example, Frank (1940), who expresses another version of the working assumption of much Aristotelian scholarship in this century. The eminent historian of philosophy, Etienne Gilson, writing about Aquinas' decision to build his own philosophy on that of Aristotle rather than that of Plato, claims in relation to the latter two that 'reduced to their bare essences, these metaphysics are rigorously antinomical; one cannot be for the one without being against all those who are with the other, and that is why Saint Thomas remains with Aristotle against all those who are counted on the side of Plato'. See Gilson (1926-7) 127f. I owe this reference to Francis O'Rourke. By contrast, Boas (1943), atypically, identifies Aristotle's 'protophilosophy' as being thoroughly Platonic. See also Merlan (1953), 3-4, who argues for the 'Neoplatonic' character of Aristotle's interpretation of Plato as well as the Neoplatonic character of 'some fundamental doctrines of Aristotle'.

2. See Diogenes Laertius, 5.1: γνησιώτατος τῶν Πλάτωνος μαθητῶν.

3. See especially Dillon (1977) and Tarrant in Chapter 1 of this volume, on Antiochus of Ascalon. Cicero, *Fin.* 5.7, says, 'as you have heard Antiochus say, in the Old Academy are included not only those who are called Academics ... but even the old Peripatetics, of whom Aristotle is the first and best'.

4. See Cicero, *Acad.* 1.17: 'But on the authority of Plato, a thinker with a variety of complex and fecund thoughts, a type of philosophy was initiated that was united and harmonious and known under two names, the Academics and the Peripatetics, and they agreed substantially while differing in their names'. Also, *Acad.* 2.15, '*Peripateticos et Academicos, nominibus differentes, re congruentes* ...'.

5. See Dillon (1993), especially the introduction and commentary. That the Platonist Atticus (fl. 175 BC) apparently wrote a treatise titled *Against Those Who Claim to Interpret the Doctrine of Plato Through That of Aristotle* actually supports the view that the harmony between Plato and Aristotle was the prevailing view. Evidently, Atticus believed that matters were getting out of hand.

6. The Greek term translated here as 'harmony' and usually used by Neoplatonists to indicate agreement between Plato and Aristotle is συμφωνία. Plato, *Symposium* 187b4, uses συμφωνία synonymously with ἁρμονία. The latter term tends to be reserved among the Neoplatonists for a more technical use in scientific theory. See Lloyd (1967), 272-325, for a broad outline of the principle of the harmonists.

7. See Sedley (1996b).

8. One thinks of the great painting by Raphael, *The School of Athens*, with the image of Plato and Aristotle strolling through the Academy together, Plato with finger raised upward to the heavens and Aristotle with finger pointed downward to the earth. Countless generations of students have heard the misinterpretation of this painting to the effect that Raphael is contrasting the 'otherwordly' Plato with the 'down to earth' Aristotle.

9. Here, for the sake of the analogy, we should focus especially on the empirical adequacy of Newtonian mechanics within a circumscribed domain. Quantum mechanics provides a deeper and more comprehensive explanation. I thank Dirk Baltzly for insight into this analogy.

10. See, e.g., Simplicius, *In Cat.* 6.27-30. See also *In Phys.* 8.9-15.

11. See *Physics* I.1, 184a16-18. Cf. *Nicomachean Ethics* I.2, 1095b3. Plato's *Timaeus* provides the most important example of Plato's treatment of nature on the basis of principles articulated for the intelligible world. It begins with an argument for the existence of a demiurgic god and then proceeds to deduce the manner and scope of his creative activity ending in the creation of the sensible world.

12. See his *In Phys.* 1249.12-13, where Simplicius contrasts the apparent verbal difference (in ὄνομα) between Plato and Aristotle with a putative real difference (in πρᾶγμα). The reason for the verbal difference is the different starting-points of the two philosophers.

13. See *Parmenides* 128a-e.

14. See Numenius, fr. 8 (des Places). The level of generality at which Numenius means to compare Moses and Plato is difficult to judge without a context for the remark. See, also, for example, Richard Sorabji's general introduction to the series of translations of the Greek Aristotle commentaries, where he refers to the idea of harmony as a 'perfectly crazy proposition' though he allows that it 'proved philosophically fruitful'. One might well wonder why, if harmony is a crazy idea, the attempt to show it should be other than philosophically fruitless.

15. See, for example, Ammonius, *In Cat.* 3.9-16 and the anonymous *Prolegomena to Platonic Philosophy* attributed to Olympiodorus, 5.18-30, which explains that 'Peripatetic' is a term that comes from *Plato's* habit of walking around while philosophizing. Accordingly, Aristotle (and Xenocrates), as followers of Plato, were called 'Peripatetics', though the former taught in the Lyceum while the latter taught in the Academy.

16. See, for example, Proclus, *In Tim.* I 210.27ff; Simplicius, *In DC* 731.25-9.

17. See I. Hadot (1996), 57-8, where she points out that Simplicius held that Aristotle's obscure style is intended to reserve his 'revelations' for the philosophically adept. But this is not I take it equivalent to attributing to Aristotle himself Neoplatonic religious practices. I think that this is the case even for Iamblichus who was especially eager to emphasize the continuity of Platonism with the religion of the ancient sages of Egypt and Persia.

18. For example, Neoplatonists differed concerning the relationship between intellect and intelligibles, specifically how to interpret the relationship in Plato's *Timaeus* between the Demiurge and the Forms; they differed on the nature and knowability of the first principle of all, on the relationship between intellect and soul, and so on. See Syrianus, *In Metaph.* 109.33-110.7 and Proclus, *In Tim.* I 306.31-307.4; 322.20-6; 323.1-22, etc. See I. Hadot (1990), 177-82, on divergences among the Neoplatonists in their understanding of the elements of harmonization.

19. See Donini (1988), 27-8, for some critical remarks on the use of the terms 'eclectic' and 'syncretic' among historians of ancient philosophy in the nineteenth and twentieth centuries.

20. One may compare in this regard Catholicism and Protestantism as types of Christianity. Despite their opposition on various points, it is not implausible to

Lloyd P. Gerson

insist on their underlying harmony owing to their shared principles. On this analogy, for Neoplatonists, Platonism is Christianity, Plato's philosophy is Roman Catholicism, and Aristotelianism is a type of Protestantism.

21. See O'Meara (1989), 210-11, on Iamblichus' unique and influential role in the Neoplatonic interpretation of Plato. Iamblichus was particularly concerned to harmonize Plato with Pythagoras, something that is not found at all in Plotinus, Porphyry, or to a great extent in Proclus. Iamblichus is also reported by Proclus as criticizing Porphyry for saying things that are neither Platonic nor true (οὔτε Πλατωνικῶς οὔτε ἀληθῶς) and for introducing alien elements into Platonism (ἀλλοτρίως τοῦ Πλάτωνος εἰσαγομένας). The implication of the former remark is that 'Platonic' and 'true' are least logically distinct. See Proclus, *In Tim.* I 307.4; I 152.29; III 65.9. I owe these references to John Dillon.

22. See Photius, *Biblioteca* cod. 251, 461a24-39. See Düring (1957), 332-6, for a compilation of the texts from the Neoplatonists relating to harmony. At 214.8, 173a18-40, Hierocles makes the bolder claim that all those from Aristotle up to Ammonius 'who had a reputation for wisdom' were in agreement with Plato. And all those 'born of the sacred race' from Ammonius up to Plutarch of Athens were in agreement with the purified version of Plato's philosophy (διακεκαθαρμένη φιλοσοφία). The qualifications obviously are intended to exclude genuine non-Platonists such as Stoics and Epicureans. More importantly, Hierocles here recognizes the need to grasp Platonism 'purified'. This purification must include the elimination of false interpretations, a claim that rests upon the momentous assumption that Plato must be interpreted.

23. See Suda Π 2098.8-9 (= fr. 240T Smith). On the meaning of the term αἵρεσις in this period see Glucker (1978), 166-93.

24. See Schibli (2002), 27-31, with nn. 98, 100, who notes the prevailing view that Hierocles got from Porphyry his idea that Ammonius taught the harmony of Plato and Aristotle. See n. 96 for references and Dodds' dissent from this view. Whatever the case, Schibli goes on to suggest that Porphyry's attribution of a teaching of harmony to Ammonius is dubious. But Schibli's principal reason for saying this is that Plotinus, Ammonius' greatest pupil, must not have been a harmonist because he criticized Aristotle. Two points can be made here. First, the *Enneads* of Plotinus amply confirm Porphyry's claim (*VPlot.* 14) for the profound effect Aristotle's thinking had on Plotinus. Second, Plotinus' (sometimes severe) disagreements with Aristotle on various issues did not preclude his assuming a harmony between the two on a deeper level any more than, say, Porphyry's disagreements with Plotinus precluded the former's recognition of *their* harmony with each other and with Plato.

25. See Diogenes Laertius, 1.19-20, where ten philosophical schools are listed. Diogenes also here refers to another historian, Hippobotus, who gives a similar list. See Suda, s.v., αἵρεσις as well. It is, of course, possible that the division between the Peripatetic and Academic 'schools' is sharper than that between Aristotle and Plato.

26. According to Glucker (1978), 206-25, philosophers began declaring themselves as Platonists in the second century BC. But see Cicero, *ND* 1.73 for an exception.

27. See especially the two great works Cherniss (1944) and Cherniss (1945).

28. See, for example, Berti (1962).

29. See Jaeger (1948), whose seminal work still dominates Aristotle exegesis today, perhaps even unconsciously in the minds of some scholars.

30. See, for example, von Arnim (1924), who applies Jaeger's general developmentalist hypothesis to Aristotle's ethical theory, Solmsen (1929), who applied it Aristotle's logical theory, and Nuyens (1948), who applies it to Aristotle's psychological theory. See also on the presumed evolution of psychological doctrine Block (1961) and Lefèvre (1972). More recently, Graham (1987) has applied it to Aristotle's metaphysics. Rist (1989) has reapplied Jaeger's general developmentalist approach and arrived at somewhat different specific results.

31. See Rist (1989), who sets out to redo the work of Jaeger and arrive at a more accurate chronology of Aristotle's development. But Rist retains Jaeger's Platonist/anti-Platonist hypothesis. See Wians (1996), for a good summary of Jaeger's position as well as a number of stimulating papers showing the dominance of Jaeger, despite many objections and reservations. There is also an excellent bibliography that includes all the major studies in this area. Tigerstedt (1974) shows that the impetus to developmentalism has its roots in the revolution in Platonic studies caused by Schleiermacher at the beginning of the nineteenth century. For it was he who spearheaded the rejection of the principal interpretative approach within Platonism, namely, that of Neoplatonism. And, with a Plato viewed other than as the leading figure with the system that is Platonism, the gap between Aristotle and Plato seemed all the greater.

32. I am going to largely ignore what I regard as the now discredited thesis of Karl Praechter that Athenian Neoplatonists believed in harmony but Alexandrian Neoplatonists did not. See Praechter (1909) and the refutation by I. Hadot (1978) summarized in I. Hadot (1991).

33. Stoics provide a special case, for they are in some sense 'top-down' theorists, though they strive to be consistent materialists. Briefly, the Neoplatonic (i.e. mainly the Plotinian) response to Stoicism is that it cannot coherently maintain both materialism and the top-down explanatory framework.

34. See Porphyry, *In Cat.* 91.19-27. Cf. Dexippus, *In Cat.* 45.5-12; Ammonius, *In Cat.* 9.17-24. Graham (1987) makes a strenuous effort to show that the clearly diminished priority of sensible substances in *Metaphysics* is an 'unfortunate lapse into Platonism' on Aristotle's part. See Wehrle (2001), 20-5, for a thorough refutation of Graham. Mann (2000) argues that *Categories* represents a radical break from Platonism.

35. See Porphyry, *In Cat.* 57.6; 91.19-27; Plotinus, *Enneads* VI.3.9.23-40, argues against taking the universal as an explanation of the presence of an attribute. See Simplicius, *In Cat.* 82.35-83.10, who says that that which is common (τὸ κοινόν) must be understood in three senses: (1) that which transcends the particulars and is the cause of what is common in them owing to its nature; (2) that which is common in particulars; and (3) that which exists in our concepts owing to abstraction. According to Simplicius, when Aristotle is in *Categories* speaking about (2) and (3), he is simply ignoring, not rejecting, (1). Also, see Asclepius, *In Metaph.* 193.9; 433.9-436.6, who cites Syrianus as making a similar distinction. See also Porphyry, *In Cat.* 90.30-91.18; Ammonius, *In Isag.* 41.10-42.26 and 68.25-69.2; and his *In Cat.* 41.8-11, where a distinction between intelligible and sensible genera and species is assumed; Proclus, *ET* Prop. 67.

36. See especially Asclepius' *In Metaph.* 433.30-434.5, where Asclepius refers to Syrianus as using the term 'universal' in two senses: (a) that which is posterior and in the mind and (b) that which is substance (οὐσία), even if it be predicated of [a subject] (εἴ γε κατηγορεῖται αὐτῶν). The two senses of 'universal' are paralleled by two senses of 'predication'. In the first sense, that which is predicated does not have an independent existence; in the second sense, that which is predicated is the independent existent in which individuals participate. There is hence no contra-

Lloyd P. Gerson

diction in holding that Socrates participates in universal and separate whiteness (in sense b), whereas universal whiteness (in sense a) is not separate.

37. See *Categories* 8.10a27ff.

38. This is the case with the so-called resemblance theory of universals.

39. See *Metaph.* VII.10, 1035b34-6a1; 11, 1036a28-9.

40. See Owens (1951), 381-95, for a particularly clear defence of this claim. More recently, Lear (1987) argued the position.

41. See *Metaph.* VII.17, 1041b7-9 with b27-8 and VIII.2, 1043a2-3. Cf. I.10, 993a19-21; XII.3, 1070a22-3.

42. See *Metaph.* VII.13, 1038b8-15.

43. See Porphyry, *In Cat.* 75.24-9; 81.11-22, for the claim that the nature is prior to individuality and universality. Graham (1987), 288, argues 'that when Aristotle identifies form with substance ... he makes an unnecessary and damaging concession to Platonism'.

44. *In Parm.* 979.2-8. Cf. *Parmenides* 135b5-c3; *Sophist* 259e4-6, where the συμπλοκὴ τῶν εἰδῶν is the condition for (διὰ) the possibility of logos.

45. *Theaetetus* 175c5-6.

46. Ibid. 176a5-c5. Cf. *Timaeus*, 90b1-d7. See also *Republic*, 518d-e, 589d, 590d.

47. For example, Irwin (1995) mentions it not at all. Notable exceptions are Merki (1952), Roloff (1970), Annas (1999), ch. 3, and Sedley (1999).

48. See Annas (1999), 70-1.

49. *Phaedo* 64a5-6. Cf. 67d7-10.

50. *Phaedo* 65c11-d2. Cf. 66e6-67b2.

51. *Phaedo* 67c5.

52. *Phaedo* 69b8-c3.

53. *Phaedo* 82a10-b3. Cf. 69b6-7, where this sort of virtue is called an 'illusory façade' (σκιαγραφία), fit for slaves. Cf. *Republic* 365c3-4 and especially 500d8 with 518d3-519a6 where the 'popular' virtues are identified as the 'so-called virtues of the soul'.

54. See, for example, Porphyry, *Sententiae* 32, a somewhat more elaborate division of the virtues, essentially based on the distinction between the political and theoretical.

55. Cf. *Enneads* I.2.3.31.

56. *Enneads* I.2.1. See, for example, Porphyry, *Sententiae* 32, a somewhat more elaborate division of the virtues, essentially based on the distinction between the political and theoretical.

57. *Nicomachean Ethics* I.1, 1094b11. Cf. VII.8, 1141b23, where Aristotle says that the political 'habit' (ἕξις) is the same as 'practical wisdom' (φρόνησις), though they differ in essence. The difference, roughly, is that the former is concerned with the state and the latter with the individual.

58. *Nicomachean Ethics* X.6, 1176a30-2. See also X.7, 1177b26-1178a22.

59. *Nicomachean Ethics* I.6, 1098a16-18.

60. Nussbaum (1987), 377, argues that it is odd for Aristotle here to propose a 'sketch' of happiness since that is exactly what he has done in book I chs 1-7. But though book I does indeed tell us what happiness is in general, that it is virtuous activity of the soul, it does not tell us what is the most complete virtue.

61. *Nicomachean Ethics* X.7, 1177a12-19. See I.5, 1097a25-b21, X.5, 1175b36-117.

62. *Nicomachean Ethics* X.7, 1177b16-24.

63. *Nicomachean Ethics* X.7, 1177b24-5.

64. Sedley (1997) being a notable exception. At 335, he says, 'It seems to have

14. The harmony of Aristotle and Plato according to Neoplatonism

gone unnoticed by scholars how accurately *the main structure of Aristotle's ethics* reflects this passage of the *Timaeus* [90a-d]' (my italics). Sedley's argument is expanded somewhat in Sedley (1999). Gauthier (1970), 875, says à propos the reference to the 'divine' in this passage that 'La divinité de la partie rationnelle est une idée chère à Aristote de la période platonicienne'.

65. Remarkably, Jaeger (1948), ch. 9, does both. He concedes that *Eudemian Ethics* is Platonic in its orientation, connecting it closely with *Protrepticus*, but then concludes that it must therefore be an early work. The more mature *Nicomachean Ethics*, however, with its 'rich and humane urbanity' (243), reduces the talk about divinization and immortality to rhetorical frill. Nowhere does Jaeger explain why substantially the same remarks mean one thing in *Eudemian Ethics* and another in *Nicomachean Ethics* apart from the assumption that the development of Aristotle's ethics follows the development of theology within his metaphysics. See Defourny (1937) for a refutation of Jaeger's position. Also Schütrumpf (1992). In contrast to Jaeger, Gauthier (1970), v. 2, 874-5, thinks that the Platonism of these passage shows that *Nicomachean Ethics* is closely related to *Protrepticus*. Cf. Nuyens (1948), 192-3, who also thinks that the doctrine of *Nicomachean Ethics* is associated with *Protrepticus*. In addition, Nuyens thinks that *Nicomachean Ethics* must antedate *De Anima* since it does not have the sophisticated notion of the composite human being that is found in the latter. Nussbaum (1987), 373-7, grants the Platonism of the passage, as well as similar passages outside of *Nicomachean Ethics*, and suggests that, though it is probably Aristotle's, it mighty have been inserted by someone else. This despite the fact that 'ethical Platonism of some sort exercised a hold over Aristotle's imagination in one or more periods of his career. We should, then, view the fragment X.6-8 as a serious working-out of elements of a position to which Aristotle is in some ways deeply attracted, though he rejects it in the bulk of his mature ethical and political writings' (377). A similar view is taken by Monan (1968), 108-11, 133-4, 151-2, and Roche (1988).

66. Kraut (1989), especially ch. 3, argues with considerable force for the integrity of the primacy of the theoretical life in book X and the conception of happiness in book I. Kraut argues for a hierarchy of virtues, with the ethical virtues as inferior to the theoretical, adding the important point that the former have a causal relation to the latter (178-9). Also, 'The best amount of ethical virtue to engage in, from one's own point of view, is the amount that will best promote one's theoretical interests' (156). See also Tuozzo (1996), who argues for the instrumentality of ethical virtue in leading the best, i.e. contemplative, life. As Tuozzo notes, à propos of VI.13, 1144a1-3, the instrumentality of ethical virtue does not preclude its being choiceworthy in itself.

67. Cf. *Nicomachean Ethics* IX.4, 1166a22-3: δόξειε δ' ἂν τὸ νοοῦν εἶναι ἕκαστος ἢ μάλιστα; IX.8, 1168b31-3: ὥσπερ δὲ καὶ πόλις τὸ κυριώτατον μάλιστ' εἶναι δοκεῖ καὶ πᾶν ἄλλο σύστημα, οὕτω καὶ ἄνθρωπος. Cf. *Protrepticus* B62, 85-6. See Cooper (1975), 168-77, who gives substantially the same interpretation, noting that the identification of the self with the intellect is 'inherited from Plato' (175) and the same as in *De Anima* (176).

68. At *Nicomachean Ethics* IX.4, 1166a32, 9, 1170b6-7, Aristotle calls a friend 'another self' (ἄλλος αὐτός, ἕτερος αὐτός). Cf. *Magna Moralia* II.15, 1213a24, where we find ἕτερος ἐγώ. I take it that in these passages Aristotle is not making the point that a friend is another human being. The distinction between human being and 'self' (αὐτός) is authentically Platonic. See *Alcibiades*, *Laws*. Eriksen (1976), 89, who rejects a Platonic orientation of the above passages says, '... one may say that

217

Lloyd P. Gerson

Aristotle in his account of νοῦς makes the highest part of the soul exclusively dominating in a way that blurs his general anthropology. It might not be correct to say that Aristotle has two doctrines of man. But if he has one, it surely falls into two parts. The part concerning man as a natural species of body and soul presents another picture than the part concerning man as a philosopher and scientist with νοῦς'.

69. For example, John Philoponus, *In GC* 21.1-10, says that Plato treats of the generation of elements (in *Timaeus*), but that this treatment is not extended to the generation of living things. That is, the principles employed in the former cannot be applied to the latter. By implication, Aristotle's account of the latter is available and is not out of harmony with Platonism.

70. Simplicius, *In Phys.* 3.16-18. Cf. 10.35-11.3; 316.23-6. Cf. John Philoponus, *In Phys.* 241.3-27, who gives the same two lists, adding two further important points: (1) Aristotle does not use the paradigmatic cause added by Plato because he is confining himself to the science of nature and (2) Aristotle assimilates the instrumental contributory cause to the material cause. Later, 244.14-23, he adds that Aristotle assimilates the paradigmatic cause to the form. Thus, Aristotle collapses the six Platonic causal principles into four. I use the term 'telic' for τὸ τελικόν rather than 'final' simply in order to avoid begging any questions by the unintended connotations of the latter.

71. See Simplicius, *In Phys.* 1359.5-7.

72. See Aristotle, *Physics* I.9, 192a13-14: ἡ μὲν γὰρ ὑπομένουσα συναιτία τῇ μορφῇ τῶν γιγνομένων ἐστίν, ὥσπερ μήτηρ. Cf. *Metaph.* V.5, 1015a21, where the examples are breathing and food which are necessary for an animal to live.

73. *Timaeus* 46c7-e6.

74. Cf. *Timaeus* 29a, 76d-e; *Philebus* 53e; *Republic* 530a5-7; *Epistle II* 312e.

75. See *Timaeus* 30c-31a, 52a.

76. See Timaeus 52a4-6: τὸ δὲ ὁμώνυμον ὅμοιόν τε ἐκείνῳ [the unchanging Form], 53b5, where these are identified with shapes and numbers: εἴδεσί τε καὶ ἀριθμοῖς. Cf. 53c5; 54d4-5; 55d8. Cf. Simplicius, *In Phys.* 295.12-296.9.

77. Cf. Simplicius, *In Phys.* 1.16; Proclus, *In Parm.* 705.37; 839.33; 1053.11; *Commentary on Timaeus* I 3.2; I 10.14; II 25.2; II 36.29. The usage goes back at least to Alexander of Aphrodisias, *In Metaph.* 178.33; 360.4-5; 373.23; 639.14-15, where it is specified as applying to the 'sublunary'. Two passages from Plato were typically used to justify the terminology, *Phaedo* 102e, where Plato speaks of the 'largeness in us' as opposed to 'Largeness itself' and *Parmenides* 130e, where he speaks of the 'likeness in us' as opposed to 'Likeness itself'.

78. Actually, there are two passages in Plato where the term ἡ ὕλη does appear in something other than its common meaning of 'wood'. See *Timaeus* 69a6, where Plato is evidently using the term metaphorically to refer to the 'building blocks' of his cosmology, namely, the cooperating principles of reason and necessity. See also *Philebus* 54c1, where 'raw materials' in the process of becoming is perhaps the sense, though the term is certainly not thematized here and in any case it does not refer to matter in the sense in which Aristotle and the Neoplatonists believed that Plato was talking about matter. On the other hand, Plutarch, *On the Defect of Oracles* 414f4-415a1, says that Plato discovered the concept of matter, though the term was introduced later. Cf. Alcinous, *Didaskalikis* 8, who, too, assumes that the receptacle is another name for matter.

79. Cf. Simplicius, *In Phys.* 363.8-10, 'In general, if enmattered forms are participations in primary Forms, they are images fashioned in their likeness. Every image, then, is related to its model'.

80. Proclus, *In Tim.* I 2.16-4.1. Cf. III 222.7-27 and *ET*, Prop. 56, on the instrumental character of 'secondary' causes in relation to 'primary' causes.

81. See Simplicius, *In Phys.* 223.16-20, where he argues that nature cannot be a productive cause because it is a moved mover. The productive cause must be identified with the Demiurge. See also 315.10-16 and 287.7-30 where Simplicius compares the instrumental causality of nature with the primary causality of soul in both Plato and Aristotle.

82. *Physics* VIII.3, 253b5-6.

83. See *Republic* 510b-511c and Simplicius, *In Phys.* 1194.24-30.

84. See Simplicius, *In Phys.* 317.4-28, where Simplicius argues that a true principle of change must be unchanging. Therefore, even soul, a self-mover, is not, strictly speaking, a principle of change. The principle of change must be intellect. Proclus, *In Parm.* 785.19-786.17, argues that nature cannot be self-constituted (αὐθυπόστατος) because it cannot be self-moving and it cannot be self-moving because it is corporeal, that is, it has parts outside of parts. For example, nothing can cause itself to be heated as a whole at the same time that it is caused to be heated. So, if nature is not self-constituted, that is, roughly, self-explanatory, then there must be a cause of it outside of nature.

85. See Guthrie (1955) for a clear defence of the position that Neoplatonists were not misled in thus identifying Plato's view.

86. *De Anima* I.1, 403a27-8 with 403b15-16.

87. *Parts of Animals* I.1, 641b8-9 (= Pseudo-Simplicius, *In DA* 2.27-8). See also *Metaph.* VI.1, 1026a16.

88. See Pseudo-Simplicius, *In DA* 96.3-10.

89. Pseudo-Simplicius, *In DA* 3.14-28.

90. Pseudo-Simplicius, *In DA* 102.21-2.

91. *De Anima* II.3, 414b20-415a3. See Ross (1956), 223, who emphasizes that this passage does not take back what is said at 412b5-6. Pseudo-Simplicius, *In DA* 106.33-107.14, argues that there is a single general account of the soul but it is not univocal; rather, it is equivocal, with a primary and derivative references. The primary here would be the simplest soul which is present in all the more complex versions.

92. See, for example, Blumenthal (1996), 94-7, who thinks that this comment is 'difficult to reconcile with the text of Aristotle' and most likely a 'piece of residual Platonism which Aristotle for some reason never excised'. Hamlyn (1993), 87, dismisses the passage as 'a lecturer's aside'. Robinson (1983), 128-31, defends the analogy of the sailor on the basis of his dualistic interpretation.

93. See Wedin (2000), especially chs 5-6; Wedin (1989) and Cohen (1992). See also, for example, Wilkes (1992), especially 125-7. Caston (1999), 224, suggests that if this chapter were to have dropped out of the text, we would not have 'missed anything significant at regards the psychological *mechanisms* of thought'. Instead, what these few lines are supposed to do is explain 'how mind fits into the world and where it tends, and above all, how we, like the heavenly spheres, are moved in all we do through our imperfect imitation of God'. Contra see Heinaman (1990), 100-2, who offers several cogent reasons for rejecting functionalism, all of which amount to denying that psychical activities can be attributes of bodies.

94. See Robinson (1983) who argues for this position. His account of 'Aristotelian dualism' would I think do equally well as an account of Platonic dualism of the embodied person. For another version of Aristotelian dualism see Heinaman (1990). Heinaman, 91, argues that Aristotle is an 'emergent dualist' with respect to the soul and body. He leaves intellect out of this account. Heinaman recognizes that emergent dualism is not incompatible with a physical account unless the soul's distinctness from the body entails that it is an incorporeal entity. Its existence as such would be entirely problematic unless it could exist on its own.

95. See Pseudo-Simplicius, *In DA* 246.16-248.16 especially 245.12, for the remark on Aristotle's exegetical prowess. That most scholars today react derisively to this remark is I think only an indication of a difference in meaning of the term 'exegesis'.

96. See *Timaeus* 41c-d; 61c7; 65a5; 69c8-d1; 72d4-e1; 73d3. In none of these passages is the term 'intellect' used for the 'immortal part' of the soul, though that is the clear implication. See *Phaedo* 78b4-84b4; *Republic* 608d-612a. Themistius, *Paraphrase of Aristotle's De Anima* 106.14-107.29, explicitly identifies the intellect in *Timaeus* with the active intellect in the fifth chapter of *De Anima*. See Proclus, *In Tim.* III 234.8-235.9 and Damascius, *Commentary on Plato's Phaedo* 1.177, who record the Neoplatonic debate over whether only the rational part of the soul was immortal or both the rational and some irrational part. The latter minority view was evidently held by Iamblichus and Plutarch of Athens.

97. See *Timaeus* 30b; *Philebus* 30c; *Sophist* 249a.

98. See Gerson (1997).

99. See the famous passage at *Generation of Animals* II.3, 736b27-9: λείπεται τὸν νοῦν μόνον θύραθεν εἰσιέναι καὶ θεῖον εἶναι μόνον· οὐθὲν γὰρ αὐτοῦ τῇ ἐνεργείᾳ κοινωνεῖ σωματικὴ ἐνεργεία.

100. See John Philoponus, *In DA* 14.29-38; 161.31-162.27; 292.5-13; Pseudo-Philoponus, *In DA* 466.12-467.12.

101. *De Anima* III.7, 431a1. See III.4, 430a4-5; III.5, 430a19-20; III.6, 430b25-6; III.7, 431b17; III.8, 431b22-3. I leave out III.4, 429b9 as perhaps problematic. See also *Metaph.* XII.9, 1074b38-1075a5.

102. Cf. *De Anima* III.4, 429b30-1.

103. Victor Caston suggests to me in private correspondence that II.2, 425b12-17, provides a counterexample to the claim that Aristotle holds that the self-reflexivity of intellection guarantees the non-bodily status of the intellect. For my answers see Gerson (2005), 151 n. 84.

104. See, e.g., Syrianus, *In Metaph.* 159.33-160.5; Asclepius, *In Metaph.* 1939; 433.9-436.6; Proclus, *In Parm.* 930.6-931.9.

105. See Asclepius, *In Metaph.* 69.17-28.

106. See Kahn (1985) and De Koninck (1994).

107. See Krämer (1964), 140-9 and (1973) for a discussion of the various 'Academic Forms theories' against which Aristotle is reacting and an argument that Aristotle's own view of first philosophy is firmly rooted in an identifiable Academic approach. Plato's references to 'friends of the Forms' in *Sophist*, his implicit criticism of some theory of Forms in *Parmenides*, and his revision of the 'simple hypothesis' in *Phaedo* all indicate a self-critical stance in regard to the postulation of Forms as explanatory entities.

108. Asclepius, *In Metaph.* 69.17-27.

109. See Chen (1940), 10ff., for an argument that Aristotle's criticism of separation is directed at Academics other than Plato.

110. At *Parmenides* 133c3-d5, Parmenides characterizes Socrates' version of the theory of Forms as holding that if Forms are separate from the sensible world, then they 'are what they are in relation to each other' and not to the 'likenesses in us' or whatever we call them. Proclus, *In Parm.* 930.6-931.9, points out that if the Forms are unqualifiedly separate from us, then they will be unknowable. We need to understand Forms such that we can maintain that they are 'transcendent' (ἐξήρηνται) and not in us and at the same time are present everywhere and are participated in, while not being in their participants (930, 33-7). So, even the separation of Forms from the sensible world has to be qualified by the Platonist.

111. See Libera (1996), 105-8, on Syrianus on 'psychic Forms' as intermediary between Aristotelian concepts and separate Forms.

112. Plotinus, for example, at *Enneads* V.9.7.7-14, insists that Forms exist prior to their being thought. See also VI.6.6.8-10.

113. See Proclus, *In Parm.* 883.37-884.3, where he argues that identifying that which is common in things still leaves the question of the explanation of the origin of that which is common. In other words, identifying the fact that many things are large does not explain how many things can be large. Cf. 885.1-2. Also, see 888.18-19 on the definition of Forms as paradigmatic causes. The definition is based on Plato's *Parmenides* and *Timaeus*. See *Parmenides* 132d2; *Timaeus* 28a7; 28c6; 31a4; 37c8; 38b8; 38c1; 39e7; 48e5. Aristotle, in *On the Ideas*, according to Alexander of Aphrodisias in his *In Metaph.* 83.21-2, says that being a παράδειγμα is 'especially characteristic of Ideas'. Cf. 86.15: 'the Idea's being an Idea consists in its being a παράδειγμα'.

114. See *Metaph.* XIII.4, 1078b36-1079a2.

115. See de Strycker (1955), who argues that Aristotle, in both *Metaphysics* and *On the Ideas* presents the separation of Forms as part of an exclusive dilemma: either Forms are separate from sensibles or they are present in sensibles. But this dichotomy the Platonist need not accept. '... ne croyons-nous pas que la notion de séparation, telle quelle figure dans le Περὶ Ἰδέων et la *Métaphysique*, soit empruntée à Plato lui-même' (138-9).

116. See my recent book, Gerson (2005).

Reading Proclus Diadochus in Byzantium

Ken Parry

The purpose of this paper is to give a preliminary overview of what we know about Proclus, his readers, and his writings in the Byzantine period. It is a fact that Proclus in Byzantium is still largely *terra incognita*,[1] but then that is also true of the history of philosophy in Byzantium in general as there is no recent volume on the subject.[2]

From the evidence I have looked at there appear to be two kinds of witnesses to the influence of Proclus in Byzantium, what we might call (a) the indirect (unacknowledged influence and assimilation), and (b) the direct (either refutations of particular works or the promotion of particular works). It is noticeable that we find the majority of witnesses to the first kind of influence in the period from the sixth to the tenth century, and the second kind in the period from the eleventh to the fifteenth century. There is no doubt that the eleventh century represents a watershed in the history of reading Proclus in Byzantium.

The first indirect witness, and one of the most influential, is the unknown author of the late fifth or early sixth century who wrote under the name of Dionysius the Areopagite.[3] The earliest writer to appeal to the authority of Pseudo-Dionysius, as he is known today, is Severus, bishop of Antioch, in works written between 518 and 528.[4] Suspicions that the author was not who he claimed to be were aroused early in the East. The authenticity of his writings was first questioned in 532 by Hypatius, bishop of Ephesus, at a synod in Constantinople of Chalcedonian and Monophysite clergy called by the Emperor Justinian. Hypatius is reported to have said: 'But if none of the ancients made mention of them (the writings of Dionysius), I simply do not know how you can prove that they were written by him.'[5] At one point the Georgian Peter the Iberian (d. 491), bishop of Maiuma in Gaza, was a strong contender for their authorship. Although the debate continues most scholars accept that the works of Pseudo-Dionysius were probably written by someone from the circle of Peter the Iberian and Severus of Antioch.[6] If that is the case then Proclus may be said to have influenced moderate Monophysite christology. The Monophysites were those who rejected the particular dyophysite formula pushed through by the Greeks and Latins at the Council of Chalcedon in 451.[7]

Two clues to dating the works of Pseudo-Dionysius are (a) the death of

Proclus in 485 and (b) the first mention of his writings between 518 and 528. Like his Latin contemporary Boethius (d. *c.* 524) in *The Consolation of Philosophy*, Pseudo-Dionysius wears his Christianity lightly, but this fact does not make him less of a Christian and more of a Neoplatonist. The evidence suggests it was not an either/or situation at the time. The civil servant John Lydus (d. *c.* 565) studied at Constantinople with the last of Proclus' pupils, Agapius, and he mentions a book entitled *On the Disciples of the Great Proclus* written by the Christian poet Christodorus.[8] It seems John Philoponus refuted Proclus' views on the eternity of the world without resorting to Christian arguments, but relied instead on opposing views within the Neoplatonic tradition.[9]

Commentaries on the works of Pseudo-Dionysius by John of Scythopolis in the sixth century and Maximus the Confessor in the seventh are essential for understanding how Byzantine theologians assimilated Proclean ideas through Pseudo-Dionysius. Both commentators endeavour to vindicate the apostolic authorship of the Areopagite, but at the same time they seem to be aware that the Areopagite is using Neoplatonic terminology.[10] Their approach raises questions about the nature of the Christian assimilation of the pagan philosophical tradition in the early Byzantine period. In the past scholars have tended to use terms such as a 'fraudulent' and 'plagiarist' to describe this phenomenon, but these terms do nothing to advance our understanding of the situation. In fact the *modus operandi* of these scholiasts is related to the nature of patristic methodology and the application of that methodology to the shaping of tradition. It was the normal practice in the sixth and seventh centuries not to attribute sources or parenthesize quotations.

In the context of their time the nature of theological discourse was quite different from our own and must therefore be approached on its own terms. To this end it is a necessary to grasp the concept of 'tradition' (*paradosis*) as understood by early Byzantine theologians.[11] How they understood that concept determined what they wrote and how they wrote. They viewed both written and unwritten tradition as an essential source for the development of doctrine and made creative use of it in dealing with ongoing issues.[12] They theologized *ad mentem patrum* which meant they were steeped in the writings of the fathers and the definitions of the church councils. They quoted freely from both scripture and the fathers often with no regard for the context in which the citations appeared. They identified so closely with the authorities they were using that their own thoughts became indistinguishable from those they were promoting. They did this in order to show that they were at one with the teachings of the church and witnesses to the *consensus patrum* they believed existed. It was important in an age of doctrinal conflict to ensure that tradition was on your side, and this could mean using and engaging with, but not necessarily acknowledging, pagan sources.[13]

It is worth considering for a moment that the Neoplatonists were similarly concerned with a *consensus philosophorum* they believed existed. Just one example from Simplicius (d. *c.* 650) will suffice:

> It is necessary ... when Aristotle disagrees with Plato, not merely to look at the letter of the text, and condemn the discord between the philosophers, but to consider the spirit and track down the agreement between them on the majority of points.'[14]

We may compare this passage with one from Maximus the Confessor:

> We are to accept the reverent meaning of dogma drawn from the expressions of the holy Fathers ... that indicate unity as in no way contradictory of other statements of the holy Fathers that indicate duality [viz. regarding the two natures and energies in Christ] ... And we wisely turn away those expressions that seem somehow contrary ... and we boldly expel them from our home, that is from the Catholic and Apostolic Church of God.[15]

Both Neoplatonic philosophers and Christian theologians were keen to harmonize their respective traditions.

In the eighth century John of Damascus (d. 745) went so far as to state that his intention was to say nothing of his own, but only what had been said by others.[16] This should not be taken as a confession of plagiarism but as a statement of his working method. Canon 19 of the Council in Trullo of 692 warns church leaders against writing works of their own when they should make themselves known for their knowledge of the fathers.[17] John also stated that his method of working was like that of a bee, going from place to place gathering nectar from the best flowers. This 'labour of the bee', as he called it, was indicative of his way of working.[18] It was also a reference to his use of anthologies of proof-texts indispensable in the fight against heresy. His writings show a breadth of learning and a range of references unrivalled by other Greek authors of the eighth century.

If we keep in mind this type of approach to authorities and texts we are in a better position to understand the intention of the pseudonymous author of the *Corpus Areopagiticum* and his early commentators. The conflict theory of pagan and Christian relations still dominates the field, but the situation was not as straightforward as first appears, and not least of the complexities involved was that the monotheistic tendency was not a Judaeo-Christian monopoly.[19] Much has been written about the influence of Neoplatonism on early Christian thought, both Greek and Latin, but was the influence only one way? For instance, how far did public performance of the Christian liturgy contribute to the renewed interest in theurgy among later Neoplatonists? This interest in religious practice seems to indicate a common desire to attract adherents through spectacle as well as by persuasion. We need to look beyond the polemical rhetoric of Christian and pagan writers for a more nuanced understanding of the relationship between them.

In the Prologue to the *Corpus Areopagiticum*, attributed to Maximus the Confessor in the Migne edition, it says:

> One must know that some of the non-Christian philosophers (*tôn exô philo-sophôn*), especially Proclus, have often employed certain concepts of the blessed Dionysius ... It is possible to conjecture from this that the ancient philosophers of Athens usurped his works and then hid them, so that they themselves might seem to be the progenitors of his divine oracles ... Some say that these writings do not belong to the saint, but to someone who came later ...[20]

Although this is clearly a Christian spin on the history of philosophy it is certainly not dismissive of the Neoplatonic tradition.

Our first direct witness to the writings of Proclus in Byzantium would have been Procopius of Gaza (d. *c.* 529) had the *Refutation of Proclus' Elements of Theology* long ascribed to him been correctly attributed, but the work has been shown to be by Nicholas of Methone, a twelfth-century Byzantine bishop.[21] It was thought at one time that Nicholas had cribbed the earlier work of Procopius, but this has proved not to be the case. I will return to Nicholas later. Procopius is credited with inventing the catena or commentary on a book of scripture consisting of a collection of excerpts from earlier commentaries, each excerpt headed (but not always) by the name of its author.[22] As we have already indicated the compiling of commentaries and florilegia went on apace in the sixth and seventh centuries.[23]

The first direct witness must be John Philoponus (d. 570), who may have belonged to a Christian lay brotherhood that did good works around Alexandria, hence his nickname *philoponos*. He is well known of course for his treatise *Against Proclus On the Eternity of the World*, in which, as we have already remarked, he did not adopt an overtly Christian position.[24] We have to bear in mind that the Byzantines knew John as a Monophysite and accused him of tritheism.[25] Although he was denounced as a heretic his theological work *The Arbiter* is quoted by John of Damascus in the eighth century,[26] and he was influential in the Arab world from the ninth century. But it was probably not until the Palaeologan period and after the fall of Constantinople in 1453 that Greek scholars again gave consideration to his philosophical writings.[27]

Mention of the Arab world brings us to the selections from Proclus, or *Buruklus* as he was known to the Arabs, called the *Book on the Pure Good*, better known to Latin schoolmen as the *Liber de Causis*. Although the Arabic version seems to have originated in the circle of the ninth-century philosopher al-Kindi at Baghdad,[28] the possibility exists of there being a Greek or Syriac prototype.[29] Again this work has been associated in the past with the name of Peter the Iberian.[30] Like the pseudonymous author of the *Corpus Areopagiticum*, the anonymous complier and/or translator of the *Book on the Pure Good* was presenting Proclean ideas to yet another monotheistic readership, this time Muslim.

It seems more than likely that the works of Proclus were taken to Persia with the seven philosophers led by Damascius, the last *diadochos*, after the Emperor Justinian closed the Athenian Academy in 529.[31] The Byzantine historian Agathias (d. 582), our main source of information about their stay in Persia, does not mention the writings of Proclus among the translations commissioned by the Sasanian court.[32] But it would be rather surprising if his writings were not among those considered for translation. The philosophers were allowed to return to Byzantine territory after the Persians signed a peace treaty with Justinian in 532. The suggestion that the city of Harrân in northern Syria became their home under Simplicius has not met with universal acceptance.[33] But given that the majority of the seven were of Eastern Mediterranean origin the founding of a Neoplatonic centre in Syria is a distinct possibility. Whether it remained in operation through to the Arab conquests in the first half of the seventh century is another matter.

In a Byzantine list of manuscripts transcribed between 800 and 880 we find Proclus' commentaries on the *Timaeus* and on the *Republic*, as well as works by other Neoplatonic philosophers.[34] The presence of Proclus' commentaries among these manuscripts would seem to suggest a revival of interest in Proclus in Byzantium in this period, as well as indicating a possible source for the transmission of Greek works into Arabic.[35] In all likelihood these would have been translated by so-called 'Nestorian'[36] Christians in Baghdad and it raises again the question of whether there were in fact translations in Syriac of Proclus' works.

Photius, twice patriarch of Constantinople in the second half of the ninth century, questioned the authenticity of the writings attributed to the Areopagite, quoting from an unknown writer called Theodore who had written a pamphlet entitled *The Book of St Dionysius is Authentic.*[37] Unfortunately this work is no longer extant, but according to Photius Theodore raised several objections to the authenticity of the corpus. Like Hypatius of Ephesus before him, Theodore asked why if the writings were genuine they were not cited by later fathers. More importantly he asked why as a contemporary of the apostles the Areopagite shows knowledge of church doctrines which developed later.[38] It is interesting to observe these remarks concerning the authenticity of the *Corpus Areopagiticum* in relation to its reception in the West. It was in 827 that a copy of the works of Pseudo-Dionysius was sent by the Byzantine Emperor Michael II to King Louis the Pious of France.[39] Doubts about their genuineness circulating in Byzantium do not appear to have filtered through to the West. In Byzantium, however, a certain reserve towards some aspects of the Areopagite's thought is discernible among theologians. This is noticeable, for example, during both the Iconoclastic controversy in the eighth and ninth centuries and the Hesychast controversy in the fourteenth century.[40]

Arethas, bishop of Caesarea in Cappadocia in the tenth century, commissioned copies of twenty-four of the Platonic dialogues, some of which have glosses by him. It has been suggested that his comments on the

Gorgias derive from the lost commentary by Proclus.[41] Also from the tenth century, an encyclopaedia known as the *Suda* condemns Proclus while at the same time praising his detractor John Philoponus, a somewhat ironic statement given that John was considered a heretic by the Byzantines.[42] I suppose what we have here is a case of better a Christian of the wrong type condemning a pagan philosopher than no condemnation at all. On the other hand, the writer of the entry on Proclus in the *Suda* may have been unaware of Philoponus' theological position.

Our next direct witness is from the eleventh century. This is Michael Psellos (d. 1078) who was largely responsible for the revival of interest in Neoplatonism in Byzantium in the eleventh and twelfth centuries. He writes that after a succession of useless teachers, he turned directly to Plato and Aristotle, and from them moved on to study of the Neoplatonists, including Plotinus and Iamblichus. But it was Proclus in particular who provided him with a doctrine of perception that allowed him to advance to the study of metaphysics.[43] His interest in theurgy stemmed directly from his reading of Proclus. He was the author of a famous *Chronographia* which is full of personal details and observations on the intellectual life of Constantinople.[44] Unfortunately the revival of interest in Proclus and Neoplatonism which he helped to initiate had dire consequences for himself and some of his followers.

Psellos was forced to resign his position as 'Consul of the Philosophers' (*hypatos tôn philosophôn*) in 1054 and was obliged to retire to a monastery for awhile. He eventually returned to court when the political climate changed in his favour, but he was forced out again before his death in 1078.[45] Psellos seems to have been the first to be appointed to the office of 'Consul of the Philosophers'. The function of this office was to oversee state education in the capital and to pay the salaries of those teachers under his control. Later during the twelfth century this office was held by ordained clergy who saw their role as one of suppressing philosophy rather than promoting it. Psellos' interest in Proclus and Neoplatonism was genuine, but he found it difficult to convince his critics that he remained orthodox in his Christian beliefs. Unlike other Byzantine intellectuals Psellos was interested in Greek philosophy for its own sake, rather than using it to reach an accommodation with or as an introduction to Christianity. The process he started of freeing philosophy from Christian theology was carried a stage further by Gemistos Plethon in the fifteenth century.

His pupil John Italos succeeded him as 'Consul of the Philosophers', but he got himself into far deeper trouble than his teacher. Proceedings against him were taken in 1076 and 1082 and on the second occasion he was excommunicated for giving preference to the 'false and foolish wisdom of the non-Christian philosophers' (*tôn exôthen philosophôn*).[46] Like Psellos he was forced to resign his position and spent the rest of his life in monastic obscurity. We do not even know the date of his death. He was formally anathematized in the *Synodikon of Orthodoxy* so that his name was read out in church each year on the First Sunday in Lent and the same fate befell his pupil, the Aristotelian commentator Eustratios of Nicaea.[47] From this point on Byzantine intellectuals had to be careful not to subscribe to the opinions of the philosophers, but to pursue Hellenic studies for instruction only.[48] Actually this situation had pertained to some extent in the earlier Byzantine period as well.

The Christian Hellenism of the Cappadocian fathers in the fourth century is indicative of this situation. Basil the Great and Gregory of Nazianzus had reacted to the Emperor Julian's denial of pagan culture to Christians by claiming that Christians too were heirs to the culture and learning of the ancient world.[49] This claim is celebrated each year in the Greek Orthodox Church as the Feast of Greek Letters. Yet individual theologians like John of Damascus in the eighth century could denounce Hellenism as a source of heresy. This was in spite of the fact that John himself composed the most comprehensive collection of Aristotelian definitions in his *Dialectica*.[50] In practice, however, such denunciations did not carry that much weight. For when Stephanus of Alexandria was appointed to Constantinople as 'ecumenical teacher' (*oikoumenikos didaskalos*) in the early seventh century it was to teach the philosophy of Plato and Aristotle.[51] Although Greek in language and culture medieval Byzantium gradually became more negative in its attitude to Greek philosophy than the Arab East and the Latin West. This has led one modern commentator to observe that by the twelfth century the Latins were more Greek than the Greeks.[52]

The liturgical text of the *Synodikon of Orthodoxy* is an important document for understanding the middle Byzantine attitude to ancient philosophy. It was initially composed to celebrate the end of Iconoclasm and the 'Triumph of Orthodoxy' in 843 by lauding the names of iconophiles and denouncing the names of iconoclasts. After the ninth century additional sections were added to reflect later disputes and controversies. The sections added after the trial of Italos in 1082 show the Byzantine Church promoting itself as a guardian of higher education. Anathema 7 reads:

> Cursed are those who go through a course of Hellenic studies and are taught not simply for the sake of education but follow these empty notions and believe in them as the truth, upholding them as a firm foundation to such an extent that they lead others to them, sometimes secretly, sometimes openly, and teach them without hesitation.[53]

We should bear in mind that the general level of education in Byzantium was higher than in the West.

Italos belonged to the circle of Anna Comnena, daughter of the Emperor Alexis I and the most famous woman historian in Byzantium. She was the author of the *Alexiad*, an important source for the history of her father's life and reign.[54] Although a promoter of Aristotle and his commentators she also supported Neoplatonic studies.[55] Her uncle Isaac Sabastocrator

(d. 1118), the Emperor's brother, composed three works based on the writings of Proclus *On Providence, On Free Will* and *On the Existence of Evil.*[56] But it is said that he wrote them in such a way as to disguise all traces of Neoplatonic influence and was careful to cite only 'reputable' sources such as Pseudo-Dionysius.[57] The writings of Proclus in question have not survived in the original Greek, but they were known to Psellos and Latin translations of them were made by William of Moerbeke, who was bishop of Corinth during the Latin occupation of Byzantium in the thirteenth century.[58] Besides these translations William also translated *The Elements of Theology* and the *Liber de Causis* for his friend Thomas Aquinas.[59]

Our next direct witness is Ioane Petritsi (d. 1125). He was a Georgian who studied in Constantinople under Psellos and Italos and was associated with the revival of Neoplatonism in Byzantium. Apart from a period during the fifth and sixth centuries when Georgia supported the Monophysite cause (as witnessed by Peter the Iberian earlier), Georgia by this time was firmly entrenched in the Byzantine camp. Petritsi takes his surname from the Petritsoni monastery at Bachkovo in Bulgaria, founded in 1083 by a Georgian general serving under the Emperor Alexis Comnenus.[60] He returned to Georgia to help establish an academy at Gelati on the Black Sea coast, which, together with the academy at Iqalto, was responsible for translating many works of Greek philosophy into Georgian, preserving works which are now extant only in Georgian. He translated into Georgian Proclus' *Elements of Theology* with a commentary. It is not known to me whether his commentary has been translated into a modern European language, but I understand a Russian translation exists.

Another direct witness in the twelfth century is Nicholas, bishop of Methone in the Peloponnese (d. *c.*1165), who wrote a *Refutation of Proclus' Elements of Theology* to counteract the fashion for all things Neoplatonic.[61] This work, originally attributed to Procopius of Gaza as mentioned earlier, is a point by point refutation of the propositions of *The Elements of Theology*. It is the first direct refutation of Proclus in the Byzantine world since that of John Philoponus in the sixth century. He comments on the similarities between the Pseudo-Dionysius and Proclus and follows the tradition that the latter must be dependent on the former. Of course by this time the writings of the Areopagite were accepted as genuine by both East and West and earlier doubts concerning their authenticity seem to have evaporated. Nicholas says he was prompted to write his refutation because of the perceived threat of heresy posed by the current fascination with Neoplatonic ideas, especially the interest in theurgy. It was the interest in theurgy in particular that the hierarchy of the Byzantine Church objected to, no doubt viewing it as a demonic form of religious practice.

But if Psellos thought Proclus represented the summit of Hellenic wisdom, Theodore Prodromos (d. *c.*1180), a satirist and poet at the Byzantine court, had other ideas. In an address to the patriarch of Constantinople he distances himself from certain philosophers, including Proclus. He assures the patriarch that he does not like using the philosophical jargon of Proclus and the Neoplatonists with their talk of purgative and theurgic virtues, the henad which is in the intelligence, the source of the first beauty and so on.[62] Although Proclus by this time had become the favourite of many a Byzantine thinker he had also become part of the authorized rhetoric. His was a name to define Christianity against as he now embodied all that was incompatible with Christian doctrine. However, in the late thirteenth or early fourteenth century the historian George Pachymeres (d. after 1308) took more than a passing interest in his writings, making transcripts of his commentaries on the *Parmenides* and the *First Alcibiades*.[63]

We do not hear much of Proclus during the fourteenth-century Hesychast controversy, but we do hear mention of Pseudo-Dionysius, so I suppose the spirit of Proclus haunts this episode.[64] As far as I am aware neither Gregory Palamas for the hesychasts, nor Barlaam the Calabrian for the opposition, alludes to Proclus by name, but discussion about the relation of pagan philosophy to Christian thought was prominent in the early stages of the controversy.[65] Barlaam the Calabrian is known to have written a commentary on the works of Pseudo-Dionysius. The main issue of the controversy centred on the nature and practice of mystical prayer; something that would have been of considerable interest to Proclus himself.

Our final direct witness is George Gemistos (1360-1452). He is better known as Gemistos Plethon, because at the age of eighty he gave himself this additional name. In line with this additional name he is variously called the 'Second Plato' or 'The Last of the Hellenes'.[66] He wrote three commentaries on the *Chaldaean Oracles*, which are thought to have been influenced by Proclus' commentary on the *Oracles*.[67] Proclus' commentary itself survives only in fragments. His literary output was vast and he was considered the leading authority on Greek philosophy in his day. He was consulted by Italian humanists during his stay in Italy as a delegate to the Council of Florence in 1438-9. It was under his influence that the 'Platonic Academy' in Florence was established under the patronage of the Medici family. He may have had personal contact with Nicolas de Cusa; and his pupil Bessarion, who became a cardinal in the Roman Church, was responsible for translating many works from Latin into Greek, and quotes Proclus several times in his correspondence with his former teacher.[68]

Gemistos was accused by his detractor George Scholarios of abandoning any attempt to reconcile ancient philosophy with Christianity and of trying to promote a new religion based on Neoplatonism. Scholarios considered Proclus to be Gemistos' evil genius and the inspiration behind his religious philosophy. He further accused him of taking almost everything from Proclus without mentioning him by name. 'For those who have read Proclus,' he writes, 'and also condemned him, know as well as I do that he is the source of your arguments'.[69] One year after Gemistos' death in 1452 Constantinople fell to the Ottoman Turks bringing to an end over one thousand years of Greek Christian civilization and culture. Subsequently Scholarios, known by his monastic name Gennadios, became the first patriarch of Constantinople to be appointed under the Ottomans, and in this role he burned the books of Plethon.

It is of interest to see from this brief survey of Proclus' works those which are conspicuous by their absence. I have not mentioned, for example, the *Platonic Philosophy*, but this does not mean that it is not cited by other Byzantine writers. A more detailed search would probably reveal references to this as well as to other works not mentioned. Although this is a preliminary reading of the evidence, it would seem that Proclus was better known in Byzantium, at least by name, than other Neoplatonic philosophers, for example, Plotinus.

The reason for this, I think, is that for the Byzantines Proclus *was* the last of the pagan philosophers. Living and writing as he did in the fifth century, that is the second century of the Christian empire, he was to all intents and purposes a figure of the Christian era, who like the Emperor Julian before him, had had the temerity to propagate pagan values in a Christian society. Although portraits of Plato and Aristotle appeared in Byzantine wall paintings alongside Christian saints,[70] this was not the case for Neoplatonic philosophers such as Plotinus and Proclus. No doubt the Byzantines were happy to depict pagan philosophers of the classical period because they had less direct bearing on Christian culture. This may help to explain why the Byzantine Church authorities viewed Proclus as a fifth columnist. Proclus himself was born in Byzantium, but for him Byzantium was neither the New Rome nor the capital of the Greek Christian East.[71]

Individual Byzantine churchmen and lay intellectuals could and probably did take a different view of him of course, but his name became synonymous with a pagan tradition of philosophizing which was considered irreconcilable with Christian theology. Greek manuscripts of his work could, at least in theory, be read wherever they were available, but whether they were in fact read and how often and by whom is very difficult to assess. That his writings continued to interest Byzantine intellectuals is evident from the manuscript tradition. The re-emergence of Proclus as a formidable thinker of influence in the eleventh and twelfth centuries is of considerable interest to the historian of ideas and still requires a detailed explanation.[72] Certainly once his works were back in circulation they appear to have given palpitations to many a Byzantine bishop.

Notes

1. See the remarks by Benakis (1987), 247-59.
2. A new history would need to update certain sections of A.H. Armstrong's

15. Reading Proclus Diadochus in Byzantium

Cambridge History of Later Greek and Early Medieval Philosophy published in 1967, combined with the concept behind B. Tatakis' *La Philosophie Byzantine* first published in 1948. In addition to the Greek writings of late pagan philosophers and Byzantine writers there is an important body of work in the languages of Oriental Christianity, namely Syriac, Georgian, Armenian, and Arabic. See now the important volume of Ierodiakonou (2002), with Benakis' epilogue, 'Current Research in Byzantine Philosophy'.

3. Eusebius, *Ecclesiastical History*, 3.4.11, records that Dionysius the Areopagite mentioned in Acts 17:34 was the first bishop of Athens and he is shown wearing episcopal regalia in Byzantine depictions of the Dormition of the Virgin. Chapter 3 of the *Divine Names* of Pseudo-Dionysius is traditionally understood to refer to the Dormition.

4. On this see Rorem and Lamoreaux (1998), 11-15. Severus of Antioch (d. 538) uses the Dionysian expression 'theandric energy' as found in *Letter IV* of the *Corpus Areopagiticum*, PG 3.1072C. It has been suggested that the term *'theandrikos'* applied to Christ derives from the Arabian god Theandrites celebrated in a hymn by Proclus; see H.-D. Saffrey (1966, 1982).

5. Quoted by Rorem and Lamoreaux (1998), 18.

6. Van Esbroeck (1993); Rorem and Lamoreaux (1993).

7. For background, see Meyendorff (1989); Frend (1972).

8. John Lydus, *De Magistratibus*, III. 26. See Maas (1992), ch. 7, and Athanassiadi (1999), 257.

9. See the introduction of Lang and Macro (2001), and below.

10. Rorem and Lamoreaux (1998), 106-18 and Louth (1996), 28-32. The expression 'theandric energy' is discussed by Maximus the Confessor in his *Ambigua* 5, see Louth, 177. In his translation Louth substitutes the more familiar 'griffin' for Maximus' 'goat-stag', but does not make the connection with Aristotle's *'tragelaphos'*, *An. Po.*, II.7, 92b4-8.

11. Florovsky (1972).

12. See Parry (1996), chs 15 and 16, together with Gray (1989), 21-36.

13. Gray (1988) and Averil Cameron (1994), 198-215.

14. Quoted by Hoffmann (1987), 77.

15. *Opuscule* 7, Louth (1996), 190.

16. See his preamble in Kotter I (1969), 53.

17. Canon 19 can be found in Nedungatt and Featherstone (1995), 94-6.

18. On John see Parry (2003). The simile of the bee is taken from Basil the Great, see *Saint Basil on the Value of Greek Literature*, ed. N.G. Wilson, section 4.36. For more on John see now Louth (2002).

19. See the collection of articles in Athanassiadi and Frede (1999), and Kenney (1991). It is interesting in this respect to note the Emperor Julian maintaining that Greek culture was the prerogative of polytheists; see Pelikan (1993), 12.

20. PG 4.21a-d. Quoted by Rorem and Lamoreaux (1998), 106. On the possibility of attributing this scholion to John Philoponus, see Opsomer and Steel (2003), 6.

21. See Angelou (1984), and below.

22. On Procopius, see Wilson (1996), 31-3; Downey (1963).

23. The relation of late antique philosophical commentary and doxography to the development of the Christian catena and florilegium requires further study.

24. Besides Lang and Macro (2001), see Blumenthal (1982), 54-63; Verrycken (1990).

25. Chadwick (1997).

26. *Book of Heresies, Die Schriften des Johannes von Damaskos*, vol. IV, 50-5.

27. Geanakoplos (1989), 121-2.

28. Endress (1997).

29. On the limited number of Greek philosophical texts translated into Syriac in the pre-Islamic period, see Brock (1982), 17-34.

30. See Parry et al. (1999), 214.

31. Alan Cameron (1969); Blumenthal (1978); and, for a more recent assessment, Hallstrom (1994).

32. Agathias, *History,* B 28-30 (ed. R. Keydell). Also Averil Cameron (1970), 101-4.

33. M. Tardieu (1986, 1990). Also Athanassiadi (1999), 48-53.

34. Wilson (1996), 85-8.

35. D. Gutas tabulates forty-three Greek manuscripts (1998), 181-6.

36. See Brock (1996).

37. Wilson (1994), 26-7.

38. Wilson (1994), 26-7.

39. Luibheid (1987), 26.

40. See Louth (1997), and Meyendorff (1957), 547-53. By contrast Dionysius is cited some 1,700 times by Thomas Aquinas, Luibheid (1987), 21.

41. Wilson (1996), 121.

42. *Suda (Suidae Lexicon),* pt. iv, p. 210 Adler.

43. Sewter (1966), 174. Proclus figures in an interesting collection edited by Pontikos (1992). On the arguments for attributing this work to Psellos, see Duffy (2002), ch. 6.

44. See the important study by Kaldellis (1999).

45. Browning (1975), and Kazhdan and Wharton Epstein (1985), ch. 4.

46. See Gouillard (1967), 57, and Clucas (1981), 142.

47. Gouillard (1967), 69f.

48. Gouillard (1967), 59.

49. See Pelikan (1993), 10-20; McGuckin (2001), 117-30.

50. Kotter I (1969).

51. Lemerle (1986), 87-9. On Stephanus of Alexandria, see Wolska-Conus (1989).

52. Meyendorff (1974), 64, and also his remarks on the double intellectual life of Byzantine humanists, 106. Byzantium does not appear to have produced a form of Latin Averroism with its 'double truth' theory. The lack of interest by the Byzantines in ancient Greek philosophy and science became a sore point in Arab-Byzantine relations; see El Cheikh (2004), 103-9, and Gutas (1998), 83-95.

53. Gouillard (1967), 59. Quoted by Wilson (1996), 154.

54. Sewter (1969), and the papers in Gouma-Petersen (2000).

55. See Browning (1990).

56. See the introduction by Opsomer and Steel (2003).

57. Wilson (1996), 14.

58. Kristeller (1987), 197.

59. See Guagliardo et al. (1996).

60. Parry et al. (1999), 75, 377.

61. Angelou (1984), Introduction.

62. Cited by Angelou (1984), lvii.

63. See Gardra et al. (1989).

64. Proclus is quoted by Palamas' opponent Gregory Akindynos; see Hero (1983), 49.

65. Meyendorff (1964), Podskalsky (1977).

66. Woodhouse (1986).

67. Athanassiadi (2002), ch. 10.

68. Woodhouse (1986), 233-4.

69. Woodhouse (1986), 25, 73, 358, 360.

70. An important post-Byzantine work includes information for representing Plato, Aristotle, Plutarch, and Philo; see Hetherington (1974), 31.

71. See Marinus' *Life of Proclus*, 6, 10, in Edwards (2000). It is worth noting that Byzantium retained something of the ancient philosophical notion of '*sophia*' through the dedication of Divine Wisdom (*Hagia Sophia*) given to the Great Church in Constantinople. The title was given to other churches throughout the Byzantine commonwealth and resulted in the development of 'sophiology' among some later Russian philosophers; see Parry et al. (1999), 164, 455.

72. See Podskalsky (1976), 509-23. John Duffy in his article cited above is inclined to attribute the Proclean revival to Psellos and to accept as true his statement that 'Philosophy, by the time I came upon it, had already expired ...; but I brought it back to life, all by myself'. But given Psellos' propensity to exaggerate this seems unlikely to have been the case.

Bibliography

Aalders, G.J.D. (1968), *Die Theorie der gemischten Verfassung im Altertum*, Amsterdam.

Aalders, G.J.D. (1975), *Political Thought in Hellenistic Times*, Amsterdam.

Adam, J. (1891), *The Nuptial Number of Plato: Its Solution and Significance*, London.

Adamson, P., H. Baltussen, M. Stone (eds) (2004), *Philosophy, Science and Exegesis in Greek, Arabic and Latin Commentaries*, London.

Angelou, A.D. (1984), *Nicholas of Methone, Refutation of Proclus' Elements of Theology*, Leiden.

Annas, J. (1999), *Platonic Ethics Old and New*, Ithaca, NY.

Annas, J. and C.J. Rowe (eds) (2002), *New Perspectives on Plato, Modern and Ancient*, Cambridge, Mass.

Armstrong, A.H. (1955), 'Plotinus's Doctrine of the Infinite and its Significance for Christian Thought', *Downside Review* 73, 47-58.

Armstrong, A.H. (1966-88), *Plotinus, Text with an English Translation*, 7 vols, Cambridge, MA, and London.

Armstrong, A.H. (ed.) (1967), *The Cambridge History of Later Greek and Early Medieval Philosophy*, Cambridge.

Ashbaugh, A.F. (1988). *Plato's Theory of Explanation, A Study of the Cosmological Account in the Timaeus*, New York.

Athanassiadi, P. (1993), 'Persecution and Response in Late Paganism: The Evidence of Damascius', *JHS* 113, 1-29.

Athanassiadi, P. (ed.) (1999), *Damascius: The Philosophical History, Text with Translation and Notes*, Athens.

Athanassiadi, P. (2002), 'Byzantine Commentators on the Chaldaean Oracles: Psellos and Plethon', in Ierodiakonou (ed.) (2002), 237-52.

Athanassiadi, P. and M. Frede (eds) (1999), *Pagan Monotheism in Late Antiquity*, Oxford.

Atkinson, M. (1983), *Plotinus: Ennead V. 1, A Commentary with Translation*, Oxford.

Axelson, B. (1952), *Akzentuierender Klauselrhythmus bei Apuleius*, Lund.

Bajoni, M.G. (1994), 'Aspetti linguistici e letterari del *De Mundo* di Apuleio', *ANRW* 2.34.2, 1785-1832.

Baltes, M. (1963), 'Modes de composition des commentaires de Proclus', *MH* 20, 551-74.

Baltes, M. (1976). *Die Weltentstehung des platonischen Timaios nach den antiken Interpreten* I, Leiden.

Baltes, M. (1978), *Die Weltenstehung des platonischen Timaios nach den antiken Interpreten* II, Leiden.

Baltes, M. (1996), 'Γέγονεν (Platon, *Tim.* 28b7): Ist die Welt real entstanden oder nicht?', in K.A. Algra, P.W. van der Horst, and D.T. Runia (eds), *Polyhistor:*

237

Bibliography

Studies in the History and Historiography of Ancient Philosophy Presented to Jaap Mansfeld on His Sixtieth Birthday, Leiden, 76-96.

Baltussen, H. (2003), 'Early Reactions to Plato's *Timaeus*: Polemic and Exegesis in Theophrastus and Epicurus', in R.W. Sharples and A. Sheppard (eds) (2003), 49-71.

Barker, A. (1978), 'Symphonoi Arithmoi: A Note on *Republic* 531c1-4', *CP* 73, 337-42.

Barker, A. (1994), 'Ptolemy's Pythagoreans, Archytas, and Plato's Conception of Mathematics', *Phronesis* 39, 113-35.

Barnes, J. (1991), 'The Hellenistic Platos', *Apeiron*, 24, 115-28.

Beaujeu, J. (1973), *Apulée: Opuscules philosophiques*, Paris.

Benakis, L. (1987), 'Neues zur Proklos-Tradition in Byzanz', in G. Boss and G. Seel (eds), *Proclus et son influence*, Zurich, 247-59.

Benitez, E.E. (1989), *Forms in Plato's Philebus*, Assen.

Bertelli, L. (1962-3), 'Εἶδος Δικαιαρχικόν', *Atti della Accademia delle Scienze di Torino. Classa di scienze morali, storiche e filologiche* 97, 175-209.

Berti, E. (1962), *La filosofia del primo Aristotele*, Firenze.

Berti, E. (1997), 'L'oggetto dell' εἰκὼς μῦθος nel *Timeo* di Platone', in Calvo and Brisson (eds) (1997), 119-31.

Beutler, R. and W. Theiler (1960-7), *Plotins Shriften*, übersetzt von R. Harder, Neubearbeitung mit griechische Lesetext und Anmerkungen, 6 vols, Hamburg.

Beutler, R. (1953), 'Porphyrios', *RE* 22.1, 278-301.

Bidez, J. (1913, 1964), *Vie de Porphyre*, Hildesheim.

Bleichen, J. (1979), 'Zur Entstehung der Verfassungstypologie im 5. Jahrhundert v. Chr. (Monarchie, Aristokratie, Demokratie)', *Historia* 28, 148-72.

Block, I. (1961), 'The Order of Aristotle's Psychological Writings', *AJP* 82, 50-77.

Blumenthal, H.J. (1971a), *Plotinus' Psychology*, The Hague.

Blumenthal, H.J. (1971b), 'Soul, World-Soul, and Individual Soul in Plotinus', in *Le Néoplatonisme*, Paris, 55-73.

Blumenthal, H.J. (1978), '529 and its Sequel: What Happened to the Academy?' *Byzantion* 48, 369-85.

Blumenthal, H.J. (1982), 'John Philoponus and Stephanus of Alexandria: Two Neoplatonic Christian Commentators on Aristotle?', in O'Meara (ed.) (1982), 54-63.

Blumenthal, H.J. (1996), *Aristotle and Neoplatonism in Late Antiquity. Interpretations of De Anima*, London and Ithaca, NY.

Boas, F. (1943), 'A Basic Conflict in Aristotle's Philosophy', *AJP* 64, 172-93.

Bos, A. (1995), *Cosmic and Meta-cosmic Theology in Aristotle's Lost Dialogues*, Leiden.

Bowersock, G.W. (ed.) (1974), *Approaches to the Second Sophistic*, Pennsylvania.

Boys-Stones, G.R. (2001), *Post-Hellenistic Philosophy: A Study of its Development from the Stoics to Origen*, Oxford.

Bréhier, E. (1924-8), *Plotin: Ennéades*, 6 vols in 7, Paris.

Bréhier, E. (1958), *The Philosophy of Plotinus*, trans. J. Thomas, Chicago.

Brisson, L. (1998), *Plato the Mythmaker* (trans. G. Naddaf), Chicago.

Brisson, L. (2005), *Porphyre: Sentences*, 2 vols, Paris.

Brisson, L., M.O. Goulet-Cazé, R. Goulet and D. O'Brien (1982-92), *Porphyre: la vie de Plotin*, 2 vols, Paris.

Brittain, C. (2001), *Philo of Larissa: The Last of the Academic Sceptics*, Oxford.

Brock, S. (1982), 'From Antagonism to Assimilation: Syriac Attitudes to Greek

Bibliography

Learning', in N. Garsoïan et al. (eds), *East of Byzantium: Syria and Armenia in the Formative Period*, Washington, 17-34.

Brock, S. (1996), 'The "Nestorian" Church: A Lamentable Misnomer', in J.F. Coakley and K. Parry (eds), *The Church of the East: Life and Thought, Bull. JohnRylandsLib.* 78, 23-35.

Brown, M. (1975), 'Pappus, Plato and the Harmonic Mean', *Phronesis* 20, 173-84.

Browning, R. (1975), 'Enlightenment and Repression in Byzantium in the Eleventh and Twelfth Centuries', *Past and Present* 69, 3-23.

Browning, R. (1990), 'An Unpublished Funeral Oration on Anna Comnena', in Sorabji (ed.) (1990), ch. 17.

Burkert, W. (1972), *Lore and Science in Ancient Pythagoreanism*, trans. E.L. Minar Jr, Cambridge, MA.

Burnyeat, M.F. (1977), 'Socratic Midwifery, Platonic Inspiration', *BICS* 24, 7-16.

Bussanich, J. (1988), *The One and Its Relation to Intellect in Plotinus, A Commentary on Selected Texts*, Leiden.

Calvo, T. and L. Brisson (1997), *Interpreting the Timaeus-Critias, Proceedings of the IV Symposium Platonicum Selected Papers*, Sankt Augustin.

Cameron, Alan (1969), 'The Last Day of the Academy at Athens', *PCPS* 195, 7-29.

Cameron, Averil (1970), *Agathias*, Oxford.

Cameron, Averil (1994), 'Texts as Weapons: Polemic in the Byzantine Dark Ages', in A. Bowman and G. Woolf (eds), *Literacy and Power in the Ancient World*, Cambridge, 198-215.

Caston, V. (1999), 'Aristotle's Two Intellects: A Modest Proposal', *Phronesis* 44, 199-227.

Chadwick, H. (1997), 'Philoponus the Christian Theologian', in R. Sorabji (ed.), *Philoponus and the Rejection of Aristotelian Science*, London, 41-56.

Chen, C.-H. (1940), *Das Chorismos Problem bei Aristoteles*, Berlin.

Cherniss, H.F. (1944), *Aristotle's Criticism of Plato and the Academy*, Baltimore.

Cherniss, H.F. (1945), *The Riddle of the Early Academy*, New York.

Cherniss, H.F. (1951), 'Plato as Mathematician', *Review of Metaphysics* 4, 395-425.

Clucas, L. (1981), *The Trial of John Italos and the Crisis of Intellectual Values in Byzantium in the Eleventh Century*, Munich.

Cohen, M. (1992), 'Hylomorphism and Functionalism', in M. Nussbaum and A. Rorty (eds), *Essays on Aristotle's De Anima*, Oxford, 57-73.

Cooper, J.M. (1975), *Reason and Human Goodness in Aristotle*, Cambridge, MA.

Cooper, J.M. (1997), *Plato: Complete Works*, Indianapolis.

Cornford, F.M. (1937), *Plato's Cosmology*, London.

Cornford F.M. (1955), *Plato's Theory of Knowledge*, London.

Corrigan, K. (1996), 'Essence and Existence in the *Enneads*', in Gerson (ed.) (1996), 105-29.

Coulter, J.A. (1976), *The Literary Microcosm: Theories of Interpretation of the Later Neoplatonists*, Leiden.

Courcelle, P. (1969), *Late Latin Writers and their Greek Sources* (trans. H. Wedeck), Cambridge MA.

D'Ancona, C. (2000a), 'La doctrine des principes: Syrianus comme source textuelle et doctrinale de Proclus, 1ère partie: histoire du problème', in Segonds and Steel (eds) (2000), 189-225.

D'Ancona, C. (2000b), 'Syrianus dans la tradition exégétique de la *Métaphysique* d'Aristote, II: Antécédents et postérité', in M.O. Goulet-Cazé et T. Dorandi (eds), *Le commentaire entre tradition et innovation, actes du colloque international de l'Institut des Traditions Textuelles*, Paris, 311-27.

239

Bibliography

Dancy, R.M. (1984), 'The One, the Many, and the Form: *Philebus* 15b1-8', *Ancient Philosophy* 4, 165-76.

David, A. (2002), 'Plato and the Measure of the Incommensurable. Part II. Plato's New Measure: The Mathematical Meaning of the Indeterminate Dyad', *The Saint John's Review* 46, 25-61.

De Koninck, T. (1994), 'Aristotle on God as Thought Thinking Itself', *Review of Metaphysics* 47, 471-515.

De Lacy, P. (1972), 'Galen's Platonism' *AJPh* 93, 27-39.

De Lacy, P. (1978-84), *Galeni De Placitis Hippocratis et Platonis*, 3 vols (= CMG V 4.1.2), Berlin.

De Strycker, E. (1955), 'La notion aristotélicienne de séparation dans son application aux Idées de Platon', in A. Mansion (ed.), *Autour d'Aristote*, Louvain, 119-39.

Defourney, P. (1937), 'L'activité de contemplation dans les Morales d'Aristote', *Bulletin de l'Institut Historique belge de Rome*: 89-101.

Delatte, A. (1922), *Essai sur la politique pythagoricienne*, Liège.

Delatte, A. (1948), 'La Constitution des États Unis et les Pythagoriciens', *Académie royale de Belgique: Bulletin de la Classe des Lettres et des Sciences Morales et Politiques, 5 Série-Tome 34*, Brussels, 383-412.

Den Boeft, J. (1970), *Calcidius on Fate. His Doctrine and Sources*, Leiden.

Des Places, É. (1984), 'Les Oracles chaldaïqes', *ANRW* II 17.4: 2300-35.

Dihle, A. (1957), 'Der Platoniker Ptolemaios', *Hermes* 85, 314-25.

Dillon, J.M. (1971), 'Harpocration's Commentary on Plato: Fragments of a Middle Platonic Commentary', *California Studies in Classical Antiquity* 4, 125-46.

Dillon, J.M. (ed.) (1973), *Iamblichi Chalcidensis in Platonis Dialogos Commentariorum Fragmenta*, Leiden.

Dillon, J.M. (1977), *The Middle Platonists*, London.

Dillon, J.M. (1983), '*Metriopatheia* and *Apatheia*: Some Reflections on a Controversy in Later Greek Ethics', in J.P. Anton and A. Preus (eds), *Essays in Ancient Greek Philosophy*, II, Albany, 508-17; repr. in Dillon (ed.) (1990), vol. VIII.

Dillon, J.M. (1987), 'Iamblichus of Chalcis (*c.* 240-352 AD)', *ANRW* II 36.2, 862-909.

Dillon, J.M. (1990), *The Golden Chain*, Aldershot.

Dillon, J.M. (1993), *Alcinous: The Handbook of Platonism*, Oxford.

Dillon, J.M. (1996), *The Middle Platonists*, 2nd ed. with Afterword, London.

Dillon, J.M. (1997), 'The Riddle of the *Timaeus*: Is Plato Sowing Clues?', in M. Joyal (ed.), *Studies in Plato and the Platonic Tradition, Essays Presented to John Whittaker*, Aldershot, 25-42.

Dillon, J.M. (2002), 'The Platonic Philosopher at Prayer', in T. Kobusche and M. Erler (eds), *Metaphysik und Religion. Zur Signatur des spaetantiken Denkens*, Munich and Leipzig, 279-95.

Dillon, J.M. (2003), *The Heirs of Plato*, Oxford.

Dodds, E.R. (1928), 'The *Parmenides* of Plato and the Origin of the Neoplatonic One', *CQ* 22, 129-43.

Dodds, E.R. (1960), 'Numenius and Ammonius', in *Les sources de Plotin*, Geneva, 3-32.

Dodds, E.R. (ed.) (1963), *Proclus: Elements of Theology, Translation, Text and Introduction*, Oxford.

Donini, P. (1988), 'The History of the Concept of Eclecticism', in J.M. Dillon and A.A. Long (eds), *The Question of Eclecticism*, Berkeley and Los Angeles, 15-33.

Dorandi, T. (1991), *Filodemo, storia del filosofi: Platone e l'Academia*, Naples.

Dörrie, H. (1976), *Platonica Minora*, Munich.

Bibliography

Downey, G. (1963), *Gaza in the Early Sixth Century*, Norman.

Duffy, J. (2002), 'Hellenic Philosophy in Byzantium and the Lonely Mission of Michale Psellos', in Ierodiakonou (ed.) (2002), ch. 6.

Düring, I. (1957), *Aristotle in the Ancient Biographical Tradition*, Göteborg.

Dyke, A.R. (ed.) (2004), Cicero: *De Legibus*, Ann Arbor.

Edwards, M. (2000), *Neoplatonic Saints: The Lives of Plotinus and Proclus by their Students*, Liverpool.

El Cheikh, N.M. (2004), *Byzantium Viewed by the Arabs*, Cambridge, MA.

Endress, G. (1997), 'The Circle of Al-Kindi', in G. Endress and R. Kruk (eds), *The Ancient Tradition in Christian and Islamic Hellenism*, Leiden, 43-76.

Eriksen, T. (1976), *Bios Theoretikos: Notes on Aristotle's Ethica Nicomachea X. 6-8*, Oslo.

Erler, M. (1978), *Proclus. Über die Existenz des Bosen*, Hain.

Evangeliou, Ch. (1982), 'The Ontological Basis of Plotinus' Criticism of Aristotle's Theory of Categories', in Harris (ed.) (1982), 73-82.

Evangeliou, Ch. (1987), 'The Plotinian Reduction of Aristotle's Categories', *Ancient Philosophy* 7, 147-62.

Evangeliou, Ch. (1988), *Aristotle's Categories and Porphyry*, Leiden.

Ferrari, G. (2000), *BMCR* review of G. Press (ed.) *Who Speaks for Plato?*

Festugière, A.J. (1953), *La révélation d'Hermès Trismégiste III: Les doctrines de l'âme* (repr. 1983, Paris).

Festugière, A.J. (1963), 'Modes de composition des commentaires de Proclus', *MH* 20, 77-100.

Festugière, A.J. (1967), *Proclus: Commentaire sur le Timée*, II, Paris.

Festugière, A.J. (1969), 'L'ordre de lecture des dialogues de Platon au Ve/VIe siècle', *MH* 26, 218-96.

Flamand, J.-M. (2003), *Plotin: Traités 7-21*, Paris.

Florovsky, G. (1972), 'The Function of Tradition in the Ancient Church', in his *Bible, Church, Tradition: An Eastern Orthodox View*, vol. 1, Belmont, MA, 73-91.

Ford, L.S. (2002), 'Process and Eternity: Whitehead Contemplates Plotinus', in Harris (ed.) (2002), 195-210.

Fowden, G. (1982), 'The Pagan Holy Man in Late Antiquity', *JHS* 102, 33-59.

Frank, E. (1923), *Plato und die sogennanten Pythagoreer. Ein Kapital aus der Geschichte des griechischen Geistes*, Halle.

Frank, E. (1940), 'The Fundamental Opposition of Plato and Aristotle', *AJP* 61, 34-53; 166-85.

Frend, W.H.C. (1972), *The Rise of the Monophysite Movement*, Cambridge.

Gadamer, H.-G. (1960), *Wahrheit und Methode: Grundzüge zu einer hermeneutischen Logik*, Tübingen.

Gaiser, K. (1988), *Philodems Academica*, Stuttgart.

Gardra, T.A. et al. (eds) (1989), *George Pachymeres, Commentary on Plato's Parmenides*, Athens.

Gatti, M.L. (1996), 'Plotinus: The Platonic Tradition and the Foundation of Neoplatonism', in Gerson (ed.) (1996), 10-37.

Gauthier, R. and J. Jolif (1970), *L'éthique à Nicomaque*, Louvain and Paris.

Geanakoplos, D.J. (1989), *Constantinople and the West. Essays on the Late Byzantine (Palaeologan) and Italian Renaissances and the Byzantine and Roman Churches*, Madison.

Gersh, S. (1986), *Middle Platonism and Neoplatonism: The Latin Tradition*, 2 vols, Notre Dame.

Bibliography

Gerson, L.P. (ed.) (1996), *The Cambridge Companion to Plotinus*, Cambridge.

Gerson, L.P. (1997), "'*Epistrophe pros heauton*": History and Meaning', *Documenti e studi sulla tradizione filosofica medievale* 8, 1-32.

Gerson, L.P. (2001), 'Plotinus on Being and Knowing', in Gregorios (ed.) (2002), 111-32.

Gerson, L.P. (2005), *Aristotle and Other Platonists*, Ithaca, NY.

Gill, C. et al. (1998), *Reciprocity in Ancient Greece*, Oxford.

Gilson, E. (1926-7), 'Pourquoi Saint Thomas a critiqué Saint Augustin', *Archives d'histoire doctrinale et littéraire du moyen age*, 1, 5-127.

Glucker, J. (1978), *Antiochus and the Late Academy* (= *Hypomnemata* 56), Göttingen.

Glucker, J. (1988), 'Cicero's Philosophical Affiliations', in J.M. Dillon and A.A. Long (eds), *The Question of Eclecticism*, Berkeley, 34-69.

Goodenough, E. (1928), 'The Political Philosophy of Hellenistic Kingship', *Yale Classical Studies* 1, 55-102.

Goodenough, E. (1938), *The Politics of Philo Judaeus. Practice and Theory*, New Haven.

Göransson, T. (1995), *Albinus, Alcinous, Arius Didymus*, Gothenberg.

Gouillard, J. (ed.) (1967), 'Le Synodicon de l'orthodoxie: edition et commentaire', *Travaux et Memoires* 2, 57.

Gouma-Petersen, T. (2000), *Anna Komnene and Her Times*, New York and London.

Graham, D.W. (1987), *Aristotle's Two Systems*, Oxford.

Gray, T.R. (1988), 'Forgery as an Instrument of Progress: Reconstructing the Theological Tradition in the Sixth Century', *Byzantinische Zeitschrift* 81, 284-9.

Gray, T.R. (1989), '"The Select Fathers": Canonizing the Patristic Past', *Studia Patristica* 23, 21-36.

Gregorios, P.M. (ed.) (2002), *Neoplatonism and Indian Philosophy*, Albany.

Gregory, A. (2000), *Plato's Philosophy of Science*, London.

Gruppe, O.F. (1840), *Über die Fragmente des Archytas und der alteren Pythagoreer*, Berlin.

Guagliardo, V.A., C.R. Hess, and R.C. Taylor (trans.) (1996), *St.Thomas Aquinas: Commentary on the Book of Causes*, Washington, DC.

Gurtler, G.M. (1988a), 'The Origin of Genera: *Ennead* VI 2 [43] 20', *Dionysius* 12, 3-15.

Gurtler, G.M. (1988b), *Plotinus: The Experience of Unity*, New York.

Gutas, D. (1998), *Greek Thought, Arabic Culture*, London.

Guthrie, W.K.C. (1955), 'Plato on the Nature of the Soul', in *Recherche sur la tradition platonicienne*, Geneva, 3-19.

Guthrie, W.K.C. (1965), *A History of Greek Philosophy*, vol. 2, Cambridge.

Hackforth, R. (1945), *Plato's Examination of Pleasure*, Cambridge.

Hackforth, R. (1952), *Plato's Phaedrus*, Cambridge.

Hadot, I. (1978), *Le Problème du néoplatonisme alexandrin: Hiéroclès et Simplicius*, Paris.

Hadot, I. (1990), *Simplicius. Commentaire sur la Catégories*, vol. 1, Leiden.

Hadot, I. (1991), 'The Role of the Commentaries on Aristotle in the Teaching of Philosophy according to the Prefaces of the Neoplatonic Commentaries on the Categories', in J. Annas (ed.), *Aristotle and the Later Tradition*, Oxford, 175-89.

Hadot, I. (1996), *Commentaire sur le manuel d' Épictète*, Leiden.

Hadot, P. (1963), *Plotin ou la simplicité du regard*, 1st edn, Paris.

Hadot, P. (1968), *Porphyre et Victorinus*, Paris.

Hadot, P. (1995), *Philosophy as a Way of Life*, trans. M. Chase, Oxford.

Hadot, P. (1997), *Plotin ou la simplicité du regard*, last edn, Paris.

Hager, F.P. (1962), 'Die Materie und das Böse im antiken Platonismus', *MH* 19, 85-103.

Hallstrom, G. (1994), 'The Closing of the Neoplatonic School in AD 529: An Additional Aspect', in P. Castren (ed.), *Post-Herulian Athens*, Helsinki, 141-60.

Hamlyn, D. (1993), *De Anima: Books II and III (With Passages from Book 1)*, Oxford.

Harris, R.B. (ed.) (1982), *The Structure of Being: A Neoplatonic Approach*, Albany.

Harris, R.B. (ed.) (2002), *Neoplatonism and Contemporary Thought*, Albany.

Harrison, S.J. (2000), *Apuleius: A Latin Sophist*, Oxford.

Harvey, F.D. (1965), 'Two Kinds of Equality', *Classica et Medievalia* 26, 101-46.

Heath, T. (1921), *A History of Greek Mathematics*, Oxford.

Heinaman, R. (1990), 'Aristotle and the Mind-Body Problem', *Phronesis* 35, 83-102.

Heiser, J.H. (1991), 'Plotinus and the Apeiron of Plato's *Parmenides*', *The Thomist* 55, 67-72.

Henry, P. and H.R. Schwyzer (eds) (1964-82), *Plotinus, Enneads*, Oxford, cited as HS^2. (Previous edition HS^1, 1951, Brussels.)

Hero, A.C. (1983), *The Letters of Gregory Akindynos*, Washington, DC.

Hetherington, P. (trans) (1974), *The 'Painter's Manual' of Dionysius of Fourna*, London.

Hijmans, B.L. (1987), 'Apuleius Philosophus Platonicus', *ANRW* II.36.1, 395-475.

Hoffmann, P. (1987), 'Simplicius' Polemics', in R. Sorabji (ed.), *Philoponus and the Rejection of Aristotelian Science*, London.

Hunink, V. (1996), 'Apuleius and the *Asclepius*', *Vig. Chr.* 50, 288-308.

Ierodiakonou, K. (ed.) (2002), *Byzantine Philosophy and its Ancient Sources*, Oxford.

Jaeger, W. (1948), *Aristotle: Fundamentals of the History of his Development*, Oxford.

Jahns, G. [Wilhelm] (1850), *De Iustitia in Plat. Civ. Exposita*, Diss. Warsaw.

Jones, W.H.S. (trans.) (1923), *Hippocrates*, vol. 2, London and New York.

Joyal, M. (2000), *The Platonic Theages: An Introduction, Commentary, and Critical Edition* (= *Philosophie der Antike*, Bd. 10), Stuttgart.

Kahn, C.H. (1985), 'The Place of the Prime Mover in Aristotle's Teleology', in A. Gotthelf (ed.), *Aristotle on Nature and Living Things*, Pittsburgh and Bristol, 183-205.

Kaldellis, A. (1999), *The Argument of Psellos' Chronographia*, Leiden.

Kazhdan, A.P. and A. Wharton Epstein (1985), *Change in Byzantine Culture in the Eleventh and Twelfth Centuries*, Berkeley and Los Angeles.

Kenney, J.P. (1991), *Mystical Monotheism: A Study in Ancient Platonic Theology*, Hanover, NE.

Kirk, G.S., J.E. Raven, and M. Schofield (1983), *The Presocratic Philosophers*, 2nd ed., Cambridge.

Klein, J. (1965), *A Commentary on Plato's Meno*, Chapel Hill.

Klein, J. (1968), *Greek Mathematcial Thought and the Origin of Algebra*, trans. E. Brann, Cambridge, MA.

Klein, J. (1985), 'The Concept of Number in Greek Mathematics and Philosophy', in R.B. Williamson and E. Zuckerman (eds), *Lectures and Essays*, Annapolis, 43-52.

Kotter, B. (ed.) (1969, 1981), *Die Schriften des Johannes von Damaskos*, vols I and IV, Berlin and New York.

Krämer, H.J. (1964), *Der Ursprung der Geistmetaphysik*, Amsterdam.

Bibliography

Krämer, H.J. (1973), 'Aristoteles und die akademische Eidoslehre: Zur Geschichte des Universalienproblems im Platonismus', *Archiv für Geschichte der Philosophie*, 55, 118-90.

Kraut, R. (1989), *Aristotle on the Human Good*, Princeton.

Kristeller, P.O. (1987), 'Proclus as a Reader of Plato and Plotinus, and his Influence in the Middle Ages and in the Renaissance', in Pépin and Saffrey (eds) (1987), 191-211.

Kroll, W. (1916), 'Iamblichos', *RE* 9, 645-51.

Kühn, C.G. (ed.) (1821-33), *Claudii Galeni Opera Omnia*, vols 1-20, Leipzig.

Lamberz, E. (1987), 'Proklos und die Form des philosophischen Kommentars', in Pépin et Saffrey (eds) (1987), 1-20.

Lang, H.S. and A.D. Macro (trans) (2001), *Proclus: On the Eternity of the World*, Berkeley.

Lang, U.M. (2001), *John Philoponus and the Controversies over Chalcedon in the Sixth Century: A Study and Translation of the Arbiter*, Leuven.

Langstadt, E. (1937), 'Zu Philos Begriff der Demokratie', *Occident and Orient. Being Studies for Haham Dr. M. Gaster's 80th. Birthday*, London, 349-64.

Larsen, B. (1974), 'La place de Jamblique dans la philosophie antique tardive', in *De Jamblique á Proclus*, Entretiens Hardt 21, Geneva, 1-26.

Lear, J. (1987), 'Active Episteme', in A. Graeser (ed.), *Mathematics and Metaphysics*, Bern and Stuttgart, 149-74.

Lefèvre, C. (1972), *Sur l'évolution d'Aristote en psychologie*, Louvain.

Lemerle, P. (1986), *Byzantine Humanism: The First Phrase*, Canberra.

Lernould, A. (2001), *Physique et Theologie. Lecture du Timée de Platon par Proclus*, Villeneuve d'Ascq.

Lewy, H. (1956), *Chaldean Oracles and Theurgy: Mysticism, Magic and Platonism in the Later Roman Empire*, Cairo.

L'Homme-Wery, L.-M. (1996), 'La notion d'harmonie dans la pensée politique de Solon', *Kernos* 9, 145-59.

Libera, A. de (1996), *La querelle des universaux: de Platon à la fin du Moyen Âge*, Paris.

Lilla, S. (1971), *Clement of Alexandria: A Study in Christian Platonism and Gnosticism*, London.

Lloyd, A.C. (1967), 'The Later Neoplatonists', in Armstrong (ed.) (1967), 272-325.

Lloyd, G.E.R. (1996), 'Theories and Practices of Demonstration in Galen', in M. Frede and G. Striker (eds), *Rationality in Greek Thought*, Oxford, 255-77.

Long, A.A. (1988), 'Socrates and Hellenistic Philosophy', *CQ* 38, 150-71.

Long, A.A. (1998), 'Plato's Apologies and Socrates in the *Theaetetus*', in J. Gentzler (ed.), *Method in Ancient Philosophy*, Oxford, 113-36.

Louth, A. (1996), *Maximus the Confessor*, London.

Louth, A. (1997), 'St Denys the Areopagite and the Iconoclast Controversy', in Y. de Andia (ed.), *Denys l'Aréopagite et sa postérité en Orient et en Occident*, Paris, 329-39.

Louth, A. (2002), *St John Damascene: Tradition and Originality in Byzantine Theology*, Oxford.

Luibheid, C. (trans) (1987), *Pseudo-Dionysius: The Complete Works*, New York.

Lycan, W.G. (2004), 'The Superiority of *HOP* to *HOT*', in Rocco W. Gennaro (ed.), *Higher Order Theories of Consciousness*, Amsterdam.

Maas, M. (1992), *John Lydus and the Roman Past: Antiquarianism and Politics in the Age of Justinian*, London and New York.

Bibliography

Majercik, R. (1989), *The Chaldean Oracles: Text, Translation and Commentary*, Leiden.

Mann, W.-R. (2000), *The Discovery of Things: Aristotle's Categories and Their Context*, Princeton.

Mansfeld, J. (1994), *Prolegomena. Questions to be Settled Before the Study of an Author, or a Text*, Leiden.

Martin, R.M. (1982), 'On Logical Structure and the Plotinic Cosmos', in Harris (ed.) (1982), 11-23.

McGuckin, J. (2001), *Saint Gregory of Nazianzus: An Intellectual Biography*, New York.

Merki, H. (1952), Ὁμοίωσις Θεῷ. *Von der platonischen Angleichung an Gott zur Gottähnlichkeit bei Gregor von Nyssa*, Freiburg.

Merlan, P. (1953) and (1968), *From Platonism to Neoplatonism*, 1st and 3rd eds, The Hague.

Merlan, P. (1970), 'Greek Philosophy from Plato to Plotinus', in Armstrong (ed.) (1967), 14-132.

Meyendorff, J. (1957), 'Note sur l'influence dionysienne en Orient', *Studia Patristica* 2, Berlin, 547-53.

Meyendorff, J. (1964), *A Study of Gregory Palamas*, London.

Meyendorff, J. (1974), *Byzantine Theology*, New York.

Meyendorff, J. (1989), *Imperial Unity and Christian Divisions: The Church 450-680 AD*, New York.

Michel, P.H. (1950), *De Pythagore à Euclide. Contribution a l'histoire des mathématiques préeuclidiennes*, Paris.

Minar, E.L. (1942), *Early Pythagorean Politics in Practice and Theory*, Baltimore.

Monan, J. (1968), *Moral Knowledge and its Methodology in Aristotle*, Oxford.

Monroe, H.L. (1854), 'On the Interpretation of a Passage in the *Nicomachean Ethics* of Aristotle', *Journal of Philology* 1, 344-8.

Moreschini, C. (1966), *Studi sul* De Dogmate Platonis *di Apuleio*, Pisa.

Moreschini, C. (1978), *Apuleio e il platonismo*, Florence.

Moreschini, C. (1991), *Apulei opera philosophica*, Stuttgart.

Morgan, K.A. (2000), *Myth and Philosophy from the Presocratics to Plato*, Cambridge.

Morrison, J.S. (1956), 'Pythagoras of Samos', *CQ* 6, 135-56.

Morrison, J.S. (1958), 'The Origins of Plato's Philosopher-Statesman', *CQ* 8, 198-218.

Mugler, C. (1948), *Platon et la recherche mathématique de son époque*, Strasbourg-Zürich.

Mugler, C. (1958), *Dictionnaire historique de la terminologie géométrique des Grecs*, Paris.

Nedungatt, G. and M. Featherstone (eds) (1995), *The Council in Trullo Revisited*, Kanonika 6, Rome.

Nightingale, A.W. (1993), 'Writing/Reading a Sacred Text: A Literary Interpretation of Plato's *Laws*', *CP* 88, 269-300.

Nussbaum, M. (1987), *The Fragility of Goodness: Luck and Ethics in Greek Tragedy and Philosophy*, Cambridge.

Nutton, V. (1979), *Galeni De Praenotione* (= CMG V 8 1), Berlin.

Nutton, V. (1980), 'Review of *PHP* Books I-IV', *Medical History* 24, 98-100.

Nuyens, F.J.C.J. (1948), *L'évolution de la psychologie d'Aristote*, Louvain.

O'Brien, D. (1971), 'Plotinus on Evil. A Study of Matter and the Soul in Plotinus' Conception of Human Evil', in *Le Néoplatonisme* (Paris 1971), 1.

245

Bibliography

O'Meara, D.J. (ed.) (1982), *Neoplatonism and Christian Thought*, Norfolk.

O'Meara, D.J. (1989), *Pythagoras Revived. Mathematics and Philosophy in Late Antiquity*, Oxford.

O'Neill, W., trans. (1965), *Proclus: Alcibiades I, a Translation and Commentary*, The Hague.

Opsomer J. and C. Steel (2003), *Proclus: On the Existence of Evils*, London and Ithaca, NY.

Osborne, C. (1996), 'Space, Time, Shape and Direction: Creative Discourse in the *Timaeus*', in C. Gill and M.M. McCabe (eds), *Form and Argument in Late Plato*, Oxford, 179-211.

Owens, J. (1951), *The Doctrine of Being in the Aristotelian Metaphysics*, Toronto.

Parry, K. (1996), *Depicting the Word: Byzantine Iconophile Thought of the Eighth and Ninth Centuries*, Leiden.

Parry, K. (2003), 'Byzantine and Melkite Iconophiles under Iconoclasm', in Ch. Dendrinos et al. (eds), *Prophyrogenitia: Essays on the History and Literature of Byzantium and the Latin East presented to Julian Chrysostomides*, Aldershot, 137-51.

Parry, K. et al. (1999), *The Blackwell Dictionary of Eastern Christianity*, Oxford.

Pearcy, L.T. (1998), 'Medicine and Rhetoric in the Period of the Second Sophistic', *ANRW* II. 37.1, 445-57.

Pelikan, J. (1993), *Christianity and Classical Culture: The Metamorphosis of Natural Theology in the Christian Encounter with Hellenism*, New Haven and London.

Pépin, J. and H.D. Saffrey (eds) (1987), *Proclus: lecteur et interprète des anciens*, Paris.

Podskalsky, G. (1976), 'Nikolaos von Methone und die Proklosrenaissance in Byzanz', *Orientalia Christiana Periodica* 42, 509-23.

Podskalsky G. (1977), *Theologie und Philosophie in Byzanz: Der Streit um die theologische Methodik in der spätbyzantinischen Geistesgeschichte (14./15.Jh.), seine systematischen Grundlagen und seine historische Entwicklung*, Munich.

Pontikos, I.N. (1992), *Anonymi Miscellanea Philosophica: A Miscellany in the Tradition of Michael Psellos (Codex Baroccianus Graecus 131)*, Paris and Brussels.

Praechter, K. (1905), 'Procli Diadochi in Platonis Timaeum commentaria ed. Diehl', *Göttingische gelehrte Anzeigen* 7, 505-35.

Praechter, K. (1909), 'Die griechischen Aristoteleskommentare', *Byzantinische Zeitschrift* 18, 516-38.

Press, G. (1997), 'The Dialogical Mode in Modern Platonic Studies', in G. Press (ed.), *Plato's Dialogues – the Dialogic Approach*, Lewiston, 1-28.

Reale, G. (1997), 'Plato's Doctrine of the Origin of the World, with Special Reference to the *Timaeus*', in Calvo and Brisson (eds) (1997), 149-64.

Redfors, J. (1960), *Echtheitskritische Untersuchung der apuleischen Schriften* De Platone *und* De Mundo, Lund.

Regen, F. (1971), *Apuleius Philosophus Platonicus*, Berlin.

Reynolds, L.D. (1983), *Texts and Transmissions: A Study of the Latin Classics*, Oxford.

Rist, J.M. (1962), 'The Neoplatonic One and Plato's *Parmenides*', *TAPA* 93, 389-401.

Rist, J.M. (1967), *Plotinus: The Road to Reality*, Cambridge.

Rist, J.M. (1989), *The Mind of Aristotle: A Study in Philosophical Growth*, Toronto.

Bibliography

Robinson, H. (1983), 'Aristotle's Dualism', *Oxford Studies in Ancient Philosophy* 1, 123-44.

Rocca, J. (2003), *Galen and the Brain: Anatomical Knowledge and Physiological Speculation in the Second Century AD*, Leiden.

Roche, T. (1988), '"Ergon" and "Eudaimonia" in *Nicomachean Ethics* I: Reconsidering the Intellectualist Interpretation', *JHistPhil* 26, 175-94.

Roloff, D. (1970), *Gottähnlichkeit, Vergöttlichung und Erhöhung zu seligem Leben; Untersuchungen zur Herkunft der platonischen Angleichung an Gott*, Berlin.

Rorem, P. and J.C. Lamoreaux (1993), 'John of Scythopolis on Apollinarian Christology and the Pseudo-Dionysius' True Identity', *Church History* 62, 469-82.

Rorem, P. and J.C. Lamoreaux (1998), *John of Scythopolis and the Dionysian Corpus: Annotating the Areopagite*, Oxford.

Rosenthal, D. (2002-3), 'Unity of Consciousness and the Self', *Proceedings of the Aristotelian Society* 103, 325-52.

Ross, W.D. (1951) *Plato's Theory of Ideas*, Oxford.

Ross, W.D. (1955), *Aristotelis Fragmenta Selecta*, Oxford.

Ross, W.D. (1956), *Aristotle's De Anima*, Oxford.

Rossetti, L. (ed.) (1992), *Understanding the* Phaedrus, Sankt Augustin.

Runia, D.T. (1997), 'The Literary and Philosophical Status of Timaeus' Prooemium', in Calvo and Brisson (eds) (1997), 101-18.

Runia, D.T. (2000), 'Timaeus, Logician and Philosopher of Nature', in J. Spruyt and M. Kardaun (eds), *The Winged Chariot*, Leiden, 105-18.

Rutherford, R.B. (1995), *The Art of Plato*, London.

Ryffel, H. (1949), ΜΕΤΑΒΟΛΗ ΠΟΛΙΤΕΙΩΝ. *Der Wandel der Staatsverfassungen. Untersuchungen zu einem Problem der griechischen Staatstheorie*, Berne.

Saffrey, H.-D. (1966), 'Un lien objectif entre le Pseudo-Denys et Proclus', *Studia Patristica* 9, Berlin, 98-105.

Saffrey, H.-D. (1975), 'Allusions anti-chrétiennes chez Proclus, le diadoque platonicien', *Revue des Sciences Philosophiques et Théologiques*, 59, 553-63.

Saffrey, H.-D. (1982), 'New Objective Links Between the Pseudo-Dionysius and Proclus', in O'Meara (ed.) (1982). 84-94.

Saffrey, H.-D. (1984a), 'Théologie Platonicienne de Proclus, fruit de l'exégèse du *Parmenides*', *Revue de Théologie* 116, 1-12.

Saffrey, H.-D. (1984b), 'Le "Philosophe de Rhodes": est-il Théodore d'Asine?', in E. Lucchesi and H.-D. Saffrey (eds), *Memorial André-Jean Festugière: Antiquité paienne et chrétienne*, Geneva, 65-76.

Saffrey, H.-D. (1990), 'How did Syrianus Regard Aristotle?', translated from the French of 1987, in Sorabji (ed.) (1990).

Saffrey, H.-D., A.-Ph. Segonds, and C. Luna (eds) (2001), *Proclus ou Sur le bonheur*, Paris.

Saffrey H.-D. and L.G. Westerink (eds) (1968-97), *Théologie platonicienne*, 6 vols, Paris.

Santa Cruz, M.I. (1997), 'Le discours de la physique: eikôs lógos', in Calvo and Brisson (eds) (1997), 133-9.

Sayre, K.M. (1969), *Plato's Analytic Method*, Chicago.

Schibli, H. (2002), *Hierocles of Alexandria*, Oxford.

Schofield, M. (2003), 'Religion and Philosophy in the *Laws*', in S. Scolnicov and L. Brisson (eds), *Plato's Laws: From Theory into Practice*, Sankt Augustin, 1-13.

Schroeder, D.N. (1981), 'Aristotle on Law', *Polis* 4, 17-31.

Schütrumpf, E. (1992), 'Einige wissenschaftliche Voraussetzungen von W. Jaegers

Aristotelesdeutung', in W.M. Calder (ed.), *Werner Jaeger Reconsidered*, Atlanta, 209-25.

Scott, D. (1987), 'Platonic Recollection Revisited', *CQ* 37, 346-66.

Sedley, D. (1996a), 'Three Platonist Interpretations of the *Theaetetus*' in C. Gill and M.M. McCabe (eds), *Form and Argument in Late Plato*, Oxford, 79-103.

Sedley, D. (1996b), 'Philosophical Allegiance in the Greco-Roman World', in J. Barnes and M. Griffin (eds), *Philosophia Togata* I, Oxford, 97-119.

Sedley, D. (1997), 'Becoming Like God in the *Timaeus* and Aristotle', *Interpreting the Timaeus-Critias*, in Calvo and Brisson (eds) (1997), 327-39.

Sedley, D. (1998), *Lucretius and the Transformation of Greek Wisdom*, Cambridge.

Sedley, D. (1999), 'The Idea of Godlikeness', in Gail Fine (ed.), *Plato 2. Ethics, Politics, Religion and the Soul*, Oxford, 309-28.

Sedley, D. (2002), 'The Origins of Stoic God', in D. Frede and A. Laks (eds), *Traditions of Theology*, Leiden, 41-83.

Segonds, A.Ph. (1985), *Proclus sur le premier Alcibiade de Platon*, Paris.

Segonds, A.Ph., et C. Steel (eds) (2000), *Proclus et la Théologie Platonicienne, Actes du colloque international de Louvain (13-16 mai 1998)*, Leuven and Paris.

Senn, F. (1927), *De la justice et du droit*, Paris.

Sewter, E.R.A. (trans.) (1966), *Fourteen Byzantine Rulers: The Chronographia of Michael Psellos*, Harmondsworth.

Sewter, E.R.A. (trans.) (1969), *The Alexiad of Anna Comnena*, Harmondsworth.

Sharples, R.W. (1990), 'The School of Alexander?', in R. Sorabji (ed.) (1990), 83-112.

Sharples, R.W. and A.D.R. Sheppard (2003), *Ancient Approaches to Plato's Timaeus*, *BICS* supp. vol. 78, London.

Sheppard, A.D.R. (1980), 'Studies on the 5th and 6th Essays of Proclus' Commentary on the Republic', *Hypomnemata* 61, Göttingen.

Sheppard, A.D.R. (1982), 'Proclus' Attitude to Theurgy', *CQ* 32, 212-24.

Sheppard, A.D.R. (1987), 'Proclus' Philosophical Method of Exegesis: The Use of Aristotle and the Stoics in the Commentary on the *Cratylus*', in Pépin et Saffrey (eds) (1987), 137-51.

Shiner, R.A. (1974), *Knowledge and Reality in Plato's Philebus*, Assen.

Siorvanes, L. (1996), *Proclus: Neo-Platonic Philosophy and Science*, Edinburgh.

Sleeman, J.H. and Pollet G. (1980), *Lexicon Plotinianum*, Leiden.

Sodano, R. (1964), *Porphyrii in Platonis Timaeum Fragmenta*, Naples.

Sodano, R. (1966), 'Porfirio commentatore di Platone', in *Porphyre. Entretiens sur l'antiquité classique*, Entretiens Hardt 12, Vandouvres Geneva, 93-228.

Solmsen, F. (1929), *Die Entwicklung der Aristotelischen Logik*, Berlin.

Solmsen, F. (1975), *Die Entwicklung der aristotelischen Logik und Rhetorik*, Zürich.

Sorabji, R. (1983), *Time, Creation and the Continuum*, London.

Sorabji, R. (ed.) (1990), *Aristotle Transformed: The Ancient Commentators and their Influence*, London.

Steel, C. (1997), 'Breathing Thought: Proclus on the Innate Knowledge of the Soul', in J. Cleary (ed.), *The Perennial Tradition of Neoplatonism*, Leuven, 293-309.

Steel, C. (2001), 'The Moral Purpose of the Human Body: A Reading of *Timaeus* 69-72', *Phronesis* 46, 105-28.

Steel, C. (2003), 'Why Should we Prefer Plato's *Timaeus* to Aristotle's *Physics*? Proclus' Critique of Aristotle's Causal Explanation of the Physical World', in Sharples and Sheppard (eds) (2003), 175-87.

Striker, G. (1970), *Peras und Apeiron*, Göttingen.

Sumi, A. (1985), *Noetic Infinity and Intelligible Matter: Reexamination of the*

Fundamental Structure of the Philosophy of Plotinus, M.A. thesis, Old Dominion University.

Sumi, A. (1993), *The One's Knowledge in Plotinus*, Ph.D. diss., Loyola University, Ann Arbor.

Sumi, A. (1997), 'Plotinus on *Phaedrus* 247D7-E1: The Platonic *Locus Classicus* of the Identity of Intellect with the Intelligible Objects', *American Catholic Philosophical Quarterly* 71, 404-20.

Sumi, A. (2002a), 'The Omnipresence of Being, the Intellect-Intelligible Identity and the Undescending Part of the Soul: An Essay on the Dispute about Indian Influences on Plotinus', in Gregorios (ed.) (2002), 45-70.

Sumi, A. (2002b), 'The Psyche, the Forms, and the Creative One: Toward Reconstruction of Neoplatonic Metaphysics', in Harris (ed.) (2002), 211-56.

Tarán, L. (1971), 'The Creation Myth in Plato's *Timaeus*', in J.P. Anton and G.L. Kustas (eds), *Essays in Ancient Greek Philosophy*, New York, 372-407.

Tarán, L. (1975), *Academica: Philip of Opus, and the Pseudo-Platonic Epinomis*, Philadelphia.

Tarán, L. (1987), 'Proclus and the Old Academy', in Pépin and Saffrey (eds) (1987), 227-76.

Tardieu, M. (1986), 'Sabiens coraniques et "sabiens" de Harran', *Journal Asiatique* 274, 1-44.

Tardieu, M. (1990), *Les paysage reliques: routes et haltes syriennes d'Isidore à Simplicius*, Louvain and Paris.

Tarrant, H. (1985), *Scepticism or Platonism? The Philosophy of the Fourth Academy*, Cambridge.

Tarrant, H. (1993), *Thrasyllan Platonism*, Ithaca, NY.

Tarrant, H. (1995), 'Introducing Philosophers and Philosophies', *Apeiron* 28, 141-58.

Tarrant, H. (2000a), *Plato's First Interpreters*, Ithaca, NY, and London.

Tarrant, H. (2000b), 'Recollection and Prophecy in the *De Divinatione*', *Phronesis*, 45, 64-76.

Tarrant, H. (2004), 'Must Commentators Know their Sources? Proclus *In Timaeum* and Numenius', in Adamson et al. (eds) (2004), vol. 1, 175-90.

Tarrant, H. (2005a), *Recollecting Plato's Meno*, London.

Tarrant, H. (2005b), 'Socratic *Synousia*: A Post-Platonic Myth?', *JHP* 43, 131-55.

Tarrant, H. (2006), 'Antiochus: a New Beginning?', in R. Sharples and R. Sorabji (eds), *Post-Hellenistic Philosophy*, forthcoming, London.

Taylor, A.E. (1926), *Plato: The Man and His Work*, London.

Taylor, A.E. (1928), *A Commentary on Plato's Timaeus*, Oxford.

Taylor, T. (1816), *The Theoretic Arithmetic of the Pythagoreans*, London.

Tejera, V. (1997), 'How Compatible are the Dialogic and the Doctrinal Approaches in Plato's Dialogues', in G. Press (ed.), *Plato's Dialogues – the Dialogic Approach*, Lewiston.

Teloh, H. (1981), *The Development of Plato's Metaphysics*, University Park.

Thesleff, H. (1961), *An Introduction to the Pythagorean Writings of the Hellenistic Period*, Åbo.

Thesleff, H. (1962), 'Okkelos, Archytas, and Plato', *Eranos* 60, 8-36.

Thesleff, H. and W. Burkert (1971), *Pseudepigrapha I, Entretiens sur l'antiquité classique*, Geneva, 23-102.

Tigerstedt, E.N. (1974), *The Decline and Fall of the Neoplatonic Interpretation of Plato*, Helsinki.

Toeplitz, O. (1933), 'Bemerkungen zu der vorherstehenden Arbeit von Konrad

Müller', *Quellen und Studien zur Geschichte der Mathematik, Astronomie und Physik*, Abteilung B: Studien, Band II, 286-90.

Trapp, M.B. (1990), 'Plato's *Phaedrus* in Second Century Greek Literature', in D.A. Russell (ed.), *Antonine Literature*, Oxford, 141-73.

Trouillard, J. (1955), *La purification plotinienne*, Paris.

Trouillard, J. (1958), '"Agir par son être même". La Causalité selon Proclus', *Révue des Sciences Religieuses* 32, 347-57.

Tuozzo, T. (1996), 'Contemplation, the Noble, and the Mean: The Standard of Moral Virtue in Aristotle's Ethics', in R. Bosley (ed.), *Aristotle Virtue and the Mean*, Edmonton, 129-55.

Vallejo, A. (1997), 'No, it's not a Fiction', in Calvo and Brisson (eds) (1997), 141-8.

Vallette, P. (1960), *Apulée Apologie et Florides*, Paris.

Van den Berg, R. (2000), 'Towards the Paternal Harbor: Proclean Theurgy and the Contemplation of the Forms', in Segonds and Steel (eds) (2000), 425-43.

Van den Berg, R. (2003), '"Becoming like God" According to Proclus' Interpretations of the *Timaeus*, the Eleusinian Mysteries, and the *Chaldaean Oracles*', in Sharples and Sheppard (eds) (2003), 189-202.

Van den Broek, R. (1982), 'Apuleius on the Nature of God (*De Plat.*, 190-191)', in J. den Boeft and A.H.M. Kessels (eds), *Actus: Studies in Honour of H.L.W. Nelson*, Utrecht, 57-72.

Van der Waerden, B.L. (1943), 'Die Harmonienlehre der Pythagoreer', *Hermes* 78, 163-99.

Van Esbroeck, M. (1993), 'Peter the Iberian and Dionysius the Areopagite: Honigmann's Thesis Revisted', *Orientalia Christiana Periodica* 59, 217-27.

Van Lieshout, H. (1926), *La théorie plotinienne de la vertu: essai sur la genèse d'un article de la Somme théologique de saint Thomas*, Diss. Fribourg.

Van Winden, J.C. (1959), *Calcidius on Matter. His Doctrines and Sources*, Leiden.

Vander Waerdt, P.A. (1989), *The Stoic Theory of Natural Law*, Diss. Princeton.

Vander Waerdt, P.A. (1994a), 'Philosophical Influences on Roman Jurisprudence? The Case of Stoicism and Natural Law', *ANRW* 36.7, 4851-900.

Vander Waerdt, P.A. (1994b), 'Zeno's *Republic* and the Origins of Natural Law', in P.A. Vander Waerdt (ed.), *The Socratic Movement*, Ithaca, NY, 272-308.

Verrycken, K. (1990), 'The Development of Philoponus' Thought and its Chronology', in Sorabji (ed.) (1990), ch. 11.

Vlastos, G. (1939), 'The Disorderly Motion in the *Timaeus*', *CQ* 33, 71-83.

Vlastos, G. (1965), reprint of Vlastos (1939) in R.E. Allen (ed.), *Studies in Plato's Metaphysics, London*, 379-99.

Volkmann-Schuluck, K.-H. (1966), *Plotin als Interpret der Ontologie Platos*, Frankfurt am Main.

Von Arnim, H. (1924), 'Die drei Aristotelischen Ethiken', *Sitzungsberichte der Wiener Akademie der Wissenschaften, Phil.-hist. Klasse* 202.

Von Leyden, W. (1985), *Aristotle on Equality and Justice: His Political Argument*, New York.

Von Staden, H. (1995), 'Anatomy as Rhetoric: Galen on Dissection and Persuasion', *Journal of the History of Medicine*, 50, 47-66.

Wagner, M.F. (2002), 'Scientific Realism and Plotinus' Metaphysics of Nature', in Harris (ed.) (2002), 35-70.

Wallis, R.T. (1972), *Neoplatonism*, London.

Wedin, M. (1989), 'Aristotle on the Mechanics of Thought', *Ancient Philosophy* 9, 67-86.

Bibliography

Wedin, M. (2000), *Aristotle's Theory of Substance. The Categories and Metaphysics Z*, Oxford.

Wehrle, W. (2001), *The Myth of Aristotle's Development and the Betrayal of Metaphysics*, Lanham.

Westerink, L.G. (1962), *Anonymous Prolegomena to Platonic Philosophy*, Amsterdam.

Westrup, C.W. (1939), *Introduction to Early Roman Law* III, Copenhagen and London.

Whittaker, J. (1969a), '*epekeina nou kai ousias*', *Vigiliae Christianae* 23, 91-104.

Whittaker, J. (1969b), 'Neopythagoreanism and Negative Theology', *Symbolae Osloenses* 44, 109-25.

Whittaker, J. (1975), 'The Historical Background of Proclus' Doctrine of the *authupostata*', in O. Reverdin (ed.), *Entretiens sur l'Antiquité Classique* XXI (De Jamblique à Proclus), Geneva, 193-237.

Wians, W. (ed.) (1996), *Aristotle's Philosophical Development: Problems and Prospects*, Lanham.

Wieland, W. (1982), *Platon und die Formen des Wissens*, Göttingen.

Wilkes, K. (1992), 'Psuche Versus Mind', in M. Nussbaum and A. Rorty (eds), *Essays on Aristotle's De Anima*, Oxford, 109-27.

Wilson, N.G. (ed.) (1994), *Photius, The Bibliotheca. A Selection Translated with Notes*, London.

Wilson, N.G. (1996), *Scholars of Byzantium*, rev. ed., London and Cambridge, MA.

Wolska-Conus, W. (1989), 'Stéphanos d'Athènes et Stéphanos d'Alexandrie. Essai d'identification et de biographie', *Revue des Études Byzantines* 47, 5-89.

Woodhouse, C.M. (1986), *Gemistos Plethon: The Last of the Hellenes*, Oxford.

Wright, M.R. (2000), 'Myth, Science and Reason in the *Timaeus*', in M.R. Wright (ed.), *Reason and Necessity*, London, 1-22.

Zeller, E. (1923), *Die Philosophie der Griechen in ihrer geschichtlichen Entwicklung*, Leipzig.

Zeyl, D.J. (trans.) (2000), *Plato: Timaeus*, Indianapolis.

Index Locorum

References to the page and note numbers of this book are given in **bold**.

Index of Ancient Names

For authors see also the Index Locorum.

265

Index of Modern Names

Index of Selected Topics

apatheia, see *metriopatheia*
assimilation to god, 14, 18, 92, 95-8, 102-3n3, 170
Atlantis, 22-3
authorship (Apuleian), 43n1
autozôion, 88n42
Bacchants of Philosophy, 125-33
body (in physics), 144-5
categories, 201-2
causes, 136-7, 140-1, 144, 205-7
commentaries, 20, 135-67
common notions, 13-18
creation, 24-5, 156-7; of soul, 25-7, 107
demiurge, 26-7, 34-40, 42, 140-1, 146-7, 148n7, 177, 190, 210
diaphônia, 15
diarthrôsis, 13
disorderly motion, 67-70
division of text, 137-8, 152-5, 163
duty, 92-4
eclecticism, 14-18, 197
eikos, 27-8
eikôs mythos, 151-67
eikotologia, 159
elements, four or five, 190
enodatio, 13
epistemology, 12-16, 186-8
epistrophê, 141
epopteia, 128
ethics, 202-5
evil, 61-72
Forms, 188-90, 209-11
gods: invisible, 40-2; traditional, 42
harmonics, 109-12
harmony (of soul), 120n19

harmony of Plato and Aristotle, 6-7, 15-16, 169-70, 185-221
hermeneutic principles, 136-41, 152-5, 160-2
images, 155-6, 162
immortality, 191-3, 207-9
lemmata, 152-5
logos, 158-9
mathematics, 5, 107-23,
matter, 61-70, 206
medicine, 49-59
metaphor, 64-5, 129, 131, 136, 156-7
metriopatheia and *apatheia*, 93-4, 171-2
mysteries and rituals, 128, 169-72, 174-7
myth, 68, 107, 128-31
nature, 83, 138-41, 151, 160
prayer, 141-2
prokopton, 14
prooemia, 23, 148n8, 151-67
recollection, 12-17
sage, 14, 91-2, 94
Second Sophistic, 49, 52, 55
skopos, 136-7, 160-2
theôria and *lexis*, 151
theurgy, 169, 176-7, 183
tripartite soul, 50
universals, 188-90
virtue: civic (political, constitutional), 93-5, 102, 171-3; contemplative (theoretic), 97-8, 102, 171-3; hieratic, 100, 172-4, 183; moral (ethical), 100, 102, 173; natural, 100, 102, 173; paradigmatic, 98-102, 172-3; purificatory, 95-7, 102, 169-84; theurgic, 101-2

268